Future
of
Law and Justice

Future
of
Law and Justice

Dr. Gokulesh Sharma
LL.D.

Foreward by
Justice MN Venkatachaliah
Former
Chief Justice of India
Chairperson, National Human Rights Commission

Manas Publications
New Delhi-110 002 (INDIA)

Manas Publications
(Publishers, Distributors, Importers & Exporters)
4858, Prahlad Street, 24, Ansari Road, Darya Ganj,
New Delhi - 110 002 (INDIA)
Ph.: (O) 23260783, 23265523, (R) 27131660, 27143052
Fax: 011 - 23272766
E-mail: manaspublications@vsnl.com

First Published: 2004

ISBN 81-7049-163-0

Typeset at
Manas Publications

Printed in India at
Shree Balaji Printer
and Published by Mrs Suman Lata for
Manas Publications, 4858, Prahlad Street,
24, Ansari Road, Darya Ganj,
New Delhi - 110 002 (INDIA)

Foreword

Law, it is said, is politics by other means. In dysfunctional societies law and justice mean different things to different people. They merely symbolise the perpetual tension in the apportionment of the resources and good things of life. The traditional judicial scenario is seen as a contest between the positivists and natural lawyers. Social scientists, however, observe law's empire from beyond its frontiers. By inviting himself to speculate on these irresolvable issues of the province and function of law and their destiny, through his eminently readable "Future of Law and Justice", Dr. Gokulesh Sharma has joined the band, which Lord Goff would call, of "pilgrims on the road to unattainable perfection".

Speaking of the future of legal institutions, one is tempted to recall a conversation when the Lord Chancellor is said to have enquired of the then Chairman of Law Commission in Australia as to what he thought of the future of Courts. The latter seems to have expressed his happiness that the Lord Chancellor thought they had a future at all!

But then, Dr. Gokulesh Sharma's is a serious and sincere inquiry. His `Introduction" brings out his vision of the chapters on the concepts of jurisprudence, of law and justice and their ultimate purposes. They bear the imprint of a serious minded legal scholar. That a working judge could develop the temperament and find time for such academic pursuits is in itself an indication of his higher and loftier interests.

The philosophical foundations of the Common Law are more social than metaphysical. The system grew in rugged isolation from its continental neighbour -the Civil Law System and imparted primacy to the role of judges in judicial law making. That process was not anonymous. However, the classicist days of the school men of the neat philosophical classifications and institutionalized ideologies seem to be yielding place to greater interdisciplinary and interactive legal institutions. Science and technology, particularly the New Biology and Genetics, will profoundly influence the next society. Legal reforms will need to address these profound social changes. International Human Rights Regime, the Post Marrakesh International Intellectual Property Regime and the issues of equality in the international economic order will greatly influence our legal and economic institutions. Possner held law to be a junior branch of economics. In short, the next decade will be an era of unprecedented change.

Amidst these high winds of global change, the lamp of personal liberty and freedom of spirit must burn trim and bright -eternally. Dicey saw the Sovereign Parliament as a great protection of liberty. That was in the context of the divine right the kings had asserted against their own parliaments and people. But where parliament itself came to be perceived as a mere majoritarian symbol and democracy degenerated into electoral despotism, limitations on parliament in the form of written constitutions with entrenched `Bill of Rights' became necessary. 'Public opinion' and `the ordinary law of the land' were the other traditionally perceived sources of protection of the liberties of the individual. Now treaty obligations of the State under the Human Rights regimes are claiming center-space and are demanding their way into municipal laws. Alexis de Tocquevile believed that there was more in the customs of the people than in their laws to protect their liberty. With a massive universal thrust towards democratic ways, the concepts of law and justice can not remain static. Justinian had said "knowledge of law amounts to little if it oversees the persons for whose sake the law is made. (`Institutes')

The debates will, as time moves, acquire wider range, greater depth and sharper and more critical edge. Dr. Sharma's book and the issues it raises will contribute to and enrich this debate. Dr. Gokulesh Sharma and his work deserve serious attention and generous appreciation.

Justice MN Venkatachaliah (Retd.)

Preface

Which came first whether the hen or the egg? It is still undecided. It is also undecided that what is the specific and real meaning of law and justice and more particularly of *Dharma* or *Nyaya.* It is roughly known to all that this kind of study is carried under the subject "Jurisprudence'. Jurisprudence is roughly called the knowledge of law but the real jurisdiction and scope is still not known. Simply it may be said that the study of jurisprudence is about law and justice.

No specific book has been written which deals about law and justice particularly touching Indian oriental philosophy. I have tried in this book to present a comparative legal philosophy, on one hand, of the Hindu, Muslim and Chinese thought relating to the eastern world and communist philosophy of Russia, and on the other hand, western philosophy of Greek, Roman, British and American thinkers. Although brief role of German, Australian and other thinkers of various other nations have also been taken up for consideration. I have tried to give a complete picture of various faces and theories of law, justice and jurisprudence. The book will also suggest a proper guideline for the future.

The book is divided into seven chapters. The first chapter deals with a brief outlook of the whole subject. Second chapter gives a description of the real meaning of jurisprudence. The scope of jurisprudence and the relation of jurisprudence with other social sciences have also been taken up for study. Third chapter describes the meaning of law. A good discussion of thought of available philosophers of law has been taken up along with a new approach to existing law and future trends.

Fourth chapter deals with the purpose of law and classification. Fifth chapter is about, the administration of justice and morals. It also provides the natural keys to various theories of punishment, whether of civil or criminal type: Sixth chapter shows a comparative table of law and justice in western concept with the concept of *Dharma* and *Nyaya* of Indian oriental philosophy.

Finally the seventh chapter sums up the entire material. The relevant juristic opinion, quotations and remarks from respectable and eminent jurists have been included. All relevant and available case laws have been referred. I humbly invite suggestions for improving and updating of the book and removing of mistakes if any.

The book is dedicated to my elder brother, Late Pandit Sunder Lal Sharma, whose high inspirations have always guided me to work for all possible legal reforms in the society.

I am highly indebted to my wife Smt. Neeta Sharma and my friends who have cooperated with me in the preparation of the book and helped me a lot, which is unforgettable.

Lastly I am personally obliged to Shri V.K. Garg of Manas Publications, Delhi, who has published the book in a very short time. I think the book will be useful for Judges, Advocates and not only to legal experts but also to each and everyone who is interested in the legal field or have a specific interest in law and justice.

Dr.Gokulesh Sharma
Judge, Civil Court, Kanpur

Contents

CHAPTER 1

Introduction

"Jurisprudence", according to Laski, *"is the eye of law. It gives the law its insight into the environment of which it is the expression. It relates the law to the spirit of the time, and richer the jurisprudence of a given system in a given era, the nearer will be the law of that system to the needs of its time.*[1],

Justice Desai said that essentially, jurisprudence for those who believe is an insight to law. That necessarily takes care of its science as well as social philosophy. Jurisprudence activates the law to take care of the needs and demands of the community. Justice, according to law, therefore, mostly comprehends social urge, commitments and values. But it is ridiculed as "Legal Justice" not being akin to "Justice" by those who believe that jurisprudence does not give insight to law of time and situation. To Justice Iyer: "Jurisprudence is simply an organized knowledge of law."[2]

Justice according to law they feel has therefore no strength to satisfy the urge of the community. It is being considered diagonally opposite to the 'Social Justice,' which alone has a capacity to meet the public urge. They hold that legal justice and social justice are different conceptually and in their intendment.

Civilization has the foremost thirst for "Justice". Dennial Webster held that "Justice has been the highest interest of man, which he seeks persistently, fights for it resolutely, expects confidently from the Ruler and neighbours. Denial or absence thereof he reacts bitterly."[3]

Justice is held to be the *alma mater* for mankind, and phenomena of over persuasive value. Also it is a foundation of human relations.

People can sense the phenomena conveniently, but find it difficult to put it aptly in written words. Harold Potter has therefore remarked that many people believe that they understood the meaning of justice but their notions are not clear.[4]

Expressions of man have not yet attained the proficiency to define it. Language of a man has yet to translate the term "Justice" in a most cohesive manner. Rosoe Pound explains:[5]

"Justice is the totality of values as to human relations intuitively recognized through collective experience."[6]

His emphasis was on the values of human relations gathered through collective and common interaction. For the Greek, David Miller says:

"The sense in which justice was equivalent to virtue in general."[7]

Greeks had an ancient culture which had its foundation on morality and ethics.

David Miller then attempted to give practical contents to the term "Justice" by defining it as "to each according to his right, desert and need". This finds proximity with the concept in the developing civilized society.

Justice is as free as air or water. It has a relation with every sphere of human activity. Its pursuit, when confined to courtrooms, invites a serious debate as regards its form and content. Yet an isolated quarter believes that the concept of justice has no substantive contents. Rawls found himself in difficulty when he said that "there is no single conception of justice which can rationally be defined."[8]

Perhaps to him justice has no sole or single foundation and conceptually it is variable. Variance, if any, can only be in sensing. "Justice" however cannot have indefinite contents.

David Miller asserts: "Indeed the most valuable definition of justice is that which brings out its distributive character most plainly; justice is *summum cuique* to each his due."[9]

He has stressed on functional results.

For the subject, just and fair arbitration on rival or competing claims or interest in a set-up, is by and large understood to be an essence of justice to be administered by the court. And that is also an unimpeachable virtue of justice simplistic in all formats. 'Justice' has a sole and single foundation that is in being just and fair, with regard to man and material. It could however have numerous facets within itself, and they have no independent entity outside the broader concept.

All have an urge for justice and a mission for community interest, but divergence in thinking to guide oneself. This is the root of ideological crisis. In a society of progressive people, the term justice bears numerous brands, patents and labels, viz, Legal, Social, Distributive, Human, People's, Colonial, Imperial, so on and so forth. And each one of them is held to be independent as well in contradistinction with the other.

Any State–socialistic, or otherwise—which thinks in terms of the well-being of its inhabitants, has to take care of even the last person of its soil. In a nation with limited resources like ours, the need to treat those unfortunate millions, by distributing higher dividends cannot rationally be debated. This is the supporting treatment to the less equals to minimize the imbalance. This the civilized society ordains. It takes shape of constitutional objectives, which are, however, to be accomplished by the *modus operandi* evolved and within the parameters prescribed by the Constitution itself.

Justice Iyer is one of the leading lights of this country(India). A man with crystallized wisdom and thinking, his precepts are reflective. A jurist with a distinction of being a humanist and an activist, he is an adjudicator of the commoner. Sensitivity of his mind has a depth of an ocean and the height of a mountain. Prevalent judiciary system seems to him to be unmindful of the weaker section of the society. This supplies fuel to his burning heart. His words bear potency and are being valued to a great deal. His ceaseless campaign for Social Justice has gathered considerable momentum. His mission is exemplary. In his view, law cuts the wings of justice administered by the court and accordingly is inadequate to meet the demands of time.

With a solace he makes a mention that –

"The socialist justices are very fond of quoting Lord Denning of Great Britain, Justice Murphy of Australia, Justice Earl Warren of America, who never waited for legislative intervention and moulded the law so as to serve the need of time."[10]

Lord Denning has asserted (as for justice vs. law) that the proper role of a judge is to do justice. If any rule of law impairs him in doing so, it then is the providence of the judge to do all he can legitimately do to avoid that rule or even change it so as to do justice. "He need not wait for the legislature to intervene because that cannot be of any help in the instant case. I would further emphasize the word 'legitimately'. The judge is himself a subject to law and must abide by it."[11]

The proclamation carved out the premises is:

(a) Notion of justice need not necessarily be in commensuration with the relevance of law.

(b) For doing justice according to the notion, the judge is within his competence even to brush aside the law, but

(c) the judge, being subject to the authority of law, must adhere to it and has to do justice legitimately.

Rosoe Pound has described that philosophical legal thinking of the past is a force in the administration of justice of the present. Indeed the everyday work of the court was never more completely shaped by abstract philosophical ideas than in the nineteenth century when lawyers affected to despise philosophy and analytical jurists believed they had set up a self-sufficient science of law, which stood in no need of any philosophical apparatus.

In all stages of what may be described fairly as legal development, philosophy has been a useful servant. But in sum it has been a tyrannous servant and in all but forms a master.

Two needs have determined philosophical thinking about law. On the one hand, the paramount social interest in the general security, which as an interest in peace and order dictated the very beginnings of law, has led man to seek some fixed basis of a certain ordering of human action which should restrain magisterial as well as individual wilfulness and assure a firm and stable social order. On the other hand, the pressure of less immediate social interests, and the need of reconciling them with the exigencies of the general security and of making continual new compromises because of continual changes in society have called for readjustment, at least of the details of the social order. They have called continually for overhauling of legal precepts and for refitting them to unexpected situations. And this has led men to seek principles of legal development by which to escape from authoritative rules which they feared or did not know how to reject but could no longer apply to advantage.

These principles of change and growth, however, might easily prove inimical to the general security, and it was important to reconcile or unify them with the idea of a fixed basis of the legal order. Thus the philosopher has sought to construct theories of law and lawmaking and has sought to unify them by some ultimate solution equal to the task of yielding a perfect law, which should stand fast forever. From the time when law givers gave over the attempt to maintain the general security by the belief that particular bodies of human law had been divinely dictated or divinely revealed or divinely sanctioned, they have had to wrestle with the problem of proving to mankind that the law was something fixed and settled, whose authority was beyond question, while at the same time enabling it to make constant readjustments and occasional radical changes under the pressure of infinite and variable human desires.

The philosopher has worked upon this problem with the materials of the actual legal systems of the time and place or with the legal materials of the past upon which his generation is built.

Hence in closer view, philosophies of law have been attempts to give a rational account of the law of the time and place, or attempts to formulate a general theory of the legal order to meet the needs of a given period of legal development, or attempts to state the results of the two former attempts universally and to make them all-sufficient for law everywhere and for all time.

Historians of the philosophy of law have fixed their eyes chiefly on the third. But this is the least valuable part of legal philosophy. If we look at the philosophies of the past with our eyes upon the law of the time and place and the exigencies of the stage of legal development in which they were formulated, we shall be able to appreciate them more justly, and so far, as the law of the time and place or the stage of legal development is similar to or different from the present, to utilize them for the purposes of today.

We may understand the materials upon which Greek philosophers were working if we look at an exhortation addressed by Demosthenes to an Athenian jury. Men ought to obey the law, he said, for four reasons: because laws were prescribed by God, because they were a tradition taught by wise men who knew the good old customs, because they were deductions from an eternal and immutable moral code, and because they were agreements of men with one another binding them because of a moral duty to keep their promises. It was not long since, that men had thought of legal precepts as divinely revealed, nor was it long since, that law had been a tradition of old customs of decision. Philosophers were seeking a better basis for them in eternal principles of right. In the meantime in political theory, at least, many of them were the agreements of Athenian citizens as to how they should conduct themselves in the inevitable clashes of interests in everyday life. What was needed above all was some theory of the authority of law, which should impose bonds of reason upon those who were subject to law in such an amorphous legal order.

A sure basis of authority resting upon something more stable than human will and the power of those who govern to impose their will for the time being was also required for the problem of social control in the Greek city-state. In order to maintain the general security and the security of social institutions amid strifes and factions in a society organized on the basis of kingship and against the wilfulness of masterful individuals boasting descent from gods, in order to persuade or coerce both the aristocracy and the mass of the law born to maintain in orderly fashion the social status quo, it would neither tell them that law was a gift of God, nor that what offended the aristocrat as a radical bit of popular legislation enacted at the instance of a demagogue which was yet to be obeyed because it had been so taught by wise men who knew the good old customs, nor that Demos chafing under some items of a class-possessed tradition was bound by it as something to which all citizens had agreed. The exigencies of the social order called for a distinction between law and rule of law. The Minos, which if not actually a dialogue of Platos, seems clearly Platonic and very close to Plato in time, is taken up with this distinction and gives us a clue to the juristic problems of the time.

Another example may be seen in Aristotle's well-known discussion in the Nicomacbean Ethics. It is significant that Greek thinkers always had couple of customs and enactments: things that we contrast today. These were the formal bases of legal authority. So Aristotle considers, not natural law and positive law, but what is just in itself, just by nature or just in its idea–and what derives its sole title to be from convention or enactment. The latter, he says, can be just only with respect to those things, which by nature are indifferent. Thus when a newly reconstituted city took a living Spartan general for its eponymous, no one was bound by nature to sacrifice to Brasidas as to an ancestor, but he was bound by enactment and after all the matter was one of convention which, in a society framed on the model of an organized kindred, required that the citizens have a common heroic ancestor, and was morally indifferent. The distinction was handed down to modern legal science by Thomas Aquinas. **{AQ}** was combo died in Anglo-American legal thought by Blackstone, and has become staple. But it is quite out of its setting as a doctrine of *mala prohibita* and *mala in se*. An example of the distinction between law and rule of law has become the basis of an arbitrary line between the traditionally antisocial, penalized by the common law, and recently penalized infringements of newly or partially recognized social interests. Although the discrimination between what is just and right by nature and what is just because of custom or enactment has had a long and fruitful history in philosophical jurisprudence and is still a force in the administration of justice. I suspect that the permanent contribution of Greek philosophy of law is to be found rather in the distinction between law and rule of law, which lies behind it and has significance for all stages of legal development.

Roman lawyers came in contact with philosophy in the transition from the strict law to the stage of enquiry and natural law, and the contact had much to do with enabling them to make the transition. From a purely legal standpoint Greek Law was in the stage of primitive law. Law and morals were still largely undifferentiated law and morals, lent itself to the identifications of the legal and the moral in juristic thinking, which was characteristic of the classical Roman law. But the strict law obviously was indifferent to morals and in many vital points was quite at variance with the moral ideas of the time. The Greek distinction of 'just by nature' and 'just by convention or enactment' was suggested at once by such a situation. Moreover the forms of law at the end of the Republic and at the beginning of the Empire invited a theory of law as something composite, made up of more than one type of precept and resting immediately on more than one basis of authority.

Cicero enumerates seven forms of law. Three of these are not heard of thereafter in Roman juristic writing. Evidently already in Cicero's time they belonged to the past and had ceased to be effective forms of actual law. The remaining four, namely, statutes, resolutions of the senate, edicts of the magistrates, and the authority of those learned in the law, come to three–legislation, administrative edicts, and juristic reasoning on the basis of the legal tradition. And these correspond to the three elements, which made up the law. First, there was the *ius ciuile*: the Twelve Tables, subsequent legislation, interpretation of both, and the traditional law of the city. Second, there was the mass of rules, in form largely procedural that was contained in the edicts. The growing point of the law had been here and to some extent growth was still going on through these means. Indeed this part of the law reached its final form under Hadrian. Third, there were the writings of the jurisconsults. The growing point of the law had begun to be here and this was the most important form of law in the classical period from Augustus to the third century. This part of the law got its final form in the Digest of Justinian.

Of the three elements the first was originally thought of as declared and published custom. Later it was thought of as resting on the authority of the state. It was obviously local and peculiar to Rome. In form it rested on the legislative power of the Roman people, supplemented by a mere interpretation of the legislative command with only the authority of customary acceptance. In Greek phrase it rested on convention and enactment. The second purported to the rules observed by civilized people, and on points of commercial law may well have been an approximation thereto.

Apart from this, however, according to ancient ideas of personal law, the rules, which obtained among civilized people, were eminently a proper law to apply between citizen and non citizen. In Greek phrase it was law by convention. The basis of the third was simply reason. The jurisconsult had no legislative power and no imperium. The authority of his responsum, as soon as law ceased to be a class tradition, was to be found in its intrinsic reasonableness: in the appeal, which it made to the reason and sense of justice of the index. In Greek phrase, if it was law it was law by nature.

Natural law was a philosophical theory for a period of growth. It arose to meet the exigencies of the stage of equity and natural law, one of the great creative periods of legal history. Yet, as we have seen, even the most rapid growth does not permit the lawyer to ignore the demand for stability. The theory of natural law was worked out as means of growth, as means of making a law of the world on the basis of the old strict law of the Roman city. But it was worked out also as a means of directing and organizing the growth of law so as to maintain the general security. It was the task of the jurists to build and shape the law on the basis of the old local materials so as to make it an instrument for satisfying the needs and wants of the whole world while at the same time ensuring uniformity and predictability. They did this by applying a new but known technique to the old materials. The technique was one of legal reason; but it was legal reason identified with natural reason and worked out and applied under the influence of a philosophical ideal. The conception of natural law as something of which all positive law was but declaratory, as something by which actual rules were to be measured, to which so far as possible they were to be made to conform, by which new rules were to be framed, and by which old rules were to be extended or restricted in their application and was a powerful instrument in the hands of the jurists and enabled them to proceed in their task of legal construction with assured confidence.

But the juristic empiricism by which the *ius ciuile* was made into a law of the world needed something more than a theoretical incentive. It was a process of analogical development by extension here and restriction there, of generalization, first in the form of maxims and later by laying down broad principles, and of cautious striking out of new paths, giving them course and direction by the method of trial and error. It was a process very similar to that by which Anglo-American judicial empiricism had been able to make a law of the world on the basis of the legal precepts of seventeenth century England. Such a process required something to give direction to juristic reasoning, to give definite content to the ideal, to provide a reasonably defined channel for juristic thought. This need was met by the philosophical theory of the nature of things and of the law of nature as conformity thereto. In practice just-made and judge-made laws have been moulded consciously or unconsciously by ideas as to what law is for; by theories as to the end of law.

In the beginnings of law, man had no more ambitious conception than a peaceable ordering of society at any cost. But the Greeks soon got a better conception of an orderly and peaceful maintenance of the social status quo–a form which expresses its nature, a perfect form of the social organization of a given civilization–that which the legal order is to further and maintain. Thus judge and jurist obtain a guide, which has served them well ever since. They are to measure all situations by an idealized form of the social order of the time and place and so to shape the law as to make it maintain and further this ideal of the social status quo. We shall meet this idea in various forms throughout the subsequent history of the philosophy of law. It constitutes the permanent contribution of Rome to legal philosophy.

As soon as scientific legal development begins in the Middle Ages the law once more comes in contact with philosophy through the study of both in the universities. What was the need of the time for which philosophy was called upon to satisfy? Following an era of anarchy and disunion and violence men desired order and organization and peace. They called for a philosophy that would bolster up authority and rationalize their desire to impose a legal yoke upon society.

The period was one of transition from the primitive law of the Germanic people to a strict law, through reception of Roman law as authoritative legislation or through compilation of the Germanic customary law more or less after the Roman model, as in the north of France, or through declaration of the customary law in reported decisions of strong central courts, as in England. Thus it soon became a period of strict law. Scholastic philosophy, with its reliance upon dialectic development of authoritatively given premises, its faith in formal logic, and its central problem of putting reason as a foundation under authority, responded exactly to these demands. It is no misnomer to style the commentators or post-glossators of the fourteenth and fifteenth centuries as the "scholastic jurists." For it was in large part the philosophy that met the needs of the time so completely which enabled them to put the Roman law of Justinian in a form to be received and administered in the Europe of nine centuries later. While they made the gloss into law in place of the text and moulded many things over, as they had to be made over if they were to fit a wholly different social order, the method of dialectical development of absolute and unquestioned premises made it appear that nothing had been done but to develop the logical implications of an authoritative text. Men could receive the law of Bartolus so long as they believed it, but the logical unfolding of the pre-existing content of the behinding legislation of Justinian. It is interesting to note in *Fortes cue* an application of this to the rules of the common law in its stage of strict law. He assumes that these rules are the principles of which he reads in the Commentators on Aristotle and that they may be compared to the axioms of the geometrician. The time had not yet come to call rules or principles or axioms in question. The need was to rationalize man's desire to be governed by fixed rules and to reconcile, in appearance at least, the change and growth which are inevitable in all laws with the need men felt of having a fixed, unchangeable, authoritative rule. The scholastic philosophy did notable service in these respects and, I venture to think, left as a permanent contribution to legal science the method of ensuring certainty by logical development of the content of authoritatively defined conceptions.

On the breakdown of the feudal social organization, the rise of commerce and the era of discovery, colonization, and exploitation of the natural resources of new continents, together with the rise of nations in place of loose congeries of vassal-held territories, called for a national law unified within the national domain. Starkey proposed codification to Henry VIII and Dumoulin urged harmonizing and unifying of French customary law with eventual codification. The Protestant jurist–theologians of the sixteenth century found a philosophical basis for satisfying these desires of the time in the divinely ordained state; in a natural law divorced from theology and resting solely upon reason, reflecting the boundless faith in reason which came in with the Renaissance. Thus each rational jurist might work out his own interpretation and might interpret the word of God for himself as his own reason and conscience showed the way. On the other hand, the Catholic jurists of the Counter-Reformation found a philosophical basis for satisfying these same desires in a conception of natural law as a system of limitations on human action expressing the nature of man, that is, the ideal of man as a rational creature, and of positive law as an ideal system expressing the nature of a unified state. For the moment these ideas were put at the service of a growing royal authority and bore fruit in the Byzantine theory of sovereignty, which became classical in public law. In private law they soon took quite another turn. For a new period of growth, demanded by the expansion of society and the breaking over of the bonds of authority, was at hand to make new and wholly different demands upon philosophy.

Glossators and commentators had made or shaped the law out of Roman materials for a static, locally self-sufficient, other-worldly society revering authority because authority has saved it from what it feared, regarding chiefly the security of social institutions and neglecting the individual life because in its policy the individual lived his highest life in the life of another whose greatness was the greatness of those who served him. In the seventeenth and eighteenth centuries, jurists were required to make or shape a law out of these medievalized Roman materials to satisfy the wants of an active and shifting, locally interdependent, worldly society, impatient of authority because authority stood in the way of what it desired, and jealously individualist, since it took free individual self-assertion to be the highest good. In England the strict law made for feudal England out of Germanic materials, sometimes superficially Romanized, was likewise to be made over to do the work of administering justice to a new world. A period of legal development resulted which is strikingly analogous to the classical period of Roman law. Once more philosophy took the helm. Once more there was an infusion into law of ideas from within the law. Once more law and morals were identified in juristic thinking. Once more men held as a living tenet that all positive law was declaratory of natural law and got its real authority from the rules of natural law, which it declared. Once more judicial idealism led the jurist to survey every corner of the actual law, measuring its rule by reason and shaping, extending, restricting, or building anew, in order that the actual legal edifice might be a faithful copy of the ideal.

But the theory of natural law, devised for a society organized on the basis of kingship and developed for a society organized on the basis of relations, did not suffice for a society, which conceived itself as an aggregate of individuals and was reorganizing on the basis of competitive self-assertion. Again the convenient ambiguity of *ius*, which could mean not only right and law but also "a right", was pressed into service and *ius naturale* gave us natural rights. The ultimate thing was not natural law as before, not merely principles of eternal validity, but natural rights, certain qualities inherent in man and demonstrated by reason, which natural law exists to secure and to which positive law ought to give effect. Later these natural rights came to be the bane of juristic thinking. Yet they achieved great things in their times. Under the influence of this theory jurists worked out a scheme of "legal rights" that effectively secures almost the whole field of individual interest of personality and individual interests of substance. It put a scientific foundation under the medieval scheme of the claims and duties involved in the relation of king to tenants- in-chief, out of which the judges had developed the immemorial rights of Englishmen, and enabled the common-law rights of Englishmen to become the natural rights of man, entrenched as such in our bills of rights.

Thus it served as a needed check upon the exuberance of growth–stimulated rigidly in a time when law threatened to become wholly fluid. And this steadying influence was strengthened from another quarter. The Roman jurisconsult was teacher, philosopher, and practitioner in one. As a lawyer he had the exigencies of the general security ever before him in that he felt the imperative need of being able to advise with assurance what tribunals would do on a given state of facts. The seventeenth and eighteenth century jurists were chiefly teachers and philosophers. Happily they had been trained to accept the Roman law as something of paramount authority and so were able to give natural law a content by assuming its identity with an ideal form of the law which they knew and in which they had been trained. As the Roman jurisconsult built in the image of the old law of the city, they built on idealized Roman lines. If Roman law could no longer claim to be embodied authority they assumed that, corrected in its details by a juristic-philosophical critique, it was embodied reason.

Both these ideas of natural rights and an ideal form of the actual law of the time and place as the jural order of nature were handed down to and put to new uses in the nineteenth century. In the growing law of the seventeenth and eighteenth centuries they were but guides to lead growth into definite channels and ensure continuity and permanence in the development of rules and doctrines. Whether natural rights were conceived as qualities of the man or as deductions from a compact which expressed the nature of man, the point was: not that the jurist should keep his hands off lest by devising some new precept or in reshaping some old doctrine or infringe a fundamental right, but that he should use his hand freely and skillfully to shape rules and doctrines and institutions, that they might be instruments of achieving the ideal of human existence in a "state of nature."

For, the state of nature, let us remember, law was a state, which expressed the ideal of man as a rational creature. If a reaction from the formal over refinement of the eighteenth century came to identify this with a primitive simplicity, in juristic hands, it was the simplicity of a rational ideal in place of the cumbrous complexity of legal systems which had become fixed in their ideas in the stage of the strict law. Thus Pothier, discussing the Roman categories of contract and rejecting them for the "natural" principle that man, as a moral creature, should keep his engagements, declares that the complex and arbitrary system of Roman law, made up of successive additions at different times to a narrow primitive stock of legally enforceable promises, is not adhered to because it is "remote from simplicity."

Again the ideal form of the actual law, which gave content to natural law, was not an ideal form of historically found principles, constraining development for all time within historically fixed bounds, as in the nineteenth century, but an ideal form of the *ratio legis*–of the reason behind the rule or doctrine or institution whereby it expressed the nature of the rational human being guided only by reason and conscience in his relations with similar beings similarly guided. Attempts to fix the immutable part of law, to lay out legal charts for all time, belong to the transition to the maturity of law. The eighteenth century projects for codification and the era of codification on the continent, which the result of two centuries of growth were put in systematic form to serve as the basis of a juristic new start, in form rested upon the theory of natural law. By a sheer effort of reason the jurist could work out a complete system of deductions from the nature of man and formulate them in a perfect code. **'Go to let him do so!'** This was not the mode of thought of a period of growth but rather of one when growth had been achieved and the philosophical theory of a law of nature was called upon for a new kind of service.

At the end of the eighteenth century Lord Kenyon had determined that "Mansfield's innovations" were not to go on. Indeed some of them were to be undone. Equity was soon to be systematized by Lord Eldon and to become "almost as fixed and settled" as the law itself. The absorption of the law merchants was complete in its main lines although in details it went on for two decades. Moreover the legislative reform movement, which followed, only carried into detail the ideas; which had come into the law in the two preceding centuries. For the time the law was assimilating what had been taken up during the period of growth and the task of the jurist was one of ordering, harmonizing, and systematizing rather than of creating. Likewise law had been codifying on the continent.

Down to the end of the nineteenth century the codes, whatever their date, in reality speak from the end of the eighteenth century and with few exceptions are all but copies of the French code of 1804. Where there were no codes the hegemony of the historical school led to a movement back to the law of Justinian, which would have undone much of the progress of the last centuries. The energy of jurists was turned for a time to analysis, classification, and systematize as their sole task. Where codes obtained, analytical development and dogmatic exposition of the text, as a complete and final statement of the law, was to occupy jurists exclusively for the next hundred years. We may well think of this time, as it thought of itself, as a period of maturity of law. The law was taken to be complete and self-sufficient, without antinomies and without gaps, wanting only agreement, logical development of the implications of its several rules and conceptions, and systematic exposition of its several parts. Legislation was in need occasionally in order to get rid of archaisms, which had survived the purgation of the two prior centuries. For the rest, history and analysis, bringing out the idea behind the course of development of legal doctrines and unfolding their logical consequences, were all the apparatus, which the jurists required. He soon affected to ignore philosophy and often relegated it to the science of legislation, where within narrow limits it might still be possible to think of creating.

Yet the nineteenth century was no more able to get on without philosophy of law than were its predecessors. In place of one universally recognized philosophical method we find four well-marked types. But they all come to the same shackles upon juristic activity. They are all modes of rationalizing the juristic desires of the time, growing out of the pressure of the interest in the general security by way of reaction from a period of growth and in the security of acquisitions and security of transactions in a time of economic expansion and industrial enterprise.

In the United States, since the natural law of the eighteenth century publicists had become classical, we relied largely upon an American variant of natural law. It was not that natural law expressed the nature of man. Rather it expressed the nature of government. One form of this variant was due to our doctrine that the common law of England was in force only so far as applicable to our conditions and our institutions. The attempt to put this doctrine philosophically regards an ideal form of the received common law as natural law and takes natural law to be a body of deductions from or implications of American institutions or the nature of our polity. Within a generation the Supreme Court of one of our states laid down dogmatically that primogeniture in estates **tail** (which by the way is still possible in one of the oldest of the original states) could not coexist with "the axioms of the constitution," which guarantees to each state a republican form of government.

More generally, however, the American variant of natural law grew out of an attempt at philosophical statement of the power of our courts with respect to unconstitutional legislation. The constitution was declaratory of principle of natural constitutional law that was to be deduced from the nature of free government. Hence, constitutional questions were always only in terms, questions of constitutional interpretation. They were questions of the meaning of the document, as such, only in form. In substance they were questions of a general constitutional law which transcended the text; of whether the enactment before the court conformed to principles of natural law "running back of all constitutions" and inherent in the very idea of a government of limited powers set up by a free people. Now that courts with few exceptions have given over this mode of thinking and the highest court in the land has come to apply the limitations of the fifth and fourteenth amendments as legal standards, there are some who say that we no longer have a constitutional law. For how can there be law unless a body of rules declaring a natural law which is above all human enactment? The interpretation of a written instrument, no matter by whom enacted, may be governed by law, indeed, but can yield no law. Such ideas die hard. In the language of the eighteenth century our courts sought to make our positive law, and in particular our legislation, express the nature of American political institutions; they sought so to shape it and restrain it as to make it give effect to an ideal of our polity.

Later in the nineteenth century natural law as a deduction from American institutions or from "free government" gave way to a metaphysical-historical theory worked out in continental Europe. Natural rights were deductions from a fundamental metaphysically demonstrable datum of individual free will, and natural law was an ideal critique of positive law whereby to secure these rights in their integrity. History showed us the idea of individual liberty realizing itself in legal institutions and rules and doctrines. Jurisprudence developed ssthis idea into its logical consequences and gave us a critique of law whereby we might be delivered from futile attempts to set up legal precepts beyond the necessary minimum for ensuring the harmonious coexistence of the individual and his fellows. This mode of thought was well suited to a conception of law as standing between the abstract individual and society and protecting the natural rights of the former against the latter, which American law had derived from the seventeenth century contests in England between courts and crown. It was easy to generalize this as a contest between the individual and society, and it became easier to do so when the common law rights of Englishmen secured by common-law courts against the crown had become the natural rights of man secured to individual men as against the state by the bill of rights.

Others in England and America turned to a utilitarian-analytical theory. The legislator was to be guided by a principle of utility. That which made for the greatest total of individual happiness was to be the lawmaker's standard. The jurist was to find universal principles by analysis of the actual law. He had nothing to do with creative activity. His work was to be that of an orderly, logical development of the principles reached by analysis of what he found already given in the law and improvement of the form of the law by system and logical reconciliation of details. As a result the legislator was to be busied with formal improvement of the law and rendering it, as Bentham put it, more "cognoscible," while the jurist was exercising a like restricted function so far as he could work with materials afforded exclusively by the law itself. No unnatural, metaphysical and historical and analytical jurists at the end of the century were quite willing to say that their several methods were not exclusive but were complementary.

Towards the end of the last century a positivist sociological thinking tended to supersede the metaphysical historical and the utilitarian analytical. All phenomena were determined by inexorable natural laws to be discovered by observation. Moral, social and hence legal phenomena were governed by laws as completely beyond the power of conscious human control as the movement of the planets. We might discover these laws by observation of social phenomena and might learn to submit to them intelligently instead of rashly or ignorantly defying them. But we can hope to do no more.

Except as he can learn to plot some part of the inevitable curve of legal development and save us from futile flying in the face of the laws by which legal evolution was inevitably governed, the jurist was powerless. Many combined this mode of thought with or grafted it on the metaphysical legislation of the last decade of the nineteenth century and the first decade of the present century with this reinforced juristic pessimism as a base. Superficially it appeared that the Greek idea of the naturally just, which in its Roman form of natural law and its eighteenth century form of natural rights had made for a creative legal science as long as such a science had existed, and at length exhausted its possibilities.

Today, however, we hear of a revival of natural law. Philosophy of law is raising its head throughout the world. We are asked to measure rules and doctrines and institutions and to guide the application of law by reference to the end of law and to think of them in terms of social utility. We are invited to assume questions of law and of the application of law under the social ideal of the time and place. We are called upon to formulate the jural postulates of the civilization of the time and place and to measure law and the application of the law thereby in order that law may further help in civilization and that the legal materials handed down with the civilization of the past may be made an instrument of maintaining and furthering the civilization of the present.

We are told that observation shows us social interdependence through similarity of interests and through division of labour as the central fact in human existence and are told to measure law and the application of law functionally by the extent to which they further or interfere with this interdependence. For the era of legal self-sufficiency is past. The work of assimilating what had been received into the law has been done. The possibilities of analytical and historical development of the classical materials have been substantially exhausted. While jurists have been at these tasks, a new social order has been building which makes new demands and presses upon the legal order with a multitude of unsatisfied desires. Once more we must build rather than merely improve; we must create rather than merely order and systematize and logically reconcile details. One has but to compare the law of today on such subjects as **torts** or public utilities or administrative law with the law of a generation ago to see that we are in a new stage of transition; to see that the juristic pessimism of the immediate past, which arose to save us from taking in more, while what had been taken already remained undigested, will serve no longer; and to see that the jurist of tomorrow will stand in need of some new philosophical conception of the end of law, and at the same time will want some new steadying philosophical conception to safeguard the general security, in order to make the law which we hand down to him achieve juristic in his time and place.

We have seen that law and justice are complementary to each other. They cannot survive without each other. There was a time when justice was dispensed as per law. It is still like that but now there is a change in the conception. Now it is the feeling that law must be according to justice. Justice should not be according to law. It is clear that there are several faces of the real meaning of the law. Likewise there are several aspects of real meaning of justice. Here we have to examine in detail the real faces of law and justice, particularly in Indian conditions.

Notes:

1. Quoted by Justice V.R.K. Iyer in book - *Law & Life*
2. *Justice VS Jurist* - A.D. Desai
3. Forword to National Jurisprudence - B. A. Masodhkar.
4. *The Task of Law*—Rosoe Pound
5. *Supreme Court of India as an Instrument of Social Justice*—Bakshish Singh
6. *The Task of Law*—Rosoe Pound
7. *Social Justice* - David Miller
8. Ibid
9. Ibid
10. *Justice VS Jurist*
11. In search *of Social Justice*—Justice V.R.K. Iyer.

CHAPTER 2

Concept of Jurisprudence

" Jurisprudence is the first of the Social Sciences to be born," says Wurzel.[1]

What is this world and its creature's only philosophers can describe? What is the position of planets, we can find it out only through astronomy. The mental position of a person can be detected only by the study of psychology. In brief we can know the real meaning and position of a particular subject only through the study of its philosophical aspects. The same clue is with regard to the study of law and legal system. If we have to study law, we first have to know what is jurisprudence. Only lawyers and legal minded persons can describe it, because they have conceived it through the study of similar subjects. Law, in its abstract sense, can be explained only by the study of jurisprudence.

Chamber and Oxford Dictionaries have defineds jurisprudence as follows:

1. "Jurisprudence is the science or knowledge of law."
2. "Jurisprudence is the knowledge or skill in law. The science, which deals with human laws, written or unwritten in general. The philosophy of law. A system or body of law." These definitions are general without scientific contours.

Generally jurisprudence is regarded as an etymological study of the science of law in itself.

Now we have to analyse in detail the changing faces of the various aspects of jurisprudence in various ages starting from ancient time.

1. Eastern Continental Thoughts:

Eastern thoughts consist of Hindu, Mohamedan and Chinese systems. These may be arranged as follows:

(a) Ancient Hindu Concept:

In the ancient Hindu period the civilization and culture were at an exorbitant peak position. So many eminent writers had discussed the ancient position of Hindu Jurisprudence. U.N.Ghosal,[2] has brightly analysed and appreciated the old Indian legal system. He has called it a "Genius of India". He has transcripted some ideas of the Great Indian thinker Sri Aurobindo Ghosh from his inspiring book Renaissance in India, which has pointed out characteristics of Indian Genius and their influence in moulding Indian civilization. The three qualities of Ancient Indian spirit are: (1) Her spirituality, the master key of Indian mind; (2) Her stupendous vitality, her inexhaustive power and joy of life; (3) Her strong intellectuality at once austere, rich, robust, minute, powerful and delicate, massive principles and curious in detail. Under the impact of these three factors elaboration of all life into a science and an art assumed great dimensions in the history of ancient Hindu Jurisprudence, from the time of Ashoka the Great. Dr. Radhakrishnan[3], former President of India, also supported these basic Indian qualities of life and law.

Referring to another characteristic of the Indian mind–the Indian sense of balance and rhythm, of its synthetical tendency which prevented pursuit of the opposite extremes of life from resulting in chaos and confusion, Sri Aurobindo has illustrated his point from 'Indian Attitude towards Social ideas and Institutions' in the following memorable words: "In life the ideal of opulent living and the ideal of poverty were carried to the extreme Royal splendour and the extreme of satisfied spirituality. If Indian spirit was obliged to stereotype caste as a symbol of its social order it never quite forgot, as the caste spirit is apt to forget that the human soul and the human mind are beyond castes.... Its spiritual extremism could not prevent it from fathoming through a long era of the life of the senses and its enjoyment, and there too it sought the utmost richness of séance detail and the depth and intensities of sienna's experience."

Element of Spirituality: Let us see the influence of these three qualities of Indian Genius referred so far, and their part in Shaping the growth and development of our ancient political, social and legal theory under jurisprudence.

Taking the element of spirituality first, we quote A.K. Pavithran,[4] "Hindu jurisprudence and law is a code of duties and the ancient scriptures are full of duties (Dharma) rather than rights. Life itself is made subordinate to Dharma (Virtue), the key-note of which was not conventional morality based on Tradition, but righteousness in profession and practice in the attainment of true knowledge (Gyan) through devotion and action (Bhakti and Karma)." The exhibiting extortion in Taittareyya Upanishad, the true practice of Dharma (Satya Vada Satya Chara) points to the predominant element of spirituality of the Indian mind. The King as Danda Dhara was the fountain of justice, who identified himself completely with his subjects. The Smritis introduce us to see the concept of the welfare state, ensuring freedom from hunger and want. Apasthamba deliberately rejected the standard of wealth (Artha) in favor of virtue (Dharma), while we come across Arthashastra, the advocacy of a line of statecraft honoring as well as violating the moral standard. The writings of the followers of Lord Buddha reacted violently against the teaching of economics and also condemned politics as a dismal science, but pleaded for the application of principles of righteousness to the conduct of government affairs. The transcendental position given to righteousness under the influence of the Buddhist teaching is to be seen in the starting statement of Emperor Ashoka, that all men are his children and that the chiefest conquest is the conquest of righteousness, which he illustrated so beautifully in the administration of his vast empire.

Element of Vitality: The second factor relates to the stupendous vitality of the ancient Indian mind. The history of Indian legal theory legions with the Vedic Samhitas which means that it has existed for a period of at least 3000 years, if not more. This one factor is sufficient to testify to the extraordinary vitality of the ancient Indian mind. It may be further stated that Indian legal ideas and concepts are spread over practically the whole field of our extensive and astonishing literature.

Element of Intellectuality: Coming to the third element of India's strong intellectuality the Vedic Samhitas and the Brahmans present us with the concept of the omnipotent Cosmic Divine law. The doctrine of the supremacy of law of the social order and that of the multiple bases of the rights and duties of the King and the application of the rationalism to politics are discussed in the early Smritis. Manu and Bhisma, in particular, have added other principles of equal importance. Bhisma's forceful advocacy for the application of the principles of violence and of righteousness and the administration of the Government, his enunciation of the four-fold basis of sound statecraft: (1) Sacred Canon, (2) Custom, (3) Reason, and (4) Expediency are cases in point. In direct opposition to the Brahminical dogma of the origin of the social order, it formulated independent theories of cosmic or divine evolution as well as the evolution of man and his institutions, such as property, government and society. The greatest contribution made by our ancient jurists for the careful study and rational treatment of the principles of problem of the government including rule of diplomacy and interstate relations. According to Hindu ideas of jurisprudence, which was permeated by the central idea of 'Dharma' that applied to king and his subject without any distinction. As Jamini says what is signified by a command of God and of divine and leads to common benefit is called 'Dharma'. "Jurisprudence is the science which endeavour's to ascertain the fundamental principles of which law is expression."

Hence in conclusion we can say, after going through analytically the entire religious scriptures, that in Hindu concept law and legal system was not different from religion. In other sense religion kept the key to all types of affairs whether religious, legal, political or social, etc. Hence jurisprudence in Hindu aspect is the study of the rules and principles laid down in Hindu scriptures, imposed by divine power as proper for man as being capable of eternal existence governing all his activities whether of any type in this world.

In order to understand and appreciate ancient Indian jurisprudence it is necessary to start from its foundations upon which the theoretical superstructure was built. Some of the theories were, afterwards, modified or conditioned and to some extent even forsaken or abandoned, due to the exigencies of social and political life of later ages. Invasions by other people and influence of foreign ideas created great tensions and consequent re-adjustments, which are reflected in the evolution of legal theory, as we shall notice hereafter. To understand the philosophic base of law we must directly turn to the Rig-Vedic thought, which is considered as the sheet anchors of Indian culture and civilization wherein the Indian mind is seen embedded with all its potency, vitality and simplicity. This mind, which is latent with us, can still be considered to be the substratum for a legal reconstruction of the present Indian life. To achieve our objective a review of theories about the creation of this universe, the nature of law, the theory of karma, the nature of wrong, evil and suffering, and the theory of the ends of life become relevant. Such a review will also help find out the fiber of legal thought out of which its whole pattern emerged.

In theories of creation, we find certain considerations, objectives and preferences, which continue to take precedence in Indian mind. Our investigation brings forth three predominant views. The first is embodied in the Rig Veda (X Mandal, 90 Sukta) wherein we find that creation starts with yajna or sacrifice. In yajna or sacrifice the Pursha (jivatma) is sacrificed. Yajna expresses an aspiration for an ideal social life, which is sought in the Vedic prayer thus:

- Assemble (Sam); speak in harmony (Sam)
- May your minds be of one accord (Sam)
- Your prayer (Mantra) be common (Samana)
- Your assembly be common (Samana),
- Common (Samana) your mind united your thoughts.
- I counsel you to common (Samana) purpose and
- I worship with your (Samana) obtain.

(Rig Veda X 191. 2-3)

Yajna contains in itself all the main elements of a system, organization and must have been an original mode of Aryan life, even before emergence of political and other institutions like territorial state, private property, marriage, slavery, etc. It was based on common living and sharing the goods of existence with all its attendant dangers and advantages.

Law is reflected, at first, in the Yajnic way of common social life. It is a mixture of custom, legend, doctrine, myth, magic and religion. It is only at a later stage that state comes into being and law begins to be associated with it and then it is institutionalized and its knowledge is enriched and specialized and consolidated by a class of persons for the purpose of maintaining 'Dharma' and ordaining life in a strait-jacket of morals, religion and law. Yajna, as we have already seen, is the manifestation of 'Dharma', which later on was established as law. If Yajna seems burdensome than it ceases to be yajna. This jural attitude we need in our people when they obey law. Without it law is bound to be frustrated. Modern positivistic theories of law cannot generate this type of attitude. They merely bank upon 'force' or 'coercion' as the sole guarantee for the obedience of law, which is only an indirect and external control sanctioned by law. On the other hand, yajna as law is voluntary and a willing act and, therefore, operates directly. In it the person participates himself and feels one with it. What an irony that modern thinkers have begun to realize the importance of reverting to the idea of 'willingness' as an indispensable part of the nature of law. To a great extent it is an admission of failure on the part of the so-called scientific thinkers of law. In fact, law cannot yield its meaning to any reactionary or extremist thinker. It is essentially a synthetic product. Ancient religion-juristic philosophy of India is a reminder of this view. Modern thinkers like Ehrlich have begun seeking law in society besides its official modes and formalistic expressions. This is not new to Indian thinkers.

The notion of Yajna has seen a revival in the hands of Vinoba Bhave. He has started two movements—(i) Bhoodan Yajna and (ii) Sampatidan Yajna–which are juristically relevant. According to him the main object in launching these movements is to achieve, without the aid of parliament, the goal of social justice, which has a great jural relevance. Such campaigns can be correctly designated as social legislation by the society itself for the upliftment (economic) of the community. The concept of Yajna has inspired him to deny individual's ownership of land and to assert the ultimate ownership in God. He is claiming land for the landless and wealth for the poor. To him dan (giving away) is not just charity but the just distribution. These movements are a prelude to what the social legislators would like to do in future. Thus, in essence, these are jural postulates as they provide a theoretical basis for future Indian law.

In yet another description of 'creation' in Rig Veda we find the idea of will and intelligence without which human action and progress becomes impossible. Thus in Sukta 129 of the Rig Veda (X Mandal) there is a manifestation of the teleological view of creation of this universe, which has become famous as Nasadiya Hymn.

Whatever, the mystery of creation, be it untold or unknown, it is atleast certain that desire 'the first seed of mind' is the attribute to the Absolute reality, which at this cosmic level implies creative force and will, behind this Universe. A will and mental process implies original intelligence that was the basic urge of creation. This intelligence is not something outside the world or something above it. It is a part of the world. This Vedic Cosmic 'teleos' gives sanction to construct theories and to have purposeful thinking about law and life. Law like any other subject becomes a system and science, i.e., Shastra. Law or dharma becomes known and fit to be realized and obeyed in life and so is formulated in tests. This being so, Nyaya (logic) and Mimansa (interpretation) are recognized as essentials for any systematized development of law and there is ample evidence of their use in the historical evolution of ancient law.

As an extension of this systematic urge, dharma, artha, kama and moksa become the ends of life. Consideration for common goods gets its place in the theory of justice: the concept of duty, whether legal or moral, gets rationale and expresses the need to cope with the direction of this metaphysical intelligence. When duty or dharma is forgotten by people it gives rise to litigation which is termed as Vyavahar. In order to redress the disputes a king was needed to wield 'Danda' (Sceptre) (Manu vii. 18 to 24). To uphold Dharma judicial administration starts with the purpose of maintaining public order and enforcement of dharma or law including sacred or religious duty. Interpretation of law, which is nothing but an application of dynamic creative intelligence upon the static text of law, becomes necessary to re-determine it for making it suitable to life and its purposes.

Due weight is to be given to the circumstances of time, place and habits of people. All these considerations, which find place in the Indian legal philosophy, can be seen as progeny of this creative intelligence, which is metaphysical with this universe. The mythical support of the axiomatic truth that Danda is related to Brahmana (God) in the same way as Dharma, finds favor with Manu who says: "For the King's sake the Lord formerly created his own son. Punishment, the protector of all creatures, an incarnation of dharma or the law, is formed of Brahmana's glory." Kautilya reinforces this view in the following lines:

"That sceptre, on which the well-being and progress of the science of logic, Veda and commerce depend, is known as punishment. That which treats danda is the law of punishment or science of government."

He further observes that in the happiness of the subjects lies his (King's) happiness; in their welfare his welfare. Whatever pleases his subjects he shall consider as good. Intelligence had its operation in the dynamics of law. Indian jurists of the past have always recognized reason (viveka) as the source of law. Though in poetical literature mythological form of explanation is given, yet Nyaya or logic plays its own part in dispensing justice. Punishment or the force of law is not merely a coercion exercised at the command of the Austinian superior but is impregnated with intelligence which takes into account the purposes of life and law. It will not allow a purely materialistic or positivistic or spiritual approach to life but a synthetic approach bringing in its fold all these three, thus reaching the high watermark of human intelligence.

Another important theory of creation is embodied in the hymn No.190 of X Mandals of Rig Veda, which gives us the twin ends of living as 'Rita' and 'Satya'. It is the height of Indian genius that order (also law) and truth which are abstractions are considered as creations prime to all other concrete creation in this Universe. Rita, that seems to be the oldest juristic concept of human civilization expresses itself in the mind of the Rig Vedic seers as an ordering concept. Law is first envisaged as an order in cosmos and then in human life. It is the eternal law. Rit or law as order in human socio-political life is an extension of cosmic order. Therefore, the juridical law has its rationale of existence in the general concept of 'Order'. This law as order is also expressed in the form of prescription as 'dharmani'–eternal statutes. If order is the nature and necessity of human society and a guarantee of its existence, it also becomes a theory of obligation. Duty has to be imposed to do one's function well to maintain order. This order or law is later spoken as 'dharma', which holds this universe and society together. Hence, it becomes the duty of everyone to follow law or order called dharma, which is the metaphysical 'Is' and social or juristic 'Ought'.

The whole idea of social solidarity that is now posed in the West as juristic ideal is grounded in Rit or order as conceived by the ancients. If order is the value in itself, then conforming to order is 'right' or 'good' and its violation a 'wrong' or 'evil' which invites suffering. This suffering, when inflicted by authority, becomes punishment (Danda). Danda as the enforcement of this order is nothing but an aspect of Rit and in its later transformation, Dharma. To saints and sages this order becomes spiritual peace (Shanti) with the message of universal peace as visualized by the ancients in India.

Predominance and foremost consideration is given to truth when it is stated as one of the born and one of the twin ancestors of our world. Metaphysically, this 'truth' is the truth of the Existence, i.e. 'Reality'. Truth is satya (real), i.e., existence. This aspect is explored to its furthermost limit in Indian legal philosophy. In social relations this 'truth' is the agreement or coherence with precepts or actual state of facts. The judicial trial, after the Rig Vedic period, is spoken by the Sastrakars as an enquiry into truth, i.e., what has actually happened. Justice is impossible in the absence of ascertainment of truth. Justice is a deliberate act establishing coherence with truth. In other words, it reduces disorder into order and thus truth becomes the concomitant of Rit, the order as law, because one enforces the other. Truth is as great as order. It is identified in Vedas with God. Similar is the view of Mahatma Gandhi who formulated the natural law doctrine of 'Satyagrah', i.e., the theory of non-cooperation with unjust law, by applying the principle of 'Truth'.

Law is not only a prescribed behavior from outside but also recognition from within. It tends towards harmony and order in society. In the theory of justice this ordering is done according to law whose purpose is to uphold truth, which inspires faith in law. Justice in India is not born of conflicts in society. It has not arisen as a judgment presupposing a fight between adversaries. In Indian history there were no conflicts of intuitions and waging of constitutional battles, or revolutions like those we have had in the West, where law could be seen at one extreme as the will or command of the ruler and at the other extreme as an expression of the greatest amount of political and social freedom of the individual portrayed by the doctrine of 'rights of man'. It is beyond our nascent ancient Indian mind to think of law as the sole monopoly of the State. The ancient Indian could never think of supremacy of political order over social order in generating law. The law or 'Dharma' is considered as ruler of rulers. To do one's duty according to it is called rights. The nineteenth century notion of rights as subjective to man and at times subversive of legal order, boosted as securities or reservations against State were not needed, because the idea of security was already built in the concept of 'Dharma' itself. This Dharma, the 'Right', implies 'harmony' or 'Samanvya' and is conducive to welfare. It gives spiritual peace and later, in the hands of religious thinkers, tends towards the religion of non-violence. Dharma, therefore, is considered as the summum bonum of civilized existence. In order to understand and to construe the ancient Indian legal philosophy, it is also relevant to examine the theories regarding this universe, Karma, evil and ends of life[4]. From these theories issue forth the supreme position of law with its autonomy, dynamism and idealism; the role of reason in administration of justice and interpretation of law and a positive approach to its problems.

Some Criticism: On the question of the nature and extent of our ancient legal thoughts foreign writers have subjected us to a number of criticisms. The classical statement of Prof. Max Muller[4] about the paucity of our legal and political ideas is what strikes one at the outset:

This is what he wrote: "The Hindus were a nation of philosophers, their struggles were the struggle of thoughts, their past the problem of creation, their future the problem of existence. It might therefore justly be said that India has no place in the legal and political history of the World." This criticism is based upon the erroneous interpretation of the spirit of our civilization, because in our ancient society all types of activities whether political or legal, social etc., were governed and controlled by religion itself. Religion was wider enough for its application anywhere. So we can say religion, law and politics as they were separated by Max Muller were inseparable in India. But Prof. Max Muller has not understood the basic concept of Indian legal and political system and has understood religion in a very narrow concept governing only spiritual or policies relating to God and divinity only. The other answer of this criticism is that our civilization consists of three elements (discussed above). Sri Aurobindo Ghosh says, spirituality does not flourish on earth in the vaccum even as our mountaintops do not rise like those of an enchantment of dreams out of the clouds without a base. So this criticism ignores all three elements and disregards the vast and varied range of our old intellectual interests and pre-occupations. Thinking does not occur in vacuum and political ideas or theories generally relied on are invariably related to actual problems and existing conditions are indeed inseparable from them.

Another charge that is some times levied against Indian people is that they were too saturated with dogmatic belief in the divine creation and ordering of the world that they never attempted to inquire into the rational of their social, political and legal institutions. This betrays a lamentable lack of understanding of the genius of Indian culture. The inclusive spirit of Indian culture is totally different from the exclusive attitude of West. This criticism is also baseless because the Indian principles and policy of religion is too much scientific than many scholars have inquired and found them to be reasonable and rational one. It is not necessary for all to go and inquire about them and to waste time foolishly. Further a survey among a cross section of English people showed, says Prof. Basham of London University,[5] that fifteen percent of church going Christians believed in the Hindu doctrine of transmigration, which from Christian point of view would be absolutely heresy.

So I think that persons who have faith and belief in God or in any religion cannot reproduce this criticism. At a talk on January 28, 1964, at Trivendrum, Prof. Basham said[5] that the Westerner tended to see everything as either black or white. To him a preposition was either false or true. There could be no half way; this spirit found expression in the old expression, "Those shall not have any other God, but me." As distinguished from this in Shreemad Bhagwad Gita, Lord Krishna said, "Whatever god you may worship I shall answer from your prayer."

The Westerner could not accept both as true from the logical point of view unless some strange dispensation of providence part of one and part of other could be right. Another aspect, which distinguishes between the two, is the doctrine of transmigration. It is a rare doctrine and an essential part of Indian religious thoughts, which is also legal. The religious concept of West is that man on the earth is born once and only once. Life thus became very real and earnest as man stood to be saved or condemned forever. In Hinduism there are indefinite chances for everybody to achieve something better. So Indian religion would not have taken a hysterical turn, but for its belief in transmigration as provided in Gita, emphatically. So it cannot be the criticism of one another, but are two different branches of world going contradictory to each other. As regards criticism that Hindu Jurisprudential principles are dogmatic, Dr. Radhakrishnan observed,[6] "Religion in India is not dogmatic. It is a rational synthesis, which goes on gathering into new conceptions as Philosophy progresses. It is experimental and provisional in its nature attempting to keep pace with the progress of thoughts. The common criticism that Indian thought on its emphasis on intellect, puts philosophy in the place of religion, brings out the rational character of religion in India. No religious movement has ever come into existence without developing as its support, a philosophical content, referring to the general belief in the Vedas as the only authoritative source of knowledge. Generally these Vedic truths refer to the experiences of the seers with which any rational rendering of reality must take into account. The appeal to the Vedas does not involve any reference to an extra-philosophical standard."

There is yet another criticism which is urged against the tendencies and characteristics of our ancient political and legal thoughts. Willoughby[7] states, "the ideas of the ancient civilized people of the East were so much vitiated by confusion between law and religion that they failed to develop jurisprudence and political science as an independent branch of knowledge."[8] This criticism has already been repelled in detail.

So in conclusion we may refer to the idea of Brye[9] (study in history and jurisprudence), which we find proper and reasonable to be placed. "Hindu system of law and jurisprudence was suited to the needs of the people whose social relations it had to adjust and regulate."

Muslim (Mohammedan) Concept: According to the opinion of Bihariy,[10] "The object of knowledge of Muslim Law is to secure happiness in the eternal world of the hereafter. Islam like Hinduism regards this life as only transient and evanescent, a fitful flicker of a fading light." Here similarity stops and differences begin. Islam believes that life so long as it lasts is for living whereas Hinduism divides this worldly life in four parts:-

(1) Celibacy (2) Householder
(3) Hermit in forest (4) Renunciation

The Holy Quran describes: **(i)** there are some men who say O Lord give us good in this world, but such shall have no portion in the next world and there are others who say, O Lord give us good in this world and also good in the next world and deliver us from the torment of the fire. They shall have a portion of that which they have gained. God is swift in taking into account. Holy Quran again preaches, "But seek the abode of the hereafter in that which God hath given thee and neglect not thy position of the world and be thus kind even as God hath been kind to thee and seek not corruption on the earth! God loved not corruption."

According to Muslim belief, law originated from the direct command of God to real sovereign and law giver. It was interpreted and expanded by messengers of God who were certain chosen human guides, along with reason to help them in the conduct of life with a view to induce them to do which is good and abstain from what is evil. Those chosen ones pointed out what God commanded regarding good and evil and these injunctions of prophet were and are regarded absolute, final and reasonable. The Holy Quran and Hadith (Traditions) satisfied the needs of Muslim society of that time. But this could not serve long after the death of the prophet and subsequent progress of community, men could not be satisfied by the sayings or doings of the Mohammad; the result would have been disastrous and the whole fabric of "Fiqh" would have gone under but for the fact that express provisions were made in law for further expansion and elaboration. The Muslim jurists also had taken a hand, after the death of the prophet, to make the divine law flexible and elastic to meet the demands of the society. The result was the emergence of a comprehensive and compact system of law, which served all the purpose of Muslims. Some of its terms may be improper too, but strictly for the good of the community.

So we can say that Muslim law was ushered into this world to guide the followers of Islam to follow a regulated and righteous life in this world similarly with such changes as situation demands.

So in conclusion we can say according to Muslim point of view, "jurisprudence is the study of those guidelines and principles which regulate the life of the human beings in world as righteous keeping in view the Mohammadan Law."

Chinese Conception: The fundamental fact in the history of China (Ancient) is the development of a great empire in almost complete isolation from the current and crosscurrent of other civilized states. Other great civilizations for a long time were a closed book to her.

Some aspects of orthodox Chinese concept of life and law and humen relationships have to be borne in mind, and foremost in Chinese thoughts, was its conception of nature and man's relationship to nature. At the outset, it may be stated that Chinese view of life and law was diametrically opposed to Western era. The latter looked upon nature as an enemy to be conquered and controlled to gain material freedom. As far human nature is concerned, the difference perhaps is even deeper. According to the Christian concept man is always born a sinner and the only way in which he can hope to have some kind of spiritual freedom is by carrying on an incessant fight against nature in which he could not always be sure of success. The Chinese, on the other hand, conceived nature as a personification of kindness and not cruelty. Wrter Forke[11] says, "An object which attracts and not repels, a friend not a foe. Man therefore cooperates and does not compete with nature. Instead of fighting man tries to fit or fuse into the natural scheme of things and by this process produces a good thing on the earth and all that is necessary to sustain life. Both nature and human nature are good and if there is evil, it is an outcome of man's disregard of the natural laws of things, a downright departure from the principles of nature, and not due to the original sinful nature of man."

So in China, natural law and man made law were applicable and adjusted in such a manner that produced good things on the earth to sustain life. So in this view both nature and man made (positive) law are good enough. The fact should be noticed here that in Hindu and Muslim era man made law and its conception was not recognized at all, but it was regarded and recognized in China during that time. Apparent cause for this was isolation of China's civilization from other civilizations of the world for a long period and kingship (Empire) Rule by one voice was recognized by the law.

So in conclusion we can say jurisprudence in this conception is the study of those rules and principles both natural and man-made, adjusted in such a manner to produce only and exclusively for the well being of society and the community.

Western Thoughts:

Lord Loyd[12] summed up the position of jurisprudence as follows: "Recent trends in jurisprudence exhibit a variety of movement linked by an increasing awareness of the fruits of interdisciplinary cooperation, and buttressed by a more sophisticated methodology. It is apparent that, within its increasing professionalization, jurisprudence has now moved, lately, into the twentieth century."

Now we shall consider the contributions of various important jurists in western countries. What they have thought about jurisprudence or what they are thinking. Let us consider from the initial stage.

Holland[13] has made great contribution regarding the idea of jurisprudence. He said, "For the beginning of the science which reduces legal phenomenon to order and coherence the world is indebted to the Romans. It is also from their language that the science derives its name."

"JURISPRUDENTIA" in its original use, was merely one among several phrases signifying knowledge of the law just as "REIMILITARIS PRUDENTIA" signified knowledge of the conduct of warfare. The following terms are used synonymously with JURISPRUDENTIA – Legum PRUDENTIA, Legum SCIENTIA, Legitima SCIENTIA, PURIS NOTITIA, Cognitio, IURIS, IURIDS NOTITIA, and CIVILIS SCIENTIA. The phrase IURIS PRUDENS is employed by Pompons—

Legum Prudens. So the sort of knowledge which the term denoted may be gathered from Cicero's description of a juristconsult as one who must be skilled in the laws and in the usages current among private citizens and in giving opinions and bringing actions and guiding his clients right.

From this practical conception of legal knowledge the Roman jurists subsequently raised jurisprudence to a far higher one. The rudiments of this may already be traced in the writings of Cicero, who enumerates the civil law along with astronomy, geometry, and dialectic among the arts, which have to do with the pursuit of truth. He tells us that the study of law must be derived from the depth of philosophy and that by an examination of the human mind and of human society, principles may be discovered in comparison with which the rules of positive law are of but trivial importance.

Holland further says, "Thus the way was prepared for Utopian's who described jurisprudence, 'as the knowledge of the things human and divine, the science of just and unjust'." Although this definition is nearly the translation of the definition of jurisprudence by Stoic modified by the addition of a clause specifying the particular kind of wisdom intended. The first clause of Utopian's definition has been with little reason, thought by some to have reference to the distinction between IUS SACRUM and the other branches of law.

Thus Holland says, jurisprudence was conceived as a branch of the philosophy and such an elevation of the idea of legal study was naturally accompanied by the corresponding elevation of its professors. Utopian claims for himself and his learned brother that they are the "priests of justice" engaged in the pursuit of philosophy that is truly such and not counterfiet. The Roman had, in fact, attained by this time to the idea of a science of those legal principles that exist independently of the institutions of any particular country. No technical term could be borrowed from the Greek language to denote what was of purely indigenous growth and thus it has happened that a phrase which at first had been one among several signifying in a homely and quite unscientific sense, a knowledge of law came at length by an accident of Latin Philosophy, to express the new idea of a legal science.

The nations of modern Europe are fortunately in the habit of calling the various branches of knowledge by non-vernacular names adopted by common consent from the classical language so that a science is generally known by the same Greek or Latin term wherever Western civilization extends. It is, therefore, natural and convenient that most of the European nations should express the idea of science of law by a word, which they have borrowed from the language of those by whom the idea was first conceived. Even the Germans who have vernacular names for so many of the sciences recognize jurisprudence as well as "Richtswissens chart."

But the term is unfortunately also borrowed on the modern language to express other ideas, which might be better expressed in the vernacular. Thus upon the analogy of certain loose expressions of the Roman writers who sometimes use "JURIS PRUDENTIA" to denote a current view of law, there has sprung up in French the use of such phrases as Jurisprudence Constants–Jurisprudence des arrets de la Cour de cessation, in the sense of the view which the courts are in the habit of taking certain questions still less judiciable, is the use of English and French from the jurisprudence. The imposing quadri-syllable is constantly introduced into a phrase on grounds of the emphony alone. Thus we have books upon equity jurisprudence, which are nothing more or less than treatise upon the law administered by court of equity and we hear about the jurisprudence of France or Russia when nothing else is meant than the law that is in force in those countries respectively. This sacrifice of sense to sound might more readily be pardoned had it not misled serious and accurate thinkers. Bentham[14] for instance divides jurisprudence into expository which ascertains what the law is and censorial which ascertains what it is ought to be. Now an exposition of existing law is obviously quite another thing from a science of law and criticism upon the law with a view to its amendment is the subject not of jurisprudence, but as Bentham himself states that it is an art of legislation. Bentham carries the confusion further by proceeding to sub-divide expository into authoritative and un-authoritative. By first he means nothing more or less than law emanating from legislative power, by second he means rest of that which is not covered by the first. So, textbooks on law and works on jurisprudence without special reference to any one country can be called universal jurisprudence.

If we are right in considering that censorial jurisprudence should be called an art of legislation, that authoritative jurisprudence is nothing more or less a body of law and unauthoritative local jurisprudence is a mere commentary and unauthoritative universal jurisprudence is alone entitled to bear the name of science and should bear the name simply without the addition of epithets intended to distinguish it from department of the subject which are not existent. Jurisprudence ought, therefore, to be used without qualifying epithet as the name of science.

Holland further considers jurisprudence and inquires whether what kind of science it is–formal, analytical as opposed to material, that is to say, that it deals rather with the various relations which are regulated by legal rules than the rules themselves which regulate those relations. Although Roman Jurist Cicero clearly describes, "It is an analytical science of law because there always floated before the uses of the Roman Jurist a vision of a 'JUS Natural' an universal code from which all particular systems are derived or to which they are lent, atleast to approximate a set of rules, the matter of contents of which is the universal application." But Holland says, "This was not indeed the whole scope of the science as conceived by its founder like quoted above. But in point of fact, and in the very pursuit of this material unity they were led to elaborate a system of formal unity, to catalogue the topics with which every system of law has to deal. However, each may differ from the rest in its mode of dealing with them. They performed for law a service similarly to that which was rendered to language by the Greeks of Alexandra, when by invention of grammar (syntax, part of speech, clause etc.) and under the formulae of which are the phenomenon of any language find appropriate place."

Holland further thinks, "The assertion that jurisprudence is a formal science may perhaps be made clear by an example, if any person should accumulate knowledge of every system of law holding each apart from the rest in chambers of his mind, his achievements would be best described as an accurate acquaintance with the legal system of Europe. If each of these systems were entirely unlike the rest, except when laws have been transferred in the course of history from one to another. Such a distinguished jurist could no more than endeavor to hold fast and to avoid confusing the heterogeneous information of which he had become possessed. Suppose, however, as in the case, that the laws of every country contain a common element that they have constructed in order to affect similar objects and involve the assumption of similar moral phenomenon everywhere existing. Such a scheme would be a formal science of law presenting many analogists to grammar the science of those ideas of relation, which in greater or less perfection, and often in the most dissimilar ways, are expressed in all the languages of mankind. To each of these formal sciences there ministers a science that supplies it with materials."

Just as similarities and differences in the growth of different languages are collected and arranged by comparative philosophy and facts thus collected are the foundation of abstract grammar, similarly comparative law collects and tabulates the legal institutions of various countries and from the result thus obtained, the abstract science of jurisprudence is enabled to set forth an orderly view of the ideas and methods which have been variously realized in actual systems. It is for instance the office of comparative law to ascertain what have been at different times and places the period of prescription or the requisite of good marriage. It is for jurisprudence to elucidate the meaning of prescription in its relation to ownership and to action or to explain the legal aspect of marriage: We are not indeed to suppose that jurisprudence is impossible unless it is preceded by comparative law. A system of jurisprudence might conceivably be construed from the observation of one system of law only. Such, however, has not been in point of fact the mode of its evolution which must have been at extreme yards, but for impossibility of separating the essential elements of science from its historical accidents by comparing together laws enforced in the same country at different epochs and indigenous laws with the differing though resembling laws of foreigners. So Holland says, "Jurisprudence is, therefore, not the material science of those portions of the law which various nations have in common. But the formal science of those relations of mankind which are generally recognized as having legal consequences."

Holland further says, it must be sufficient to present without further explanation that jurisprudence is not a science of legal relations, a prior, as it might have been, or should have been, but is abstracted posteriori from such relations as have clothed with a legal character in actual systems; that is to say from law which has actually been imposed or positive law. It follows that jurisprudence is a progressive science. Its generalization must keep pace with the movement of systems of actual law.

Lord Hall of England has observed, "It cannot be supposed that Roman Laws can be wholly exempt from the common fate of human beings. Parliament has taken off and abridged many of the titles about which the law was concerned. Usage and disusage have antiquated others, and it shall not be ai together impertinent to give some instances herein of several great titles in the law which upon those occasions are at this day in a great measure antiquated and some that are much abridged and reduced into a very narrow compass and use. As time and experience and use and some acts of parliament have abridged some and antiquated other titles, so they have substituted or enlarged other titles, for instance action upon the case, devices, election and diverse others."

The interesting remarks of Sir Henry Maine on the prohibition that general adoption of a system of registration of titles would render comparatively unimportant such topics as possession; Bonitarean ownerships although these have been recognized as belonging to what may be called the osseous structure of jurisprudence.'

Last question for the consideration of the conception of jurisprudence in the eyes of Holland is whether the science of jurisprudence is divisible in several sciences. In this inquiry Holland first takes the view of Austin that science of jurisprudence is of two types–general and particular jurisprudence. Austin says " Particular jurisprudence is the science of any actual system of law or any portion of it, the only practicable jurisprudence in particular." The proper subject of general, or universal jurisprudence is description of such subjects and ends of law as are common to all. System and of those resemblances between different systems which are bottomed in the common nature of man or correspond to the resembling points in these several portions. Now particular jurisprudence may mean either two things. It may mean a science derived from observation of the laws of one country. If so the particularity attaches not to science itself which the same science whensoever derived, but to the source whence the materials of it are gained.

A science of law might undoubtedly be construed from knowledge of law of England alone, as science of geology might be and in great part was constructed from an observation of the strata in England only. Yet as there is no particular science of geology, so neither is there a particular science of law, for a science is a system of generalization which though may be derived from observation extending over a limited era will nevertheless hold good everywhere, assuming the object matter of the science to possess everything; the same characteristics. Principles of geology elaborated from the observation of England alone hold good all over the globe insofar as the same substance and force are everywhere present and the principles of jurisprudence, if arrived at entirely from English data would be true if applied to the particular laws of any other community of human beings, assuming them to resemble in essentials the inhabitants of England. The wider the field of observation, the greater, of course, will be the chance of the principle of science being lightly and completely uninitiated, but so far as they are scientific truths at all they are always general and of universal application, the phrase may, however, and probably does mean, an aquittance with the laws of particular people and the impropriety of describing such merely empirical and practical knowledge by a term which should be used only as the name of science has been already pointed out.

In either sense, therefore, the term is misnomer and it follows that the existence of a particular jurisprudence not being admitted, the employment of the opposed term "General Jurisprudence" becomes un-necessary both expressions should be discarded and science should be treated as incapable of being divided into these two branches -(1) historical or (2) philosophical. It may be said that the unity, which makes jurisprudence a science, exists only in India that while it has a side upon which it is closely allied to ethics and metaphysics. It is, on the other hand, no less intimately connected with archaeology and history that its phenomenon grow from any independent roots and are formed and coloured according to the character of the various soils from which they have sprung. But to say this, is only to say that the facts from which jurisprudence generalizes are furnished by history, the record of human actions. The unity which is the main business of jurisprudence to exhibit as underlying all the phenomenon which it investigates, is the late discovery of an advanced civilization and was for a long time unperceived while whose phenomenon were accumulating, the facts can only be presented by history may be studied with the sole view of discovering this class of facts. But this is not the task of jurisprudence, which may only begin when these facts begin to fall into an order other than the historical and arrange themselves in groups, which have no relation to the variety of human race. The province of jurisprudence is to observe the wants for the supply of which laws have been invented and the manner in which those wants have been satisfied. It then digests those actual wants and the modes in which they have actually been satisfied, irrespective of their historical or geographical distribution, according to a logical method one work on jurisprudence may contain more of historical disquisition which in another philosophical argument may predominate, but such differences are incidental to the mode of treatment and afford no ground for a division of science itself.

But though the science is one it may have as many heads or departments as there are departments of law. It would, therefore, be unobjectionable to talk of criminal, civil, public and private jurisprudence.

Holland concludes in these words: "To sum up, the term jurisprudence is wrongly applied to actual system of law or to current views of law or to suggestions for its amendment, but is the name of science. This science is formal, analytical rather than a material one. It is a science of actual positive law. It is wrongly divided in general and particular, or into historical or philosophical. It may, therefore provisionally be defined as the formal science of positive law."

In the Western culture Keeton[15] has also paid a rich contribution to jurisprudence. Keeton has considered the idea of jurisprudence as follows:

The subject matter of jurisprudence is the relations of man to society and to his fellowmen, insofar as the law regulates the relations. It will thus immediately be apparent that jurisprudence is a social science closely allied to political science, economics, and ethics. The study of jurisprudence presupposes knowledge of law or of some particular branch of it, but the amount of law, which must necessarily be known before the subject may be undertaken profitably by the students varies to some extent, according to the method which the student proposes to employ. That is to say that there is more than one approach to the science of Jurisprudence.

Originally jurisprudence meant merely knowledge of law. Thus Justinian placed at the beginning, both of the digest and of the institute says," Jurisprudential est. divinarum at quehumana-rum renum Notitia JUSTI Atque IN JUSTI SCIENTIO. "It is to be noticed that this definition contains two parts. The first part stating that jurisprudence is merely a knowledge of human and divine things and second stating that it is the science which distinguishes the just from unjust. The second part, which recognizes an abstract principle, which the first does not, is not only historically connected with the first, it does not inevitably proceed from it. In Roman law jurist first stated what the law was. Later in their history they deduced from their knowledge the principles upon which their law was founded. Such is the development, which has taken place in the science of jurisprudence. In other words science of jurisprudence may now be considered to be the study and systemic arrangement of the general principles of law.

Thus jurisprudence considers the elements necessary for the formation of a valid contract but it does not attempt to enter into a full exposition of the detailed rules of law of contract i.e. in English law or in any other system. It analysis the notion of status and considers the most important examples; but it does not consider exhaustively the points in which persons of abnormal status differ from ordinary persons. Again, jurisprudence deals with the differentiation between public and private law and considers the contents of the principle departments of the law. To do more than this would be to attempt a treatise upon the substantive law of some particular state.

In the present day, there exist certain textbooks, which purport to discuss–medical jurisprudence, dental jurisprudence and similar topics. They are compilation of facts, useful to the profession concerned and as such fulfill an exceedingly useful function. But on account of the inclusion of word jurisprudence in this title these works have incurred the censure and abuse of several writers upon the science of jurisprudence. The employment of what Prof. Holland calls "The imposing quadri-syllable" for these works is greatly to be regretted, but probably arose from the fact that lawyers frequently find these works useful in dealing with cases involving medical and dental questions. On the other hand, the employment of words like "Jurisprudence" when considering compilation of the laws of some country or some particular court is not wrong. It has become merely so historically. The early Roman lawyers would have considered each compilation to be true jurisprudence. The later Roman lawyers would not, nor do we at the present time. The writers who entitle such compilation have not thus perceived the change, which has taken place in the science. From this it follows that if the writers upon medical jurisprudence confined their labour to setting forth the law, which related to medical profession, the use of the word would be less reprehensive though it would still be inaccurate.

Although it cannot be strongly emphasized that there is only one science of jurisprudence, there are many methods of approach to it. It is customary in studying the science to employ one method principally although occasionally recourse may be had to others. Some of these methods of approach may be collected together in groups since they possess some common factor. Thus three very important methods (1) Historical, (2) Analytical, and (3) Critical (to qualify the name of science itself), are united by the time factor. Each method of approach contemplates the subject matter–law, from a different standpoint in time consequently reaching different but mutually supplementary conclusions.

Historical jurisprudence examines the manner of growth of legal system. It should be carefully distinguished from legal history, which records simply the changes, which have occurred in the development of law. It is the function of legal history to set forth the development of law, allotting to each phase its true position in the completed narrative. Legal history, however, is not critical, except unconsciously it indicates the processes of change and is therefore descriptive.

It is the function of historical jurisprudence to interpret those changes and to expose the forces, which have brought them about, taking a view of the whole system. It explains the inner significance of each change in the structure of the system. As Sir Polecat[16] puts it the historical method is nothing else than the doctrine of evolution applied to human societies and institutions.

Analytical Jurisprudence takes a legal system as it actually exists and resolves it into fundamental conceptions. This was the method of the later Roman jurist. It was also the method of John Austin who may be said to have founded the Modern English school of Analytical Jurisprudence. Salmond[17] calls it Systematic Jurisprudence. Critical Jurisprudence estimates the value of existing legal institutions and from them deduces, that changes in the law are desirable. Some jurists argue that such considerations are not properly within the sphere of jurisprudence at all, but are a portion of allied science of legislation. Prof. Gray[18] would limit the critical function of the science of jurisprudence to cases in which the law upon a particular topic is not yet settled, but adds later that it might be extended to include a case in which there was a possibility that an already existing rule of law might be extended to analogous groups of facts. But Keeton thinks it a question of hypothetical or speculative jurisprudence but also this term is a misnomer for there can be no jurisprudence where there is no law and Prof. Gray has already admitted that the law on the topic does not exist. It is, therefore, difficult to see upon what principle the cases that Prof. Gray enumerates can be differentiated from a general discussion of what the law ought to be. They are either within critical jurisprudence or within the science of legislation. The science of Critical Jurisprudence or of legislation depends naturally upon the science of Analytical and Historical Jurisprudence and is impossible without them.

It is an undoubted fact that such a science performs an exceedingly useful function, intimately connected with the progress of law. Glimpses of it, indeed, may frequently be discovered in practically every work dealing with jurisprudence. Moreover without conclusions relating to legal progress, jurisprudence would be a somewhat barren science and both historical and comparative methods of approach would lose much of their value. Therefore, there can be no philosophy of law in the true sense of word.

Two further methods of approach i.e. (1) known shortly as Civil or Municipal-and (2) International Jurisprudence may be differentiated according to the communities over which the legal system extends. Speaking generally only law, which is administered within states or community, is considered in jurisprudence. International Jurisprudence is concerned with the principles upon which the law existing between states is based. A third classification of methods of approach possesses as its differentiating characteristics the number of legal systems. Examined thus we have particular, comparative, and general jurisprudence.

(i) "Particular Jurisprudence is the science which examines any actual and single system of law."

(ii) Comparative Jurisprudence considers the development of two or more systems of law. The term has more than one meaning. The science may have for its object the discovery of those legal rules, which are common to the legal system studied or again it may discuss those relations of individuals, which have legal consequences together with an inquiry how those relations find expression in the legal systems considered more frequently. This type of jurisprudence selects various legal topics and explains fully their method of treatment. The comparative jurisprudence has only recently received its recognition as a science. The Roman lawyer habituated to the classic symmetry of his own system, despised the confusion and archaism of English Law while the common lawyers rich in the accumulated wisdom of Brocton, Coke, could scarcely conceive that any other system might furnish illustration, which it would be profitable for him to study. Even for practical purposes, the science of comparative jurisprudence might prove to be of extreme value.

Lastly there is General Jurisprudence. This term has more than one meaning. It contemplates a compression of all the legal systems of the world. Libnitz[19] proposed a work of this type when he declared that if he lived long enough, he would set forth the legal systems of all the systems in parallel columns. In Libnitz's day this would not have been the practical impossibility that it is now, for the only legal system, which he would have profitably, and accurately compared would have been the Romans with its offshoot, the product law of Germany, the English and possibly the Mohammedan. Today in order that such a science could be construed, cause duration of all Hindu, Muslim, English Chinese, Japanese as well as Roman and English and other systems would be necessary together with some notice of the laws and customs of numerous uncivilized and semi-civilized peoples at all stages of social development. Such study would be far too big, besides it is exceedingly doubtful whether it would serve any practical end. Keeton says that Holland has rightly said that jurisprudence is a progressive science.

Thereby indicating that such generalization is possible, Prof. Buckland[20] supplies necessary note of caution when he writes, "What is likely to be the fate of a principle found in the law of, say, then states which go on developing on different lines? The probabilities are against its continuance as a general principle and the notion that some other general principles will arise, to take its place appears to be rather an article of faith then a proposition on which a science can be based." Prof. Buckland further proceeds to demonstrate that the generalizations that Prof. Holland wishes to make about the systems of law themselves may be made about the privileges according to the Institutions and juristic notions of various communities themselves change. In this particularly the science of jurisprudence approaches very close to the sciences of anthropology and sociology, but all three gain by this proximity. The point that Prof. Buckland made when replying to Prof. Holland is also implied in Pollock's note on the book of Maine–Ancient Law, in considering the order of growth of community institutions from consideration of the various influences affecting this growth of Human Institutions. It would appear that no two systems of law ever develop along precisely similar lines.

The term General Jurisprudence may be used with a second and quite different meaning to denote the study of those legal rules that are found in all legal systems of law. Just as the science of jurisprudence when considered as the science, which compares the legal system of the whole world, is too vast so the science of general jurisprudence when bearing its second meaning is altogether too small to be of any value. Prof. Gray notes: "The list of rules of law received simper, unique, it omnibus from Kamschatka to Patagonia is likely to be a short one." The list would not contain a single rule that is to say that the science of general jurisprudence, in this sense, has no practical existence. In any case it is doubtful whether the list, when made would do more than indicate that some particular group of rules had been borrowed universally from some well established system on account of their extreme utility.

There is a third and more usual meaning attached to the term General Jurisprudence i.e. a statement of the most important general legal principles and institutions as they occur in civilized communities. Understood in this sense, General Jurisprudence already possesses a considerable literature of which Berolz Hummer's world's legal philosophy may be taken as a good example.

Sir Vine Gradoff[21] has summed up the work of this school of jurists as follows: "But suppose that after drawing up your table of contents you proceed to define law, rights, etc. You will, not only find that many of your colleagues disagree with you."

This is inevitable in any case but it will be difficult to deny that the ideas of the Greeks about justice as the end or the Roman conception of absolute property and view of canonist of crime and sin do not coincide with the teaching of modern jurists and are not likely to coincide with the doctrine of their probable successors. There is bound to be more substantial agreement as regard methods of legal thoughts insofar as these rest on an application of logic because former logic is built upon universally accepted rules as to the operation of reasoning. So to sum up, General Jurisprudence of 19th century can hardly stand for anything else than an encyclopedia survey on juridical principles of individualistic society. In this sense it deserves full attention because it expresses the tendency of the legal mind to coordinate and harmonize its concept in the coherent and reasonable whole on a given bases the basis of individualism. So in conclusion Keeton observes that jurisprudence, therefore, is the science of general principles and may be approached from many points of view, as Mr. Harrison has pointed out the three main and most important methods of approach are the historical, the analytical and comparative.

Eminent jurist Prof. G.W. Paton[22] has provided the concept of jurisprudence. He says the writer of jurisprudence is the fortunate or unfortunate position of being able to determine the boundaries of his subject with rather more freedom than remains in other legal courses. Stern conflict rage concerning its nature and scope. But this certainly introduces a liveliness into many consider a dull pursuit, but it has corresponding disadvantages because controversy absorbs much of the energy that should be spent in pursuing the subject itself.

Modern jurisprudence trenches on the field of social sciences of philosophy. It digs into the historical past and attempt to create the symmetry of a garden out of the luxuriant chaos of conflicting legal system. The breadth of its scope covering a voluminous literature written in many tones make it a difficult subject to master. But in spite of difficulties inherent in the subject the problems of jurisprudence can be expressed in fairly simple language, though, of course, opinions may well differ as to real solution.

Jurisprudence is some time used merely as imposing synonym for law as when we speak of medical jurisprudence. This is not the use to which the term is put in this work. In

France law, jurisprudence covers what we should term case law. But Paton says jurisprudences a particular method of study not of the law of one country, but of the general notion of law itself. Holland describes it as a formal science of positive law. Allen defines it scientific synthesis of the essential principles of law. However, it may be defined as a study relating to law. Although the term law may seem to the uninitiated a simple one, analysis reveals that there are many uses of this word.

Hence one of the first tasks of jurisprudence is to attempt to throw light on the nature of law. At first sight it would seem to be the most logical procedure, first to define law and then to discuss the scope of jurisprudence. But there are various ways of approaching the problem and each school of jurisprudence tends to set up its own definition. Thus to take only one point for purpose of illustration is wrong, law has a two-fold aspect. It is an abstract body of rules and also social machinery for securing order in community. The sensible approach is to admit that both these sides of law must be considered. Clearly a jurist who considers only the theoretical rules of the books will be very different from one that attempts to study law in action. Hence study of schools of jurisprudence will provide a clear glance to any misconception of jurisprudence.

Veno Gradoff, a jurist, has also contributed to jurisprudence in the basic language. He says, "In contrast to the simple rules and divisions of positive law which strikes across the history of all nations there arises a science of law, jurisprudence which aims at discovering the general principles underlying legal enactment and judicial decisions. It speculates on the processes of thought, which take place in the mind of legislators, judges, pleaders and parties. This theory of law enable men to frame and use their laws deliberately and scientifically instead of producing them over or less random under the stress of circumstances. The study of jurisprudence is therefore, by no means a mere expedient and the schools, contrived in order to introduce beginners to the term and principal directions of this art. Though, of course, jurisprudence does help in this respect while on its way towards the solution of scientific problems, nor does it exist chiefly for the purpose of classifying and cataloguing, scattered notices as to rules and remedies. The most perfectly systemized chapters and paragraphs of a code would not render a general theory of law superfluous, for the prime consideration is not so much to establish the sequences of laws as to discover rational interdependence and ultimate significance, for the intricate maze of common law which like Anglo-American is based on judicial decisions. The help rendered by the jurisprudential classification is especially welcomed, may be necessary, but even apart from that a theory of jurisprudence is needed to strengthen the scattered agreements by treating them as parts of a coherent body of legal thoughts. Observations and rules, which may seem casual and arbitrary when memorialized for practice, obtained their justification or called forth for criticism when examined in the light of general theory. John Salmond[23] has also laid down new concept of jurisprudence as follows:

In a generic and primary sense jurisprudence includes the entire body of legal documents. It is jurisprudentia – the knowledge of law. In this sense all law books are books of jurisprudence. By law in this connection is meant exclusively the civil law, the law of land as opposed those other bodies of rules to which the name of law has been extended by analogy. If we use the term science in its widest permissible sense, as including the systemized knowledge of any subject of intellectual inquiry, we may define jurisprudence as the science of civil law.

Salmond gives two meanings of jurisprudence, one in the widest sense and the other in the narrow sense. In the widest sense jurisprudence is the science of civil law. It is a science not an art. It is the law of the land, law of lawyers and law of courts. It is confined only to those rules that are enforced by the court; there are three branches of jurisprudence in this sense–legal exposition, legal history and science of legislation.

Legal exposition means the actual contents of particular legal system as it exists today or as it has existed in the past. Legal history deals with the various stages through which law has passed. Science of legislation means the study of law as it ought to be in the future in an ideal state or as it has been in past.

In the narrow sense, jurisprudence is the science of the first principles of Civil law. It deals with the abstract principles of law, which are basic in the legal system. It is well-considered and profound knowledge of the ultimate principles, which underline specific and concrete provisions of law.

According to Rosoe Pound[24]: "Jurisprudence is the science of law using the term in judicial sense as denoting the body of principles recognized as enforced by public and regular tribunals in the administration of justice."

Prof. Gray[25] has defined this term as follows: "Science of law, statement and systematic arrangement of the rules followed by the Court and the principles involved in those rules."

According to Lee[26]: "Jurisprudence is the science, which endeavors to ascertain the fundamental principles of which the law is the expression. It rates upon the laws as established facts, but at the same time it is a power in bringing law into a coherent system and in rendering all parts thereof subservient to fixed principles of justice."

According to Clarke[27]: "Jurisprudence is the science of law in general. It does not confine itself to any particular system of law, but applies to all the systems of law or most of them. It gives the general idea, conception and fundamental principles upon which all or most of systems of laws of the world are based."

John Austin[28] has laid a definition of jurisprudence in these words: Jurisprudence is the philosophy of positive law.

According to Dr. Julins Stone[29]: "Jurisprudence then in the present hypothesis is the lawyer's extra version. It is the lawyer's examination of precepts, ideals and techniques of the law in the light derived from present knowledge in discipline another than the law."

It is an attempt which must always remain imperfect to fulfill for the law the object strikingly posed by the late Mr.Justice Holme of showing the rational connection between your fact and the frame of Universe, "to be master of any branch of knowledge you must master those which lie next to it."

Dias and Hughes[30] have noted as follows: "Jurisprudence today is thus envisaged in an immeasurably broader and more sweeping sense than in which Austin understood it. Buckland described the change vividly. "The analysis of legal concepts, he says, is what jurisprudence meant for the student in the days of my youth. In fact it meant Austin was a religion. Today he seems to be regarded rather as a disease, he cannot be replaced on his pedestal. The intentionally individualistic habit of mind of his day is out of fashion. At present jurisprudence may tentatively be described as any thought or writing about law other than a technical exposition of the branch of the law itself. So if X writes a book about the economic effects on the families of convicted prisoners on their conviction this will be called a contribution to jurisprudence. If Y writes a book on theories of justice in the ancient world, this too will be a contribution to jurisprudence. If Z describes how the development of English case law is governed by the psychology of the judges this would also fall within the scope of our subject, sometimes qualifying adjectives are lacked on to the noun so that X's book might be called a study of economic jurisprudence, Y's book an example of philosophical jurisprudence and Z's book one on psychological jurisprudence, but with or without the qualifying adjectives.

"It would be within the modern sense of the word to describe all three books as being works of jurisprudence.

"Criticism of Positive and Formal Positive Law: many writers have criticized the theory of formal positive law as follows:

"It has been pointed out that jurisprudence is not only a formal science of positive law but also material science.

According to Gray, jurisprudence is, in truth, no more formal science than physiology. As bones and muscles and nerves are the subject matter of philosophy so the acts and forbearance of men and the events that happen to them are the subject matter of jurisprudence and physiology could as well dispense with the former, as jurisprudence with the later. Again the real relation of jurisprudence to law depends upon not what law is treated, but how law is treated. A treatise on jurisprudence may go into the minute particulars or be confined to the most general doctrine and in either case deserves it name. What is essential to it is that it should be an orderly, scientific treatise in which the subjects are duly classified and subordinated."

According to Jenks[31]: "Can jurisprudence be truly said to be a purely formal science, not it is submitted unless the word formal is used in a strained and artificial sense. It is true that a jurist can only recognize a law by its form, for it is the form which, as has been said causes the manifold matter of the phenomenon to be perceived but the jurist having got the form, as it were on the operating table has to dissect it and ascertain its meaning. Jurisprudence is concerned with means rather than with ends though some of its means are ends in themselves. But to say that jurisprudence is concerned only with forms is to degrade it from the rank of a science to that of a craft."

But we find that there is confusion in the agreement of Jenk's because he does not make any distinction between a formal science and a formalistic manner of its approach. Holland does not say that jurisprudence is concerned merely with forms, what he says is that jurisprudence deals in a formal or abstract manner with those relations of mankind which are generally recognized as having legal consequences.

Adamson[32] says, "The notions of form and formal relations are by no means so simple and free from ambiguity that by their aid one can at once solve a complicated problem of philosophic arrangement."

P. J. Fitzgerald[33] described as follows: "Jurisprudence is the name given to certain type of investigation into law, as investigation of an abstract general and theoretical nature which seeks to lay bare the essential principles of law and legal system."

It is a subject, which differs in kind from other subjects, for the typical legal subjects i.e. contract or tort–consists of set of rules and principles to be derived from authoritative sources and applied to factual situation in order to solve practical problems. So jurisprudence does not constitute set of rules, is not derived from authority and is without practical application. One result of this difference is that far less agreement is to be found in different jurisprudence text books than in the textbooks on other legal subjects, where much the same ground is covered and much the same picture presented, for the simple reason that, whatever the writer's view, the legal rules remain the same whereas jurisprudence which is without rules, allows a far greater play to the writer's own personal approach. Another consequence of this difference is that the method of inquiry apt for jurisprudence will not necessarily be that used in the study and practice of ordinary or typical legal subjects. In jurisprudence we are not concerned to derive rules from authority and apply them to problems, we are concerned rather to reflect on the nature of legal rules or the underlying meaning of legal concepts and on the essential features of legal systems.

In this jurisprudence comprises philosophy of laws and secondly order subject whose object is not to discover new rules, but to reflect on the rules already known. Just as the philosopher of science concerns himself with scientific laws already discovered rather than with the discovery of new laws.

Now the basic features of a legal system are chiefly to be found in its authoritative sources and the investigation of the nature and working of legal authority naturally form a subject of jurisprudential inquiry such as pros and cons codification, strict system of judicial precedent. Another branch of jurisprudence consists of the analysis of legal concept such as right, possession etc., in various forms and from various point of views. But whether discussing nature of law or analyzing legal concept, jurisprudence should not confine to logic. Legal theory is concerned with law as it exists and functions in society and the way in which it is created and enforced.

The classification of aspects of jurisprudence by Austin, in general and particular, has been criticized by Holland and Salmond. We have considered Holland at length. But the criticism of Holland is based on the assumption that the law has the same characteristic all over the world, but this is opposed to human experience.

According to Mainland: "Races and nations do not travel by the same road and at the same rate."

Bryce tells[34]: "The law of every country is the outcome and result of the economic and social conditions of that country as well as the expression of its intellectual capacity for dealing with these conditions."

According to Buckland[35]: "Law is not a mechanical structure like geological deposits. It is a growth and its true analogy is that of biology."

According to Savings: "Law grows with the growth and strengthens with the strength of people and its standard of excellence will generally be found at any given period to be in complete harmony with the prevailing ideas of best class of citizens."

By Puchta[36]: "The progress in the formation of law accordingly keeps pace with the progress in the knowledge of the people of the facts which they observe and hence it is, that law has its provincialism no less marked than language."

Salmond has also discarded Austin's classification of the aspect in these words: "The error in Austin's idea of general jurisprudence lies in the fact that he assumes that unless a legal principle is common to many legal systems it cannot be dealt with in general jurisprudence. There may be many schools of jurisprudence, but these are not different kinds of jurisprudence. Jurisprudence is one integral social science, the distinction between general and particular jurisprudence is not proper. It is not proper to use such terms, as Hindu

Jurisprudence, Roman and English Jurisprudence. Actually what we are dealing with are not the different kinds of jurisprudence but the different systems of law. It is more appropriate to use the term jurisprudence alone without any qualifying epithet. Jurisprudence is a social science, which deals with social institutions, which are governed by law. It studies them from the point of view of their legal significance."

In western countries one fact is clear at least, that no single school of thought can provide complete guideline and concept of subject like jurisprudence. Positive, natural, historical, sociological or realist schools individually cannot provide the correct description of jurisprudence. The position of eastern continental countries is little bit complex. Here in India and China religious and legal principles cannot be separated from each other. Legal and religious principles are united and inseparable. It shall not be wrong to say that legal principles, to a large extent, are an offspring or side product of religious principles or dogmas. Hence to describe the real picture and concept of jurisprudence in India we have to take into account western thoughts and our own cultural and unique religious way, which had set down the path for justice delivery system in society.

Paton[37] described jurisprudence as follows: "The writer on jurisprudence is in the fortunate (or unfortunate) position of being able to determine the boundaries of his subject with rather more freedom than remains in other legal courses. Stern conflicts rage concerning its nature and scope. This certainly introduces liveliness into what many consider be a dull pursuit, but it has corresponding disadvantages, for controversy absorbs much of the energy that should be spent in pursuing the subject itself."

Modern jurisprudence trenches on the field of social sciences and philosophy. It digs into the historical past and attempts to create the symmetry of a garden out of the luxuriant chaos of conflicting legal systems. The breadth of its scope, covering a luminous literature written in many languages, makes it a difficult subject to master. There is a danger that excessive learning may obscure the real problems that must be faced. Too many works contain such a wealth of reference to the learning of the past and present that they become tedious and unintelligible, save to one who is as erudite as the author of the work concerned.

Moreover, even if the work is written in a language with which we are familiar, we are sometimes tempted to repeat the old quip that language was given to us to conceal our thoughts. It is true that it is difficult for any system of knowledge to use the terms of popular speech, for, unless the vague meaning given to his terms by the average man is made precise, confusion results. It is not easy to preserve a balance between the use of common words in a strange sense and the invention of terminology that baffles the reader. Thus one writer may use such a common term as 'possession' in a sense entirely his own, causing confusion to all save the most acute; another invents such a technical apparatus that it is necessary to furnish a glossary of eighteen pages. As in modern politics, -isms abound. Some difficulties of terminology there must be, for even such a term as law has many meanings. But the besetting sin of jurists is to conceal threadbare thoughts in elaborate and difficult language. In spite of the difficulties inherent in the subject, the problems of jurisprudence can be expressed in fairly simple language, though, of course, opinions may well differ as to the real solution. Hence a short discussion of the schools of jurisprudence seems to be the clearest way to approach the question. To cover the learning of many centuries is impossible, but it is also unnecessary, as the problem remains the same, though the answers may differ.

Dias[38] describes as follows: "Writings on jurisprudence are not concerned with expositions of law, but with disquisitions about law."[39] Various branches of substantive law, for example, teach how rights and duties are acquired whereas jurisprudence would investigate such questions as: What are rights and duties? How are they used? How do they work? It also improves the use of law by drawing together insights from different branches, criminal, constitutional etc., in the solution of problems. Thought about law is also a story of movements in outlook and ever-changing ideas, and developments are taking place in contemporary, physical, moral and other social sciences, which make it difficult to decide once and for all how, if at all, these should be taken into account.

'Thought about law' suggests that an important, if not essential, prelude to jurisprudence study should be of some thought about thought. The overall aim is not to teach students what they need to know, but how to think profitably and for themselves, as well as to educate and equip them to be efficient lawyers. Thinking is inseparably bound up with the meaning and use of words. This is an aspect of philosophy, known as semantics, which is of especial interest to lawyers since, as Lord Macmillan said, "The lawyer's business is with words. They are the raw material of his craft"[40]. Laws are articulated in language; logic is controlled by it. Some of the needless difficulties that have arisen in jurisprudence are of linguistic origin. This is because words are not only tools of thought, but also control it. People tend to think in terms of their language structure. Accordingly, learning how to think profitably will be assisted by a sharpened awareness of the possibilities of language, not only to lead thought but also to mislead it.

He further describes about jurisprudence: books called "Jurisprudence" vary so widely in subject matter and treatment that the answer to the question, what is 'Jurisprudence' is that it means pretty much whatever anyone wants it to mean–a depressing start indeed. This kind of answer suggests that something is amiss with the question. It would be better to ask: How is this word used or more pertinently, what is this book going to do? The Latin expression, Jurist Prudential, means either 'knowledge of' or 'skill in law.'

The Roman jurists, however, never developed any subject as 'Jurisprudentia'[41]. In the sense of 'knowledge of law', the word sometimes describes expositions of particular branches of the law. For e.g., the name 'Equity Jurisprudence' was once given to a textbook on Equity[42]. This use of the word, current on the continent, is no longer fashionable in common law countries. In a wide sense it ''is also used to describe the legal connections of any body of knowledge: so 'Dental Jurisprudence',' Architectural Jurisprudence' or 'Medical Jurisprudence' would be titles for expositions of such aspects of dentistry, architecture or medicine as may be important in law. Some criticisms of this use of the term are somewhat misconceived.

There has been a tendency to suppose that the word 'Jurisprudence' has, or should have, some 'proper' meaning, which makes it applicable to this kind of study[43]. As will appear, no word, least of all 'Jurisprudence', has a 'proper' meaning. There is also the argument that such studies as these are not 'scientific[44], which presupposes some special meaning of the word 'science'. The reason for avoiding a term like 'Medical Jurisprudence' is that this kind of expression is no longer current in English-speaking countries, although occasional instances may still be found[45]. It may be noted that in French law, la jurisprudence is the term applied to the body of law built up by the decisions of particular courts[46].

In English it was not until the time of Bentham and his disciple Austin in the early part of the nineteenth century that the word began to acquire a technical significance among English lawyers. The former distinguished between examination of the law as it is and as it ought to be ('expositorial' and 'censorial' jurisprudence), and he was also much concerned with law reform ('decontogy'). The latter, who was the first professor of Jurisprudence in the University of London, occupied himself with 'expository' Jurisprudence, and his work consisted mainly of a formal analysis of the structure of English law. Analytical exposition of the type that Bentham pioneered, and Austin developed, has dominated

English legal thought almost to the present. It was therefore inevitable that the word 'Jurisprudence' came to mean in this country almost exclusively the analysis of the formal structure of law and its concepts. This was the nearest that the word came to bearing a precise meaning.

Towards the end of the nineteenth century changing human affairs had brought about an ever-increasing preoccupation with conflicting ideologies and troubled social conditions, which resulted in a decisive shift in outlook with the result that jurisprudence came to be envisaged in a broader sense than in Austin's day. Buckland described the change vividly. 'The analysis of legal concepts', he said[47], 'is what Jurisprudence meant for the student in the days of my youth. In fact it meant Austin. He was a religion; today he seems to be regarded rather as a disease'. The breadth of the modern attitude is well summed up by Julius Stone who described jurisprudence as:

"The lawyer's extra-version. It is the lawyer's examination of the precepts, ideals, and techniques of the law in the light derived from present knowledge in disciplines other than the law[48]."

So vast coverage may be summed up in the proposition that Jurisprudential study nowadays concerns thoughts about law, its nature, function and functioning, on the broadest possible basis, and about its adaptation, improvement and reform. A convenient way of obtaining an idea of its compass is by explaining this description.

Hence it may be concluded:

Jurisprudence is the overall study of those principles or rules, which are meant for the enforcement and maintenance of justice universally, individually, or jointly to persons or things of the society for the purpose of working and administration of that society or world. (Jurisprudence is thinking and thought line on law, justice and legal system.)

I think that the definition is wider enough to take into all types of study in law, legal system and justice because the entire legal phenomenon moves round about the object of justice.

New Jurisprudence

Sri P.B.Mukherji[49] writes that New Jurisprudence is both an intellectual and idealistic abstraction as well as behaviouristic study of man in society. It includes political, social, economic and cultural ideas. It covers the study of man in relation to state and society. It may be concluded that Sri Mukherji has an idea about jurisprudence that it is like a shining but unfulfilled dream of a world governed by reason. For some, it is a buried system, details of which they do not know. For another, familiar with the details of the system, it is laid in the depth of an unreal literature. For others, known with the subject, it is laid in the hope of a future enlightenment. For all, it is just around the corner. Hence jurisprudence is the part of history, economics, sociology, ethics and a philosophy of life. Hence it is as big as law and bigger.

This world needs a new jurisprudence for the new age. Law and jurisprudence have a universal quality. It also has a timeless element. They are "Alphabets of law." It is therefore essential in civilized jurisprudence to find out common basic elements, but subject to the demands of the universality. The jurisprudence of the country cannot afford to be entirely exotic for the simple reason that law is its ultimate analysis, remains the relative expression of the life and spirit of the land and community it serves. Vast growth, rise in mental and physical sciences and their application to life, the changing theories of political theories and manifold plans for social and economic development require a new jurisprudence to support corresponding objectives. The slow and placid legal procedure of a bygone and feudal age is a hindrance. If the Roman Jurisprudence was not enough for the rise and growth of England, it requires little effort to realize that other American and continental Jurisprudence, in case of study of new Jurisprudence is to meet this challenge of country is self-evident.

Constitutional Jurisprudence

In the sphere of Constitutional Jurisprudence a new integration is required to lay the ghost of perpetual conflicts between state and subjects. This conflict is historic legacy dating its ancestry from Hobbesion and Austeim theory of law and sovereignty. The concept of an absolute state and traditional doctrine of sovereignty are today inadequate in law and jurisprudence. The old trinity of ideas, state, law and sovereignty has changed radically but constitutional jurisprudence has largely failed to adjust with it. From the notion of the Police State, Tax collecting state the idea grew of pursue state and his pursued subject. Law largely comes to be understood as rules of this pursuit. In the modern idea of welfare state with pluralistic origination of state and democratic legislature, it is necessary that the new constitutional jurisprudence should accord its recognition to this established fact. The old theories that state is like an alien organization apart from subject and its counterpart in the protection theory that the subject always needs a kind of perpetual shelter and protection from grabbing state require a new reconciliation by a new Constitutional Jurisprudence. The Romantic theory of civil liberty developed as a corner stone of Conservative Jurisprudence has lost its importance. We, now, have to fight not against king and feudal lords but modern counterparts; the bureaucracy and administration.

Criminal Jurisprudence

The Criminal Jurisprudence has become too backward to meet the challenge of modern age. Doctrine of man's need is eclipsing. The onus of proof, burden of proof, innocence of accused and other theories of Criminal Jurisprudence are no longer good in present conditions.

Civil Jurisprudence

The picture of law of properties, succession, contract, tort inheritance, revenue and labor cases is one of date. The triple concept of capitalism, socialism and communism have their respectable on this subject but the mechanism of adopting these concepts to the contemporary demands of current social needs in a viable Jurisprudence need not wait till the final solution of these contending philosophies which may never come. There is similar position of the law of contact, tort, etc.

Traditional Juristic Concepts

Old Jurisprudence concerning right, obligation, duties and privileges are crumbling down. The great task before the present generation of jurists, judges and lawyers is to help to formulate an integrated system of multidimensional modern jurisprudence, expansive enough to recognize new challenges and stresses.

Old Jurisprudence has become a dead classic. Much of it is good, deal in legal sense and rest is today at best only in legal history. Every jurist has his own notion of the subject matter and the proper limits of jurisprudence depend upon his ideology and the nature of society. Moreover, the growth and development of law in different countries has been under different social and political conditions. The words used for law in different countries convey different meanings. The words of one language do not have synonyms in other languages conveying the same meaning. The word "Jurisprudence" is not generally used in other languages in the English sense. In French, it refers to something like "case law". The evolution of society is of a dynamic nature and hence the difficulty in accepting a definition by all. New problems and new issues demand new solutions and new interpretations under changed circumstances. However, scientific inventions have brought the people of the world closer to each other, which help the universalisation of ideas and thoughts and the development of common terminology.

Jurisprudence and Sociology

According to Salmond[23], Jurisprudence is the knowledge of law and in that sense all law books can be considered as books on jurisprudence. Among the phenomena studied by sociologists is law also and that makes sociology intimately connected with jurisprudence. The attitude of the sociologists towards law is different from that of a lawyer who, in his professional capacity, is concerned with the rules, which have to be obeyed by the people. He is not interested in knowing how and to what extent those rules actually govern the behavior of the ordinary citizen. A book on the law of torts, of contract, deals with the rules relating to torts and contract but does not mention how often torts and breaches of contract are committed. A lawyer is essentially interested in those who frame the rules and execute them in a given society.

There is a separate branch of sociological jurisprudence based on sociological theories and is essentially concerned with the influence of law on society at large, particularly social welfare. The sociological approach to legal problems is essentially different from that of the lawyer. In the case of crime in society, its causes are to a very great extent sociological and to understand their pros and cons, one must have knowledge of society.

Sociology has helped jurisprudence in its approach to the problem of prison reforms and has suggested ways and means of preventing social wrongs. Previously, judges and legislators came to their conclusions regarding the effect of punishment by depending upon popular opinion and personal impressions, but now they have at their disposal precise data through the efforts of criminologists. Their decisions are no more conjectural but are based on solid facts. There is a general indignation against hanging as the extreme form of punishment and hence its abolition in many countries of the world.

Behind all legal aspects, there is something social. The causes of crimes are partly sociological and an understanding of sociology helps the legislators in their task of prison reform and prevention of crime. Topics like motives, aims and theories of punishment and the efficacy of the various types of punishments are considerably helped by sociology. The birth and growth of sociology has given a new orientation to the study of jurisprudence.

There is a distinction between sociological jurisprudence and the sociology of law. The latter differs mainly from the former in that "it attempts to create a science of social life as a whole, and cover a great part of general sociology and political science." In the sociology of law, the emphasis is on society but in sociological jurisprudence emphasis is on the relation between law and society. The sociology of law is a branch of sociology dealing with law and legal institutions in the light of sociological principles, aims and methods.

The view of Paton[22] is that the relationship between law and social interests can be usefully studied by jurisprudence for three reasons. It enables us to understand better the evolution of law. For example, an attempt to explain law on a purely logical basis ignoring social interests is equivalent to interpreting a graph of the vibrations in a speeding motorcar without taking into account the surface of the road. Although man's view of ethics and his social needs have changed over the centuries, the element of human interest provides a greater substratum of identity than the logical structure of law. Although German law adopted the subjective theory of contract and English law has preferred an objective approach, each has been forced to adapt its theoretical basis to the needs of modern commerce. Although the view of certain jurists like Kelsen that jurists should not discuss the question of social interests is attractive, yet such a study is essential to a lawyer in order to enable him to properly understand the legal system.

Jurisprudence and psychology

Psychology has been defined as the science of mind and behavior. It is recognized that no human science can be discussed properly without a thorough knowledge of the human mind and hence its close connection with jurisprudence. In the study of criminal jurisprudence, there is great scope for the study of psychological principles in order to understand the criminal mind behind the crime. Both psychology and jurisprudence are interested in solving such questions as the motive for crime, a criminal personality, whether a criminal gets pleasure in committing crime, why there are more crimes in one society than in another and what punishment should be given in any particular case. In criminology, psychology plays an important part. It is the duty of a lawyer to understand the criminal and the working of a criminal mind.

It is the duty of a lawgiver to understand man and not to pass judgments and say what man ought to do or ought not to do. Psychology can help the lawmaker considerably, in the approach to the problem of not only making the law but also in executing it. Jurisprudence is concerned with man's external conduct and not his thoughts and mental processes, but penology has benefited from the knowledge made available by psychological researches.

There is a school of jurists, which holds the view that the sanction behind all laws is a psychological one. Study of negligence, intention, motive and other cognate mental conditions forms part of both jurisprudence and psychology.

Jurisprudence and Ethics

Ethics has been defined as the science of human conduct. It deals with how man behaves and what should be the ideal human behavior. There is the ideal moral code and the positive moral code. The former belongs to the province of natural law, while the latter deals with the rules of positive or actual conduct. Ethics is concerned with good or proper human conduct in the light of public opinion. Public opinion varies from place to place, from time to time and from people to people. Dr. Sethna writes: "It changes in the furnace of social evaluation, social culture and social development. What may be a rule of good morality at one time may be bad moral today."

Jurisprudence is related to positive morality insofar as law is considered as the instrument through which positive ethic tries to assert itself. Positive morality is not dependent upon the good actions of a good man only. It requires a strong coercive influence for maintaining public conscience. There is a separate branch of ethical jurisprudence, which tries to examine the existing ethical opinions and standards of conduct in terms of law and makes suggestions for necessary changes so that it can properly depict the public conscience.

There are many ethical rules of conduct, which are not considered as crimes. The law ignores trifles. It may be immoral to tell a lie but it is not a crime. Many acts are unethical but all unethical acts are not necessarily criminal. One has to consider the problem of laws, which are considered undesirable by society. All that is prohibited by law is not necessarily immoral. For enforcing certain ethical conduct, ethics depends upon law through the instrumentality of the police, law courts, judges and the system of courts and punishment. Legislation must be based on ethical principles. It must not be divorced from human values. No law can be a good law if it is not based on sound ethical principles.

Ethics lays down the rules for human conduct based upon higher and nobler values of life. Laws are meant for regulating human conduct in the present and subordinating the requirements of the individual to that of society at large. A jurist must be apt at the science of ethics because he cannot criticise a law unless he examines that law through the instrumentality of ethics.

Although Austin separated jurisprudence from ethics, jurisprudence must not be divorced from ethics altogether. The reason is that if ethical values are excluded from jurisprudence, it shall be in "the formalistic vacuum of the sanctuary of the state barring the road to all contacts with life or society". It shall be reduced to a "system of rather arid formalism."

Dr.Sethna writes: "In mirror of a community's laws are reflected its culture, its ideology and its Miranda. On the high level of its laws is perceived the glory of a country's civilization the depth of its positive ethics. Hence the relationship between ethics and jurisprudence."

Jurisprudence and Economics

Economics studies man's efforts in satisfying his wants and producing and distributing wealth. Economics is the science of wealth and jurisprudence is the science of law. There is a close relationship between the two. Very often, economic factors are responsible for crimes. Economic problems arise from day to-day and it is the duty of the lawgiver to tackle those problems. The aim of the economist is to improve the standard of life of the people and also to develop their personality. Jurisprudence teaches legislators how to make laws, which will promote social and economic welfare. Both jurisprudence and economics aim at the betterment of the lives of the people. There are laws relating to workmen's compensation, factory legislation, laws relating to labor, insurance, maternity welfare, bonus, leave facilities and other concessions given to workmen. There are laws for the benefit of the agriculturists such as the Zamindari Abolition Acts, Agricultural Debtors Relief Acts, Acts preventing the fragmentation and sub-division of agricultural holdings and regulation of agricultural labor. Both jurisprudence and economics help each other in furthering the welfare of society.

The intimate relation between economics and jurisprudence was first emphasized by Karl Marx and the interpretation of jural relations in the light of economic factors is receiving serious attention at the hands of jurists.

Jurisprudence and History

History studies past events in their different perspectives. The relation between jurisprudence and history is so close that there is a separate historical school of jurisprudence. History furnished the background in which a correct idea of jurisprudence can be realized.

Jurisprudence and Politics

Friedmann[50] rightly points out that jurisprudence is linked at one end with philosophy and at the other end with political theory. Politics deals with the principles governing governmental organization. In a politically organized society, there exist regulations which may be called laws and they lay down authoritatively what men may do and what they may not do.

Synthetic Jurisprudence

The necessity for synthetic jurisprudence arises from the fact that it is necessary to determine the truth from all aspects and from different angles. Analytical jurisprudence, studied separately, does not give anything more than an understanding of the legal concepts as they prevail in various legal systems. This in itself is useful but we cannot stop after merely analyzing the problem. We will be in a better position if we discuss the historical aspects of the legal ideas, problems or principles and go further in the light of philosophical norms and sociological requirements. The historical jurists lay emphasis on historical jurisprudence and refuse to recognize the other branches of jurisprudence.

The first thing to be done in the study of jurisprudence is to understand the fundamental principles analytically. When that is done, we should turn to its historical aspects. We must trace the origin of the legal ideas and principles and sources of law. Our knowledge and experience of the past would help us to be wise in the present and forewarned for the future. Philosophical jurisprudence enables us to trace the philosophical basis of our laws and consider the legal principles in the light of philosophical norms. A comparative study of law is useful, as a thorough study of the legal systems of other countries enables us to improve the legal machinery of our own country. Sociological jurisprudence helps us to study the fundamental principles of law.

Knowledge is a synthetic whole and cannot be divided into watertight compartments. It is our duty to amalgamate half-truths in order to form the whole truth. Synthesis enables us to reconcile the conflicting theories. In synthetic jurisprudence, we study the various topics and theories from the point of view of synthesis. We analyse, we retrospect, we compare, we philosophies, we socialise and we synthesise. The fruits of synthesis are well-balanced and well-digested truths. The advocates of synthetic jurisprudence consider jurisprudence as a study of fundamental legal principles, including their historical, philosophical, scientific and sociological basis and including an analysis of legal concepts. They point out that jurisprudence is history; it is philosophy; it is a science and it is concerned with altruistic utilitarianism.

There are many advocates of synthetic jurisprudence. Prof. Jerome Hall is an advocate of integrated jurisprudence in the United States. His view is that "if we could cultivate the aesthetic impulse of the system-builder, we would have all the interests needed to achieve a significant synthesis of jurisprudence thought". He wants that the legal philosophers should concentrate upon legal theory, which has been constructed slowly, and painstakingly over the centuries by specialists in contracts, torts, criminal law and other basic branches of law, as the bridge between jurisprudence and law.

Though Dean Roscoe Pound[51] does not speak of synthetic jurisprudence, his treatment of the subject is similar to that of Hall. He explains all the methods of jurisprudence and then discusses the various topics of jurisprudence in a systematic form, after giving an account of the various schools of jurisprudence. He deals with the nature of law and justice according to law. He explains the scope and subject matter of law and also the sources, forms and modes of the growth of law. He discusses under various headings all the branches or types of jurisprudence and applies practically all the recognized methods.

Julius Stone deals with all kinds of jurisprudence, whether analytical, comparative, philosophical, historical or sociological, in a systematic manner. He does not stand for a hotchpotch of them but he believes in dealing with all types of jurisprudence in one book. Cicero has described, "Jurisprudence is the philosophical aspect of the knowledge of law." Allen has also described, "Jurisprudence is the scientific synthesis of the essential principles of law." Lord Dennis Lloyd is also an advocate of synthetic jurisprudence. In his book Introduction to Jurisprudence, he has advocated the necessity for synthesis.

Dr. M. J. Sethna is the strongest exponent of synthetic jurisprudence in India. According to him, jurisprudence is the study of fundamental legal principles, including their philosophical, historical and sociological basis and an analysis of legal concepts. Dr. Sethna refers to his definition of civil law. According to him, civil law is all that body of principles, decisions and enactments made, passed or approved by the legally constituted authorities or agencies in a state for regulating rights, duties and liabilities and enforced through the machinery of the judicial process, securing obedience to the sovereign authority in the state. The view of Dr. Sethna is that his definition of civil law gives a complete idea of civil law as it includes both abstract and concrete aspects of civil law. Dr. Sethna also refers to his theory of negligence. According to him, negligence is the faulty behavior arising out of the lethargy of the mind or faulty thinking. Negligence is a faulty negative act. It is a failure of the duty to take as much care as a normal person is expected to take under the circumstances. Negligence is both objective and subjective.

Dr. Sethna refers to his quasi-realist theory regarding the personality of corporations. According to the fiction theory, the personality of a corporation is not real but fictitious. According to the realist theory, a corporation has real and not a fictitious personality. According to Dr. Sethna, the correct view is the synthetic view according to which the personality of the corporation is neither completely real nor truly fictitious. It is quasi-real and quasi-fictitious.

The view of Dr. Sethna is that every topic should be fully considered from all angles–historically, philosophically, analytically, comparatively and sociologically. It is only then that a true picture emerges. If we deal with the subject of property, we should analyse the concepts of property, proprietary rights, personal rights, legal and equitable rights, etc. We should make a comparative study of those concepts and examine them historically and critically. What Dr. Sethna emphasises is that all the jurisprudential aspects of the subject must be considered at one place. He does not believe in having separate chapters on analytical jurisprudence, historical jurisprudence, philosophical jurisprudence or sociological jurisprudence. He stands for combining all the types and thus gives a synthetic discussion under each topic heading.

Salmond has said as follows: "Now we have seen that, in general, jurisprudence is a subject without applicability. But if the value of the ordinary legal subject lies in its practical use, what possible value then can there be in an abstract, theoretical subject like jurisprudence? There is of course its own intrinsic interest, in which it resembles any other subject of serious scholarship. Just as, for example, the mathematician investigates number theory, not with the aim of seeing his findings put to practical use, but by reason of the fascination which it holds for him, so the writer on jurisprudence may well be impelled to his subject by nothing more than its intrinsic interest. And this should in no way surprise us, for speculation and theory have a natural appeal, whatever the subject; it is natural to speculate of the nature of law as on the nature of light. The fascination of a subject however is no guarantee of its worth. A life devoted to the solution of chess problems seems less worthwhile than one devoted say to historical or mathematical research, because this has a general sort of relevance to thought and life which chess problems do not possess. Number theory has significance for general mathematical thought, which in turn has implications for science, philosophy, logic and indeed the shade spectrum of human thought. Similarly researches into jurisprudence may well have repercussions on the whole of legal, political and social thought.

"But jurisprudence is not without practical value, albeit of a long-term character. In science and mathematics progress has been largely due to increasing generalization, which has unified branches of study previously distinct, simplified the task of both scientist and mathematician, and enabled them to solve by one technique a whole variety of different problems. But in law too generality can mean improvement. The English law relating to negligence, for example has progressed from a host of individual rules about particular types of situation to a general principle. And indeed one of the tasks of jurisprudence is to construct and elucidate organising concepts serving to render the complicities of law more manageable and more rational; and in this way theory can help to improve practice.

"Finally jurisprudence also has an educational value, since the logical analysis of legal concepts sharpens the lawyer's own logical technique. In addition, the study of jurisprudence can help combat the lawyer's occupational vice of formalism, which leads to excessive concentration on legal rules for their own sake, to interest in legal from rather than in social realities, and to resulting disregard of the social function of law. This is best remedied by setting the law in its proper context, by considering the needs of society and by taking note of advances in related and relevant disciplines. A proper grasp of the law of contract may well need some understanding of economics and economic theory, a proper grasp of criminal law, some knowledge of criminology and psychiatry, and a proper grasp of law in general, some acquaintance with sociology. English lawyers, rooted as they are in the common law with its worship of precedent, have a natural tendency to turn to history, to look backwards instead of forwards and to regard every question as a historical one. Jurisprudence can teach him to look, if not forwards, at least sideways and around him, and to realise that the answers to new legal problems must be found by consideration of present social needs rather than in the distilled wisdom of the past."

The Crises In Jurisprudence

Justice Markanday Katju, senior Judge of[53] Allahabad High Court and an emminent jurist, wrote as follows:

Western Jurisprudence has come to a grinding halt. Despite the creation of a host of schools and theories in the 20th century it now seems to have exhausted possibility of any other further development. However solutions to vital problems still elude it. In this article we shall discuss the reasons for this crises and consider the way out.

The unchallenged sway of Austinian positivism up to the end of the 19th century corresponded to the unchallenged sway of Newtonian physics up to the same period. At the end of the 19th century both Austinian jurisprudence and Newtonian physics underwent a severe crisis. But while physics emerged from the crisis victorious, refreshed, and with a deeper understanding of nature, jurisprudence never made a genuine recovery.

Nineteenth century positivist jurisprudence was followed in the twentieth century by a host of intricate theories – sociological jurisprudence (including its varieties; e.g., the autonomous law school, Pound's functionalism, realism, Ehrlich's living law school, institutionalism, the psychological theory, juridical sociology, etc.), positivism (including Kelsen's normatism, the Hart concept, neo-thomism, phenomenology, etc.

Indeed the multiplicity of schools is a striking feature of the 20th century jurisprudence, reflecting the myriad social structures in today's world and the tussles between them.

However, these various schools have all been found wanting in certain basic respects (which have been pointed out by the writer in his earlier articles). Some of these schools staged a come-back after having earlier yielded ground to a newcomer, e.g. natural law, which have yielded first place to positivism in the 19th century, staged a temporary revival after World War II. Others, having been displaced from their original habitat found refuge elsewhere, e.g. Kelsen's pure theory, which have been declined in Europe became popular in Latin America. This intellectual jugglery, however, did not solve basic problems. Jurisprudence is still lying caught in quagmire, making little headway.

It is submitted that the reason for the current stagnation and crisis in jurisprudence has been that the subject is not treated as a science, and instead it is utilized as an ideological apology or tool for serving vested interests. The way to break out of the morass and move forward, therefore, is to raise jurisprudence to the level of a science, and to insist on treating the subject scientifically.

Here the question arises whether jurisprudence can be made a science at all. It is submitted in reply that it can. And to prove this two propositions will sought to be established:

1) Social science is a science, and

2) Jurisprudence can be social science.

These are discussed below.

Is the social science a science?

Science is the systematic study of nature. Since man is the part of nature (having evolved from simpler forms), the study of man in society should be regarded a science.

However, an objection is immediately raised that the human beings have free will, while animals, plants and inanimate matter do not, and hence there cannot be laws to describe how human beings will actually behave. This argument is also put thus: Science deals with law governing recurrent or repetitive events, and since man's actions are not predictable there can be no science of human social behavior.

Now it is no doubt true that the social sciences cannot be identified with the natural sciences. The materialist philosophers of the 17th and 18th century who tried to create a "social physics" which would explain social behavior with the same mathematically exact laws as those of physics had grossly oversimplified, and thereby distorted reality.

However, it would be also untrue to say that there cannot be a science of social behavior. The free will of man is limited by his objective material conditions. Our actions, our thoughts, etc., are largely conditioned by the mode of production which is not created by man of his own free choice but is a product of historical development that proceed in accordance with certain laws. Those who argue that there cannot be reoccurrence in human social behavior argue against facts. For example a historian who studied the laws, customs, morals, etc., of ancient tribal societies (Typees, Samcans, Irequis etc.) discovered an amazing similarity between them. This was because of the primitive-communal mode of production common to these societies. It is true that each of these societies had also some distinct features of their own, but that was not basic. In modern industrial societies also, as contrast to agricultural societies, the basic features are strikingly common.

The recurrence of phenomena cannot of course be the same in different fields of reality. The simpler the phenomenon the more apparent is the recurrence of its properties. As we ascend to higher forms of evolution, from a study of inanimate matter (physics, chemistry, etc.), to a study of plants and animals (biology), and then to the study of human society we find that recurrence of phenomena becomes more complex and diverse. From this, however, it cannot be concluded that there is no recurrence in human life. For example, most humans get married. An investigation, therefore, is called for as to how the marriage institution originated, what is its true purpose, etc. Similarly various other institutions like the state, the legal system, economic systems etc., often recur in certain societies (in their basic features), and this requires investigation.

Moreover, it is not necessary that science must always deal with recurrent events. The birth of our solar system, the extinction of Dinosaurs, etc., were unique events, but nevertheless scientists do enquire into them.

It is then said that in science we can experiment but there can be no experiment with humans. Here again it can be replied that a lot of science is observation and inference without experimentation, for e.g., the discoveries of quasars and black hole. Also, there is nothing to prevent experiment on human beings, provided necessary safeguards are taken. For example, experiments are often made in the economic system by putting a certain economic theory into practice, e.g. Keynes' theory, Marxist Theory, etc.

The arguments of those who deny the status of science to the social sciences are thus unfounded.

Can jurisprudence be a science?

In jurisprudence we study law from the most general point of view viz. its origin, its nature, its role in society, its form, the concepts, which it uses, its future, etc.

Economics, Sociology, Anthropology, etc., are fairly well recognized as social sciences. This is not so, however, in the case of jurisprudence. In fact jurisprudence is often defined as the 'Philosophy of Law' rather than the science of law.

However, since law has an objective existence, as a part of the social reality there is no reason why the systematic study of its nature, origin, etc., should not be a science.

To make jurisprudence scientific, however, we must free it from prejudices, subjectivism and vested interest. Unfortunately, as pointed out earlier, jurisprudence has not been free from the unscientific approach. Consciously or unconsciously jurists have been creating theories which are apologies or justifications for social systems in which vested interests dominate, instead of pursuing truth in a detached, scientific manner. For example, Kelsen's pure theory, which rigorously shuts out any social evaluation of the law, was readily accepted in Latin America where the generals naturally wanted to keep the people away from raising awkward questions.

To make jurisprudence a science the foremost requirement is to introduce the scientific methodology into the subject. This implies:

1. Careful and detached observation
2. Necessary general inferences from such observation

The most striking feature of the law, which one observes is that it is heavily dependent on the economic system. Thus, for example, it is noticed that customary law corresponds to agricultural society (which is relatively stable), while statutory law corresponds to industrial society (which is relatively dynamic). Since law is so heavily dependent on the economic base how can one study it in isolation to discover its true nature and purpose? A priori theories of the origin of law, e.g. Kelsen's theory, are thus unscientific as they shut their eyes to realities. All that Kelsen examines is the form of the law that is, its hierarchy, its types, etc., but he refuses to enquire into its background e.g. its origin, its role in society, its connection with the economic system, etc. According to Kelsen, all such questions are outside the scope of jurisprudence. Thus, far from answering key questions in jurisprudence, Kelsen refuses to allow them to be even put. It is true that law has a normative nature. But the question remains as to why a particular set of norms exists in one society while another set exits in another. Norms, too, on deeper analysis, are found to be products of a certain mode of production. Hence the "Is" and the "Ought" do not exist in worlds apart, as Kelsen imagines, but in one and the same world.

The positivists, while making a significant contribution to our understanding of the law by clearly differentiating it from morals religion, etc., sought to shut out any enquiry as to the origin and nature of law, its role in society, its social evaluation, etc. They thus sought to reduce jurisprudence to a mere descriptive study. But a scientist has to keep an open mind, and he cannot shut out relevant enquires; otherwise his approach will become dogmatic. In fact the social evaluation of the law, its origin, nature, function, etc., are all very important questions in jurisprudence and one cannot turn a blind eye to them.

Sociological jurisprudence no doubt perceived law as a part of the social reality, instead of a thing existing in isolation. However, having started from his correct approach sociological jurisprudence soon went off the rails and ended up by becoming an apology for the existing social system in the west e.g. Pound's functionalism, which only seeks or 'harmonizes' the deep contradictions prevalent in the American social fabric. The sociological jurists never went really deep. They did not scientifically investigate the origin and real nature and function of law. Many of them (e.g. the autonomous law school) merely sought to shift the center of gravity in the legal order from legislation to judge-made law, as if that is a panacea for all ills.

The other schools of jurisprudence in the 20th century e.g. 'received' natural law, neo-Theorism, neo-positivism, phenomenology, etc., were all clumsy, superficial approaches which never seriously tackled the subject. Having experimented with all these theories and having found them all unsatisfactory, Western jurisprudence is now lying exhausted. It has reached its nadir.

In the series of articles that the writer has been writing (many of them have been published in S.C.C) he has submitted his theory of 'progressive positive law' as the new jurisprudence for the scientific era. It is a theory which may show a way out of the present crisis.

Progressive positive law is the law which utilizes the scientific discoveries of the laws of the social development for the forward movement of man in history. Progressive positive law seeks to alter social relations where they are outdated, irrational or unjust. Such a law does not merely keep pace with social advance; it anticipates and helps in planned social order, where social relations are harmonious and rational, where science advances at accelerating speed and where friction is eliminated.

The word 'positive law' indicates that in modern times it is man-made law (as contrasted to custom or natural law), which is required. The whole progress of man has been from helplessness before nature to mastery over nature, and correspondingly the progress in law has been from spontaneously created law (which was irrespective of human will) to consciously created, man-made law. The scientific era requires precision, and therefore more and more positive law.

The word 'progressive' indicates forward movement. This is axiomatic in the scientific era. The word 'progress' here indicates not spontaneous, unplanned and haphazard movement but conscious progress on scientifically planned lines, taking into accounts the laws of social development. Thus, progressive positive law overcomes the defects of positivism by linking the law with social development.

The theory of progressive positive law can be utilized by legislators, judges and others connected with the legal order in the discharge on their functions. Thus, for example, when a judge is faced with a case where he has several options, he should take a decision, which takes society forward in history.

Even a cursory view of the law will show that till now it has largely been property based, and one of its important functions has been to preserve the status quo as regards property relations in society. This situation will change in the future. Instead of being property based, the law of the scientific era will be science-based, and its function will be not to protect vested interests but to regulate society on a scientific basis, and to promote scientific development. Indeed the law will then become a powerful engine of social progress in the future.

Notes

1. Method of Juridical Thinking
2. History of Indian Political Ideas
3. Indian Philosophy.
4. Vendanta Philosophy
5. The Wonder What the India was
6. Indian Philosophy
7. Nature of State

8&9. •Quoted by A.K.Pavithran in his book International Law East & West

10. Quoted by A.K.Pavithran in his book International Law East & West
11. An Introduction to Jurisprudence
12. An Introduction to Jurisprudence

13. Elements of Jurisprudence
14. An introduction to the Principles of Moral and Legislation.
15. Elementary Principles of Jurisprudence.
16. Essays in Jurisprudence and Ethics.
17. Jurisprudence
18. The Nature and Sources of the Law.
19. Jurisprudence
20. Some Reflections on Jurisprudence
21. Outlines of Historical Jurisprudence
22. A Text Book of Jurisprudence
23. Jurisprudence (edited by Fitzgerald)
24. Jurisprudence in Action
25. Nature and Sources of the Law
26. Nature of Jurisprudence
27. Jurisprudence
28. Lectures on Jurisprudence
29. Province and Functions of Law.
30. Jurisprudence
31. New Jurisprudence
32. The Theory of Legal Science
33. Latest Addition of Salmond on Jurisprudence
34. Studies in History & Jurisprudence
35. Some Reflections on Jurisprudence
36. On the Vocation of our time for Legislation & Jurisprudence.
37. Textbook of Jurisprudence by G.W.Paton
38. Jurisprudence-Dias
39. King 'Propositions about Law' (1951) II CLJ 3I.
40. Macmillan Law and Other Things
41. Ulpain's remark in the Digest, quoted in the opening of Justinian's Institutes, 'Jurist prudentiaest divinarum atque human arum rerun notitia, justi atque injusti scientia' (D i.i.io.2; inst i.e.: jurisprudence is the concept of things divine and human, knowledge of the just and the unjust), was only a piece of rhetoric not pursued by the Romans.
42. Ames Equity Jurisprudence. See the comments of Stone. The Province and Function of Law
43. Holland Jurisprudence
44. Gray The Nature and Sources of the Law

45. The term 'medico-legal Jurisprudence' has largely been superseded by 'forensic medicine'.
46. The equivalent of 'Jurisprudence' in its Anglo-American sense is Theorie du droit. .
47. Buckland Some Reffections in Jurisprudence
48. Stone Legal system and Lawyers' Reasonings
49. New Jurisprudence
50. Legal Theories
51. La & Morals
52. Synthetic Jurisprundence
53. Law in Scientific Era

CHAPTER 3

Concept of Law

Law has various types of meaning according to various points of views. It may be used in practical as well as in general or abstract form. From time immemorial law has been divided into two major concepts: (1) Eastern world concept (2) and Western world concept.

The position of the Eastern world may be obtained from the study of ancient Hindu, Chinese and Muslim concepts of law.

Law according to Hindu Concept of life: Law in this sense has been defined by Dr.S.N. Sen[1]. as follows:- "As these rules of conduct authoritatively imposed by divine power for men, as a being capable of eternal existence governing all his activities public or private and effecting inseparably in spiritual and temporal interests."

Rita and Dharma: The Hindu concept of law and social custom and political ideas in ancient India are closely coupled with two inseparable and dynamic ideas of an omnipotent cosmic or divine law. *Rita,* and an all prevailing custom, *Dharma* which runs through the oldest works of our sacred literature viz. *Rig Veda* and *Atharvaveda, Samhitas* and which were developed more fully in the sacred works of the immediately following period viz. *Yajur-Sameritas* and the *Brahmans* and to still later works on the Bramhimical sacred law viz. *Smritis* (Rita) originally meant the ordered course of thing. The rising and the setting of the sun, the waxing and waning of the moon, the regularity of the seasons, etc. In the mantras its meaning is extended to include not only the rhythm, regularity and uniformities of nature and natural order but also moral order based on natural justice. Gods are called-guardians of Rita and practitioners of Rita—who reward the good and punish the wicked, those who observe the rules of Rita are the good ones, those who follow the opposite path are the wicked ones. In *Brahmans,* which speak of the efficacy of sacrifices rites, rites become identical with the object, with Yagna or sacrifice. Sacrificial rites are performed with the object of attaining prosperity and happiness here and thereafter. Rita and Yagna imply that each action carries its own reward and Dharma means right activity or duty, activities which promote virtues and induce man to live in harmony and peace with the world. These two concepts of Rita and Dharma have anticipated to a very great extent the law nature, as developed on the stoic philosophers of ancient Greece and perfected by early Roman lawyers.

Dharma: Dharma is the core and center of Hindu legal theory. It is not creed or religion, but a mode of life or a code of conduct, which regulated a man's activities as a member of society and was intended to enable him to reach the full height of his stature, the goal of human existence. It, thus, corresponds to Acquinas's Eternal Law- the name given to this first law which is the source of all other laws. It is no wonder, therefore that as already stated Hindu law began with duties rather than with rights as in the Western countries.

C les Drekmier of Stanford University: (U.S.A.) has shown that in Hindu concept of life duty occupies the central position and in European thought it belongs to the concept of natural rights and freedom. We are justified in saying that civil obligation rather than rights formed the basic of relation of state and subject.

The ancient Hindu philosopher-law-givers exclaimed the truth that maintenance, harmony and tolerance in life should be the highest objective of mankind and that same can be achieved by a balance of duties and not by conflict of rights. We are reminded of Alexis de Toequeville's statement,- "Ancient Hindu communities were, however, no strangers to the concept of rights. But there are specific rights to old Vedic idea of social order, which is concerned with the application of the principles of the supremacy of law to the individuals and the social units". In the text of *Satapatha Brahmans* - It is said that "the waters are the law (Dharma). Hence, whenever the waters come down to this world everything here comes to have accrued with Dharma. But whenever there is drought then the stronger sides prevail upon the weaker for the waters— the dharma". From the extract, it is clear that nature without law is synonymous with anarchy and that law is the foundation of the individual and collective security. "Dharma is the word which has been defined variously. It's most ordinary meaning is duty, but its more appropriate meaning in the sense in which it has been used by ancient law givers, appears to be virtue or what is true knowledge. Data used the word in the sense of "that totality of human duties and of human life in all its occupations, pursuits and daily action. It was this fundamental philosophy of life that permeated the life of individuals as well as nations in ancient India and influenced them in moulding their religious, moral, legal and social intercourse. All creatures grow on the growth of righteousness. Righteousness is called Dharma. Dharma was not only justification for state but its ultimate cause and support. There are various sources of Hindu law—1. Vedas, 2. *Sruti,* 3. *Smirti,* and 4. *Vyavahara*—rules relating to positive law such as marriage, separation etc., 5. *Achara*—rules relating to customs and usages, and 6. Payathitha—rules relating to religious and moral observance and expiation.

Danda: According to ancient Hindu belief the temporal sovereign was not a source of law. Law is divinely ordained, so *danda* (the spirit of punishment) also is divinely planned.

The law was the king of kings and there was nothing higher than law, says one Upnishad Manu Smriti-[2] says. Danda is above the king. The whole world is kept in order by punishment (danda) for a guiltless man is hard to find. The king is just an inflector of punishment. A true king is the one who is truthful and wise and who knows the respective value of virtue (dharma), wealth (artha) and pleasure (Kama) and who holds righteousness. Manu further says, "even the king as deviating from one path of dharma is struck by danda." So, it is the duty of the king to wield power and deal with punishment for breaches of dharma. Dharma was itself deemed to be the real restraining power over the king's office. According to Charles Drekmeier "the Hindu king never enjoyed the immunity that accompanied the European concept of the divine right of kings, rather than divine right. We must speak of divine obligation, the duty of the king to protect the social order. Many passages that appear to glorify the king are in fact reminder of duties implied in his office, the function of the king and not the king himself, are usually equated with the Gods. We never find the idea that Ruler is accountable to God."

A great work on positive law, *Narda Smriti*—in its 18th title dealing with law, strikes a modern note of positive law by saying that it is "transgression of king's commandments that gives rise to action in courts. Law personified as a king roams on earth visibly with a thousand eyes. Mortal cannot live at all if they transgressui his commandments."

Sanctions: Where all laws were traceable to God and the decrees of the Almighty were revealed to the people in the Vedas by saints and sages who had knowledge of them. Sanction is necessarily a religious and moral one. The basic for obedience of law in ancient India was their divine origin. In ancient Hindu society where religious and secular rules were interwoven and intermixed, fear of consequences in the other world, dread of divine displeasure always acted as a deterrent for every infringement of duty, the individual is subject to two punishments, one immediate and other remote. There was no distinction made between crime and sins by Hindu jurists, the punishment inflicted upon these (offenders) was based on expiatory theory, common in Europe in the Middle Ages.

Nairajya or the law of nature: The Hindu concept of law of nature—*nairajya*-bears a close resemblance to that developed in the west, namely, the power or principle imminent in the universe which Aristotle called Nature. In Mahabharat a we have one *sloka* attributed to Bhisma which means that originally, prior to the evolution of organized states in the world there was no kingdom i.e. government or states.

There were no things, no laws, no person to administer, and that in such a state men used to protect each other according to dharma or dictates of their conscience.

Dharma that protected men in such a society was a law that was neither laid down nor enforced by any external authority but was what the stoics considered as reason and which according to them was a universal force prevailing the whole universe as the basis for law and justice. Natural law is the law dictated by conscience, which reflects nature inherent in man. It is a reform, a law of moral reason, the postulate of which must be of universal application binding all men everywhere. This law attributed to divine authority is eternal and unchangeable, binding at all times upon all people; this is what Dharma means, conscience or right reason which man focused in protecting each other. Law, in its generic sense, is the rule of action. 'Rit' which appears also as jural law starts with this meaning. It is the dynamics of action in the world whether cosmic, human or divine. It is because of this conception of 'Rit' that the Aryan race has been called a juristic race par excellence. At its cosmic level, Rit expresses the idea of order and is spoken of as eternal law. It is identified with the Divine itself. Later, due to historical reasons, Dharma takes place of Rit. Dharma is the mystic force as well as the social obligation and as such holds this world and society together in its fold. It is the ultimate good, revealed in the Vedas which themselves are impersonal and for guidance, which, is codified in socio-legal codes called Dharmasastra. When justice is administered by king's court it is spoken of as *Vyavahar* or positive law. *Danda* or punishment is a means of the enforcement of Dharma. Thus *Danda* or punishment is identical with Dharma. Punishment is not to repress the criminal but must work as Dharma or justice, which has its justification in the welfare of the criminal and the society equally in which he lives. For this purpose there should not be a mechanical application of law only. Indian jurists of the past evolved a systematic theory of the interpretation of law. Again, law is not to be seen as imprisoned in a code but has plural sources outside it, like custom, traditions, reason, etc. To keep alive the spirit of enquiry and revision of views, Dharma (i.e., law, ultimate knowledge of Dharma), at its highest level is said to be mysterious. It's meaning is not always knowledge to one person. This keeps alive the urge for reform of law and its adaptation in the light of human welfare and in social milieu. This law, at all levels, remains impersonal and objective, and in the highest sense typifies the doctrine of the 'Rule of Law,' which has become the touchstone of modern democracies. This law, or Dharma, integrates matter and life on cosmic scale, and regulates the function of man in society, and institutions, in the best interests of the whole, which is again spoken of as Dharma.

If this universe is dynamic having a logical progression, it should generate actions and reactions in the physical, social and moral world. 'Karma' as law of action, expresses this law of causation. By doing right actions (Karmas), man keeps pace with the purposes of this universe and partakes in this world process by progressively realizing his own personality or self. Self is not only the individual self but a portion of the universal self, the former has to work in harmony with the latter. The law or the rule of law then gets authority for its imposition and criterion of its validity in the theory of Karma. The law of Karma, which is eternal, ordains that a man has to bear the fruits of his 'Karma,' be they good or bad. The theory of punishment is based upon this theory of causation, i.e. the theory of Karma of which it (punishment) is a voluntary and conscious participant.

Wrong, in early Vedic thought, is disorder 'Arit' or deviation from the straight course of Rit. Mimansa which keeps alive this Vedic idea says that evil is also the deviation from part of the law. The deviation, which is brought about by one's limitations, can be restored and man can keep pace with the rhythm of this law. Good is only the conformity with law. Good actions result in happiness. Happiness, in other words, consists in so ordaining one's actions as to be in conformity with law. Sin or evil is then the state of deviation. Where there is evil, there is suffering or reverse movement of the law of progression. As evil is merely a negation of good, i.e., law, it cannot be called real or positive. Evil is only non-conformity with law. It can be remedied. In Vedic thought and life evil plays only a minor part. But in Buddhism this evil assumes the form of 'World tragedy' which prompted Buddha to visualize world full of sorrow but truth. Buddha's emphasis upon suffering is philosophical. He wants to solve the problem of death, decay and disease. He becomes a rationalist and shows a positive approach to life at a time when Vedic rituals degenerated into wastage and violence, reduced themselves to state forms, devoid of spirit and became unsuitable for rational enquiry. Puranas resound with the note of optimism and heighten the dignity of man even more than God's. The assertion of the dignity of man is the confirmation of theory of Karma.

According to B.K. Purohit[3], law in Indian sense can be described as follows: "The first idea of law that arose in the Indian mind is that of 'Rit' i.e. 'Order'. This order is inclusive of physical as well as legal, social, moral and ritualistic ones. More than that, it is also the order of ideas and signifies the very concept of idea or form by which alone comprehension or cognition can be possible of thoughts and actions. This is the 'form' or category of understanding and the aspect of the movement of the dynamic reality. The first cosmological creations were the twins of 'Rit' and 'Satya'. From ethic-legal point of view Rit is law and Satya is truth. But from the point of view of reality, Rit is order and Satya is existence *(Satta)*. Both are the aspects of reality. Thus order and existence go together. They sanctify each other and are the warp and woof of Indian civilization and culture. Gods and other beings were created afterwards in the list of creation. Rit as eternal order or eternal law is mentioned first, as without form no matter of reality can be manifested. Reality has been expressed as ordered whole and material essence, which culminates in the *atmaṇ* or *brahman* of the Upanisadic philosophy. Because of the concept of Rit, as omnipresence and comprehension of complete cosmos, it has been called the 'Crude Precursor' of *Vedantic Brahman*—the epitome of Indian philosophy.

Indian thinking in law starts from this concept of Rit. It is said in *Rig Veda* that Divinity manifests itself through splendour and through law. The all-pervading Being is born of eternal law and is eternal law itself. In its literal meaning Rit is the course of things. In its primary or physical sense Rit is the path of Zodiac with which apparent motions of 'Devas' (luminaries) are confined and which is dotted by Nakshatras. The devas are said to be born in Rit and are governed by it. From this primary and physical sense, the meaning of Rit as an ordering principle of the universe extends to human life in society, in its normative and secondary sense it is understood as ethical, religious, legal and social order.

Rit also means 'proper' or 'right'. 'Right, a derivative of Rit, means literally straight and thus implies straight or right conduct as against 'crooked' or tortuous path of life. In old English it is 'right' in German 'recht' and in Latin 'rectus'. It is surprising that even French 'droit' and Italian 'diritto' we find an echo of the sound of 'Rit'. Rit becomes the expression of order, organization and system of every type of social life. In religion, Rit is the order created by sacrifice that enables the performer of ritual to live in harmony with gods, In order to achieve social harmony, it is submitted, the division of society into classes called as 'Varna' system was also in a large measure a reflection of this 'rit'; and in aesthetics it is the expression of that beauty which expresses through order and symmetry. In ethics, Rit is right ordering of conduct; and as law 'Rit' is the preservation of order and awarding of punishment to wrongdoer when there is a violation of the 'seven laws' by 'an-riti' acts. Rit is order and coherence; its negation 'An-rit' is chaos, disorder and death. In human dealing it is complementary to *Satya* or *Sattva* the standard of truthfulness in conduct, which squares, with the whole 'Existence of Society'.

In ancient Indian legal theory there is no lawmaker. Law in its essence is not the command of the king or the sovereign. Ontologically, Rit is not even the creation of gods, as gods are said to be created afterwards. Gods are only the keepers or guardians of law. Agni declares law; Brahspati is the son of law; Usa (dawn) obeys law. Indian thought, from its earliest stages, expresses the idea of the "supremacy of law." On a cosmic scale this law works by itself but on the social science we hear of the seven laws, as stated above which constituted Rit or law. These seven laws, referred to, in *Rig Veda* were, it seems, the predecessors of the later formulation of law in *Sutras* and *Smritis.* In the Vedas, Rit is associated with all gods but special mention is made of Varun who is the keeper of Rit. Association of Rit with Varun has also juristic significance. There are many reasons for it. Firstly, he maintains the rigour of law and inspires awe. Varuna is the purest of gods and is the highest ethically. He is so pure and holy that a mere performance of sacrifice will not ensure his favor for he abhors sin, or anything which does not conform to Rit. Secondly, he commands awe and respect. Thirdly, Varun is always aware of the deeds of men and is omnipresent in the theistic as opposed to pantheistic sense. Two men, even in the most secret of places, or at the end of the earth, cannot make plans or enter into contract— a third person, Varuna is always there to witness the transaction. This may not sound as strange because in secular law as in ancient Roman Law we find the presence, on such occasions of an anomalous personage, the libripens. The whole idea in both the cases was to provide evidence of the transaction. Fourthly, his ubiquity ensures that there is no escape for the sinner. He catches and binds the evildoers in his snare, so that they become diseased, especially with dropsy, and when they die they descend to the 'House of Clay' apparently a sort of gloomy subterranean region. Fifthly, in *Atharvaveda,* Varun is seen as mighty emperor sitting in a great palace in heaven, often associated with most important of these was Mitra, a god mainly connected with 'Vows and Compacts'. The contracts were enforced by Mitra, Varun sat with his scouts or spies who flew all over the world and brought back reports on the conduct of mortals. This points out the fact that in later age, law began to be associated with king and state. Law of contract and crime must have been the early expressions of Rit. The association of Rit with Varun, after giving proper discount to the theological description indicates that Rit expressed the jural law. It was considered quite efficient in controlling society and some sort of organization or legal system must have been in existence for the purpose of the enforcement of this law.

At least five concepts of law were prevalent in the Vedic age. First, we have the idea of a divinely ordained rule or set of rules for human action as in the conception of *Vratam* and secondly in *Purvi* and *Dirga Sratra* where we have an idea of law as tradition of old customs which perhaps proved acceptable to the gods and hence point the way in which man walks with safety. A third and closely related idea is contained in Vedic *maryada,* an idea conceiving law as the recorded wisdom of old who learnt the safe course of human conduct. (*Rig Veda* X.5.6.). Herein we find also the idea of law as a system of principles discovered philosophically, and perhaps, expressing the nature of things, to which, therefore, man ought to conform his conduct. In the fifth place, law seems to have been thought of as a reflection of the divine reason. For such creatures who are amenable to reason, it (law of divine reason) can only appeal and for those who are not endowed with reason it leaves them to be governed by this law. The former because of their free will may violate the law, the latter, however, cannot do anything else than to obey it. How interesting, that a parallel idea is found later, much later in the Western Jurisprudence by the Schoolmen as reflected in the writings of St. Aquinas.

These ideas of law, of course according to Radha Binod Pal[4], are not presented to us as distinct from each other, but everyone of them is grafted on the other and on the idea of law as the order, the harmony, the status quo of the universe, i.e. Rit. The idea of *Vratam*, to which a reference has been made a little earlier, is the embodiment of Rit. It expresses the idea of authority in law and makes it violable and its non-observance is met with punishment at the hands of gods whose *Vratam* is violated. *Vratam* is the ordinance of gods. Vedic Rishis considered it a guidance to mortals. It has been maintained that *Vedic Swadha* is also derived from Rit.

This *Swadha* is conceived as quality or disposition of nature, the essence of a person or thing as derived from its growth, i.e. its nature and potency, developing from within from spontaneous energy inherent in material objects without the intervention of any external agency. Here it seems to lie the authority of custom or usage, *Purvi* and *Dirga Sratra*. What is found in past and what has long tradition demands our respect because its observance and repetition makes it consistent with nature. What is not contrary to *Swadha* is liable to be repeated frequently. This is similar to Aristotelian 'nature of the thing'. Dharma in its meaning reflects *Swadha* when it has the meaning of 'nature of the thing' or its characteristic function.

In later Vedic age we see a major change. The word 'Rit' falls into disuse. In *Atharvaveda* it becomes one of the expressions of 'Dharma'. It is also identified with truth. There were many reasons for this transformation. Firstly, the prestige of Varun, the Keeper of Rit, began to wane and he was consigned to the position of an Indian Neptune. Secondly, Aryans had to fight wars constantly for a couple of centuries before they could establish themselves in India. They needed more of the blessings of the war god 'Indra' who was at first merely a tribal god but later shot into prominence at the cost of 'Varun'. Thirdly, to fight wars for a long time it became necessary to plan the function of organization by a division of labor for all time, to gear up the war machinery. The society was divided by the principle of division of labor to bring in the highest degree of efficiency. The concept of Rit was not so appropriate to govern the relations of these classes inters. Some new orientation was needed which was affected by the concept of Dharma. Fourthly, Rit being rigid and inflexible, was suitable only to govern a simple collective life where procedure was rudimentary and trial must have been mechanical having its mode in ordeals. The Rit-era was that state of social existence where there was not much of private property and no division of classes. King was only a leader in war, state was not territorial, and observance of law was more a matter of habit or custom. Later a distinction between Rit and Vratam arose. It was thought that Rit could not be violated willfully whereas Vratam as commands of gods could be so violated. Willful wrongs were then associated with 'Vratam'. Lastly, Rit was replaced by 'Dharma' to complete Budhistic influence of 'Dharma'. *Dharman,* an old Vedic word, meaning law as eternal statute suffered a change of gender from neuter to masculine and *dharman* became Dharma to offset Dhamma of Buddhism which was gaining popularity.

Idea of Order in Post-Vedic Juristic Thought

(a) The theory of the creation of Dharmas Social Order: As has been adverted before at the end of Rig Vedic age the society was divided in four classes and the concept of Rit was found ill-suited to govern the relations of these classes inters. It was, therefore, necessary to so construct the social order as would avert the mutual clashes and conflicts, which might lead to disorder and chaos. Since 'Rit' was found inadequate, a concept like Dharma became indispensable and consequently the juristic mind of ancient India found in the latter an appropriate remedy to deal with the ills of the time. How this was rationalized becomes evident from the following description in *Brahadara-nyaka Upanishad,* which is told in the form of a myth.

The Creator, Prajapati, first created the god Brahma. He represented intelligence. But the Creator was not satisfied only with that. He felt that he should create other gods also if creation were to be a complete manifestation of the various powers in him. He created the Ksatriya gods, Indra, Varuna, Soma, Rudra, Prajanya, Yama and others. They were the embodiments of power, valour, brilliance, fearlessness, the tendency to govern and such other qualities.

But the Creator was not satisfied even with these gods. He saw that there was still something wanting in creation. So he created the Vaisya gods, the eight Vasus, Aditya, the Maruts and so on.

But then he saw that the society of gods he wanted to evolve was not yet complete so he added Pusan to the creation. He represents the 'Sudra principle,' namely, manual labor and service.

Even this did not satisfy the Creator. He, therefore, created *Dharma* or the law, which binds all, which keeps all in their own places and which strengthens all who act according to it. Those who do not follow law, they fall away, however, strong they might be. Those who follow the law are stronger than the strongest because they adhere to the law. He who speaks the law, speaks the truth. He who speaks the truth, speaks the law. Truth and the law are one. Corresponding to this creation of his in the heavens, Prajapati created human society on the earth also on the same pattern and laid down the law for all the four Varnas. The law lays down the functions of the four pillars of the social system. Those who follow the law and perform their functions accordingly have nothing to fear. They are stronger than the strongest and they are bound to be happier than the happiest.

Intelligence, sacrifice, disinterested service is the characteristics of the Brahmins. Valour, chivalry, forgiveness, ability to rule are the characteristics of the Ksatriyas. Trade, co-operation, agriculture and distribution of material wealth are the characteristics of the Vaisyas. Ungrudging manual labor and service are the characteristics of the Sudras.

To choose our functions according to our powers and to attune our powers to the functions that we take up is the only way to follow the law and maintain social harmony.

In Plato's Republic, which is later in chronological order, we find echo of this ordering scheme where society was divided into classes. He also expresses such division in the form of a myth: God used gold for the composition of rulers, silver for soldiers, and iron and brass for that of the class of farmers and craftsmen. The proposed classification was meant for the purpose of attaining excellence through specialisation. Plato's principle of justice like Dharma is conditioning of the proper functioning of society. It is like Dharma 'the citizen's sense of duty of his station'. It is that righteousness which is the result of performance of duties. Justice is the conception of social morality and a definition of the code of social ethics, which is no less than law, and perhaps even more than law, underlies the play of social relations. In his theory of justice Plato gave a theory of right. The Greeks "had no word corresponding to the Latin Jus. Jus implies not only right but also, and still more, Remedy: it is something concrete, 'which is recognized, and can be enforced, by a human authority'. It is the sum of the actual rules, whether created by usage or by judicial decision or by Statute (lis), on which courts proceed." While, the Romans thus thought and spoke of a single concrete jus and of lax as a part thereof, the Greeks thought and spoke of an abstract and absolute right, by the side of which they set, as the one expression of concrete law, the old and traditional use whether written or unwritten, of the community. While the scheme of social order remained a dream in Greece it has already become a living reality and a principle of integration in India. In Greece a mere theoretical formulation of the ordering principle of society as the principle of Justice or Right proved 'fatal to any concrete law, and ideal Justice resident in the pure reason of the philosopher-King, was made to abolish all law and all legislation'. Due to the political orientation of Greek culture it initiated a struggle between Right and Law or usage, which has culminated into a controversy between natural law and positivism. Plato, himself was conscious of it. He thought that Ideal Justice was opposed to traditional usage of the Greek State.

Dharma then owes its creation to the need of order. But it is not merely a social obligation and a characteristic function but also the ultimate social value. As a mystic force it is the ruling spirit of this world. According to Indian thinking, this world is sentient and intelligent and as such it is realized that in order to achieve victory of good over evil and to progress in the direction, some all-pervading and all inclusive concept ought to be accepted. The ancients find 'Dharma' as a fulfilment of this urge.

(b) Danda as preservation of Order in Civil Society: The function of law as order is not merely the preservation of order in physical, social and moral spheres but is also to ensure administration of justice by the instrument of the coercive mechanism in a civil society with its political institution like the state and thus to maintain order. Rit orders life by nature, Dharma by imposing duty to perform proper function and Danda (punishment) by exerting force. The primary meaning of Danda is a stick. Its secondary meaning may be easily inferred from it. Danda may be translated as 'military force', 'coercion', 'punishment', 'a fine', or according to its functions as 'justice'. Ancients had not always a good opinion about human nature and they thought Danda was needed. In the benighted ages in which most ancient writers on law and morals believed themselves to be living, mankind could only be disciplined to observe the sacred law by fear of punishment. According to Manu, Danda (punishment) alone governs all created beings, Danda alone protects them, Danda watches over them while they sleep, the wise declare Danda to be identical with Law (Manu-VII-18). The whole world is kept in order by punishment for a guiltless man is hard to find; through fear of punishment the world provides enjoyment. The Source from which the word 'Danda' orignates is 'Dama' which means to restrain. According to Sukraniti 'Dama' is weaning away from wrong conduct, this is achieved by punishment. The means by which a person is restrained (from misconduct) is Danda. In describing the King's duties. Yajna Valkya and Narad use the expression *Sthapayetpathi* as meaning 'put him back on the right path', which Mitakshara interprets as "having punished (a person) according to the nature of the wrong, the King must re-establish the person in the performance of Swadharma."In ethic-religious legal theory of ancient India, Jurisprudence is sought in the theory of creation of Danda. Manu says: "The Lord created his own son and made him law incarnate for the protection of the entire living world; it was endowed with Brahma's own vigor as Law's administration as Danda." (Manu-VII-17). Manu believed that before the administration of justice by king arose there was the state of self-help. It was the age of Matsya Nyaya in which bigger fish devoured the smaller one. This view is supported by Kautilya when he says "when the law of punishment is kept in abeyance a great fish swallows a small one; for in absence of magistrate, the strong will swallow the small and the weak, but under his protection the weak resists the strong. The object of keeping men to their paths is accomplished by punishment. Here law of punishment is equated with science of government and it is said that progress of the science of logic, the three Vedas, and commerce depend upon Danda which alone can procure safety and security to life and these in turn are dependent upon discipline." With this end in view the procedural and administrative rules multiply and police regulations and safety measures are formulated with varied needs of well-organized state like that of Mauryan State in times of Kautilya. The end of law administered by State is expressed as *Kantak Sodhana* i.e. removing the thorns; maintaining peace and order in society. "Kantak Sodhana" sets forth different measures such as police regulations and administration of criminal law with a view to get rid of such thorns or obnoxious people who are a danger to the country. This process starts from Manu and culminates in Kautilya and becomes the justification for the development of a 'special law' as ordinance of king called *Raj Shasana* or administrative law.

Order is the first and the ultimate justification of law. This has been partially proved by having a review of ancient Indian thinking about law. It is our business now to test the validity of this proposition in the light of Western theories of law. We should know that though the idea of Rit or order is complete as it reveals the nature, function and ideal of law, it can be better understood when viewed together with its doublet 'Satya' which is not only the metaphysical reality (Existence) but also the social reality imbued with all the value considerations involved in the existence of man in society. In fact, in later Vedic age Rit was identified with Truth. Rit then inheres all the juridical idealism, which is a necessary aspect of the existence of law and is vital to its understanding and knowledge.

Law according to Muslim concept of thoughts: In Muslim law language, law is called *Figh*. Law is variously defined by clerical Muslim Jurist Abu Hanifa. He defined law as: "Knowledge of what is for upon one." In other words it means the science of the Rights and obligations of man having regard to the contents and the conception of *Figh*. The scope of law of land is really wider, the former regulates the internal affairs of the state in dealings with the subjects in its executive, legislative, judicature, scientific development and social welfare department of activities.

So, according to Muslim belief, law originated from the direct command of God, the real sovereign and lawgiver interpreted and expanded by messenger of God who was a certain chosen human guide.

Law according to Chinese conception: Definition of any Chinese jurist regarding law is not available. But certain views regarding the definition of law are available. Ancient China although recognized both law of nature and positive law in balanced sense. Foremost Chinese thought was its conception of nature and man's relationship to nature. The positive law, at the very beginning, was developed because China was governed by pure empires in very strict sense. The Chinese people at that time could not go outside and they were in habit of thinking that their country was the entire world so they became familiar with positive law (Command of thing empire which has to be obeyed in verbatim).

We have seen the ancient Eastern and oriental concepts regarding law.

Now, we shall try to analyse, the western world views of some famous and eminent jurists.

Holland's views:

At the initial stage of his book[5] Holland refers a very rough meaning of law: "In the language of Benthem as - law or the law, says Benthem, taken indefinitely is an abstract or collective term which when it means anything can mean neither more or less than the sum total of numbers of Individual laws taken together."

This simple statement is in striking contrast with a multitude of absorptions upon the subject which however are less frequently made with reference to the English form of law than to its equivalents in other languages. The form Lus, Richte, Droit, etc., cannot be said to express nothing more than sum total of a number of individual laws taken together. It happens that all these forms denote not only sum total of laws but also sum total of Rights (IORA, Richhe, Droits), when we say that jurisprudence is science of Lus, Richte, or Droits we may mean in each case that it is the science anyone of three following things viz.-

1. of Law; **2.** of Rights; **3.** of Justice.

And unless this ambiguity be borne in mind many expressions having apparent reference to law will be quite unintelligible but a coherent science cannot be constructed upon an idea which has complex or shifting meanings, one or other meaning must be chosen and when chosen must be made the sole foundation of the edifice. It is therefore a piece of good fortune that when we say in English that Jurisprudence is the science of law, we are spared the ambiguities, which beset the expression of that proposition in Latin, German and French and have greatly obscured its exposition in those languages. This form of "law" is free from any suggestion of the aggregate of Rights or of the aggregates of just things. It is of course suggestive of all the meanings in which the concrete law "a law" is employed in our language and have, unfortunately been so numerous as to involve the abstract idea in considerable obscurity. Hence it is that so many of the definition which have been given of that mysterious non-entity strike us as being vague or merely eulogistic. Many of them have reference to that divine order which pervades the unanimity universe even more than the actions of rational being and those of them which have reference to human action deal quite as often with the voluntarily observed norms of society as with Rules which are supported by the authority of state so as the sense of term "Alow" may at first right appear the connection between them is not hard to trace nor is the earliest use widely different from the latest and most accurate.

Its earliest use: The shepherd who guides his flock, or on a larger scale the head of the family who regulates its encampment and employment seems to have been the earliest law givers and his directions as orders given by one who has power to enforce their observance are the earlier laws. The original and still the popular conception of a law is a command, disobedience to which will be punished, prescribing a course of action, this conception necessarily implies that of a law giver, who has power to enforce his command from this vague original use of the term, has arisen that large developments of uses some proper some merely metaphorical out of which the jurist has to select that he admits into his science, the strong intellectual tendency of man-kind is the Anthropomorphie. If a man is mystery to himself, external nature is a still great mystery to him and he explains the more by the less obscure. As he governs his flock and his family, so he supposes that unseen being govern the waters and winds. The greater the regularity which he observes in nature the fewer much being does he suppose to be at work, in her till at length he rises to the conception of one great being whose laws are obeyed by the whole universe or it may be that, having thus arrived at the notion of a universe moving according to law he holds fast to it even while he laces his hold on the idea of existence of a supreme law giver. Men have also, almost always believed themselves to be acquainted with certain rules intruded for the guidance of their action and either directly revealed to them by a superhuman power or gathered by themselves from such indications of will of that power as are accessible. They are supposed that they have discovered by self-analysis a master part of themselves, to the dictate of which they owe allegiance. They have observed that in order that their senses may receive certain impressions from external objects, those objects must be arranged in certain ways and order. It is easy enough upon consideration of these facts to account for the existence of such phrases as laws of nature, laws of God, laws of morality and others, which will at once suggest themselves.

The employment of the same name to denote things so different may appear to us imply on extraordinary confusion to the topics appropriate to theology, to physics, and to jurisprudence. But the wonder will be less if we remember that separation of sciences to which we are accustomed and which we take for granted, was unknown to remote antiquity. The world with all its varied phenomena was originally studied as a whole. The fact of nature and the doings of man were either conceived or ordained by the gods. The constitutions of states and customs and laws of all the peoples of the earth were as much of divine contrivance as the paths of the planets. The great problems, thus, presented for the study of mankind was gradually broken up into number of minor problems there occurred a division of sciences. A distinction is drawn between those, which dealt with external nature, and those, which dealt with the actions of men. Then, later, the practical were thus severed from the theoretical sciences and the term law, which had been ambiguously in the discussion on both sets of topics before their severance has two distinct histories. In the theoretical science, it is used as the abstract idea of the observed rejections of phenomena be those relations instances causation or of were succession and co-existence. In the practical science the modern science is used to express the abstract idea of the Rules, which regulate human actions.

Use of term law in physical sciences: In theoretical science or in modern sense or in physical science law is used to denote the method of phenomena of the universe, a use which would imply in accordance with the primitive meaning of the term that method is imposed upon the phenomenon either by the will of God or by the obstruction called nature or through minor abstractions called gravitation, electricity and the like. The phenomena, themselves are unable to inform us, so to remove this misconception of mind. We must use the term law merely to convey to our minds the idea of order and method and we must be aware of importing into this idea, any of the association called up by term when it is employed in the practical sciences.

Its use in these sciences is speaking very generally, to express a Rule of human action and sciences of human action being those in which the term is most used and indeed is most needed. It is reasonable to say that this is its proper meaning and that its use in the theoretical science is improper.

The first step, therefore, towards clearing the form law of ambiguity for the purposes of jurisprudence is to discard the meaning in which it is employed. In the physical science where it is used by a mere metaphor, to express the method or order of phenomena and to adopt as its proper meaning that which it bears in the practical sciences where it is employed as the abstract of Rules of human action.

Law as the order of the universe.

Holland himself cites this definition of law in his book:

(1) **Vedas**-"Law is king of kings, far more powerful and rigid than there can be nothing mightier than law on whose aid and that by the highest monarch even the weak may prevail over the strong."

(2) **Pindar**-Law, the king of both mortals and immortals.

(3) **Demonsthens**-"Since also the whole world and things divine and what we call the seasons, appears if we may trust what we see to be regulated by law and order."

(4) **Chrysippus**-"The common law which is the right reason moving through all things identical with Zeus the supreme administration of the universe."

(5) **Cicero**-*Lex Vera Atque prin-eps, apta ad lubendum it advintendum Ratiaert recta summi Lovis.*

(6) **Hooker**-Of law there can be no less acknowledged than that her seat in the bosom of God her voice her money of the world all things in Heaven and earth die her homage, very least as feeling her care and the greatest as not exempted from her power both angels and men and creatures of what condition suaver through each in different sort and manner yet all with uniform consent admitting her as the mother of their peace and joy.

Law as the Rule of action

(1) **Cicero**-*Lex est recta ratio imperandi Atque prohi bendi.*

(2) **Celsus**-*Lus est ats boni it aequi.*

(3) **Hooker**-Any kind of Rule or canon whereby actions are framed that which reason is such sort defines to be good that it must be done.

(4) **Kant**-The sum total of conditions under which the personal wishes of one man can be combined with the

personal wishes of another man in accordance with the General law of freedom.

(5) **Hegel**-The Abstract expression of the General will existing in and for it.

(6) **Krause**-The organic whole of the external conditions of life in conformity with reason.

(7) **Savigny**-"The Rule whereby the Invisible Borderline is fixed within which the being and activity of each individual obtains a secure and free space."

Holland further says that the term law is employed in jurisprudence not in sense of abstract idea of order but in that of the abstract idea of rules of conduct. But of these rules only a particular class are "Laws" in the strict sense of the term. So that although the jurist is in no danger of getting entangled in question of physical sciences, he is obliged to busy himself in marking the boundary, which separates his own department of study from the wider field of morality. His task is to narrow and deepen the popular conception of law in the sense of rule of action as to fit it for his own purposes before entering upon which it may perhaps be as well to point how various characters are those precepts for the guidance of the life and conduct of man to which the term law is with more or less proprietly applied. While some of these precepts are received wherever human beings are gathered together, others are limited to the followers of particular religion while some of them deal with the fundamental Institution of Society. Some are enforced by the whole power of great empires while others may be violated by anyone who is not afraid to encounter the banter of his acquaintance. They possess certain common characteristics. They are either, or they be, expressed as distinct propositions. They are further propositions addressed to the will of Rational beings of the two kinds of proposition, which may be so addressed. They are commands, that is to say, precepts in which the cause of obedience depends on the will on him who commands, not counsels, which are precepts in which reason of obedience is taken from the thing itself which is revised. Being commands they are accompanied by a sanction, that is to say, they imply, if that do not express, an intimation that author will see to their being obeyed, not necessarily by a threat of punishment as such, but also by a suggestion of interference to prevent disobedience or to ruin state things in the position in which they were before the act of disobedience. Lastly there are general commands that relate to courses and conduct as opposed to special commands, which enjoin only a particular action. Black-stone on the other hand makes the generality of law depend on its being addressed to a class of persons. Law, therefore, in the vague sense of rules of human action are proposition commanding the doing or abstaining from certain classes of action, disobedience to which is followed, or is likely to be followed by some sort of penalty or inconvenience.

The rules of human action which are most often confused with laws proper, are those which are called laws of God, laws of nature and laws of morality. So closely indeed are these topics connected with those proper to jurisprudence, that many of the older works on the subject are occupied as much with the laws of God or of nature as with law proper. Sir Walter Releigh, for instance, brings a dissertation upon law, by stating that laws are of three kinds (1) Eternal Uncreated, (2) Natural (Internal), (3) and those which are imposed or in addition, which are explicatory and perfecting to law of nature or either human or divine both of which kinds are again variously subdivided.

It will therefore be necessary to touch briefly on those classes of so-called laws which are occasionally compared with laws properly.

Laws as the Rules of human action

The use of term law in any of the sciences called practical or moral that is to say which have to do with the human will is irrelevant for our purposes but the difficulty is that to draw a sharp line of distinction between the meaning in which this term is used in jurisprudence in which it is used in the other practical sciences.

The common characteristics of moral sciences covering of human action and including all violations whether accompanied or not by the external movement may be summed up as follows: They postulate a will, free at any rate so far as to be influenced by motives presented to it, they postulate the determination of that will by other causes than the mere sensations of the moment and more specifically by respect for rules of life and conduct. They have many fundamental ideas in common, such as freedom, act, obligation, ideas which they are not bound to analysis strictly, but employ in accordance with the usage of ordinary language. It might be accepted by widely opposed schools of speculation, each science must be defined, and classify such ideas so far as is necessary for its own purposes, leaving their full and final investigation to psychology and metaphysic.

The resemblances and differences in the employment of the "Term law" in the several practical sciences must be explained on the resemblances and the differences between the sciences themselves. The grand division of sciences in between that which deals with state of the will, irrespectively of their outward manifestation in act and those which deals with states of the wills only so far as they are manifested in action. The former regards, which later disregards those without, acts of the will, which do not result in outward acts of the body. The former kind of Science is ethic the latter kinds possess no received collective name, but may perhaps be provisionally designated "nomology". So, Ethic is the science of the conformity of human character to a type, nomology of the conformity of actions of Rules. So, ethic is the science mainly of duties, while nomology looks rather to the definition and preservation of Rights. The terms Rights and Duties are co-relatives and are common to both ethic and nomology. But the former science, in accordance with its more inwards nature looks rather to the duties, which are binding on the conscience. The latter looks to the Rights, which are the elements of social life.

Prof Kant has described such: "Ethic is concerned with laws for which external legislation is impossible. It is the science of those rules, which when known are themselves adopted on the will as its object or aims. This Rightness of will can never be enforced by external legislation, but must be free choice of Individual. All external legislation can do is to effect the external expression of the will enact and this, not by a rectification of the aim itself of the will, but by causing the will to follow out enact another aim." Kant define Nomology further as "the science of the totality of the Rules for which an external legislation is possible." So, the moral science, having thus grouped under the head of Ethic in which object of Investigation is the conformity of the will to Rule and of nomology in which the object of investigation is the conformity of acts to a rule we pass by the former as foreign to our subject.

Nomology is divided in two groups:

(1) A science of Rules enforced by indeterminate Authority.

(2) A science of Rules enforced by determinate Authority.

(1) Enforced by indeterminate Authority: What may be vaguely called "Moral laws" are of very various origin and obligation. Their common characteristic is that although no definite Authority can be appealed to in case of their infraction-as in case of (i) Law of fashion, (ii) Law of honour, (iii) Law of Morality, (iv) Law of ettquitte, (v) Law of Nature, etc.

So far as sanction of law of fashion and honor is concerned, it seems nothing because the infraction of these are called vice only, and not condemnation by public or bad public opinion. So far as law of morality is concerned, the business of jurist is to accept at first place as an undoubted fact, the existence of moral principles in the world differing in many particulars in different nations at different epochs, but having certain broad resemblance and in second place to observe the sort of sanction by which these principles are made effective. He will then be in a position to draw unanswering by the line, which divides such moral laws from the laws, which are the subject of Legal Science, or proper science, which have the broad resemblance of the moral principles. As mankind is universally admitted the occasional divergences between them are frequently lost sight off. The truth upon the point is admirably expressed by Paley. "Moral approbation," he writes, follows the fashion and institution of the country we live in which fashion and also Institution themselves, have grown out of the exigencies, the climate, situation or circumstances of country or have been set up by the authority of an Arbitrary Chieftain or unaccountable caprice of the Multitude. As regards sanction of Moral Rules, Locke says that "no man escapes the punishment of their censure and dislike who offends against fashion and opinion of the company he keeps and would recommend himself to it." Such Rules are thus by no means without their appropriate sanction. In the presence or absence of compulsion the diniding characteristic between morality and law, that portion of Morality which supplies the more important and universal Rules for the governance of the outward acts of mankind is called the law of nature. This is a plain and true account of a subject upon which a vast amount of mystical writing has been expended. Such of the received precepts or moral relating to overt acts and therefore capable of being enforced by a political authority or are enforced by such Authority or are supposed to be fit so to be enforced are called laws of nature. They are precepts obedience to which, whether it be or not commanded by the State, is insisted upon by deep-rooted public sentiment, resting totally upon public sentiments, they are rules of Morality. But having reference only to such outward actions as are thought fit for political endorsement, they form only one class of such Rules. After what has been said as to the origin and Authority of moral rules in general, it will be unnecessary to discuss at length the origin and Authority of such moral rules as are called natural laws. Whatever may be the character the objective of those laws whether they should be identified with the will of God or should be supposed to be some sort of guides even of that will, it is enough for the jurists that they certainly rest like other Rules upon the support of public sentiment, while there has been much difference of opinion as to the contents of the laws of nature. The existence of such a law has been generally admitted. At the time when the social sciences were first separated from the Physical sciences speculation recognized in the former nothing, but what is variably and arbitrary thus, Democrats thought, that institutions were of human devising while atoms and vacuum exist by nature. It was the stock sophistical doctrine that moral distinctions, specifically Justice, are the creatures of law, which is itself a mere compromise, securing each man against injury on condition that he surrenders the luxury of ill-treating his neighbors. The purely conventional character of Morality is absolute conclusion drawn by Hero Dotus from the contradictory views and customs, which he found to prevail among different nations.

But a contrary view found early expression in literature. Sophocles makes Antigen appeal from the orders of King Kreon to unwritten and read fast customs of God.

Aristotle fully recognizes the existence of a natural as well as of a legal justice. He mentions as an ordinary device of rhetoric the distinction which may be drawn between written law and common law, which is in accordance with nature and immutable. Stories were in the habit of identifying nature with law in the higher sense and of opposing both of these terms to law, which is such by mere human appointment. "Justice", he says, "is by nature and not by imposition. It proceeds from Zeus and common nature."

The same view finds expression in Roman law. "Law", says Cirere, "is the highest reason implanted in nature which commands these which ought to be done and prohibits the reverse. The highest law was born in all ages before any law was written or state was formed. We are by nature inclined to love mankind, which is the foundation of law. Law did not then begin to be when it was put into writing. But when it arose that is to say at the same moment with the mind of

God." It may be worthwhile to add a few instances from later writers of the times in which the law of nature has been spoken of:

Hobbes-Reason suggests convenient articles of peace, upon which men may be drawn to agreement, these articles are they which otherwise are called laws of nature.

Taylor-The law of nature is the universal law of world or the law of mankind concerning common necessities to which we are inclined by nature, invited by consent, prompted by reason, but is bound upon us only the command of God.

Thomas Equinas - *"Participation legis acternea in Rational creaturalex naturalize dicitur."*

The term "Law of nature" besides the sense in which we have just explained, it has been employed in wider and also in a more restricted sense. The wider is that of well known - *"Ius Naturals"* of Ulpian, which he says, prevails among animals as well as men regulating the nurture of the young and the union of the sexes. It is obvious that the courses of action oriented by Ulpian are followed in pursuance not of a precept addressed of a rational will, which alone is properly called a law, but rather of a blind instinct resembling the forces, which sway the inanimate world. Such an employment of the term is, in fact, fully as meta- phorical as its use to express the order of the Universe. A law for the nature of offspring is no more intelligible than a law of gravitation. It is, in pursuance of this law, which is supposed to cover the relations of men before they have originated. Any of these institutions which mark superiority to the merely animal creation, that all men are asserted to be equal "before any laws were in existence no differences between man and man were recognized by law. Ulpian's *sius naturals* is therefore merely metaphorical phrase leading to consequences, which, however, magniloquently, they may be expressed turn out upon analysis to be dangerous truism. All legal right and wrong had its origin after human society was put in motion and began to reflect and act. To talk of law and Right is applied so mankind at a supposed period anterior to society beginning to think and act is contradiction in terms.

In narrower sense it is the identification of natural law with *Ius Gentium*. Its origin, a system of positive law enforced among the Romans and the races with whom they were brought into commercial contact, was conceived of doubtless as early as second century B.C., as the body of principles which was found in the laws of all nations and which therefore point to a similarity in the needs and ideas of all peoples by the introduction of these precepts. The narrow and strict law of Rome was gradually enriched and expanded. It was an afterthought to give them a higher authority and philosophical significance by identifying them with the Naturals-as is done even by Ciceroby Gaius.

Ulpian's width meaning of term "Law" never seems to have gained currency. It was on the other hand long and generally used in restricted sense of an equivalent for what the Romans meant by the *"Ius Gentium."*

Its suitable and convenient use is the same in which it was employed by Aristotle was also resorted by such writers as Grotius, Gentile, Oldendrop, etc.

A brief of various practical conclusions, which have been drawn from the *Doctrine Ius naturals,* is as follows:

1) Acts prohibited by positive law, but not by the natural law, are said to be mala prohibited not mala in se.

2) Natural law, or natural equity, has been often called in to justify a departure from the strict rules of positive law.

3) In cases for which the law makes no provision the courts are sometimes expressly authorized to decide in accordance with the principles of Natural Law. This is so, for instance, in the Austrian-German-Civil Codes and the commissioners for preparing the body of substantive Law for India recommended that the judges should decide the cases in the manner they deem most consistent with the principles of equity. justice and good conscience, the new Swiss Civil Code which came into operation in 1912 provides that in default of express enactment, a judge is to decide in accordance with "Le Droit Coutumier" failing both of these sources he has to apply such rules as he would lay down as a legislator.

4) The exceptional rules of law, "law merchant have been explained as derived from natural law."

5) When English courts refuse recognition to a foreign judgment, as being opposed to natural justice, the objection is limited to the procedure by which the judgment was obtained. But this ground of objection u/s 14 of CPC (India) is of wider application.

6) The International Law is based upon the rather scaffolding, than law of nature.

7) Positive laws have been said to be invalid when they contradict the law of nature. Hooker Para Phasing Thomas says, "Human laws are measures in respect of men, whose motions they must direct. How be it such measures they are as have also their higher rules to be measured by, which rules are two, the law of God and law of nature so the laws must be made according to the General law of nature and without contradiction to any positive law of scripture, otherwise they are ill-made."

Blackstone says: "The law of nature being coexistence with mankind and dictated by God himself, is of course superior obligation to any other. It is binding all over the globe in all countries and at all times, no human laws are of any validity if contrary to this and such of them as are valid, derive all their force and all their authority from their original." Lord Coke In Bonham's case says, when an act of Parliament is against common right, reason or repugnant, or is impossible to be performed the common law will control it and void. Lord Hobert says, "Even an act made against nature equity as to make a man a judge of his own cause is void to itself." In Day v/s Savage these dictas were approved. But in Hondon v/s Wood Lord Holt says though these dictas are correct but appears never to have been followed in practice.

Rules enforced by Determinate Authority:

i) **Divine Laws:** Among such rules would, no doubt, be included Rules imposed or thought to be imposed upon mankind by God or God's direct revelations of the will of a supernatural power or indirect intimation of that will as each man may find in his own conscience have described as laws of God. It has been believed that infractions of higher class of God's law, generally known as sins, are sooner or later to be redressed, it may differ in religion to religion. The law of God resembles in almost every kind other than point of sources and sanction.

ii) **Human laws:** Now, we shall come to those which are set by a definite human authority and here we draw the final distinction between the case when such authority is and the case when it is not a sovereign political authority, rules set by such an authority are alone properly called 'laws' by a successive narrowing of the rules for human action. We have at length arrived at such of those rules, as are laws. A law, in proper sense of the term, is therefore a General Rule of human action taking cognizance only of external acts, enforced by a determinate authority, which authority is human and among human authorities, is that which is paramount in a political society more briefly a general Rule of external human action enforced by sovereign political authority. All Rules of human action for its guidance are called law merely by analogy. A law in the sense in which that term is employed in jurisprudence is enforced by a Sovereign Political Authority. It is thus distinguished not only from all rules which like the principles of morality and the so-called laws of honor and of fashion are enforced by a Indeterminate Authority; But also from all rules enforced by a determinate authority, which is higher super human or politically subordinate.

In order to emphasise the fact that laws in the strict sense, are thus authoritatively imposed they are described as positive laws. Some definition will be found to have reference:

Hobbes: Positive are those which have not been from eternity. But have made laws by the will of those that have had the sovereign power over others , "the speech of him who by Right commands some what to be done or omitted".

Demonsthenes: "This is law, to which all men ought to yield for many reasons and specifically because every law is a discovery and gift of God and at the same time a decision of wise man and a righting of transgression, both voluntarily or involuntarily and common covenant of a State in accordance with which it be sums all men in the State to lead their lives."

Xeonophon: "Whatever the Ruling part of the State after deliberate as to what ought to be done shall enact is called a law."

Anaximenes: "Law is a definite proposition, in pursuance of common Agreement of a State intimating how everything should be done."

Joh Erskine: "Law is a command of sovereign, containing a common Rule of life for his subjects and obliging them to obedience."

Bents: "A portion of discourse by which expression is given to an extensively applying and permanently enduring act or State of the will of a person or persons in relation to whom he is, or they are, in a state of superiority."

Savings: "Positive Rights, embodied in language and invested with absolute power is called the law."

Bruns: "The objective, maxims of Right which are set forth by the highest State Authority."

Jhering: "The sum total of compulsory Rules which prevails in state and the state is a sole source of law."

Daruburg: "That ordering of the relations of the life which is upheld by the General will."

Regarding the evolution of law Keeton further says as follows: "In order to arrive at a true appreciation of the term law an attempt will be made to indicate the principal steps in the development of law in regarding society. First, however, it is necessary to remember that when we speak of the growth of law, in general, terms we are discussing largely a hypothetical growth for unfortunately all legal systems do not pass through the same stages. This is due to variety of reasons. Some societies have not developed within themselves their laws except in comparative by crude forms. Others seem to jump directly from an early stage to a vary advanced one through contracts with culture more developed than their own. Legal systems do not grow up entirely cut off from each other. There is constant and increasing interchange of Institutions and ideas." But at the same time Pollock has pointed out all development. In law follows a certain sequence, "what we do mean is that the order (i.e. of progress) is not found reserved chalk is not everywhere in England nor red sand stone. But where red sandstone is we know that chalk is not below it."

Sir Henry Maine wrote[6], "historical Jurisprudence looked no farther back than early Roman and Greek law. Since then the field of inquiry has been greatly widened to include the customs of uncivilized tribes, as well as highly civilized laws of Ancient Kingdoms of China and Egypt. It is exceedingly hard to produce General conclusions which will fit all those communities."

All of them, however, seem to have passed through patriarchal stage, which the traces of a prior matriarchy are far from definite. In this patriarchal stage, the power of the paterfamilias is extensive, his wife, children are subject to his authority and his commands are laws. On the other hand his children on his death have an inalienable right to share the family property among themselves, perhaps with the special provision of a special position for the eldest son. When families no longer disintegrate on the death of the paterfamilis another stage is legal, as well as political development has been reached, within the family. The power of the paterfamilis remains, but in the relations of members with members of other families within the clan custom administered by the elders of law, operates within all families comprising the law there is a common clan cull centering round the veneration paid to the semi-legendary founder who is considered to be the common ancestor of all and whose name is borne by all members of the clan as patronymic. Social relations outside the clan are regularly and usually regulated by force. The stranger who is not taken in adoption is enslaved, whilst the murder of the member of a clan is punished by the declaration of blood feud against all members of murder clan. Greek and Rome also followed this stage, in earlier stage. But there were records of clan feud in the time of earlier Chinese Rulers and among less advanced people of South Europe. The vendetta survived until late historical times among many people although not universally (Chinese never passed such age) at the period when a rude mentary State organization is coming into existence through federation of number of tribes into a common wealth, law becomes closely associated with religion. This seems to be direct consequences of the development of an elaborate ritual, associated with the clan-cult, which is based on Bottom and more particularly for the founder of clan. Such a clan cult is found among all peoples where a patriarchal society has developed into State from a federation of clans. The best example is found in Rome and Greek in the period before XII table; gradually the central Authority becomes stronger and dominated by some single person usually a capable leader in battle. Thus, we have seen monarchies in which kings themselves deliver judgments or dooms in the disputes of their subjects in accordance with the customs pre-existing with their own interpretation. This is the condition of Society in the heroic age of Homer. These customs were not laws in the modern sense of law, rather they were a mixture of laws, rules of good conduct and religious observance. There was no clear line of demarcation between *jus, Fas* and *bonimores,* three trends to separate with the advance of Society.

Following this comes another stage in the evolution of law. The dominated order in the State not unnaturally utilizes its privileged position for its own benefit. This leads eventually to an insistent demand, from the people as a whole, for a code of law, which shall be available for all men to read. Better bad law which is known, they say in effect, than law which is uncertain, for the former may at least be avoided accordingly the popular demand is altogether satisfied. But codification is the turning point in the early legal history of any people. Roman law was codified at favorable comparative moment. *Jus* and *Fas* had at length become atmost comparatively separated so that XII table is almost secular code and basic of all subsequent development. In Roman law although, Sir Fedrick Pollock-points out, codification of Roman law has tended to perpetuate a form of Legal procedure by way of contrast, the codification of Hindu Laws of Manu occurred when the dominating order in community had assumed a definitely priestly character and when all laws therefore subject to religious interpretation with the result that Legal development was finally arrested by the process of codification.

These important generalizations, first advanced by Sir Henry Maine based upon Roman and Greek and Hindu law, have, on the whole, strikingly stood the test of analysis necessitated as a result of archaeological discoveries since his day at the beginning of the Twentieth century on almost version of code of Hummurabi of Babylon (2000 B.C.) was discovered at Susa and subsequent researches have proved it to be the basic of the law of more important commercial nations of the east between 2000 B.C. and the expansion of Roman dominion into eastern Mediterranean. Indeed, it has been suggested that the XII table themselves are based ultimately on the Babylonian Code. However, Hummuriba's code, which was the starting point of 1500 years of Legal development, is again overwhelmingly secular. This code was anticipated by earlier codes. But all these codes, so far as we know, have one common characteristic. They are secular and on account of their adaptability to varying stages of social development they are passed on with modification from one people to another. On the other hand the much later code of Jews is throughout subject to religious influences and is expounded by priests with the result that it represents rather the idealization of legal principles than the legal clothings of every day social relations. Chinese law seems to have been codified as early 2000 B.C. recodified at about (122-255 B.C.) during Chov Dynasty and recodification once again by Han Dynasty 200 B.C. to 220 A.D. and T'sang Dynasty (600 AD to 900 AD). At no period in the long history of Chinese law does religion appears to have exercised any appreciable influence upon its development, on the other hand all great Chinese legislators seem to have attempted to frame their laws in the form of repressions of improper conduct in conformity with some philosophical conception of perfect duty on the part of individual towards his family, towards neighbors towards Emperor. All Chinese officials until revolution, had the power to punish and what they considered to be breaches of Moral duties even if performance of them is not enjoined by law, so summing up, therefore, Maine's generalization hardly seems to have any direct application to Chinese law. Among western nations, the period following codification, seems to be one in which a legal system first becomes conscious of its true function within a community. In Rome, for example, we find that XII table are followed by the establishment of praetorship and the formation of *Jus Gentium* in beginning. Ancient custom must in future give place to rules suitable for a rapidly advancing community. Eventually we get evolution of community of jurists and a period of intense juristic activity during which the very foundations of law are subjected to critical examination and the process of change is rationalized. But there is a similar progression, which is best, illustrated in the history of Roman law. But there is a similar progression in English law and in China again we have a similar line of development. As far as the body of law itself is concerned there is one fundamental change, which requires notice: In 5th chapter, Sir Henry Maine points out that early law is largely a law of status. In other words a man's right and obligations both public and private are determined by the position he holds in his family, his clan and society generally. Thus, in Roman law we have the slaves, a few citizens, married women dediticius and other several types of legal potentialities. Moreover, it is difficult and in some cases impossible to change from a position of limited capacity to one of fuller capacity, in modern law state to a considerable extent, though not entirely, disappeared. Every person who may be deemed by the law to form a proper judgment of his own interests in general, is free to enter into what legal relations involving rights and duties he chooses. This is due to the action of several Legal principles of the first importance. In the first place the family in modern law is no longer a corporate unit for legal purposes as it was in early law. The adult children are now independent legal existence and full capacity and furthermore number of artificial distinctions between man and man have been broken (such as *serurn, bibertus, Liberttnus, peregrines, Letinus,* etc.). Again in medieval European law feudalism, determined a man's public rights and duties. An individual today has a greater freedom in these matters. He can enter into or abstain from contemplated legal relations at his pleasure. In fact Maine's classic phrase, "The movement of the progressive societies has hitherto been a movement from status or contract" It seems too correct. It should be noticed that Maine informing this generalization was considering primarily material drawn from private law. It is the highest decree of doubtful whether it has an application to public law.

Now, we should consider in the language of Keeton[6A] what is the concept of law. He says as follows:

"It is obvious that we do not mean the same thing when speak of "the law" or law generally-as when we speak of "a law" meaning some particular law in most foreign languages. This distinction is still more clearly marked, different words are used to convey the different ideas-

- A law-Lex, Loi, Gesetz, legge
- The law-Jus, aroit Recht, diritto.

But in these foreign languages (third term) mean something more than law. They include Justice, Rights and Collection of Rights, etc. In English we have spared the confusion. The word law has no connection with the Abstract conception of Justice and Collection of Rights."

Sir John Salmond says, "Is this difference between English and continental terminology a reason for the divergence between English and continental juristic thoughts to which writer Good- heart applies plausible as this theory may. It is doubtful whether it is actually correct." The word "Jus" has the same double significance.

But the Romans were as essentially practical as the modern English jurist is not the difference due rather to the fact that for over six hundred years English justice has been centralized and efficient, while that on the Continent it has been in a constant state of flux. Sir John Salmond suggests that it is the difference in nomenclature which has caused the difference between English and Continental jurisprudence. But the first difference is no more a cause than the second; they are in fact, the result of more fundamental difference. The difference in law between English and continent. Mr. Goodheart indicates that the Romans, although as practical as English jurists, nevertheless preserved double significance. This seems to supply the clue. The nation whose language has contained a word denoting at once law, justice, rights have all derived their law from Rome, and it is a natural consequence that they should have derived that fundamental legal conception from the same source also. The English, however, have built up their systems from their primitive institution and their original language, therefore, naturally supplies name for the legal conception they evolve, conceptions which from the circumstances of their development are naturally different from those of the Roman Jurisprudence.

It is thus no accident that "Law" is Anglo-Saxon not derived from the Latin, to obtain a true idea of what we mean by the term law. It is necessary to examine what it implied in early society. The earliest rules requiring general observance and enforced penalties to have been those imposed by the head of the household upon those under his control. In this sense it is clear that law proceeds the state in origin. Since the state only emerges when several clans are federated for their mutual protection. At the same time, another conception of law is visible this time as the dominating force of the universe, in this sense, law becomes definitely an attribute of God and is responsible for regularity in the universe. Thus, God promises Noah, "while the earth remainth seed time and harvest and cold or heat and summer and winter and day and night shall not cease his conception of law as the guiding force behind all things appears in the philosophical conception of many other Ancient peoples." Confronted with this exceedingly general theory, we may well ask what has led mankind to assume that law is natural or a divine, ordinance regulating the universe.

The conclusion is as follows: Man endowed with reasoning faculty and confronted everywhere with phenomena which he cannot completely understand, seeks nevertheless to discover some hypothesis, which will these phenomena. He notices that one of the most striking characteristics of material universe is its orderliness and regularity. Certain things are uniform if various elements of a situation are present, a certain conclusive inevitably follows. Thus, if a stone held in the hand is released it falls again, summer always occurs between spring and autumn but never between autumn and winter. The crops sown in the spring always ripen during summer and are reaped in autumn. Turning from natural world to human affairs, he is acquainted with the extremely complex character of human desires, hopes and fears. He has a vague recollection of facts that, before the existence of human law intercourse and society, were difficult if not altogether impossible. He knows when the law is weak.

Confusion returns from these observations we can draw conclusion, just in his tribe, family or nation some individual preserve order and upholds law, so in the universe there is some person of power, omnipotent as far as human beings are concerned, who does the same.

Thus, in early times, Greek, Hindu and Hebrew philosophers were one in holding that law is command and that behind the law, there is always the lawgiver, human or divine. But it must be noticed that in ascribing a law given to law as order of universe (whether law given is God or Nature). They were arguing only by analogy. Thus, the ancient analogy, to the whole of the material universe emphasized the element of order in its composition when the extension had been accompanied. They populated a law giving theory thereby stressing the element of command to be found in law. This progression in ideas is significant and not accidental. It would be impossible to find it reversed. Investigation of the customs of primitive peoples demonstrate that the taboo of these people, although early possessed some meaning, gradually cease to have one and are ultimately observed for no other reason than the force of habits, of course there is punishment for these breaches—has the punishment itself is not based upon any conceivable reason but habit.

Thus a man who infringes a "Taboo" is not punished because his action is illegal, irreligious, or immoral, but solely because he has infringed taboo and infringements of these taboos are punished in that way. So, it is that at a much late stage of civilization, we have the laws of Medes and Persians, which are "unalterable", and societies where the penalty, for proposing a law, which was rejected by the people, was death. So, fixate of habit is preserved sometime at the cost of reason itself. Thus, we perceive in early peoples an unconscious striving after immutability in law. The laws of nature were internal and changeless and they grew in harmony. Should not human laws, starved to imitate them, besides if God gives the law what right have mere human beings to change it. Hence, in early societies the element of harmony and the formity is predominant.

Later by the evolution and rise of state, state's arbitrary power as manifested in legislation the idea of uniformity in law is gradually replaced by the idea of a law as the command of sovereign. So, Blackstone defined law as old ideas. (Law in its most general and comprehensive sense signifies a rule of action and is applied indiscriminatly to all kinds of objects whether animate or inanimate, rational and irrational.) Contrary to it Austin has defined law in other sense taking command of sovereign, sanction by State, etc. The task of defining law is not easy one. Blackstone's definition may be rejected as too wide. It includes a great deal which is not really law at all. On the other hand, Austin's definition is too narrow as it excludes international law, custom as a law, etc. For which Sir Fredric [7] follows objects: "we should hardly give the name of law to a series of unrelated and inconsistent commands enforced by arbitrary and uncertain method. The capricious orders of the crazy despot may be laws according to Austin's definition until they are revoked, but if so it is the worst for the definition." The first part of this objection seems to be valid one, but as far as second is concerned Austin would probably reply that a crazy despot is not an intelligent human being. Salmond has considered this problem in another way.

Salmond has defined law as "A body of principles recognized and applied in the administration of justice. Thus it consists of the rules recognized and action by court of justice." This definition is also open to objection. The second part of it does not necessarily mean the same as the first. Mr. Good heart[8] criticizes: "admirable as this definition may be as an ideal, it can hardly be accepted as a practical solution of the question. The obvious answer is that it does not include laws, which are unjust. Such rules nevertheless are laws. A definition of the whole must include all of the parts. A minor criticism of this definition will be that administrative law is not covered by the definition. Prof. Pound has pointed out that administrative law is developing repeatedly and many questions of it are no more justifiable by Court of law, is primary purpose of law, order, rather than justice. Law and order cannot come in conflicts but law and justice are forms, which unfortunately, contrasted.

The only valid objection to the argument of Good Heart, seems to be that it tends to subordinate the idea of justice. To the idea of order, subordination, which if accepted, would be had for the science of jurisprudence as well as for the law itself. In ancient times the characteristic of law was order and on that account extended the term law to the material world in general. But, it cannot be said that the primary purpose of law was only order. The all testaments for every single time that it mentions the orderliness of the universe mentions the justice of God in creating such a system and the laws of the Moses are based upon abstract conception of Right or justice and not upon the necessity of orderliness and in places this conception of Right trumpets over the letter of the law - nor were the jews alone in their high conception of law among Romans.

The desire of orderliness was satisfied by the existence of Civil Law. But the abstract conception of Right & Justice, higher than existing Civil law than that realized by the existing law compelled them to institute a system of equitable rules based on edicts, similarly in modern law, equity law, and inherent power of Courts etc. Venogradiff has defined law: "As a set of rules imposed and enforced by the Society with regard to the adjudication and exercise of power over persons and things." His definition is good one except it does not show the purpose of law at all. Accordingly, we can say that the purpose of law is "Administration of Justice" and one of the primary characteristics is order. The meaning of person in the sense of Venogradiff includes legal persons. It is now necessary to separate law, as understood in jurisprudence, other things improperly termed law again from other rules, which though laws are not state laws. Connected with the idea of the divine or natural. Ordinary of the whole universe, is the conception of the law of God or law of Nature, regulating the action of man. The Greeks in the course of their philosophical speculation celebrated the theory that nature through the dictates of the human region had partially revealed a code of perfect law and which all human law tended to approximate. Human law was therefore of inferior authority to natural law. This doctrine, which was most fully developed by stoic school, the Roman jurists adopted and incorporated into their works.

Thus providing a philosophical basis for the *Jus Genitium*. from the Roman jurists, the theory was transmitted to the medieval Schoolmen.

So far as we are considering law in abstract sense it will now be convenient to discuss: - "A law" - Austin defines a law a "command which obliges a person or persons to a course of conduct." This definition now admitted to be generally defective. It undoubtedly performed useful function. But as a final statement of what law is, it is impossible in the first place, all laws even Statute laws cannot be expressed in terms of a command, many of them are permissible. They say that if a certain course of conduct is persuaded the State will protect the action of the doer. Thus, if a man makes his will in conformity with the regulations of a statute the State will give effect to his will. But there is no command by the State to individual to make will. Further, there is statute, which repeal statutes. They permit things to be done which were previously forbidden. Here, again the element of command is missing.

The second objection is that: a considerable portion of law of some civilized states is made by the Judges through case law. But some times it is argued that State permits the Judge to make the rules, which appear in the form of judicial precedent. Then, this permission be considered as a command of the State, to judges to make law. But this is quite worthless argument.

The third objection to Austin's definition is one, which has already been lodged against this definition of law, in general. The definition assumes because a law is product of State activity that it was always so, the value of historical method of approach to the science of jurisprudence, lies in the fact that it teaches that law is order than State. Finally, the ethical element is completely excluded from the definition of Austin. A law is completely a command, its purpose is completely ignored. This is also the criticism of definition of Holland. Keeton's final definition of law is: "We may say, therefore, that a law is rule of conduct administered by those organs of a political society, which it has obtained for that purpose and imposed in the first instance at the will of the dominating political Authority. In that society, in pursuance of the conception of justice, which is held by the dominating political authority or by those to whom it has committed the task of making such rules."

Salmond[9] has considered the concept of law as follows: The name Civil Law though now fallen somewhat out of use in this sense and though possessing certain other meaning is the most proper and convenient title by which to distinguish the law of land from other forms of law. Such law is termed Civil as being that of the Civil as or state the name to derive from *Jus civilizes* of the Romans.

The other meanings of the term Civil Law are not such as to create confusion. It often means law of Rome as opposed to Cannon law. These being two systems by which, in middle age State Church were respectively governed. The term Civil law is also used to signify not the whole law of land but only the residue of it after deducting some particular portion, having a special title or its own. The Civil law is opposed to Criminal or Military law. The term 'Civil law' as indicating law of land has been partially superseded by improper substitute positive law. *Jus Positium* was the term invented by Medieval Jurists to denote law made by human authority as opposed to *Jus naturable,* which was uncreated and immutable. It is from this contrast the term positive derives all its points and significance. it is not permissible therefore to confine positive law to be law of the land. All law is positive that is not natural. So, international law is positive law made by human authority not less than the law itself, where the stress is on the distinction between law of land and international law. The former is commonly spoken as municipal rather than civil law. This usage is of course somewhat inconvenient having regard to the modern connotation of the adjective Municipal as relating to Municipality or borough. It is used as a synonym of Civil law, derived from *Municipalim* in the sense of self government governing political community within Roman Empire. Civilian & Municipium were closely related in meaning & use. Both terms denoted a body politics or State. The name Civil law is derived from one of them and the name Municipal law from the other.

The term law has been used in senses (1) Abstract (2) Concrete sense. In Abstract application-we speak of the law of England, criminal law and so forth. In its Concrete application we say that Parliament has enacted or repealed a law. We speak of bylaws or railway or navigation laws. So in Abstract sense we speak of law or of the law, in the Concrete sense we say of a law or of laws. The distinction demands that Concrete term is not co-extension and co-incident with the abstract and its application. Law or the law does not consist of the total number of laws, in force. A law means a statute, ordinance, decree or other exercises of legislative authority and it is one of the sources of law in the abstract sense. A law produces Statute law of Rulings of Courts (case law), which is enactment and enforced by Court of law, but not made by any law. Although laws commonly produces law. This is not invariably the case every act of Parliament is called law, but on all acts of Parliament have not their purpose and effect formulation of rules of law. Statutes are essentially the formulation of the will of sovereign legislation and this may be directed to other purposes than the alteration of the legal system. It must be borne in mind, therefore, that law and laws, the law and a law are not identical in nature and scope. All law is not produced by laws and all laws do not produce law. All the continental languages possess distinct words for two different meanings-as–

Law in concrete-Lex (Roman), Loi (French), Gesltz (German), Leggi.

Law in abstract-Jus (Roman), Droit (French), Recht (German), Diritto.

So it can be seen, it is the peculiarity of English Law that one term is used in two senses, but in Continental languages different words are used to avoid complexity. This advantage obtained by these languages at a considerable cost because the terms *Jus, Droit, Recht, Diritto* not only mean law is abstract but also include right & justice within its scope. So, it is always necessary to bear in the mind the distinction between *Jus, Droit, Recht, Diritto* in their ethical and in their significance. The same ambiguity is about the meaning of term 'equity' whether it means principles of natural justice or justice and whether the principle of law developed by Court of Chancery. Hence it is clear that all law is not made by the legislature. In England most of laws are made by the law Courts. There is more law to be found in law reports than in Statute book. But all law however is made recognized and administered by the Courts and minutes are recognized and administered by the Courts, which are not rules of law. It is therefore to the Courts and not to the legislature that we must go in order to obtain the true nature of law. The law may be defined as the body of principles recognized and applied by the State, by the Administration of Justice in other words, the law consists of the rules recognized and acted as by Court of Justice. To this definition I following objection may be made. In thus defining law by reference to the Administration of justice you have served the proper order of ideas for law is first illogical, order and the Administration of Justice. Second, the latter must, therefore, be defined by reference to the former and not vice versa. Courts of justice are essentially Courts of law. Justice in this usage of speech being merely another name of law and the Administration of justice means the enforcement of the law. The laws are the commands laid by the State upon its subjects and the law Courts are the organs through which these commands are enforced.

Legislation direct or indirect must receive adjudication. So definition of law is therefore inadequate for it runs in a circle. It is not permissible to say that the law is the body of rules observed in the Administration of justice since this function of the State must itself be defined as the application and enforcement of the law.

This objection is based on an erroneous conception of essential nature of the Administration of Justice. The primary purpose of this function of the State is that which name implies: to maintain right, to uphold justice, to protect right, to redress wrong. The Administration of Justice may be defined as the maintenance of right of justice within a political community by means of physical force of the State through the instrumentality of the States Judicial Tribunals. Law is secondary and unessential. It consists of the Authoritative rules, which Judges apply, in the Administration of justice, to the exclusion of their own free will and distinction. They are not at liberty to that which seems right & justice in their own eyes. They are bound hand & foot in the body of authoritative creeds, which they must accept without demur. This creed of Court of justice constitute the law and so far as it extends it excludes all private judgment, What a litigant obtains in the tribunal of a modern & civilized state is doubtless justice according to law. But it is essentially and primarily justice and not law. Judges are appointed in the world of judicial oath. "To do right to all manner of people and the laws and usages of this realm." Justice is the end of law merely the instrument– and the instrument must be defined with reference to its end. It is essential to a clear understanding to this matter to remember that the Administration of justice is perfectly possible without law at all. Administration of justice can be provided by any other method other than law. One court may be Court of Law as well as Court of justice. Courts may be Courts of law only but not Courts of justice. The extent of the system of law may vary indefinitely. The decree in which the free discretion of judges for doing right is excluded by predetermined Rules of law is capable of indefinite increase or diminution. The total exclusion of judicial discretion by legal principles is entirely impossible in any system; however, great may be the encroachment of law, there must remain some redidumn of justice, which is not according to law. Some activities in respect of which the Administration of justice cannot be regarded as the enforcement of the law. Law is a gradual growth from small beginnings. The development of legal system consists in the progressive substitution of rigid pre-established principles of individual judgement and to a very large extent those principles grow spontaneously within tribunal themselves. The great aggregate of rules, which constitute developed Legal system, is not a condition precedent of Administration of Justice, but a product of it. Gradually from various sources, precedent, custom, Statute, there is collected a body of fixed principles which the Court apply to be exclusion of their private judgment. The question at issue in the Administration of Justice more & more ceases to be "what is the Right and Justice of this case" and more & more assumes the alternative forms. "What is the general principle already established and accepted as applicable to such a case as this."

Justice becomes increasingly justice according to law and court of justice became increasingly Courts of law. Salmond considered the concept of justice according to law as follows:

That it is on whole expedient that Courts of justice could have become Court of law. No one can seriously doubt yet the elements of evil involved in the transformation are too obvious and serious ever to have escaped recognition. Law is in theory as Hooker says, the voice of the like reason. They are in theory the utterances of justice speaking to man by mouth of the State, but too often in reality, they fall far short of his idea. Too often, they term "judgment to worm Wood" and make the administration of Justice are preach. At present day our law has learnt in a measure never before attained to speak the language of sound reason and Good sense but it still retains the no slight degree in vices of its youth nor it is to be expected that at any time we shall altogether escape from the perennial conflict between law & justice. It is needful therefore that the law should plead and prove the grounds and justification of its existence. The chief uses of law are three in number: the first of these is that it imparts uniformity & certainty for the reason we require in great part to exclude judicial discretion by a body of inflexible law. For this reason it is that in civilized community of the Judges and Magistrates to whom is entrusted the duty of maintaining justice exercise with a free hand the *viri boniarbitrium*. The more complex our civilization becomes the more needful is its regulation by law and the less practicable the alternative method of judicial procedure but in simple and primitive society rulers & magistrates should execute judgments in such a manner as best command itself to them, but in the civilization at present any such attempt to substitute the deliverance of natural reason for principle pre-determined of law would lead to chaos. Reason, says Germany Tailor, is such a box of quick silver that it abides nowhere it dwells in no settled mansion. It is like a dove's neck and if we inquire after the law of nature, that is to say the principle of justice, "By the rules of our reason we shall be as uncertain as the discourses of the people or the dreams of disturbed fancies."

In second place that the necessity of confirming or publicly declared principles preache the administration of justice from the disturbing influence of improper motive on the part of those entrusted with judicial functions. The law is necessarily impartial. It is made for no particular person or for individual case so much in this so that the Administration of justice according to law is rightly regarded as one of the first principles of the political liberty. Locke says "The Legislative or Supreme Authority cannot assume to itself a power to rule by extemporary arbitrary decrees, but is bound to dispense justice and to decide the rights of the subjects by promulgated standing laws and known authorized judges." In the words of Cicero - "We are the slaves of law that we may free" Hooker says "Law doth speak with all indifferently and has no side respect to their persons." So it is to its impartiality far more than to its wisdom that are due the influence and reputation which the law has possessed at all times. Finally, the law serves to protect the administration from the errors of judicial judgment, the establishment of the law is the substitution of the opinion and the conscious of the community at large for those of the individuals to whom the Judicial functions are entrusted. Aristotle says - "To seek to be wiser than the laws is the very thing which is by good laws forbidden."

Justice: We have defined the term 'Civil Law' with reference to ideal as of right or justice. If this is so right of justice, comes first in order of logical conception and law comes second and is derivative. A complete analysis of term 'Law' involve, therefore, an analysis of the ethical element, so involved in it. This task pertains in the full compass to the science of ethics rather than so that of jurisprudence. But a partial examination of the question is necessary here, in view of the intimate relation which exists between the theory of law and theory of justice. We have used the term "Right" or "Justice" are as being synonymous. Justice is of two types: -

1. Natural or moral
2. Legal Justice.

The first of them is justice itself indeed and in truth, the second is the justice as actually declared and recognized by the Civil Law and enforced in Court of Law. Natural Justice is the ideal and the truth of which Legal Justice in the more or less imperfect realization and expression. Legal justice is the autorotation formulation of natural justice by the Civil Law, for the direction of the Courts by which Justice is administered. Such portions of natural justice are deemed for maintenance and enforcement by the State are formulated by the Law in rules, which must be accepted by the Courts as the authoritative expression of such justice. Natural justice as to authoritative formulated, constitutes, Legal justice of the State. Natural justice bears to legal justice the same relation. That the truth bears to an authoritative creed, which precludes inquiry.

Natural and legal duty:

Because, there are two kinds of justice, hence there are two types of duties & rights. A duty is an act required by the Rule of Justice, an act the contrary of which would be an act of justice or wrong. So, duties are of two types Natural and Legal. A duty of the first kind is one, which is required by a rule of natural justice an act the contrary of which would be an act of moral injustice. A legal duty, on the other hand is one which would amount to a violation of the law and a legal injury. A moral or natural duty becomes also a legal duty when the rule of natural justice to which it owes, its origin is recognized also by the law as a rule of legal justice.

Natural & Legal right: So also with rights, a right is an interest recognized & protected by a rule of right or justice. All the interests of men are not protected so those, which are so protected, are called rights. All right is the right of the person for whose sake it exists and who is interested in the observance of it. Rights are also of two types Natural and legal. First kind is one, which is conferred by rule of Natural or moral justice. A legal right on the other hand, is one, which is conferred by a Rule of legal justice. A natural right becomes legal right when the law, as a rule of legal justice, recognizes it also.

Both legal & natural justice represent intersecting circle. Justice may be legal, but not natural or natural but not legal or may be both. For the law is necessarily incomplete in the sense that it does not seek to cover the whole sphere of natural or moral justice or duty, as it is also necessarily to some extent imperfect and erroneous recognizing and enforcing as justice, what is not justice indeed and in truth and therefore, creating rights and enforcing duties which are legal rights and duties only and not also natural rights and duties. Before discussing true nature of this natural or moral justice, which is distinguished from legal justice, we should consider something, which is as follows:

Natural justice and ideal law:

Natural justice does not mean an ideal or perfect form of legal justice. A moral right or duty cannot be defined as one, which ought to be recognized as legal right or duty. In the first place there is a large portion of the sphere of natural or moral right & justice, which is not fit for the enforcement by State. Secondly even those, which are fit for enforcement, there is a large portion, which is not fit for reduction to rigid rules of Civil Law. So, we reason in a circle when we try to define natural Law. Right, Justice by use of word "ought" or by reference to the ideal or perfect form of civil law. The term "ought" involves in itself the conception of right and therefore, cannot be used for the purpose of defining it by the perfect or ideal or perfect form of law, can only be defined as that which most completely maintains right or justice.

Natural justice and positive morality:

In the second place, both terms cannot be formed together. Positive morality means the rules of conduct approved by the public opinion of any community. The rules which are maintained and enforced in the community not by the civil law, by the sanction of public disapprobation and ensure positive morality, bears the same relation to natural right or justice that legal right or justice does. Positive morality is a more and less incomplete and imperfect attempt by the public opinion of a community, to formulate and enforce the rules of natural right and justice even as legal justice is the attempt by the State, by its legislature and Court of justice, to do the same.

Natural law:

In the third place, natural or moral right or justice is not to be conceived as a system of authoritative and binding rules imposed upon mankind by some form of operative law. Just as legal justice, consists of rules, imposed upon by citizens by imperative law of the State to which they belong, the idea of natural or moral law lax natural, lax naturalism as a form of imperative law in which natural justice has its source just as legal justice has its source in the imperative law of State, which had played a great part in the history of human thoughts in the realm of Ethics, Theology, Politics and Jurisprudence. It was long the tradition accepted of those Sciences, but it has now fallen on evil days and it can no longer be accepted as in harmony with modern thoughts on those matters.

This imperative theory of natural right & justice has in the course of history assumed two forms and passed through two stages (i) Theological (ii) Secular. In the first of these, natural or moral law is conceived as imposed upon man the kind of God as Thomasic says - "Natural law is divine law, written in the heart of all men obliging them to do those things which are necessarily consonant to the rational nature of mankind." From the Church of Scotland, "moral law is the declaration of will of God to mankind directing and binding everyone to obedience there into". Blackstone in later days said - "the law of nature being coeval with mankind and directed by God himself, is of course superior in obligation to any other, it is binding over all the globe. In all countries and at all times, no human laws are of any validity if contrary to this and such of them as are valid, derive all their force and all their authority. In its alternative and secular form, natural and moral law is still conceived as in some part imperative. But the idea of diving imposition and command has disappeared or receded, into the background of thought and this law is vaguely regarded and spoken of as imposed authoritatively on mankind by nature or by region or by conscience. It is no longer the command of God, but the imperative idea is retained and moral law the rule of right & wrong, is conceived as the product of some form of legislative authority, possessed by man over himself, as by his region, over his passions or by his higher nature over his lower.

The idea of morality or obligation is still vaguely conceived as based on some form of imperative, imposition although no longer explicitly on diving imposition. But this secular form of natural law is merely the frustrated ghost of the natural or moral law of the Theologician. Regarded as a form of imperative law, whether from the religious and secular point of view, natural and moral law, no longer finds a recognized place in the Ethical speculation of present day. We still speak of natural justice, rights & duties, but rarely of that natural law by which they are recognized. Nevertheless the term "Natural law," if definitely freed from its early and misleading associations of command and Authorititative imposition is capable of useful service. So long as we do not suppose that natural law is the source of natural justice in the sense of imperative authority by which it is established and from which it derives authority, we may usefully continue to employ the term as meaning nothing more than the aggregate of rules of natural justice. The elimination of illegitimate imperative idea reduces natural law, from a system of authoritative imposition to a system of doctrines. A system of natural law declares and formulates or expresses the principle of natural right and justice. But it does not add compulsion to inspection. Natural justice becomes imperative when its principles are recognized as fit for compulsory enforcement by some form of human authority notably by the State through the instrumentalities of Court of justice and the Civil Law. The essential purpose and business of those Courts is to give to natural justice coercive authority, which in itself, it lacks and maintain it by the physical force of incorporate community against all who disregard it. Legal justice of State is natural justice, armed. Similarly, natural justice and law become, by another road, a system of imperative imposition and control, so far as recognized by being in corporated in that law of positive morality which has its authority in public opinion and it sanctions in the penalties of public censure.

So long as natural or moral law is conceived as being a form of imperative law analogous to Civil law, the same imperative element is carried into the derivative conception of natural or moral duties and rights. The elimination of imperative element from Natural law eliminates it at the same time from the conception of natural or moral rights & duties. The element of coercion is left to be superadded by some form of positive and imperative law and is no longer conceived as inherent in the natural or moral rights & duties themselves.

Nature of justice: If natural law & justice is not a system of command, Authority of Govt. but is merely a system of doctrines, what is the subject matter of this doctrine and what does it teaches there, significance of all human action depends in law and moral on its effect on human welfare act that have no significance either for ethics or for jurisprudence. On this question philosophers have disputed in all cases and with respect to it there are two predominant types of ethical theory. According to one of these well-beings the *summum bonums* consist in human perfection and according to other it consists of human happiness. The first of these philosophers teach us that it is the business of a man to seek perfection to attain the ideal form and nature of a man and so to fulfill nature purposes in making him. The other school teaches that business of man is to be happy and that everything is good so far as it produces happiness and everything evil so far as produces suffering and sorrow and that nothing is neither good or evil for any other reason. But those two different theories lead us to the same result. Men have no means of knowing the purpose for which nature created them. In the satisfaction of their desire and the successful accomplishment of this endeavor, they find life and happiness in the frustration of these desires and failure of these endeavors, they find pain, sorrow and death. The only perfection with man is the ability of knowing lies in his capacity. Thus to do nature's bidding and to attain the reward of his activities and the satisfaction of his desires, the only taste of perfection and the only indication of conformity to the ideal type and final cause of human are to be bound in the conditions of human happiness.

Let us say, therefore, that human well being the *summum bonum* consists in the abolition, so far may be, of suffering and sorrow and the increase, so far as possible, of all forms of desirable consciousness, so that men may lead happy lives enduring to length of days. It is from its effect on human welfare, as to conceived that all human action derives its practical significance and by reference to this effect that it must be judged. This effect is two fold an action may be considered either as to its effect on the well being of the actor himself or as to its effect on the well being of mankind at large, so the rule of wisdom. That is to say, self regarding wisdom, the prudence of self-interest instructs man how he must act in order thereby to secure and promote his own welfare. The rule of Justice instructs him how he must act in order to secure and promote the general welfare of mankind, if the interests of each individual were in all respects coincident with the interests of mankind at large. If it were possible for every man to pursue his own desires and purposes and to seek his own good without thereby interfering with the similar activities of other man there would be no need or place for rule of justice. To allow every man to take, as much of it as he can get is to waste much of what there is the rule of this appointment is rule of Justice. Justice consists in giving to every man his own. The rule of justice determines the spheres of individual liberty in the pursuit of individual welfare, so as to confine that liberty within the units which are consistent with the general welfare of mankind within the sphere of liberty so delimited for every man, by the rule of justice, he is left free to seek his own interest in accordance with rules of wisdom. So far there is no question of compulsion, command or authority. Neither the law of self regarding wisdom nor the law of natural justice, belongs to the class of laws imperative, they are practical laws in the sense in which that term has been defused, they assume or presuppose a certain end or purpose and lay down the rules of action by which that end or purpose is to be reached. The formula of every such law is not that of command, but that of advice to reach that end; this is the way, which you must take. The law of justice is in this respect of the same nature as the law of self interest. The additional element must be found in some regulative or coercive system of Govt. such as administrations of justice by the State or the control exercised by the pressure of public opinion in support of those rules which are recognized within any Society as being rule of Right, both within the sphere of justice & within the sphere of the wisdom of self interest. The concept of "ought" is of the same nature as the statement that a man ought to do a certain act presupposes some appointed ends and indicates that the acts in question is the proper means to that end. But the concept of "ought" has no application to the end itself.

The question why a man 'ought' in the watt of justice to seek the general welfare has no more meaning and therefore no more admits of an answer than the question why he ought in the way of wisdom to seek his own? We have spoken of that general welfare to which the rule of Right & justice is directed as if it was confused to the welfare of mankind, if we accept the view (Utilitarian) that the good means happiness and that evil means pain. It becomes clear that the welfare of lower animal does not differ save in degree, from the welfare, which is under guardianship of rule of right. We owe moral duties to beasts as well as to man and in the Civil law of modern community this part of natural justice has become a part of legal justice also. The capacity & needs of beasts are of little more than negligible importance as compared with the elements of woman welfare. Indeed, the civil law does not so far recognize their interests as to treat them as legal rights. All legal rights are rights of men. It is sufficient, therefore, while recognizing the subordinate claims of the lower animals to deal with the theory of right and law as if it is related to the general welfare of mankind alone.

Justice conceived as one portion of Right:

In the general sense in which we have used term justice synonymous with Right, the Rule of Justice and the rule of right are the same thing and co-extensive in their scope. All Right is justice and all wrong is injustice. Justice is conceived as being merely one part of right and not the whole of it. Similarly duties are recognized of two kinds, one of them consists of duties of justice. So, wrong is also of two types, one of them amounts to injustice. What then is the nature of the distinction thus indicated. It is based on distinction between Right & duties. Justice, it is said, means specifically the observance to rights & injustice is the violation of rights. All duties, it is said, do not correspond to rights vested in other persons. Every breach of duty, therefore, does not amount to injustice. it may be a breach of the Rule of right in general, but not breach of the Rule of justice in particular. So, justice consists, it is said by Roman lawyers, in giving to every man rights, the distinction so drawn between right in general and justice in particular does not seem capable of standing the best of logical analysis. The truth of matter would seem rather to be this that the distinction is one of the aspects and point of view rather than one nature of subject. All right & wrong conduct has two aspects and is capable of being looked from two different points of view; the point of view may be either that of duties or that of rights. We may view and judge an action with reference either to the duty fulfilled or broken by the actor or alternatively with reference to the right which is thereby preserved or violated from the point of view of duties. The acts belong to the sphere of right or wrong from the point of view of right, it belongs to the sphere of justice or injustice, but this double aspect exists in truth in all cases. There are no duties without right then there are rights without duties. Therefore, no rule of right which is not at the same time in truth a rule of justice and there is no wrong, which is not also in truth and injustice, but one aspect or point of view in some times more natural or more illuminating than the other. Sometimes, therefore, rights come into the fore ground of thought & speech and some times duties. We may test the matter by considering the nature of those alleged duties of rights, which are not also duties of justice: -

1. Self regarding duties as approved to duties towards others.
2. Duties to the public as opposed to duties of individual.
3. Imperfect duties as opposed to perfect duties:

First two do not require any specific detail. They are clear but third requires details: An imperfect duty is an act which ought to be done in observance of rule of rights. Therefore Justice includes the sphere of perfect duty only imperfect duty pertains not to justice, but to the domain of Voluntary virtue. The distinction so drawn between perfect & imperfect duty is, doubtless, one, which possesses both logical validity and practical importance. This distinction is subject to two criticisms. In the first place it is to be observed that the specific rule of the law of the term justice as denoting exclusively the sphere of perfect duty is not in conformity with established usage. Justice does not connote enforceability or consonance with an ideal system of civil law. It means due observance of rights. Whether such rights are of a nature to be properly enforced by law or not. We speak of father's treatment of his children as being unjust without any thought of enforceability or of the civil law whether actual or ideal. Natural or moral justice is natural or moral right from the point of view of interest protected by it rather than from that of the duties imposed by it and this is so whether those rights & duties are regarded as properly enforceable or not. The second criticism relates to the use, which is sometimes made of this distinction between justice & other forms of right. An attempt has been made so as to define justice in this sense that by the process of distinctive reasoning conclusions may be reached as to the proper limits of the administration of justice in the State's Court & of the interference of the legislature with private liberty. One attempt has been made by Herbert Spencer[10]—he said, "Justice divides the sphere of ethics in the first place into two parts dealing respectively with the so called self regarding duties and with duties towards others. The first part he calls the ethics of Individual life and second the ethics of social life and later he divides that in two parts dealing respectively with Justice & Beneficence. Justice includes the perfect and rightly enforceable duties. This alone is the proper sphere of law, court & legislatures, beneficence, on the other hand, includes all imperfect and on enforceable duties. The distinction between Justice & beneficence is not imperial. Scope of justice is to be deductively as curtained by reference to the definition of that form of Right." His definition is essentially like that of Kant who said, "Justice is that scheme of limitation of the Liberty of the individual whereby the liberty of each is limited only by the like liberties of all." The all-embracing formula of Justice is "every man is free to do that which he wills. Provided he infringes not the equal freedom of any other man. All that goes beyond this is in the operations of the legislature or of the law Court, is trespass and usurpation and unjusticiable transformation into legal justice of rules, which pertain not to the sphere of Justice at all. But to the definitely contrasted sphere of voluntarily well doing.

Private & Public Justice: Justice is either private or public. The former is the relation between individual persons between man & man while the latter is the relation between individual persons and Court of justice. The Rule of public justice is concerned with the dealing of the Judicial Tribunal with those who come before it as subject to its jurisdiction. Private Justice is that which the courts are appointed to maintain and enforce. Public justice is that which they are appointed to administer or dispense. The former is maintained by the Court in the same sense in which a physician administers drugs. Public justice is that which a plaintiff demands and receives from Judicial Tribunal, because he failed to obtain private justice from his antagonist, so private justice is the end for whose sake the Courts exist. Public justice is the instrument by which they fulfill their functions. Public justice is of two kinds being either criminal or civil. It is sufficient to say Criminal Justice is retributive and Civil Justice is remedial.

Professor H.C.A. Hart said as follows[11]: "The clearest and the most thorough attempt to analyse the concept of law in terms of the apparently simple element of commands and habits, was that made by Austin in the Province of Jurisprudence Determined. In this and the next two chapters we shall state and criticize a position, which is, in substance, the same as Austin's doctrine but probably diverges from it at certain points. For, our principle concern is not with Austin but with the credentials of a certain type of theory, which has perennial attractions, whatever its defects may be. So we have not hesitated where Austin's meaning is doubtful or where his views seem inconsistent to ignore this and to state a clear and consistent position.

Moreover, where Austin merely gives hints as to ways in which criticisms might be met, we have developed these (in part along the lines followed by later theorists such as Kelsen) in order to secure that the doctrine we shall consider and criticize is stated in its strongest form.

In many different situations in social life one person may express a wish that another person should do or abstain from doing something. When this wish is expressed not merely as a piece of interesting information or deliberate self-revelation but with the intention that the person addressed should conform to the wish expressed, it is customary in English and many other languages, though not necessary, to use a special linguistic form called the imperative mood, 'Go home!' 'Come here' 'Stop!' 'Do not kill him!' The social situations in which we thus address others in imperative form are extremely diverse; yet they include some recurrent main types, the importance of which is marked by certain familiar classifications. 'Pass the salt, please', is usually a mere request, since normally it is addressed by the speaker to one who is able to render him a service, and there is no suggestion either of any great urgency or any hint of what may follow on failure to comply. 'Do not kill me', would normally be uttered as a plea where the speaker is at the mercy of the person addressed or in a predicament from which the latter has the power to release him. 'Don't move', on the other hand, may be a warning if the speaker knows of some impending danger to the person addressed (a snake in the grass) which his keeping still may avert.

The varieties of social situation in which use is characteristically, though not invariably, made of imperative forms of language are not only numerous but shade into each other; and terms like 'plea', 'request', or 'warning', serve only to make a few rough discriminations. The most important of these situation is one to which the word 'imperative' seems especially appropriate. It is that illustrated by the case of the gunman who says to the bank clerk, 'Hand over the money or I will shoot'. Its disnctive feature which leads us to speak of the gunman ordering not merely asking, still less pleading with the clerk to hand over the money, is that, to secure compliance with his expressed wishes, the speaker threatens to do something which a normal man would regard as harmful or unpleasant, and renders keeping the money a substantially less edible course of conduct for the clerk. If the gunman succeeds, we would describe him as having coerced the clerk, and the clerk as in that sense being in the gunman's power. Many nice linguistic questions may arise over such cases: we might properly say that the gunman ordered the clerk to hand over the money and the clerk obeyed, but it would be somewhat misleading to say that the gunman gave an order to the clerk to hand it over, since this rather military-sounding phrase suggests some right or authority to give orders not present in our case. It would, however, be quite natural to say that the gunman gave an order to his henchman to guard the door. We need not here concern ourselves with these subtleties. Although a suggestion of authority and deference to authority may often attach to the words 'order' and 'obedience', we shall use the expressions 'orders backed by threats' and 'coercive orders' to refer to orders which, like the gunman's, are supported only by threats, and we shall use the words 'obedience' and 'obey' to include compliance with such orders. It is, however, important to notice, if only because of the great influence on jurists of Austin's definition of the notion of a command, that the simple situation, where threats of harm and nothing else is used to force obedience, is not the situation where we naturally speak of 'commands'. This word, which is not very common outside military contexts, carries with it very strong implications that there is a relatively stable hierarchical organization of men, such as an army or a body of disciples in which the commander occupies a position of pre-eminence. Typically it is General (not the sereant) who is the commander and gives commands, though other forms of special pre-eminence are spoken of in these terms, as when Christ in the New Testament is said to command his disciples. More important—for this is a crucial distinction between different forms of imperative—is the point that it need not be the case, where a command is given, that there should be a latent threat of harm in the event of disobedience. To command is characteristically to exercise authority over men, not power to inflict harm, and though it may be combined with threats of harm, a command is primarily an appeal not to fear but to respect for authority.

It is obvious that the idea of a command with its very strong connotation with authority is much closer to that of law than our gunman's order backed by threats, though the latter is an instance of what Austin, ignoring the distinctions noticed in the last paragraph, misleadingly calls a command. A command is, however, too close to law for our purpose; for the element of authority involved in law has always been one of the obstacles in the path of any easy explanation of what law is. We cannot therefore profitably use, in the elucidation of law, the notion of a command, which also involves it. Indeed it is virtue of Austin's analysis, whatever its defects, that the elements of the gunman situation are, unlike the element of authority, not themselves obscure or in need of much explanation; and hence we shall follow Austin in an attempt to build up from it the idea of law. We shall not, however, hope, as Austin did, for success, but rather to learn from our failure.

2. Law As Coercive Orders:

Even in a complex large society, like that of a modern state, there are occasions when an official, face to face with an individual, orders him to do something. A policeman orders a particular motorist to stop or a particular beggar to move on. But these simple situations are not, and could not be, the standard way in which law functions, if only because no society could support the number of officials necessary to secure that every member of the society was officially and separately informed of every act which he was required to do. Instead such particularized forms of control are either exceptional or are ancillary accompaniments or reinforcements of general forms of directions which do not name, and are not addressed to, particular individuals, and do not indicate a particular act to be done. Hence the standard form even of a criminal statute (which of all the varieties of law has the closest resemblance to an order backed by threats) is general in two ways; it indicates a general type of conduct and applies to a general class of persons who are expected to see that it applies to them and to comply with it. Official individuated face-to-face directions here have a secondary place: if the primary general directions are not obeyed by a particular individual, officials may draw his attention to them and demand compliance, as a tax inspector does, or the disobedience may be officially identified and recorded and the threatened punishment imposed by a court.

Legal control is therefore primarily, though not exclusively, control by directions, which are in this double sense general. This is the first feature, which we must add to the simple model of the gunman if it is to reproduce for us the characteristics of law. The range of persons affected and the manner in which the range is indicated may vary with different legal systems and even different laws. In a modern state it is normally understood that, in the absence of special indications widening or narrowing the class, its general laws extend to all persons within its territorial boundaries. In Canon law there is a similar understanding that normally all the members of the church are within the range of its law except when a narrower class is indicated. In all cases the range of application of a law is a question of interpretation of the particular law aided by such general understanding. It is here worth noticing that though jurists, Austin among them, sometimes speak of laws being addressed[7] to classes of persons this is misleading in suggesting a parallel to the face-to-face situation which really does not exist and is not intended by those who use this expression.

Ordering people to do things is a form of communication and does entail actually 'addressing' them, i.e. attracting their attention or taking steps to attract it, but making laws for people does not. Thus the gunman by one and the same utterance, 'Hand over those notes', expresses his wish that the clerk should do something and actually addresses the clerk, i.e. he does what is normally sufficient to bring this expression to the clerk's attention. If he did not do the latter but merely said the same words in an empty room, he would not have addressed the clerk at all and would not have ordered him to do anything: we might describe the situation as one where the gunman merely said the words, 'Hand over those notes'.

In this respect making laws differ from ordering people to do things, and we must allow for this difference in using this simple idea as a model for law. It may indeed be desirable that laws should as soon as may be after they are made, be brought to the attention of those to whom they apply. The legislator's purpose in making laws would be defeated unless this were generally done, and legal systems often provide, by special rules concerning promulgation, that this shall be done. But laws may be complete as laws before this is done, and even if it is not done at all. In the absence of special rules to the contrary, laws are validly made even if those affected are left to find out for themselves what laws have been made and who are affected thereby. What is usually intended by those who speak of laws being 'addressed' to certain persons, is that these are the persons to whom the particular law applies, i.e. whom it requires to behave in certain ways. If we use the word 'addressed' here we may both fail to notice an important difference between the making of a law and giving a face-to-face order, and we may confuse the two distinct questions: 'To whom does the law apply?' and 'To whom has it been published?'

Besides the introduction of the feature of generally, a more fundamental change must be made in the gunman situation if we are to have a plausible model of the situation where there is law. It is true there is a sense in which the gunman has an ascendancy or superiority over the bank clerk; it lies in his temporary ability to make a threat, which might well be sufficient to make the bank clerk do the particular thing he is told to do. There is no other form of relationship of superiority and inferiority between the two men except this short-lived coercive one. But for the gunman's purposes this may be enough; for the simple face-to-face order 'hand over those notes of I'll shoot' dies with the occasion. The gunman does not issue to the bank clerk (though he may to his gang of followers) standing orders to be followed time by classes of persons. Yet laws pre-eminently have this 'standing' or persistent characteristic. Hence if we are to use the notice of orders backed by threats as explaining what laws are, we must endeavor to reproduce this enduring character, which laws have.

We must therefore suppose that there is a general belief on the part of those to whom the general orders apply that disobedience is likely to be followed by the execution of the threat not only on the first promulgation of the order, but continuously until the order is withdrawn or cancelled. This continuing belief in the consequences of disobedience may be said to keep the original orders alive or 'standing', though as we shall see later there is difficulty in analysing the persistent quality of laws in these simple terms. Of course, the concurrence of many factors which could not be reproduced in the gunman situation may, in fact, be required if such a general belief in the continuing likelihood of the execution of the threat is to exist: it may be that the power to carry out threats attached to such standing orders affecting large numbers of persons could only in fact exist, and would only be thought to exist, if it was known that women, considerable number of the population were prepared both themselves to obey voluntarily, i.e. independently of fear of the threat, and to co-operate in the execution of the threats on those who disobeyed.

Whatever the basis of this general belief in the likelihood of the execution of the threats, we must distinguish from it a further necessary feature which we must add to the gunman situation if it is to approximate to settle situation in which there is law. We must suppose that, whatever the motive, most of the orders are more often obeyed than disobeyed by most of those affected. We shall call this here, following Austin, 'a general habit of obedience' and note, with him, that like many other aspects of law it is an essentially vague or imprecise not in. The question how many people must obey how many such general orders, and for how long, if there is to be law, no more admits of definite answers than the question how few hair must a man have to be bald. Yet in this fact of general obedience lies a crucial distinction between laws and the original simple case of the gunman's order. Mere temporary ascendancy of one person over another is naturally thought of as the polar opposite of law, with it's relatively enduring and settled character, and, indeed, in most legal systems to exercise such short-term coercive power as the gunman has would constitute a criminal offence. It remains indeed to be seen whether this simple, though admittedly vague notion of general habitual obedience to general orders backed by threats is really enough to reproduce the settled character and continuity which legal systems possess.

The concept of general orders backed by threats given by one generally obeyed, which we have constructed by successive additions to the simple situation of the gunman case, plainly approximates closer to a penal statute enacted by the legislature of a modern state than to any other variety of law. For there are types of law which seem prima facie very unlike such penal statutes, and we shall have later to consider the claim that these other varieties of law also, inspite of appearances to the contrary, are really just complicated or disguised versions of this same from. But if we are to reproduce the features of even a penal statute in our constructed model of general orders generally obeyed, something more must be said about the person who gives the orders. The legal system of a modern state is characterized by a certain kind of supremacy within its territory and independence of other systems, which we have not yet reproduced in our simple model. These two notions are not as simple as they appear, but what, on a common-sense view (which may not prove adequate) is essential to them, may be expressed as follows. English law, French law, and the law of any modern country regulate the conduct of populations inhabiting territories with fairly well defined geographical limits. Within the territory of each country there may be many different persons or bodies of persons giving general orders backed by threats and receiving habitual obedience. But we should distinguish some of these persons or bodies (e.g. the L.C.C. or a minister exercising what we term powers of delegated legislation) as subordinate law-makers in contrast to the Queen in Parliament who is supreme. We can express this relationship in the simple terminology of habits by saying that whereas the Queen in Parliament in making laws obeys no one habitually, the subordinate law makers keep within limits statutorily prescribed and so may be said in making law to be agents of the Queen in Parliament. If they did not do so we should not have one system of law in England but a plurality of systems; whereas in fact just because the Queen in Parliament is supreme in relation to all within the territory in this sense and the other bodies are not, we have in England a single system in which we can distinguish a hierarchy of supreme and subordinate elements.

The same negative characterization of the Queen in Parliament, as not habitually obeying the orders of others, roughly defines the notion of independence, which we use in speaking of the separate legal systems of different countries.[12]

The supreme legislature of the Soviet Union is not in the habit of obeying the Queen in Parliament, and whatever the latter enacted about Soviet affairs (though it would constitute part of the law of England) would not form part of the law of the U.S.S.R. It would do so only if the Queen in Parliament were habitually obeyed by the legislature of the U.S.S.R.

On this simple account of the matter, which we shall later have to examine critically, there must, wherever there is a legal system be some persons or body of persons issuing general orders backed by threats which are generally obeyed, and it must be generally believed that these threats are likely to be implemented in the event of disobedience. This person or body must be internally supreme and externally independent. If, following Austin, we call such a supreme and independent person or body of persons the sovereign, the laws of any country will be the general orders backed by threats which are issued either by the sovereign or subordinates in obedience to the sovereign.

Fuller has criticised Hart as follows:[13] Let me develop briefly the ambiguities implicit in the distinction with the aid of two illustrations. In the first we shall pose for ourselves the problem of classifying a rule that reads, "Where a trustee has paid out of his own pocket expenses properly chargeable to the trust estate, he has a right to reimburse himself out of trust funds in his possession." The use of the word "right" suggests a corresponding duty on the part of the beneficiary, yet the trustee has no need to enforce this duty; by a species of lawful self-help he simply affects a legally valid transfer from the trust funds to his own account. Accordingly, we may conclude that we are here dealing, with a power-conferring rule, rather than a duty-imposing rule. But suppose that the instrument creating the trust gives the beneficiary, in turn, a power on coming of age to effect a transfer of the trust estate directly to himself. Suppose, further, that the beneficiary exercises this power before the trustee has had a chance to reimburse himself out of the trust funds. Plainly the beneficiary now has a legal duty to reimburse the trustee. The fundamental principle is however, the same in both cases, namely, that the trustee is entitled to reimbursement at the expense of the beneficiary; whether he is given a power to help himself, as it were, or a right against the beneficiary (with corresponding duty) is simply a question of the most apt way of achieving the result.

My second illustration relates to a familiar rule concerning the mitigation of damages. A and B enter a contract whereby A is to construct a specially designed machine for B and B is to pay $10,000 when the job is completed. After A has begun work on the machine, B repudiates his contract. There is no question but that B is liable for damages, which would include reimbursement to A for expenses incurred up to the time of repudiation as well as any profit A would have made on the whole job.

The crucial issue is whether A can disregard B's repudiation, continue work on the machine and, when he has finished, recover the full price. The law is that he cannot charge to B any expenses incurred in performing the contract after B has repudiated it; whether he continues work or not, the limit of his recovery is set by the amount he would have been entitled to had he quit work after B's repudiation. The courts have commonly expressed this idea by saying that on the machine, the notion being that he cannot recover for costs incurred in violation of this duty.

This view has been severely criticized as obfuscating the distinction between rules that impose duties and those that grant or take away legal powers. If A foolishly continues to work on the machine after B's repudiation of the contract, B has no cause of action against A to enforce any "duty." The only sanction this misnamed duty has is that if A does continue work, he cannot recover the cost of doing so from B. Prior to the repudiation A had a legal power in that by continuing work day by day he was increasing B's possible obligation to him. Now he has lost that power. The situation is comparable to that produced by the passage of the Statute of Frauds. Prior to the Statute men had the power to create binding contracts orally; after the Statute was enacted this power, as to certain kinds of contracts, was removed. So runs an argument based on the Hohfedian analysis.[14]

This argument seems quite convincing until we reflect that in cases like that of the machine the courts start with the assumption that A ought to stop work, for by continuing he squanders his and society's resources on something that no longer serves any need. This is what the courts mean by saying A has a duty to mitigate. There is no occasion for B to sue for a breach of this duty; since he doesn't have to pay for the work done after his repudiation, he is not personally injured by A's continued performance. The Statute of Frauds, on the other hand, does not say that men to put their contracts in writing; it simply says that if certain contracts are left in oral form they will not be legally enforced. Contracting parties, familiar with the terms of the Statute, may in fact deliberately refrain from executing a written memorandum so as to preserve for their contract the status of a "gentlemen's agreement."

In the cases of the machine and the Statute, what has been called "the sanction of nullity" is employed to effectuate quite different ends. In one case it is used to make a do what he ought to do, by cutting off his pay, as it were; in the other, it is used to insure that the power to enter binding contracts will be exercised under circumstances that will protect against fraud and mistaken memory.

It is impossible to deal here adequately with the many problems that can arise out of the distinction between rules imposing duties and those conferring powers, particularly when arguments from analogy are involved.

Even the sketchy account presented here makes it plain, however, that there are two different standards for applying the distinction. The one inquires into the fundamental legislative intent; the other into the legal mechanics by means of which the aim of the rule is effectuated. A failure to perceive that these are distinct standards has mudded many attempts to put the Hohfeldian analysis to practical account.[15] On the other, if one attempts always to penetrate behind legal forms to underlying intent, the distinction loses much of its appeal and scarcely provides the pervasive illumination that the Hohfeldians expected of it. The disappointing experience with the Hohfeldian anlysis, projected against the enthusiasm with which it was originally greeted, inclines me to view with some skepticism the suggestion that the distinction Hart proposes is "a most powerful tool for the analysis of much that has puzzled both the jurist and the political theorist."

These doubts approach something like certitude when it comes to Hart's "rule of recognition." Let me express what I understand this rule to mean by the aid of an illustration of perhaps grotesque simplicity. A small country is ruled by King Rex. Within this country there is unanimous agreement that the highest legal power rests in Rex. To make this abundantly clear we may suppose that every adult citizen signs, with cheerful sincerity, a statement reading, "I recognize in Rex the sole and ultimate source of law in my country."

Now it is apparent that there is in his kingdom an accepted rule according to which Rex has the final say as to what shall be considered law. Hart proposes to call this "the rule of recognition." Certainly there can be no quarrel with this proposal. But Hart goes further and insists that we apply to this rule the distinction between rules that confer powers and those that impose duties. The rule of recognition, he declares, must be regarded as a power-conferring rule. Again, this seems almost a truism.

But Hart seems to read into this characterization the further notion that the rule cannot contain any express or tacit provision to the effect that the authority it confers can be withdrawn for abuses of it. To one concerned to discourage tendencies towards anarchy something can be said for this and Hobbes in fact had a great deal to say for it. But Hart seems to consider that he is dealing with a necessity of logical thinking. If one is intent on preserving a sharp distinction between rules imposing duties and rules conferring powers, there are reasons for being unhappy about any suggestion that it may be possible to withdraw the lawmaking authority once it has been conferred by the rule of recognition.

If Rex began to keep his laws secret from those legally bound to obey them, and had his crown taken away from him for doing so, it would certainly seem foolish to ask whether he was deposed because he violated an implied duty or because, by exceeding the tacit limits of his power, he had worked an automatic forfeiture of his office and thus became subject to "the sanction of nullity." In other words, a rule that confers a power and provides, expressly or by implication, that this power may be revoked for abuses, presents in its proviso a stipulation that straddles ambiguously the distinction between duty-imposing rules and those that grant powers.

It follows then that if Hart is to preserve his key distinction he is compelled to assume that the lawmaking authority cannot be lawfully revoked. In his whole analysis of the rule of recognition it seems to me Hart has fallen into a familiar trap properly dreaded by all of us in the field of jurisprudence. He is applying to the attitudes that bring into being and support a legal system juristic distinctions that can have no meaning in this application. There is no doubt that a legal system derives its ultimate support from a sense of its being "right." However, this sense, deriving as it does from tacit expectations and acceptances, simply cannot be expressed in such terms as obligations and capacities.

Suppose, to borrow a famous example from Wittgenstein, a mother leaving to attend a matinee says to her baby-sit term "While I'm gone, teach my children a game." The baby-sitter teaches the children to throw dice for money or to duel with kitchen knives. Must the mother before passing judgment on this act ask herself whether the baby-sitter has violated a tacit promise or has simply exceeded her authority? I suggest that she would be as little concerned with that question as she would with the one Wittgenstein himself raises: Can she truthfully say, "I did not mean that kind of game," when she never thought of the possibility of such a game being taught to her children? There are some outcomes in human relations too absurd to rise to the level of conscious exclusion. So it would be, in modern times at least, if a parliament should forget that its accepted function is, after all, to make laws and should begin to act as if it had been given the power to save souls or to declare scientific truth. And if the expectations and acceptances that underlie a parliament's power confine it to lawmaking, does not this tacitly entail further limitations? Is it not assumed, for example, that the parliament will not hold a drinking bout with the understanding that those members, still on their feet at midnight shall have the power to make the laws? And is it going much further – or even as far – to say that it is tacitly understood that the parliament will not withhold its enactments from the knowledge of those bound to obey them or express its laws in terms deliberately made unintelligible?

Hart is bent on rescuing the concept of law from its identification with coercive power. A legal system, he asserts, is not "the gunman situation writ large." But if the rule of recognition means that anything called law by the accredited lawgiver counts as law, then the plight of the citizen is in some ways than that of the gunman's victim. If a gunman says, "Your money of/for your life," it is certainly expected that if I give him my money, he will spare my life. If he accepts my purse and then shoots me down, I should suppose his conduct would not only be condemned by moralists, but also by right-thinking highwaymen. In this sense not even an "unconditional surrender" is really unconditional, for there must be an expectation on the part of him who surrenders that he is not trading sudden death for slow torture.

Hart's own distinction between the "gunman situation" and a legal system contains no suggestion of any element of tacit reciprocity. Instead, the distinction runs entirely in formal or structural terms. The gunman communicates his threat in a single face-to-face situation; the law expresses itself normally in standing and general orders that may be published, but do not constitute a direct communication between lawgiver and subject. Acting through general rules is "the standard way in which law functions, if only because no society could support the number of officials necessary to secure that every member of the society was officially and separately informed of every act which he was required to do". Every step in the analysis seems almost as if it were designed to exclude the notion that there could be any rightful expectation on the part of the citizen that could be violated by the lawgiver.

Personally, I shall not attempt to trace in detail Hart's application of the rule of recognition to a complex constitutional democracy. Suffice it to say he concedes that in this case there is not one rule of recognition, but a whole complex of rules, practices, and conventions that determine how lawmakers are elected, what the qualifications and jurisdiction of judges shall be, and all the related matters that affect the determination in a given case of what shall count as law and what not. He also concedes "that a great proportion of ordinary citizens—perhaps a majority—have no general conception of the legal structure or of its criteria of validity." Finally, he concedes that it is not always possible to draw a sharp line of distinction between ordinary rules of law and those rules that grant law-making powers. Yet he seems to insist that, despite all these concessions, the rule of recognition that ascribes legal sovereignty to the Queen in parliament can in some way summarize and absorb all the little rules that enable lawyers to recognize law in a hundred different special contexts. He seems further to assert that this view of the matter is not a juristic construction imposed from without, nor an expression of confidence in the political power of Parliament to resolve any conceivable conflicts that may arise within the system, but rather something provable empirically in the daily practices of his government.

I have difficulty in seeing how this can be. "Parliament" is, after all, only a name for an institution that has changed its nature drastically over the centuries. The memory of one such change is preserved in the gracious fiction that even today speaks, not of law-making by the Parliament, but by "the Queen in Parliament." To speak of one rule of recognition as pointing to something constantly changing is, it seems to me, almost like saying that in the given country the rule of recognition has always accorded the supreme law-making power to The Great X, where X in one decade meant an elected official, in the next, the eldest son of the last X, and in a third, a triumvirate selected by lot from the Army, the Clergy, and the Laborers' Union.

It, thus, appears in Hart's account that the pointing finger which the rule of recognition directs towards the source of law can move through a wide arc without losing its target. How wide can that arce become? It is perhaps a matter of political wisdom not to ask for too precise an answer to this question. It is well in surveying the past of one's country to see continuities even where contemporaries saw revolutions. But when the rule of recognition is used as a "powerful tool of analysis" then it becomes essential to know when there is anything towards which it can point and when it has shifted from A to a quite distinct B.

Fuller has drawn distinction between legal morality and natural law. Then again he has described legal morality law, concept of natural law. This concludes my criticism of certain theories of law. In summary of the view I have advanced I may repeat that I have tried to see law as a purposive activity, typically attended by certain difficulties that it must surmount if it is to succeed in attaining its ends. In contrast, the theories I have rejected seem to me to play about the fringe of that activity without ever concerning themselves directly with its problems. Thus, law is defined as "the existence of public order" without asking what kind of order is meant or how it is brought about. Again, the distinguishing mark of law is said to lie in a means, namely "force," that is typically employed to effectuate its aims. There is no recognition that, except as it makes the stakes higher, the use or non-use of force leaves unchanged the essential problems of those who make and administer the laws. Finally, there are theories that concentrate on the hierarchic structure that is commonly thought to organize and direct the activity I have called law, though again without recognizing that this structure is itself a product of the activity it is thought to put in order.

At this point I am sure there will be those who, though agreeing generally with my negations and rejections, will nevertheless feel a certain discomfort about the view of law I have presented as my own. To them the concept of law that underlies these writings will seem too loose, too accommodating, too readily applied over too wide a range of instances, to serve significantly as a distinctive way of looking at law.

G.W. PATON[16] described about evaluation of law as follows:

A useful classification of types of societies adopts as a criterion the method employed in earning a living. What is called 'primitive law' covers communities in the following categories: Lower hunters, higher hunters, Pastoralist, Advanced pastoralists, First Agricultural Grade, Second Agricultural Grade, and Third Agricultural Grade. The most ambitious attempt to discover if there is any correlation between the economic stages, which a tribe has reached, and its culture and legal institutions is that of Hobhouse, Wheeler, and Ginsberg.[17] The main defect of sociology and historical jurisprudence is what has been termed the method of 'illustration'. A theory is invented and then the pages of human experiences are searched for favorable examples. No theory can be proved by this method, since unfavorable examples are merely ignored. In order to obtain an objective result, these authors carefully classified all the data available on more than four hundred tribes. The results are very interesting, but certainly show the danger of rash speculation. In analysing the problem of the extent of self-help, the tables show that although the use of a regular system of justice increases as the society develops, it is impossible to say that every tribe in the third agricultural grade has reached the same level of development.[18] There is no close correlation between the economic form and the legal institution—all that can be said is that most of the tribes that are advanced economically have also correspondingly developed their legal systems. But a much greater field of evidence must be available for scrutiny before any conclusive findings can be advanced.[19]

Bearing in mind all the difficulties that have been enumerated, we now proceed to discuss some of the most sticking features in the evolution of law. The object is not to set down universal laws of legal evolution, but rather to study particular types of law: viz.

(a) Primitive law.
(b) Middle law.
(c) Classical law.
(d) Post-classical law

Primitive Law:

(a) Before the Era of Courts

It was once thought that the primitive native was automatically law abiding and, therefore, had no need of a system of law, The mores of a tribe were regarded as a confused mass of usage, custom, and religion; it was said that there was no law, no individual property, no real means (save self-help) of enforcing any 'right' which an individual might think that he possessed. What keeps the community together is fear of the unknown, of the strange spirits that may punish man. What has been done once without evil result may be done again, but to innovate is to risk a supernatural sanction. Hence the native has no desire to break the customs of the community. Early law therefore springs from a religious sanction, the fear of the unknown of the spirits that dwell everywhere.

But modern research has shown that this view needs correction. It is true that public opinion is always more powerful in a small community—it exercises much more influence in a tiny village than in a word capital. But Malinolwski asks whether it is not contrary to human nature to accept any constraint as a matter of course.[20] All customs are not on the same level—some are followed because men choose to follow them either as a matter of convenience or because they have never dreamt of doing otherwise, but others cut across human desires and passions and hence require an effective machinery of enforcement. A member of races that dwell in round huts would probably never think of constructing a square one. If he did build in a new style, his whim would not endanger the community life. But rules concerning adultery or rape may need a powerful sanction. Malinowski considers that this is the germ of primitive law. There is no sanction in the Austinian sense—a penalty imposed by a determinate body—but the law does rest on a greater force than the vague pressure of public opinion. The organization of the community protects the law. Apart from the community, primitive man is helpless, and the ultimate sanction for the 'unclubbable' (not in the literal sense) man is expulsion or death— a sentence that will not be imposed by a pre-determined tribunal but carried out by some members with the active approval of the rest. Even at a much later period when courts are fully developed, we still find a relic of the primitive expulsion in outlawry, which Brunner has described as the sentence of death pronounced by a community, which has no police constables or professional hangmen. The enforcement of economic obligations depends on a primitive anticipation of the 'stop list'—if one churlishly refuses to make a customary payment, no other member will help such a defaulter. If the Cheyenne Indians have a rule against individual hunting and it is broken, the offender is excluded from the tribe.[21]

There must be in all societies a class of rules too practical to be backed up by religious sanctions, too burdensome to be left to mere good will too personally vital to individuals to be enforced by any abstract agency. This is the domain of legal rules and I venture to foretell that reciprocity, systematic incidence, publicity and ambition will be found to be the main factors in the binding machinery of primitive law.[22]

At a very early stage the native distinguishes between a payments which is obligatory and one that is the result of generosity. There is undoubtedly here the germ of law, but whether such rules are strictly to be called law or not we leave for subsequent discussion.[23]

Before the advent of courts the sphere of pre-law (if we may invent the term) is fairly small. There are few rules concerning property but some concerning inheritance on death. There are rules of marriage (sometimes extraordinarily intricate as in the case of the Australian aborigines), which lay down the classes within which marriage may take place. Private wrongs are sometimes avenged by the victim,[24] in other cases compensation is payable. There are a few offences, which are regarded as an outrage on the community as a whole, such as incest, witchcraft, and general 'incompatibility of temperament'. A simple economic structure requires few rules for its regulation.[25]

(b) Courts

About the end of the first agricultural grade institutions begin to appear which perform, often among others, functions, which we would now recognize as those proper to courts. Before this it is rare to find definite institutions for the settlement of disputes, though a chief or patriarch may exercise a general control over the community. With the advent of the court the sphere of law becomes more definite, and the rules gradually more precise. The future history of law is largely bound up with the creation of definite institutions, which have power not only to apply the law to the settlement of disputes but also to create new law, and to secure the effective enforcement of such law as exists. Nevertheless, it is a long and slow evolution before there are institutions with the effective powers of the courts, legislatures, and the police mechanism of the modern State. If private violence is to be overcome, then the law must enforce; but if law is to remain acceptable, then there must be machinery for its reform.

The orthodox theory is that the first task of the court is to moderate the blood feud and regulate self-help.[26] The lax talons limit the aggressor to inflicting an injury similar to that which he received. Then appears the doctrine that the victim or his family may if they wish accept compensation, but that if it is not paid, physical violence may be inflicted. 'But off the spear or bear it.' As courts grow in power, the acceptance of compensation is made compulsory, save for certain offences which are regarded not as a mere private wrong but as an outrage against the community and deserving of punishment. Criminal law thus is definitely separated from civil law. For example, Roman law in 450 B.C. was in a state of transition from optional to compulsory composition.[27] Courts existed, but the methods of enforcement were still primitive, e.g. a claimant must himself secure the attendance of his opponent (apparently in the last resort by violence).[28] Such institutions as *peignoirs capio* and *manus iniectio* are obvious relics of an age of self-help. An analogy may be seen in the position of international law today—there are courts, but they do not have compulsory jurisdiction. Even if two nations submit their dispute to judicial decision; there is no machinery for the effective enforcement of decisions. In primitive communities the State finds difficulty in extending the control of the courts over the passions of men. Sometimes, in order to persuade citizens of the value of the judicial process a bribe is offered, as in the fourfold damages awarded by Roman law against a thief caught in the act. In Assyria, the State benefited itself by the forced labour imposed on criminals, gave as a solarium to the injured party a monetary compensation, and satisfied the desire for vengeance by the infliction of stripes.[29] But the ultimate reason for the triumph of royal justice is its efficiency, and the protection which it grants to those who would be too weak to stand-alone.

In some respects this orthodox theory of legal evolution must be corrected. The distinction between civil and criminal law appears much earlier than is suggested.[30] But here once again we are faced with a difficulty of terminology. If the marks of criminal law are sentence by court and the execution of the sentence by state officials, then it is a late development. But if we adopt as the test whether the wrong is regarded as a matter for a private individual only or for the community as a whole, then the distinction between criminal and civil injuries appears at the very birth of law. In some primitive communities definite rules of criminal law are enforced by superstitious practices—sorcery, or the supernatural consequences of taboo.

To avoid confusing the issue by using our modern clear-cut terminology it would perhaps be preferable to speak of public and private delicates. Even in the most primitive tribes the community itself takes action against anyone guilty of certain offences, e.g.incest witchcraft, or bestiality. What is confusing is that modern man regards murder as the crime and therefore, if we find that murder is only a matter of private compensation, the conclusion is erroneously reached that there are no offences, which the community itself punishes.[31]

Another criticism of the orthodox view is that of Diamond, who denies that the lax talons preceded the payment of compensation.[32] He considers that early law emphasized compensation for civil injuries and that corporal sanctions began to appear only in the codes of the middle period. Is not the truth somewhere between both views? The lax talons in the sense of loosely regulated self-help belong to primitive law and applies both to civil and criminal acts. But the direct infliction of corporal punishment by officials of the State belongs to a much later period.[33]

At first there is little notion of legal duty— the concept is rather that of physical liability.[34] At first, it is the community rather than the individual who is responsible—it is only gradually that an individual's obligation is distinguished from that of the group to which he belongs.

A debtor gives a hostage as security; if the debtor defaults, it is the hostage who is liable and not the debtor. Liability for debt does not mean execution against goods as in modern systems, but the physical liability of the hostage to be cut in pieces or sold into slavery—in a very real sense can a creditor 'take it out of the hide' of the debtor. When a debtor is allowed to give his own person as security, the creditor may take vengeance for any default directly upon him. The law of contract is not yet born— the debtor is regarded as one who wrongfully detains the creditor's property.[35] In early English law, debt (the action for money owed) was hardly distinguishable from detain (the gist of which was that the defendant wrongfully refused to surrender a chattel to which the plaintiff had a right to immediate possession). The notion in early law is not so much one of legal obligation (that a person ought to do something) as that of liability (that he must pay or suffer punishment). In the law of depict we see the analogous notion of, thing liability.

There has been a gradual change from liability of the person to liability of the goods, which a person possesses. This evolution of the law of execution against property is rather slow—thus in Roman law the right of *peignoirs capio* is at first exercised only to put pressure on the debtor to pay his debt, for there is no right to sell or to use the residence. When a court begins to grant execution against property, the tendency is for all the defendant's chattels to be seized, even if only a small sum is owing—to take only sufficient property to cover the debt seems an obvious procedure, but one that develops slowly.[36] Today, now that imprisonment for debt has been restricted, liability is in effect limited to a man's property and future earning power. By the device of the limited company, a man's loss may be confined to his investment in a particular venture, for the creditors can call on the funds of the company alone.

Primitive law is not rigid, nor is it largely concerned with procedural details. It is in the middle period that excessive formality develops. Law begins with rather vague and elastic rules,[37] technicality is really the result of a long period of development.

Ehrlich points out that whether in art, religion, or law, whenever we find rigid forms and we are able to trace their history, we find that there has been a hardening of what was originally soft and flexible.[38] Although there was a natural tendency, in order to secure greater reverence for the law, to emphasize its antiquity, it is an exaggeration to say that primitive man regarded the law as unchangeable.[39] Indeed, a long period of discussion and indecision may precede action if a custom is broken: only slowly does the community evolve a practicable rule of enforcement. When technicalities appear in commercial transactions, in property, or in procedure, they 'mark the end of the period of primitive law'.[40] For example, the law of contract begins in a simple way. It is only in the middle period that it becomes technical and relatively fixed. Moreover, some legal systems remain relatively free from technicality even at a late stage of development.[41]

(c) Codes

Codes began to appear, usually, at some period after the third agricultural grade. If they are classified not according to their chronological date but according to the degree of internal development, early codes may be represented by the Salic law; the middle codes extend from the *Leges Barbarorum* of the reign of Charlemagne to the more developed laws of the Pentateuch and the Twelve Tables; finally, as an example of a late code we have that of Hammurabi (which incidentally is very early historically, the date being about 1914 B.C.).[42] Maine emphasized the influence of religion on early codes: 'there is no system of recorded law, literally from China to Peru, which, when it first emerges into notice, is not seen to be entangled with religious ritual and observance'.[43] A study of materials, which have become accessible since Maine wrote shows that this view is too broad.[44] The codes of Hammurabi and of the Assyrians-45 are predominantly secular in character.

It is true that in the Hebrew Pentateuch, in the Hindu Code of Menu, and in the Roman Twelve Tables religious sanctions are to be found.[46] Diamond, however, submits the Hebrew Code[47] to a precise analysis and shows that the early code was secular and that the sections showing religious influence are priestly additions of a later date.[48] The doctrine that the community punished certain offences only because of the religious notion that the community is thereby polluted may be supported by the Hebrew text that 'the land cannot be cleaned of the blood that is shed therein but by the blood of him that shed it,[49] but this text is probably also late addition. Driver and Miles conclude that the Assyrian theory of punishment did not have a religious origin, nor is there any trace of the doctrine that crime is a pollution of the community.[50] The evidence is too meagre, however, to allow of dogmatic generalization.[51]

Proof, which Diamond attempts to give, that there is little or no direct religious influence in some early codes, does not determine the question for primitive law prior to the era of the codes. The question of the definition of religion in primitive times is nearly as difficult as that of law, but religion undoubtedly was one of the forces that went to create society and therefore the law. Maine's dictum is undoubtedly too wide, for he refers specifically to codes.

In this period, we notice a gradual growth of rigidity and technicality. What is the cause of this curious love of formalism? It has been suggested that the formalism is a relic of traditional ceremonies of religious ritual,[52] That the parties desire a religious sanction, or that some ceremony is considered necessary to create a binding sense of obligation in the minds of the parties, or to impress the witnesses so that they are likely to remember the transaction. Vinogradoff suggests that we must go back even to the early agreements between the clans which were almost in the form of international treaties.[53] But no really adequate explanation of the curious love of formalism has ever been vouchsafed. The basic explanation may perhaps be found in the fact that most human beings find it much easier to learn a formal way of performing a complicated process, than to learn why the process must be complicated or to understand the complications.

'When primitive law has once been embodied in code', Maine writes, 'there is an end to its spontaneous development', and thereafter law is brought into harmony with society by three instrumentalities; legal fictions, equity, and legislation, which appear in the historical order in which they are enumerated.[54] This dictum needs some correction. It may be true that the frequent use of legislation to change, or to create new law is a late phenomenon, but legislation appears very early. What are codes but legislation, and frequently they are mere consolidation of prior legislation.[55]

The use of fictions and equity is not confined to any one period. The fiction is useful at a time when legal stability is desired, but change in the application of the law is felt to be imperative. Maine defined the fiction in a very broad sense: 'any assumption which conceals or affects to conceal the fact that a rule of law has undergone alteration its letter remaining unchanged, its operation being modified.' Thus, in the *Actio Publiciana* of Roman law the formula ordered the index to assume that the period of prescription had already elapsed in order to give to the possessor in good faith a remedy which strictly was confined to him who was already dominos. The procedural fictions by which the English courts extended their jurisdiction are well known. But fictions are not confined to the past, for they still have their use today. What is quasi-contract but a legal fiction?[56]

Why do judges use this method? It is not, as Bentham suggests, a desire to deceive, for the fiction deceives no one. Nor is it an unbridled lust for power, although some of the fictions used to extend the jurisdiction of particular English courts are hard to defend. Partly it is 'economy of thought'—the desire to use old devices that have worked well instead of running the risk of innovation. Thus, under Scots law, dissolution of the marriage confers upon the wife *a ius relictae,* which is calculated as if the husband were already dead.[57] This device of the 'as if' can be used to extend new rules to old situations with a minimum of intellectual effort.[58] There is less apparent violence to accepted doctrines than direct reform would produce and, therefore, it is a useful weapon to a judiciary, which wishes to maintain the view that its task is but to declare the law.[59]

Moreover, the legal fiction may prove a very useful agency of development. 'The fiction is the algebra of law and a picturesque form of algebra besides.[60] Much law may be reduced to a heap of fictions piled one on top of another. Marriage may be regarded as a sale;[61] the first method of bequeathing an estate to one who is not a blood relation may be by adoption, then in the next stage a fictitious adoption may be posited as the legal basis of will.[62]

So far we have been dealing with the part played by the fiction in the evolution of law. But the term has uses other than its historical sense. Thus the brocard or legal maxim is sometimes called a fiction, e.g. the dead give seism to the living. Although not legal principles in the true sense, these maxims play a role in organizing legal knowledge. Especially before the days of writing, the use of 'catch phrases' minimizes the burden upon memory and a host of particular example may be covered by the one generalization. Although these maxims are useful at a certain stage in legal evolution, they are very likely to be misused,[63] and a true basis for classification cannot be discovered until a theoretical study creates legal principles, which can afford both cohesion and a capacity for development.

Equity

In every system of law there is a conflict between two types of judicial mind—one glories in a strong decision which upholds the logical elegance of the even at the cost of injustice or inconvenience,[64] another emphasizes that law exists for man and not man for law and that the rules must be so adapted that injustice is avoided.[65] If we like to use other language, we may emphasize the contrast between *striatum ius* and *aequitas*. In the early period the logical structure of the law has not yet sufficient rigidity to make this conflict prominent, but, once the era of formalism and technicality begins, we see the commencement of strife. Legal technique may become so absorbing that the game is played for its own sake, as in the heyday of the formalistic rules of English pleading.

English lawyers are so accustomed to think of equity as the province of a separate court that the opposition between *aequitas* and *striatum ius* is perhaps exaggerated. Yet as late as the reign of Henry VII a Chancellor could, over the dinner table, suggest to the common law judges that, if they set own house in order, the injunction which they feared would become unnecessary.[66] But the increasing technicality of the common law rendered the existence of the powers of the Chancellor a real necessity.[67] In Rome the work of the proctor in modernizing the law, enforcing the requirement of good faith, emphasizing the intention of the parties rather than the form of the agreement, is somewhat similar in effect to that of the English Chancellor.[68] If we generalize from English and Roman iaw, we may think Maine of equity as any 'body of rules existing by the side of the original civil law, founded on distinct principles and claiming incidentally to supersede the civil law in virtue of a superior sanctity inherent in those principles.[69]

Classical Law

The classical stage is marked by a sudden flowering of legal genius. The community is economically well established, but rapid social developments have left the law far behind. The primitive rules, inspite of the use of the fiction, inspite of 'interpretation', which solemnly lies down that a sacred text means what it does not mean, are too undeveloped to serve the needs of the period. There is a danger that law may become a mere chaos of specific precedents, for, although rules are many, principles are few. There is need of classification, analysis, and synthesis. The dead law of the past must be cut away in order to allow future growth to be unhampered.

Hence the search for general principles which will explain the actual rules in force and provide a ground for future development, hence the analysis of the concepts which the law uses in order to achieve clarity. This was the work performed by the Roman jurists of the classical era and by the

English judges and writers of the nineteenth century. The desire for a fully developed theory, which can stand, as a justification behind particular rules is not prompted only by an academic desire for completeness. A law that has a proper theoretical basis is more easily understood, applied, and extended than one, which lacks such a foundation. Developed jurisprudence begins in the classical age.

Post-classical Law

In the post-classical period, society becomes more complex and rapid development of the law is inevitable. We are too close to the evolution of the common law to make valid judgments, but in Roman post-classical law we find certain definite characteristics. Jolowicz[70] mentions: firstly, increasing reliance on equity at the expense of legal principle—there is lacking the desire to think out a new principle in place of the old and consequently a tendency to solve the issue merely by relying on phrases such as *benign tamen dicendum est.* The desire to achieve justice is commendable, but there is too much of a tendency to take the intellectual short cut. Secondly, he finds a desire to protect the weak at the expense of the strong, even at the expense of general security and credit. This was obviously due in part of the influence of Christianity and a growing appreciation of the value of the human personality. Thirdly, there is the increasing emphasis on intent at the expense of form: an impatience of mere technicality, which may defeat the ends of justice. These tendencies are observable to some extent in our modern system of law.

It is easy to exaggerate the value of the analogy from the human organism, which grows, reaches maturity, and then decays. Roman law after the post-classical period received a new lease of life through the reception and left its mark deep on the modern world. But there is a tendency in mature systems, as economic and social conditions become more complex, to deal with new situations by statues designed for a particular mischief only. A flood of such remedies leaves the law in a somewhat incoherent state. It is the task of the lawyer to point out how much the old order has changed and what reforms are necessary to make the body again consistent with itself. It is easy to sneer at desire for legal elegance, but if a system loses its underlying unity it becomes hard to teach and difficult to apply. Hence in the post-classical period there is a challenge to study the basis of statutory law, as in the classical period attention was concentrated on the basis of case law. Otherwise law may cease to be a system and become a collection of ad hoc rules.

At present the challenge is stronger because of the influence of new social theories of collectivism and planning. How much of the classical conception of ownership remains, so far as real estate is concerned, in the light of statutes dealing with town and country planning? Has the nature of contract insensibly changed? Is the law of tort now more concerned with adjusting social risks than awarding damages on basis of fault? These questions cannot be answered in a word, but they do demand examination if there is to be real understanding of the functioning of the law. Leaving aside debates of terminology, it is dogmatically stressed that no jurisprudence can be adequate unless it gives a better understanding of law, its evolution, and its social purpose. Legal purists may label the post-classical eras as degenerate: but that does not preclude us from studying the real nature of the world in which we live and attempting to make of law a more effective tool to achieve the ends which society demands.

The problems of definition are not as simple as they were once thought to be. According to a widely accepted method, the first task is to discover the genus to which the rest belongs and then the particular characteristics which distinguish it from other species of the same genus.

'When the notion of definition was invented by Socrates and Plato, only "real definition" was thought of. That is, it was always a rest or things that required definition, never nominal or words or concepts.'

This is not to say that the traditional process of 'real definition' is not of value. But it has often caused puzzlement and argument by confusing the identification, description, and classification of things with arguments about the use of words. 'Real definition' (i.e., the assumption that when asked for a definition what we are to define is a thing and not a word) has been valuable, although productive of confusion when applied to tasks to which it was not suited, because definition is perhaps most often seen as a matter of drawing lines or distinguishing between one kind of thing and another when language marks them off by using separate words to refer to them or so that language may do so in the future.[71]

As the purpose of one observer differs from that of another so will his emphasis on different aspects of the thing observed. To a zoologist a horse suggests the genus *mammalian quadruped,* to a traveler a means of transportation, to the average man the sport of kings, to certain nations an article of food.

If we pursue the task of defining law by the process of 'real definition' we find the method leads us into difficulties. 'There is no familiar well-understood general category of which law is a member.[72] The attempt to find some common characteristics, or an essence, enjoyed by all the instances of what in ordinary use of the word are accepted as laws, have all broken down at one point or another. Austin took the word 'law' and distinguished it, as applied to rules in systems, which he recognized as legal, from its use in other contexts—as in Divine Law, Laws of physics or chemistry. As has been seen, he fixed on the command of the sovereign as its distinguishing characteristic. But even to do this, of course, he had to recognize legal system.

The problem of defining the term 'law' may be approached form the point of view of the theologian, the sociologist, the philosopher, the political scientist, or the lawyer. Most lawyers will approach the problem from inside a particular legal system. It is not surprising therefore that for the lawyers' purposes the investigation may stop at the point where that legal system provides authoritative tests for recognizing law from not-law. Those tests will be applied by some agencies of that legal system and hence we find lawyers defining law as 'the rules recognized and acted on by courts of justice.[73] For lawyers working within a legal system such an answer may be sufficient for their purposes. But it does not assist those puzzled from a view outside a legal system as to the nature of law or the nature of legal systems. Hart says that for such people there have been three recurrent issues: 'How does law differ from and how is it related to orders backed by threats? How does legal obligation differ from, and how is it related to moral obligation? What are rules and to what extent is law an affair of rules.[74]

Much may be learnt about law by describing it in terms of its basis in nature, reason, religion, or ethics; by reference to its source in custom, precedent. Or legislation; by its effects on the life of society; by the method of its formal expression or authoritative application; or by the ends that it seeks to achieve. But no definition in terms of any one of these provides an exhaustive means by which one could distinguish legal systems from other systems in all cases or legal rules from other rules in all cases. Pound has carried out an analysis, which reveals the difficulties facing those who like their terms to be simple and clear-cut.[75] Many attempts have been made to examine the problems relating to the definition of law.[76] It is futile to attempts to be exhaustive, but an analysis of a few typical definitions is a useful approach to the problem.

In preface, it should be pointed out that the word adroit is even more ambiguous than the English term law. In its wide and objective *sense le adroit* means the totality of the rules of law and we sometimes find adroit object if (or natural law) opposed to a particular rule of positive law. Even when adroit means positive law, the word carries an undertone of right or justice, which is not present in the English term law to the same extent. In addition to these usages there is a purely subjective sense—thus *le adroit d'auteur* means the right of an author. Hence particular caution must be used in translating any phrase in which droit occurs.

Law, Ethics, And Positive Morality:

A definition of law should establish clear distinctions between rules of law and rules of ethics, and between rules of law and such social rules as those of positive morality and of etiquette.[77]

To distinguish between law and ethics is fairly easy. Ethics is a study of the supreme good—an attempt to discover those rules, which should be followed because they are good in themselves. Law tends to prescribe what is considered necessary for that time and place. Ethics concentrates on the individual rather than upon society; law is concerned with the social relationships of men rather than the individual excellence of their characters and conduct. Ethics must consider the motive for action as all-important, whereas law is concerned mainly with requiring conduct to comply with certain standards, and it is not usually concerned with the motives of men. It is too narrow, however, to say that ethics deals only with the individual, or that ethics treats only of the 'interior' and law only of the 'exterior', for ethics in judging acts must consider the consequences that flow from them and it is not possible to analyse the ethical duties of man without considering his obligations to his fellows or his place in society. It is equally misleading to concentrate upon those aspects of the law which are concerned directly with conduct and with 'exterior' factors in man's social relations,[78] to the exclusion of those which, explicitly or implicitly, are aimed at intention, motive, and the ends which men seek.

Positive Morality

Various tests have been suggested to distinguish a rule of law from a mere dictate of positive morality. Firstly, a rule of law is imposed by the State; secondly, while there may be a sanction behind the rules of positive morality, it is not applied by organized machinery, nor is it determined in advance. Thirdly, some argue that the content of law is different from that of social morality: but, while it is true that law, having a different object, covers a different scope, there is no immutable boundary to its operation. Law, positive morality, and ethics are overlapping circles which can never entirely coincide, but the hand of man can move them and determine the content that is common to all or to two or confined to one. Ethics condemns murder, but it was once accepted both by positive morality and law.

The Imperative Definition

In his well-known analysis Austin first attempts to define the genus law and then to mark the difference, which distinguish law as the subject matter of jurisprudence.[79] In the broadest sense in which the term 'law' should be used; it signifies a command which obliges a person or persons to a course of conduct. Being a command, it must issue from a determinate person or group of persons, with the threat of displeasure if the rule be not obeyed.

The person who receives the command must realize that there is a possibility of incurring some evil in the event of disobedience. This element of command clearly distinguishes a law from a mere rule of positive morality, since in the latter case the rule is not laid down by a determinate person, nor is there a definite threat of punishment.[80] But every command does not create a law, for we must distinguish between a particular order ('call me at dawn tomorrow') and an order laying down a general course of conduct ('call me at dawn every morning').[81]

Having thus discovered the genus law, Austin distinguishes the species, which is of interest to the jurist—positive law, as he terms it. Positive law is laid down by the sovereign either mediately or immediately—it is a rule laid down by a political superior for a political inferior. Austin's theory of sovereignty is discussed below;[82] here it is enough to say that he postulates, firstly, a political society, secondly, a superior in that society who is habitually obeyed by the bulk of the community and who is not the habit of obedience to any other person or body.[83] The sovereign, of course, may consist either of one person or a number of persons.

Into a detailed criticism of the Austinian definition we do not propose to go, but there are three major points:

(a) Should law be defined by reference to the State?

(b) Is a definite sanction necessary before a rule can be regarded as law?

(c) Should a definition of law contain a reference to the purpose of law?[84]

The Problem Of International Law

According to Austin's view, international law is not positive law since there is lacking a determinate sovereign whom the nation of the world habitually obeys. Perhaps on no point has Austin been so criticized as on his approach to this problem. But his conclusion follows irresistibly from his premises,[85] and many who criticize Austin show a disinclination to follow the only logical course and adopt a broader definition of law.

Attempts have been made by the Covenant of the League of Nations, the Kellogg Pact, and the Charter of the United Nations to reduce the area of self-help, but humanity must fare before there is an effective reign of law in international affairs.[86] It is true that international law of peace is seldom broken, but once grave issues arise we see flagrant disregard of accepted rules. The public opinion of the world may be a factor not lightly to be ignored, but it is harder to deal with a nation that is a law-breaker than to expel a primitive man from his community—hence while primitive and international law both lack institutional machinery, the sanctions of the former are really more effective, since they are brought to bear on the individual and not on the nation. Law can be effective only if there be a community with an accepted scale of values. Nazi Germany denied that the state4 was bound by law in its dealings with states of another colour:[87] the same doctrine was originally put forward by Soviet thinkers, but the reality of international law is recognized by contemporary Soviet theory.[88]

One significant advance has been the setting up of courts to try war criminals.[89] This step has been hailed in most quarters as a vindication of the effectiveness of international law and the dawn of a new era when sanctions will be applied against law breakers.[90] It is certainly encouraging to see the attempt made to secure the observance of certain minimum rules, but optimism must be tempered by the following considerations.[91] Firstly, it is unlikely that the threat of a prosecution for against peace (the waging of aggressive war) will ever deter a nation bent on conquest, for a crime against the peace is deliberately planned only where victory is expected. Secondly, so far as the rules of war are concerned, the principles are so uncertain that the individual is placed in a position of great difficulty. These rules are always absolute as the machinery of international conferences is too cumbrous to develop them with sufficient speed. The submarine, the aeroplane, and the atom bomb were not envisaged when the earlier rules lay down. Moreover, there is no international criminal court, which can state the law authoritatively. For a submarine commander, to kill survivors of a torpedoed vessel is a war crime:[92] the use of the atom bomb has been justified by the doctrine of military necessity.

The defense of superior orders must inevitably be rejected: but the prosecution of a private for carrying out a specific order given by his superior reveals the dilemma in which the humble soldier is placed. If he disobeys the order, immediate punishment follows: if he obeys, he may be punished if his country is defeated. Thirdly, the trials were conducted not by international courts in the full sense of the term, but by victors' tribunals. It is difficult to see what other policy could have been followed in the circumstances, but until there is permanent international criminal court we cannot expect the defeated to have full confidence in the verdicts.[93] Fourthly, the real breach of order is the use of war itself. It is impossible to fight a modern war and observe the Christian principles of morality. We must be realistic and take account of the principle of military necessity, but that is a dangerous argument because it may be carried so far as to destroy all rules. All agree that the unnecessary infliction of death, suffering, and destruction of property should be forbidden, but that principle must be thoroughly worked out before it can create rigid rules.

Before international law can be effective, a reasonable alternative to war as a solution of international problems must be found. If international law is to be developed by the judicial method, we cannot criticize the courts for creating new rules. But the decisions in the war trials should be used as the foundation for further action and not left to stand as isolated instances. The rules of war must be codified and enforced by an impartial international tribunal. The United Nations realizes these problems. It is endeavoring to create an international community by such institutions as UNESCO, but progress is necessarily slow. Politically there is still a divorce between Russia and the western world and the iron curtain leads to misunderstandings, which hinder or prevent creative effort.

The interest of these problems for jurisprudence is that they emphasize that law is ineffective without a real sense of community: that there must be machinery capable of developing the law speedily to meet new conditions: that must be an authoritative tribunal which has the confidence of those subject to it and which has the command of force to back its decisions. It is too narrow to say that international law does not exist:[94] but in the present state of civilization it is tragically ineffective.

Definition Of Law In Terms Of The Judicial Process

In America today the definition of law in terms of the judicial process is very popular. Holmes J. has said: 'the prophecies of what the courts will do in fact, and nothing more pretensions, are what I mean by law.'[95] This definition has been seized upon by the realists and has coloured their whole approach to jurisprudence.[96] To Frank J. the law for any lay person with respect to a particular state of facts is a decision of a court, and 'until a court has passed on those facts, no law on that subject is yet in existence.[97] Prior to such a decision, the only law available is 'a guess as to what a court will decide'.[98] The realists push this approach to what they regard as its logical conclusion and law is treated as a collection of decisions and not as a body of rules.

Cardozo J. is on safer ground when he emphasizes that law is a basis for prediction rather than a mere guess: 'a principle or rule of conduct so established as to justify a prediction with reasonable certainty that it will be enforced by the courts if its authority is challenged is... a principle or rule of law.'[99] The practical advantage of such an approach is that it emphasizes the fact that law is a process, that it is not a series of particular commands, but rather a body of principles slowly by the decision of concrete cases. Cardozo's definition is slightly wider than the definition of law in terms of the State, since a court may exist even where there is no sovereign. Two points arise concerning this approach. Firstly, although useful as a description, it can hardly be accepted as a definition. Much law today never comes before the courts because recourse is prohibited, as can be seen in the rapidly growing body of Administrative Law. We are so accustomed to the development of law by the courts that we tend to forget that it may be developed and applied in other ways without ceasing to be law. It may be enforced according to the whim of a Minister who by statute is given the right to determine such question with absolute finality. Secondly, the definition is but a modified form of Austin's, for he defines law in terms of the organ which creates it.

Definition Of Law In Terms Of Its Purpose

Salmond retains the emphasis on the judicial process, but considers that a reference to the purpose of law is essential. 'The law may be defined as the body of principles recognized and applied by the State in the administration of justice.'[100] Justice is the end of law, and it is only fitting that an instrument should be defined by a delineation of the purpose which is its *raison d'etre*. This raises the question of the relationship of law and justice. One theory defines law in terms of justice, but from this it follows that an unjust law cannot exist, for if it could, then on the premises there would be a fatal self-contradiction. Many writers have fallen into this simple trap. Thus earlier theories of natural law put the emphasis on justice and defined the validity of a law if it was opposed to natural justice. But slavery, condemned by natural law, yet existed in the legal systems of the time, and, though the Romans recognized this difficulty, they never succeeded in solving it.[101] Law does not cease to be such merely because it is unjust—if it did, who is to supply the criterion of injustice? Even our modes of speech contains truth—the phrase unjust law has a meaning. Whereas the term squire circle has not.[102] Is it accurate then to define law by reference to a quality, which actual laws in force may lack? Is only that law which embodies what I like?

A second means of solving the problem of the relationship of law and justice is to place all the emphasis on law and regard justice as mere conformity to law.[103] But then we are depriving ourselves of a criterion which may not be wholly subjective by which we may test the operation of legal system. In this sense law cannot be unjust, since the term 'just' is defined only as that which is legal.

Each of these approaches is founded on false premises; we must distinguish clearly between justice and law, for each is a different conception. Law is that which is actually in force, whether it be evil or good. Justice may develop, as man's understanding develops, but justice is not limited by what happens in the actual word of fact. It is wrong, however, to regard law and justice as entirely unrelated. Justice acts within the law as well as providing an external test by which the law may be judged, e.g. justice emphasizes good faith, and this conception has greatly influenced the development of legal systems.

Formal Definitions Of Law

A Study of Actual system makes many despair of finding universal elements on which a definition of law can build. Kant attacked this problem by the application of his 'critical method'. It is not possible in a short section to expound one of the difficult systems of philosophy ever conceived. All that can be achieved is to point out the bearing of Kant's method on the problem of defining law. To Kant the world of sensible experience is full of diversity and can of itself produce no principles, which are universally valid. To define law we must distinguish between form and matter; the first being 'the complex of universally valid principles presupposed in any legal judgement and the latter the changing world of social experience which those principles construe legally'.[104] To define law we should not study actual legal systems, but rather to the world of pure thought and discover those elements without which it is logically impossible to conceive law at all.

The form of human society is external regulation, as social co-operation cannot be thought of in the absence of control—since law exists to co-ordinate, it can operate only by unifying all acts of men. This analysis does not depend on any particular theory of ethics or on postulates drawn from actual legal systems. When Stammler works out his theory he does not examine an actual society but postulates an ideal community in which everyone accepts as his own all those purposes of others, which can be objectively justified. These principles of just law are based on the doctrines of respect (one must not treat another arbitrarily) and of participation (all must be allowed to share in the legal community). This picture of society is regarded as a determining form, which will condition the rules in any particular group of men.

It is unfair to attempt to describe a great system of learning in a few lines. But despite all the skill and vigour of Stammler's work, it is hard to resist the conclusion of Geny[105] that his conclusions do not really depend on his premises—they are suggested by his particular prejudices and social views. Jurisprudence, in the hands of the formal theorist, is always faced with a dilemma: if it is true to the premises on which it is built, it remains in the pure heaven of logical concepts; if it attempts to descend to earth, then these concepts are explained according to the social picture of the writer. Thus Stammler has not really solved the relationship of just law and law. Does he mean that just law effectively dominates law in every society? If so, the conclusion is demonstrably false. The abstract formulae produced are very subtle, but after all they are merely affirmed without being proved. The unity of the ideal community is merely a formal one in which there is logically no contradiction between the ends of each legal subject.

But we do not find that the legal systems of the world follow any a priori logic. The striving for justice may be the mark of ideal law, but it is not always the characteristic of actual systems. Stammler correctly emphasizes that inherent in law is the notion of purpose-but this purpose is determined, not by the logical principles of the academic jurist, but by the actual struggles of flesh and blood. The purpose of law is hardly a conditioning form, which determines the rules of every community.

Del Vecchio follows the same Kantian method, but his writings are easier to follow.[106] He defines law as the objective co-operation of possible acts aiming men, according to an ethical principle, which determines them and prevents their interference.

Definition Of Law As Social Fact

Duguit makes a determined assault on many of the traditional theories of jurisprudence.[107] He emphatically rejects any a priori method and prefers to draw his theories from an investigation of the facts of life itself. He wishes to separate jurisprudence entirely from ethics and metaphysics. Instead of beginning with a concept of the individual man and considering his rights against society, he thinks of man as living in society, bound by his own necessities to share the common life. Hence the foundation of law is not the right of the individual but the essential requirement of community life. Law arises because men live together and can only live together. Law does not depend on the will of the sovereign. Duguit rejects the notion of the personality of the State and says that a realist examination shows merely that certain people govern and that others obey. But the governing class does not create law, for it arises directly out of the facts. Law does not lay down an absolute but only an hypothetical imperative: it does not say (as does ethics) that 'this end must be pursued because it is good in itself', but rather 'if such an end is not sought, this will cause a social reaction and lack of harmony.' The ruler is bound hand and foot by law, which he cannot change. You do not need to submit to the laws of rugby but, if you want to play, you must; if you break a rule, you may be sent off the field.[112] So it is with social life, with the important difference that, while a person may exist happily without playing rugby, no satisfying existence is possible for man save in the society of his fellows. Man must realize that, if he does not observe the canons of social life, he will suffer from the displeasure of his fellows. Society rests on the need for satisfying common interests (soliarite par simitude) and the need for division of work (solidarite par division du travail).

To Duguit the only difference between morality and law is the extent of public acceptance. Moral rules accepted by the whole community are rules of law; moral rules accepted only by the intellectual elite are potential rules of law. Thirdly, there is the legal norm, which has behind it an organized sanction. If, however, we limit rules of law to those, which are recognized by the government, we are basing law on the will of the State, and this Duguit does not desire to do. The State must be limited by law. Hence Duguit considers that a rule becomes law, even before it is recognized by the State, if it has behind it the effective support of the community. Legislation does not really create law, but only defines that which already exists. The prohibition of homicide was a rule of law before it was recognized by the State; it was also a legal rule that the State feed the starving even before this humanitarian duty was embodied in legislation. Conversely, a statute does not create law until it wins popular acceptance.

The foundation of law thus depends on the sentiment of solidarity. But Duguit also recognized a sentiment of justice, which arises merely out of the facts, and he describes it as recognition by man, acquired through a study of his own personality, of the necessity for fairness and equality in the imposition of the rules on others. Solidarity, therefore, leads us to realize that a certain rule is essential to the life of the community, justice that the rule should be enforced. Only a little change of wording is necessary to transform this into the natural law theory that the basis of law is in the reason and the moral nature of man. Duguit refuses to admit this, for the sentiments of solidarity and justice are not universal ideals but mere facts of which the jurist takes note as he studies life. Law, therefore, does not depend on the will of the sovereign or the will of man, but on social realities. If we postulate a general will as the foundation of law, Duguit thinks it is too easy to make a transition to the will of the sovereign, and he desires a law, which will bind the ruler as well as the ruled.

But how is the sentiment of a community to bed discovered? Duguit grandiloquently declares that if law is only the will of the majority, it is not worth the effort of study[108] —but as, save on simple issues, unanimity is unlikely, what other method is possible if we are to avoid despotism, benevolent or otherwise? Ultimately Duguit must fall back on some system of majority rule—morals are translated into law when they are effectively accepted by the bulk of a community.

The main criticism of Duguit is that, in founding law simply on the facts, he fails to understand the true nature of ethical forces. Dr. Allen, after recognizing that Duguit has done good service to jurisprudence by emphasizing that law is essentially the product of social facts, adds: 'But he goes far beyond any sociological theory of law which has yet been advanced when he attempts to evaporate all ethical content out of law. To banish the notion of right wholly from law, as M.Duguit seeks to do, is to make it meaningless, and to violate an instinct, which is deep-seated in human nature.'[109]

In truth, as Duguit matured, he gave increasing emphasis to the sentiment of justice, and some of his own followers expressed regret that in the end he became entangled with that metaphysic which he had sworn to eschew. Although he denies that there are absolute ideals of justice, he really postulates as the basis of his theory the greatest possible cooperation of men for the highest possible ends. So interpreted, his doctrine is an unconscious natural law theory that law is based on the reasonable needs of the community life. But this phrasing uses terms, which Duguit would have scorned.

Law In The Scienticfic Era

Justice Markanday Katju, Senior Judge[108A], Allahabad High Court, wrote about law as follows:-

There are two broad conceptions of the law viz. the passive and the active. While according to the passive conception, law is a reflection of the existing social relations, according to the active conception law is an instrument of change (Friedman: Legal Theory).

The passive conception is often attributed to Savigny, the great German jurist who flourished in the early 18th century, Austin, the father of the founders of modern sociological jurisprudence, can also be said to belong to the passive school.

According to Savigny's historical school of jurisprudence, law is not consciously created phenomenon but is the gradual distillation of volksgeist (the spirit of the people). Thus, Savigny was a strong advocate of customary law and was opposed to legislation.

No doubt, the historical school made a important contribution to our understanding by suggesting that the law is not merely a set of artificial rules imposed on society but it is an outcome of the social system as it has evolved in the history. However, the historical school was essentially reactionary in character in as much as it made a fetish out of custom. As Justice Holmes said "It is resolving to have no better reason for a rule than it was so laid in the time of Henry IV." Moreover, the historical school is entirely unsuited to the scientific era. In an age of rapid technical growth people are not prepared to wait for the slow growth of custom. Legislation is in fact the dominant source of law today.

In the early twentieth century Ehrlich propounded his concept of the 'living law'. According to Ehrlich, most of the law consists not of the formal rules which are administered in law courts but the actual social norms and relationships prevalent in society. Ehrlich was against codification, and in that sense he can be regarded as follower of Savigny's school, though with many qualifications.

It would be a mistake, however, to equate the passive conception with customary law. Even positive law can be passive if it seeks not to bring about social change but to preserve the established order. Thus, the positivism of Austin aimed at reinforcing the existing social system in England rather than bringing about any change.

The active conception of law can be said to originate in modern times from the thinkers of the Enlightenment (Helvetius, Holbsch, Diderot, etc.) who regarded law as an instrument for the radical reconstruction of society. Bentham's conception of law as an instrument of bringing about "the greatest good for the greatest number" can also be classified as an activist theory, though it can hardly be called radical.

In the late 19th century Jhering, the founder of the activist school of sociological jurisprudence, conceived of law as a means of harmonizing conflicting social interests, a theory which was developed in America in the twentieth century by Roscoe Pound (see Pound jurisprudence). Pound, however, did \not contemplate a radical change in the existing social system in America.

The Marxist conception of law as an expression of will of the ruling class combines both the passive and the active elements. For while in an oppressive State the law is used to create a socialist society.

The point of view put forward in this article is that in the scientific era only the active conception of law is acceptable.

The growth of scientific knowledge has transformed man from a creature who could not understand natural and social forces, and was therefore helpless before them, to a being who has discovered many of the laws of nature and society, and can utilize this scientific view to satisfy his wants. This trend is reflected in legal history, and we may consider this in some detail.

In its inception all law consisted of unwritten customs. For thousands of years man has governed by custom, and hence had little control over his destiny.

With the invention of writing, an element of conscious legislation crept in for although the codes of Manu, Hammurabi, The Twelve Tables etc. consisted mostly of existing customs reduce to writing, there can be no doubt that each writer, however subconsciously, introduced into the text his own conception of rights and wrong, and thus slightly altered the existing customary law by his own notions of what it ought to be. Thus for example, Nanda Pandit altered Shaunak's rule of adoption in Hindu Law, and the glossators of Bolagna altered the Justinian Code.

The shift from, custom to legislation is the basic trend in world legal history that is, the shift from spontaneously created law to man-made law. With the coming of legislation man has been shaping his own destiny.

Originally legislation was mostly non-statutory, that is, in the forms of writings of eminent jurists or theologists. In the last few centuries, however, legislation has become mostly statutory, Non-statutory legislation was subordinate to custom, while statutory legislation overrides custom.

While custom merely reflects established social relationships, legislation may either seek to formalize them or to alter them. In either case legislation is a conscious human activity.

In the scientific age man utilizes hi-scientific knowledge to plan and enact laws, which will create new social relationships. Law, in this era, will gradually start proceeding, rather than following, the new social relationship. Law will be thus used to shape society according to a rational plan.

A scientific society requires precision and clarity, and hence positive, man-made law. In a modern factory, for instance, there must be a clear-cut chain of command, demarcation of duties, terms and conditions of service, etc. Vagueness in these matters will effect the smooth running of the plant.

Thus a scientific society needs more and more positive law. However, as has already been said above, positivism is a double-edged weapon; it can be used for either buttressing the existing social order or for altering it, depending on whether the legislator is conservative or progressive. Since science implies constant change it is only progressive positive law, which can be really scientific. By the expression 'progressive positive law' is meant the law, which utilizes the scientific discoveries of the laws of nature and the laws of social development for the forward movement of man in history. Progressive positive law seeks to alter social relations where they are outdated or irrational. It seeks to create a social order in which science advances; production increases, and waste and friction are eliminated.

A scientific society can only be a planned society where decisions at every level are taken on a rational, scientific basis. Anarchy in production can obviously not be scientific.

Also, there can be no room for exploitation in a scientific society, for exploitation results in strikes, agitations, etc. which hamper production. The legal structure in a scientific society will therefore ensure that there is no exploitation. Since in a scientific society there will be no suppression of one section of people by another, the coercive element in the laws of such a society will become gradually less and less. The punitive element in the law will be replaced by the reformative, and a violator of the law will be treated not as a criminal but as a patient.

The capacity to guide its own development is a unique feature of scientific society. The legislator by utilizing his scientific knowledge will function like a scientist, free of prejudices, subjectivism and vested interest. In fact in view of high degree of specialization in modern science, it can only be a specialist who can be legislator. Since there are several fields of specialization there will have to be a large number of legislators each of whom will deal with his own field, and there will also have to be co-coordinators who are specialized not only in their own field but also in co-ordination, and planning for the future. This will require a knowledge of the laws of social development.

The law of a scientific society will have a high democratic and moral content. The higher the forces of production develop and correspondingly the higher men's intellectual and cultural level, the greater is felt the need for independence and creative initiative. As Jawitsch states: "Man's social essence manifests itself particularly in his striving to effective creative activity, which is inconceivable without freedom of personal choice of variants of conduct within the limit of the social interest and objective possibilities." (Jawitsch: The General Theory of Law) When man is free of basic economic wants, which is possible only in a scientific society, then alone can he really be free, free to create and free to develop his personality.

Nowadays we read almost daily of some new scientific discovery, some new start on the edge of the known universe. Some new sub-atomic particle or some new techniques in medicine. The pace of scientific advance is accelerating constantly. Correspondingly, totally new law will be required which will serve the needs of a scientific society and help man in his endless progress towards revealing nature's mysteries and satisfying his own wants. Such a law can of course only be created on the basis of a new economic and political order, which will ensure technical advancement along with justice.

Law, Social Justice And Social Changes

Let us consider the relation of law with social justice & social changes

1. Sociological approach of law

Law is but a part of human society. Its purpose is to further and protect the interest of society. The problem of society is to reconcile selfish with unselfish social purposes and to suppress the former when they clash with the latter. Law is the sum of the conditions of social life in the widest sense of the term, as secured by the power of the state through the means of external compulsion.

According to Bentham, laws should endeavor to promote the happiness of the greatest number. In order to achieve this object, there has to be a balancing of individual interests with social welfare. As per Bentham's view such law should be made which would make anti-social behavior unprofitable.

According to Roscoe Pound, sociological approach should ensue that the making. Interpretation and application of law take account of social facts. To achieve this target, there should be.

(a) Factual study of the social effects of legal administration.

(b) Social investigations as preliminaries to legislation;

(c) A constant study of the means for making laws more effective.

Pound regards law as means of social engineering. According to him, the aim of social engineering is to build as efficient a structure of society as possible which requires the satisfaction of the maximum of wants with the minimum of friction and waste. It involves the balancing of interests. He describes interests as a "demand or desire or expectation which human beings, either individually or in groups or associations or relations, seek to satisfy, of which therefore, the adjustment of human relations and ordering of human behavior through the force of a politically organized society must take account."

Classification of interests is under:

Ihering – Law as means to an End

(1) Individual interests which include

(a) Freedom of will (b) privacy (c) honour and reputation (d) marriage (e) belief and opinion (f0 property (g) trade (h) employment

2. Social interest, which includes:-

(a) General safety (b) general health (c) peace and order (d) freedom to form political economic or religious institutions (e) conservation of human resources.

(2) Law and Poverty

Poverty is lack of opportunity. It is a state of helplessness to cope with hostile forces and exploitative institutions. It is a condition where poor people feel that equality and legal rights are enjoyed by the privileged class only. The class of poor people includes landless labourers, village artisans, disabled persons, pensioners, unemployed and underemployed labourers, small land-holders. These groups have large families with poor education. Women are prone to exploitation when divorced, widowed or deserted. The poverty forces children to labour and it implies denial of opportunity of education and other processes of development. Constitutional provisions like reservation for weaker section and protective discrimination in favour of the under-privileged groups have been introduced. But several historical, cultural, economic and sociological constraints limited the scope of access to legal services Illiteracy, destitution, economic and social bondages, cultural inhibitions and bureaucratic and political corruption seriously impaired the accessibility and assertiveness of the poorest of the poor resulting often in total denial of justice to them.[110] The heavy cost of litigation and the inordinate delay were a great barrier to the access of legal system.

Another reason for the non-use of the legal system by the poor section is the structure of the justice system itself.

Weapon of Legal aid how far effective?

Legal aid in our country is based upon the principle of equal justice for the poor. Formal equality was provided through statutory provisions. But poverty remained unaffected by legal development. The use of law for reducing economic and social inequalities and promoting social justice provided a new rationale for legal aid. But it would not be wise to assume that legal aid can eliminate property. Because the focus of legal aid is on distributive justice, effective implementation of welfare laws and elimination of discrimination. Economic inequality cannot be the subject of legal control. In the words of Mr. Madhav Menon[111] "It can increase opportunities for economic development; it can help implement Govt. welfare schemes more effectively; it can mitigate structural imbalances in the legal system functioning against the poor, it can be an essential input in development planning and social justice administration. However, legal aid cannot be a panacea for economic ills."

(3) Law and social justice

The concept of social justice is a natural progression from the theories of Laissez-faire to Marxism and Humanism. The individual justice between two parties given by the court is a narrow concept. Our Preamble talk about justice in society. Social Justice is a border concept. This border concept has been analysed in two basic elements of liberty and equality thus:

First a person is to have an equal right to most extensive basic liberty compatible with a similar liberty for others. Second, judicial and economic inequalities are to be arranged so that they are both (a) reasonably accepted to everyone's advantage, (b) attached to position and offices open to all. [112]"

This so called competition between liberty and equality is settled by the concept of social justice. Liberty is mentioned first and equality is next. It means that actual political, economic and social conditions must be such that the opportunity to exercise liberty is equal. The Constitution mentions justice first and liberty of vested interests like liberty of ownership, possession, title, trade etc. We assume liberty of thought, expression, belief and faith. When we talk of equality, we mean equality of status and opportunity.

Social justice implies equality of opportunity to those who have been denied their dues. Equality of opportunity is a consequence of the equality of status.

Equality envisages the urge to uplift the oppressed and to inspire the frustrated. It consists in bringing those on par whose levels of life have been low. When there is an equality of opportunity, everyone has a fair chance to show his merit. The state should produce an equal environment for all. Article 14 of the Constitution incorporates the doctrine of equality before law and equal protection of law. This doctrine means the denial of any special privilege in favour of any individual by reason of birth, sex, race or the like. By social justice we mean social equality. To bring social equality requires great changes in our social environment and our social institutions. "If the sentiment of social equality is carefully and wisely cultivated, it is sure to make a considerable addition to the realization of social justice.[113]"

We lack the environment of social justice. We have poverty and unemployment, failure to provide drinking water and primary education, disparity in incomes and concentration of wealth among few hands. For this failure judicial system cannot be held liable. For this failure, our political culture, corruption, planning, economy or our habits or all these factors, combined together, our responsible. Our attitudes and habits continue to be feudal, cast and status oriented and exploitative in nature. "This vice of social inequality assumes a particularly reprehensible form in relation to the backward classes and communities which are treated as untouchable; and so the problem of social justice is as urgent and important in India as is the problem of economic justice. Social justice includes both economic justice and social justice. The concept of social justice thus pays within its sweep the objective of removing all inequalities and affording equal opportunities to all citizens in social affairs as well as economic activities.[114]"

4. Social change and social legislation

Social change envisages the change in the existing pattern of social life. As the social conditions do not remain static, social change is a necessity. It also contemplates changes in attitudes or beliefs. It prepares a ground to live a better life. Gainsberg defines it, "as by social change I understand a change in social structure, e.g. the size of a society, the composition or balance of its parts or the type of its organization." Jenson called social change as modification in ways of doing and thinking of people.

The changes in social outlook and habits and resultant social action are conditions precedent to effective social change. One of the means to achieve social change is the State action in the form of social legislation. Social legislation is necessary for social reform. Economic factors also play an important role and largely generate the social change. Social changes interfere with established religious and social beliefs.

Legal measures are not effective. For example, birth control, divorce and monogamy have not found unqualified support.

When social justice is denied to certain sections of the people, laws are enacted to bring balance. These laws are called "social legislation." Social legislation tries to remove inequalities and to benefit the whole community. According to Hogan and Inni "social legislation embraces action by government authority to eliminate elements which are objectionable and provide elements for which the system does not make any provision.[115]"

According to Hogan and Inni, the primary functions of all social legislations are two:-

1. To provide for the orderly regulation of social relationship, and
2. To provide for the welfare and security of all individuals in the social unit.

According to M.C. Chagla "the mere abolition of inequality and privilege is the negative aspect of a welfare state. Its positive aspect is to provide social security to every citizen.[116]" It is gratifying to note that the Supreme Court has acted as instrument of social justice and social change. It has given adequate support to the causes of weaker sections of the society. It has utilized the Directive Principles to uphold the social welfare legislation, like prohibition, wages, and reservation. The Court has effectively intervened to forestall victimization and unfair labour practices.

Conclusion:

There is always a gap between social justice and law – the former is ahead of the latter.

Happiness of the people depends upon the promptitude with which this gap is narrowed down. This can be achieved by the Legislature by making law to confirm to social justice. For example, Minimum Wages Act, Workmen's Compensation Act, Maternity Benefit Act, Employees' State Insurance Act, Employer's Liability Act. This result can also be achieved by the judiciary by restating and updating the principles of law, as it finds them. The development of public interest litigation is one of the greatest services by the judiciary for cause of poor people. It is undertaking for the purpose of redressing any social injustice, enforcing any public duty, and protecting social interests.

Judge case, AIR 1982 SC 149 at p. 192. Asiad Case, AIR 1982 SC 1473 and Bandhu Morch's Case, AIR 1984 C 802 are three important cases.

"In India, millions of people due to their poverty conditions, illiteracy, social and economic backwardness are denied justice. Public interest litigation (one may call it judicial activism) promises them relief without cumbersome formally and heavy expenditure. With the result, new perspectives are opening before the judges, lawyers and the State Law Agencies in the task of national reconstruction and developmental activities. In pursuance of Directive Principles of State Policy law is creating new social and economic rights including freedom from indigence and discrimination as well as the right to healthy environment, right to social security and right to protection from financial, commercial, corporate or governmental oppression."[117]

Levy-Ullmann aptly says that a definition of law should have two aims: firstly, to make precise the meaning of law, and secondly, to call up in the mind of the reader a true picture of law and its operation.[118]

The existence of law presupposes a community. Implicit in the notion of community is the acceptance of a set of values dealing with the fundamental issues on which the existence of that society depends.[119] In the absence of such agreement, men cannot act together effectively. When it reaches a certain stage of development the community sets up a legal order, which determines the methods by which law is to be created, declared, and enforced. This machinery is naturally used by the most strongly organized section in order to effect their ends. Law is never ideal justice, but human justice defined by those who control the machine. What ends law has served is a question for legal history: what ends it should serve is a question for legal philosophy.

But in order to be really effective, law demands not only an active machinery for securing compliance with its rules, but also a method by which the changing conceptions of justice and the transfer of power from one class to another may be mirrored in the law itself. The sanction is a normal accompaniment of mature law, but it is impossible to lay down a priori that no rule of law can exist without a sanction. Certain constitutional convention are normally regarded as an important part of the legal order although no precise sanction can be found. The sanction, which exists, is merely a realization that the convention lies at the foundation of the order itself.

Moreover, while the sanction may be important in order to explain why a particular rule is observed, it rarely explains the acceptance of the legal order itself. Terrorism, or the domination of a small community by a ruthless neighbor, may succeed for a time, but normally the sanction is effective only if it is necessary to use it in a limited number of cases.

There are thus two sides to law: from one side it is an abstract body of rules; from the other it is a social process for compromising the conflicting interests of men.

Law may shortly be described in terms of a legal order tacitly or formally accepted by a community. It consists of the body of rules which are seen to operate as binding rules in that community, backed by some mechanism accepted by the community by means of which sufficient compliance with the rules may be secured to enable the system or set of rules to continue to be seen binding in nature. A mature system of law normally sets up that type of legal order known as the State, but we cannot say a priori that without the State no law can exist.

Broadest possible basis: -

Law is a social institution. A Society may be described as an association of people with a measure of permanence. A 'civic society' is said to comprise (1) tessitory, (2) perpetuity, (3) a measure of independence, and (4) a culture as manifested in its art, philosophy, law, morality, religion, fashion and opinion*. The last five, namely, law, morality, religion, fashion and opinion, are modes of social control in that they prescribe in various ways how people ought to behave. Law is distinguishable from the others with reference to the criteria of validity already mentioned, but the relationship between them is a matter for jurisprudential study.

More important is the inextricable inter-relation between law and philosophy, sociology, ethics and politics. The training of lawyers has hitherto failed to take sufficient account of the essential unity of law and these other disciplines. They are not just related to each other, but inter-woven; their pattern is not that of circles, which touch at their circumferences, but of circles, which overlap. Only on such an integrated basis is it possible for lawyers to approach their subject meaningfully and improve its serviceability. Indeed, Jurisprudence might well be described as the lifemanship of the law. No one can be a good lawyer who only knows law.

As Buckland well said, 'A man will be a better lawyer, as he will be a better architect or physician, if his mind is open to the movements of thought on the profound issues of life, beyond his immediate professional concerns. And, if his mind is so open he can hardly fail to have some sort of philosophy of his own.[120]

Of the philosophical aspects, which are more or less useful lawyers, that which is outstandingly relevant is logic and various kinds of reasoning. There are also questions of semantics, method and definition, which have been dealt with. Part III of this book will deal with some philosophies of law, which will reveal the manner in which people in different countries at different times have speculated about some of the problems examined in the preceding parts. It is not enough to enhance merely the technical efficiency of a lawyer, important though this is; he should also be invited to broaden his outlook by treading along paths from which he will be able to perceive new horizons and be invigorated by scholarship in other spheres. Speculations about law by past and present thinkers are part of intellectual culture. Even where theories are open to criticism they possess value and latter theories can be better understood in the light of them. This book can do no more than try to indicate directions long, which such inquiries can be pursued, and where the wisdom of great thinkers is to be found. It might be convenient to refer to a particulate alongside the discussion of the problem moose nearly concocted with ire in parts I and II; but whether one does of therefore, jurisprudential study ranges from minute analytical dissections and sharp distinctions at one end of the intellectual scale to the broad sweep of ideas and philosophies through the ages at the other.

Sociology is a theoretical study of social existence based on descriptions of social facts.[121] From the point of view of the sociologist the administration of law is an observable social fact, while from the point of view of the lawyer it is obvious that laws can only function in a social environment, that they are bound to be influenced by the prevailing climate of opinion and tendencies and that, to a lesser extent, the continued enforcement of laws does in its turn affect people's outlook. More specifically, three aspects of sociology can be singled out as being peculiarly relevant to a lawyer's understanding of law, namely history, anthropology and economics. Historical development frequently accounts for and explains present-day doctrines; anthropology increasingly provides valuable insights into institutions of the modern state; while the influence of the economics order on the structure of both laws and society has been amply demonstrated. With regard to ethics, this, again speaking broadly, is a theoretical study of what is implied by prescriptions of what ought to be or ought not to be.[122] Insofar as the 'ought' of laws imply aims to be achieved, the element of ethical evaluation inherent in the content of laws becomes clear.

"In the last, law may be defined as those 'set' of principles which are meant to conduct world by affirm for governing human conduct in temporal life only and not otherwise."

Notes

1. Essays on Hindu Jurisprudence.
2. Manu Smriti
3. Indian Philosophy
4. Outline of Indian Philosophy
5. Jurisprudence
6. Ancient Law

6A. A book of jurisprudence & law

7. Polloell – History of English Law
8. Goodheart
9. Jurisprudence
10. In the Principle of Ethics
11. Concept of Law
12. 'Addressed to the community at large', Austin
13. Morality of Law
14. 5, Corbin, Contra do to 39
15. The utility of Jurisprudence in the solution of legal problem, article published – in 5 lectures of legal topics – published by the Association of Bar – New York

16. A text book of Jurisprudence
17. The Material Culture and Social Institutions of the simpler peoples
18. Thus in the case of the lower hunters, 40 percent of the tribes have pure self-help and none of them have public justice as a regular system. In the third agricultural grade, 11 percent have pure self-help and 41 percent a regular system of public justice.
19. The most valuable characteristics of the work of Hob house, Wheeler and Ginsberg are the unscientific detachment and the caution in drawing conclusions from data that are often shown to be exceedingly difficult to classify.
20. Crime and custom in Savage Society (1932)
21. K.N. Llewellyn and E.A. Hoebel
22. B. Malinowski, crime and custom
23. Infra
24. H.I.P. Hogbin, Law and Order in Plynesia
25. This is clearly brought out by K.N. Llewellyn and E.A. Hoebel
26. For an account of blood feud in 1914, see T.G.H. Strejlow Aranda Traditions, 62; for self-help among the Cheyenners, see K.N. Liewellyn and E.A. Hoebel,
27. H.F. Jolowicz, Historical Introduction to the study of Roman law,
28. Similarly in Assyrain Law, see G.R. Driver and J.C. Miles,
29. G.R. Driver and J.C. Miles, op.cit.360. But, as is pointed out the learned authors, the text says 'they shall beat', &c., without specifying what 'they' means. The phrase apparently means that the stripes shall be inflicted by a person who has a right to do it sometimes an officer of the king, sometimes the witness, sometimes an accuser (366). The Hebrews never seem to have had a public executioner (367).
30. D. Daube, Biblical Law
31. G.R. Driver and J.C. Miles
32. A.S. Diamond, Primitive Law (2nd ed., 1950)
33. For example see G.R. Driver and J.C. Miles, op.cit.346-7. Even when the state inflicts punishment, it may make the punishment fit the crime, e.g. a man loses his lips for kissing a married woman, the wife of a man who has seduced a virgin is delivered to the seduced girl's father for prostitution. Closely related are the 'mirroring' punishment: punishment of arson

by burning, coining by boiling, removal of a boundary stone by pouching off the offender's head. Cf. H.F. Jolowicz, and the parent of the doctrine that the punishment must fit the crime': G.R. Driver and J.C. Miles, loc, cit.

34. Cf. H.F. Jowicz, Historical Introduction to the study of Roman Law, 162-3

35. For sheer barbarity, see the dictum in Dive V.Maningham (1551), I Plowden 60 at 68: ' For one be in execution, he ought to live of his own, and neither the plaintiff nor the sheriff is bound to give him meat or drink..... and if has no goods, he shall live of the charity of others, and if will give him nothing, let him die in the name of God, if he will, and impute the cause of it to his own fault, for his presumption and ill-behaviour brought him to that imprisonment.'

36. H.F. Jolowicz

37. F Pollock and F.W. Maitland, History of English Law, ii.27, speaking of the forma doni points out that it is a mistake to suppose that 'our common law starts with rigid, narrow rules about this matter. . . and rejects everything that deviates by a hair's breadth from the established models. On the contrary, in the thirteenth century it is elastic and liberal, loose and vague.' The common law of this period can hardly be regarded as primitive law, but it shows that fluidity may exist even in the early middle period.

38. Fundamental Principles of the Sociology of Law

39. A.S. Diamond

40. bid.

41. Chinese Law, for example, is much less formal than Western system. It is not sharply distinguished from ethics, but is regarded as the practical fulfillment of it. Dura Lex, sed lex seems a strange maxim to the eastern mind: J.Escarra, Archives dephil. Du droit (19935, 1-2), 70. Lord Cooper emphasizes that Scots law is less formal than English: 28 J. Comp. Leg. (1946), pt.iii.3-4.

42. This is the arrangement adopted by A.S. Diamond, op.cit.

43. Early Law and Custom

44. A.S. Diamond

45. G.R. Driver and J.C. Miles

46. A.S. Diamond.

47. His theory is that there was at first a clear-cut division between the Jurisdiction of the priest and the ruler, but as the powers and wealth of the priesthood increased not only did they seize secular powers, but they also made priestly additions to what had been a secular code: Primitive Law, ch.xi.
48. Numbers xxxv. 3.
49. The Assyrian Laws, 346-7, one possible trace of the doctrine that crime is a pollution is seen in relation to abortion.
50. D.Daube, Biblical Law
51. H.J.SSS.Maine's theory was that the formalism of the Roman lawyer could be understood only if it is realized that the jurisconsult sprang from the pontiff or priest: Early Law and Custom
52. Historical Jurisprudence, ii.
53. H.J.S. Maine, Ancient Law (ed.F.Pollock).
54. A.S. Diamond.
55. An interesting example of a recently 'fiction' in the form of an imputed license-and of its demise in Australia is to be seen in Commissioner for railways (N.S.W.) V. Cardy (1960)
56. Selsdon v. Selsdon, 50 T.L.R.469
57. J. Dabin, Technique de l'elaboration du droit positif.
58. Lon.L.Fuller, Rec.Geny. ii.157.
59. Pierre de Tourtoulon, Philosophy in the Development of Law (trans.Read).
60. Historically the institution of marriage, however, probably proceed the development of the law of sale.
61. At bottom all law is reduced to a series of fictions happed one upon another in successive layers': Pierre de Tourtoulon
62. Per Lord Wright, Lissendel v.Bosch Ltd., (1940) A.C.412 at 435. The legal maxim that husband & wife are one person in law is very misleading, unless the necessary qualifications are made: Glanville Williams, 10 Mod.L.R.(1947)16
63. In R.V.Walcott (1696). Shower 127, an attainder for treason was reversed because the words ipso vivente were omitted from the sentence. In 1908 in the U.S. a conviction for rape was annulled, because the word the was omitted from the indictment: state v.Camphell (1908), 210 Mo.202, noted 60 Harv. L.R. (1947) 406, and see Internal Revenue Commissioners v.Hinchy, (1960) A.C.748.

64. Cr. In the Matter of Davy, (1935) P.I., where the court refused to apply a technically when it would have defeated the plain intention of statute, and Rayboulds Pty. Ltd. V.Dodgshum, (1953) V.L.R.84.
65. W.S.Holdsworth, History of English Law,
66. Ibid.
67. But only some what:W.W.Buckland, equity in Roman Law.
68. Ancient Law (ed.F.Plollock),
69. H.F. Jolowicz, Historical Introduction to the study of Roman Law, ch.xxix.
70. H.L.A. Hart, Concept of Law.
71. C.Morris, How Lawyers Think.
72. J.W. Salmond.
73. Op.cit.p.
74. Legal Essays in Tribute to Mac Murray.
75. Most recently see H. Kantorowicz, The Definition of Law (1958) and H.L.A.Hart, Concept of Law (1961). Professor Hart's examination is probably the most penetrating presently available.
76. Infra, #.
77. Jurisprudence
78. Although the unorganized pressure of public opinion may provide a fairly effective sanction.
79. A law determines acts of a class, a particular command determines merely a specific act: Austin.
80. Infra
81. Austin
82. Infra
83. C.A.W. Manning, Modern Theories of Law, 224, points out that in the end Austin agreed that international law was law properly so-called, although he still denied that it was positive law.
84. H. Lauterpacht, Function of the Law in the International community.
85. The theory of the just war is accepted by H. Kelsen, but even he recognizes the difficulties: General Theory of Law and state, 334 See also A. nussbaum, 42 Mich.L.R. (1943), 453.
86. e.g. E.H. Bockhoff cited W. Friedmann, 2 Mod.L.R.(1938),194 at 199

87. R. Schlesinger, Soviet Legal Theory, 285.

88. The most authoritate account is the history of the United Nation War Crimes Commission and the Development of the Laws of War (H.M.S.O.).

89. Lord Wright, 62 L.Q.R.(1946),40.

90. 3 Res Judicatae (1947), 122.

91. 'The Peleus Trial,' Laws Reports.

92. F.B. Schick, 11 Mod.L.R. (1948), 290

93. The argument may easily become one of words, for whether International Law is such depends on our definition of law: Glanville Williams, 22 Brit.Y.B.I.L.(1945)146. While it may be futile to engage in terminological debates, it is essential to grasp the defects of the present system of international law. A brilliant treatment is that by the same writer.

94. Supra.

95. Law and the Modern Mind, 46. On this theory the U.S. Supreme Court has been called 'the court of ultimate conjecture'.

96. Growth of Law, 52:E.W.Patterson.

97. Jurisprudence

98. Infra, #29. E. Bodenheimer, Jurisprudence, 19, regards law in its purest form as that which reduces to a minimum the possibility of abuse of power by private individuals as well as by the government. The logical result of this is that law hardly exists at all in a totalitarian state. Is not this a case of defining law as ' that which achieves what I want'? Just because law is used for a purpose of which I do not approve it does not cease to be law. Cf. G.M. Bergman, 57 Yale L.J.(1947), 55 at 71, who defines law in terms of the will of the majority. The thesis is that justice is what the community accepts and, as law is based on the majority will, law be founded on justice.

99. A. Desqueyrat, L'Institution, le droit objectif et la technique positive, 199. Is an unjust law the negation of law? Droit, Morate, 48. N.S. Timasheff, An Introduction to the Sociology of Law, 270, Defines law as overapping part of ethics and power.

100. Jethro Brown, 32 L.Q.R.(1916), 180-1, suggests that justice as a concept of Jurisprudence is mere conformity to law.

101. F. Hallis, Corporate Personally, 31, for a concise account of Kantain legal philosophy see W. Fiedmann, Legal Theory (4th ed.), 106-11.

102. Science et technique en droit prive positif, vol.ii,ch.vi.stammler was apparently turn between his desire as a philosopher to establish a universal science of law and his desire as a teacher of civil law to help in the solution of actual cases. The result is an "Idea of Justice" which is a hybrid between a formal proposition and a definite social ideal, kept abstract and rather vague by the desire to remain formal': W.Friedmann, Legal Theory

103. See the Translation by J. Lislē, The formal Bases of Law. Archives de philosophie du droit (1932, 1-2) is devoted to a study of L. duguit's work: H.J. Laski, Modern Theories of Law, 52; C.K.Allen, Law in the Making

104. M. Reglade, Archives de phil. Dụ droit (1932, 1-2)

105. L.Le Fur, Archives de droit (1932, 1-2),

106. Law I the Making

107. Le Definition du droit, 132 et seq. But this may be asking too much. Perhaps the most that can be asked is that the elucidation of the meaning will provide the tests which will enable a 'true picture' to be drawn.

108. Compare A.L. Goodhart, Trans. Of Grotius society (1936)

108A. Law in scientific era

109. H.L.A. Hart, Concept of Law,

110. Legal & Justice for the poor Dr. Madhav Menon

111. Legal aid and justice for the poor.

112. John Rawis – theory of justice

113. Lord Scarman, English Law – The New Dimension

114. P.B. Gajendragadkar, Law, Liberty and Social Justice.

115. American Social Legislation.

116. Individual and the State.

117. Public Interest Litigation, Dr. Sonia Hurra

118. Johnson Sociology

119. Buckland some Reflections on Jurisprudence

120. Lord Redcliffe, The Law and its Compass

121. Generally sport Sociology; Johnson Sociology. A Systematic Introduction, Part i. Emmet

122. Emmet

CHAPTER 4

The Purpose & Classification of Law

German philosopher Karl Jasper once said that law has two sources

1. Political Will
2. Idea of Justice

Let us consider purposes of law from ancient times. Many theories of natural law attempt to define law in terms of purpose, and hence it is convenient to consider together many of the contributions of philosophy of natural law for the purpose of law. First to take up Greece.

Greece

The story of natural law begins with the philosophers of ancient Greece and its true meaning is still a matter of controversy today. The most diverse elements are gathered under the same label-Greek philosophy and medieval rationalism, Roman law and Christian theology, actual custom and moral intuition. There is much confusion and crudity of thought, but the theory is concerned with two problems, which are as vital now as when they were first formulated what is permanent underlying basis of law? What is its relationship to justice? To take only one example, 'no other philosophy moulded and shaped American thinking and American institution to such an extent as did the philosophy of natural law in the form given to it in the seventeenth and eighteenth centuries.'[1] The chief value of the older books on natural law for us in the present day does not lie so much in the systems they expound, as in the kind of legal thinking they exemplify'.[2]

The Greek traditionally regarded law as being closely both to justice and ethics.[3] Yet in the face of the diversity of the actual system of the world, wherein was a permanent element to be bound? The Imaginative notions of Plato are still freely drawn on by modern thinkers,[4] and his Republic is a constructive attempt to discover the basis of justice. Aristotle formulated more carefully the theory of justice. He regarded justice as meaning either what is lawful, or what is fair and equal. Justice, he divided into distributive and remedial justice. The first deals with the distribution of honour and wealth among the citizens and works according to the ratio of merit of particular society in question.[5]

A democracy will take different views from an oligarchy. In remedial justice the law looks to the nature of the injury, and attempts to restore the equality that existed before the wrong. Just action is a mean between acting in justly and being unjustly treated. This definition, however, applies only to the position of the citizen—not that of the judge, for in making a decision, he is not in danger of being unjustly treated.

Aristotle also made a useful distinction between natural justice, which is universal, and conventional justice, which binds only because it was decreed by a particular authority.

Stoics described the maxim, 'Live according to nature'. A thing was in accord with nature when it was governed by its own leading principle, and in the case of man this was reason. The universe itself governed by a reason similar to that which dwelt in man, and hence he who based his life on a rule of reason could face the world with confidence; for whether he understood or not the turn of fortune's wheel, a universe based on reason could not be hostile to him.

Rome

The Roman classical writers used the Stoic theory as an ornament for their texts, without really weaving its implications into their theory of the law.

Gaius writes that every system of positive law can be divided into two parts: some rules are changeable because they depend on men's wills, others are universally accepted and immutable since they depend on reason.[6] Thus *ius naturale* was the fundamental basis of legal system, for, however much conventional law may change, and rules based on nature are beyond the power of man. What was universally adopted by men was presumptively reasonable, and hence it was considered that the rules of *ius gentium* were in accord with natural law, or at least could be so treated until the contrary was proved. Thus, in Roman thought, there was a certain approximation between *ius naturale* (a philosophic theory of the fundamental element in all law) and *ius gentium* which had a twofold use: firstly, the actual common practice of mankind, and secondly, the particular rules which the *praetor peregrinus* had evolved for the use of foreigners.

Sometimes the jurists tried to draw rules from human nature itself.[7] If natural law prescribed that every man should be free, and if natural law was the fixed and immutable base of every system of positive law, how was it that all men recognized the practice of slavery? The concept of man as a reasonable being may certainly provide us with ideal standards of value by which we may test the law in force, but as civilization progresses, respect for human personality grows and the rules of law correspondingly develop. The search of *rules of law* that are unchangeable and universal is a futile one. As the Roman view got farther away from the deeper elements of Greek philosophy, it became superficial.

The Christian Fathers

The Christian Fathers extended the authority of natural law by ascribing to it a divine origin.[8] This made it easier to pour practical doctrines into the mould of natural law, for the truths of revealed religion could now be drawn upon. Hence it is not surprising that a theory of natural law should have great practical effect, since the element of reasonableness was interpreted in the light of Roman law (sometimes called *ratio scripta*) and the truths of Christianity. But, having forgotten Aristotle, the early writers treated the State as unnatural. Once, before the advent of sin, men had lived together in peace and happiness, needing not the constraint of government nor an exact division between *meum* and *tuum*. But with the fall of man, God created the State as a means of correcting the new tendencies to evil. Similarly, private property and slavery were instituted by God to correct the new sinful tendencies resulting from the fall of man. This illustrates the great gulf which separates the theory of the Christian Fathers from that of Aristotle who treated the State as a natural result of the social tendencies in man's nature.

The Middle Ages

The theory of natural law was popular in the Middle Ages due to reasons of conservatism and liberalism, of religion and of practical convenience. Firstly, we must realize that in the Middle Ages men defined law in manner very different from that of Austin. Since the fall of Rome, Europe was steering uneasily between the two dangers of tyranny and anarchy. Austinian theories might lead to the first, and, in the absence of a cohesive community, the doctrine of the general will may lead to the second. Men sought for a law that was based on something more enduring than the wills of men that could provide an element of unity in the battle against chaos and an element of protection against the arbitrary will of a sovereign. In the Germanic community, the relationship between monarch and subject was expressed by the idea of mutual fidelity rather than unilateral obedience—the king was also subject to the law.[9]

Natural law satisfied the interest of conservatism, for it had a long and 'respectable' ancestry; it could be made to satisfy the demands of liberalism (or even 'the left') because no one knew exactly what it was and many radical propositions could be drawn from the needs of man as a reasonable being. Psychologically the theory was satisfying because the very chaos of the time made universalism precious, even in a theory. Generalizing minds in their search for some principle of unity seized on natural law as the easiest method of approach. The theory satisfied the man of religion, 'economy of thought' made it easier to tread the known paths of philosophy than to strike out afresh.

In the middle ages we find the germ of theories that later became of great practical importance. In searching for a principle by which the power of the state could be justified, writers evolved the theory of the social contract. There were many varieties of this doctrine, but the predominant medieval compromise was that the monarch was above positive law, but was bound to natural law. This entails a complete break with the Roman view that natural law is the immutable and universal part of civil law. Thus even in this period we see the germ of the later theory of natural rights.

St. Thomas Aquinas (1125-74) is the most significant figure. He emphasizes that men's intellect and free will are the closest image of God in the material universe.[10] The eternal law governs the world through the will of God and according to His wisdom. For humanity this eternal law becomes the natural moral law, the basic rule being; act in conformity with your moral nature. This does not render the positive law superfluous—it is needed to work out the implications of the guiding natural law. Positive law should not conflict with natural law—if it conflicts, it is not law and does not bind the conscience of the subject. Thus law is reason and not the mere arbitrary whim of the ruler.

The elements of truth in Thomism are more clearly seen if we adopt Adler's analysis:

(a) Natural law provides the principles which determine the ends of action-the first truths of the practical reason, which are universal;

(b) Secondly, there are the precepts which are derived from these principles, and are judgement about means;

(c) Thirdly, there are the rules of law which are the application of the precepts to changing circumstances—these rules are essentially variable as conditions change;

(d) Lastly, there are the decisions—the application of the rule to a particular case.

Natural law is not directive in the same sense as positive law: the former provides the ultimate end; the latter directs a certain course of action after considering all the circumstances here and now. Natural law binds the conscience; positive law binds because of a sanction, though if it is just it will also bind the conscience. Positive law is nothing else but an ordinance of reason for the common good, made by him who has the care of the community, and promulgated. Much confusion would have been avoided if the term law had been confined to positive law and another term used for the *ius naturale,* which essentially lays down general principles rather than detailed rules. The principles of natural justice are a phrase that expresses better the medieval notion.

The Seventeenth Century

Grotius (1583-645) is the most famous representative of rationalist school. Natural law is based on the nature of man and his inward need of living in society. To discover what are the rules of natural law we must see what is in accord with the rational and social nature of man and then test our conclusions by seeing whether the rule has been adopted by all nations or at least the most civilized.[11] In Grotius's whimsical language, human nature is the grandmother, natural law the parent, and positive law the child. Human nature makes us desire society and hence creates natural law, which in its turn recognizes contracts as valid and thus sanctifies the social contract, which is the basis of the laws that Jack obeys. But he shared the naïve view that the principles of natural law could be deduced with ease—they are as evident as the physical objects we see with our eyes.

Grotius most significant contribution was in the realm of international law.

Groitus had emphasized that man had an impelling desire for society and that natural law was an outgrowth of this charters tic. To Hobbes (1588-1679), however, man in state of nature lived at war with his fellows and his life was solitary, poor, nasty, brutish, and short.[12] Hobbes was trying to build a theory on an anticipation of the finding of realism and empirical psychology. He emphasizes that he derives the rights of sovereign power from the principles of nature and according to the light of experience.[13] He claimed that he based his conclusion on the known natural inclinations of mankind. 'A law of nature is general rule, found out by reason, by which a man is forbidden to do that which is destructive for his life, or taketh away the means of preserving the same: and to omit that, by which the thinketh it may be best preserved.'[14] The fundamental law of nature is that every man ought to endeavor to obtain peace, as far as he has hope of obtaining it: and when he cannot obtain it, then he make seek, and use, all help and advantages of war. The second is that, if others are willing to follow the same rule, man should be content with so much liberty against other men as he would allow to others against himself. The third law of nature is that men perform their covenants made.[15] It is a striking commentary on the power of the tradition of the natural law that such a realist as Hobbes, who broke with accepted tradition in so many ways, should still cast his theory in the language of natural law.

The only effective way to source other was to reduce the warring wills of man by the imposition of a super-will, which could command obedience. The sovereign was the sole source of law, was above it and alone had the power to change it. The laws of nature are contrary to our natural passions and there must be the 'terror of some power to cause them to be observed.'[16] But the foundation of commonwealth Hobbes finds in the agreement of men-this shows the influence of the theory of the social contract even on one who believed in absolutism.

Hobbes aim was to justify absolutism by contrasting it with the ills of the state of the nature. Locke's[17] aim was to prove that government must necessarily be limited. Like Grotius, he believed that the moral rules could be easily discovered through reason. Locke emphasizes the imperfections of the state of the nature: there is want of established law, of an impartial judge, and of power to enforce rules—but he does not take such a gloomy view as Hobbes of the nature on\f man. He agrees with Hobbes that the organization of the state is essential, but the great difference lies in the fact that the surrender of liberty to the sovereign is not absolute but conditional—the power of state 'can never be supposed to extend further than the common good.' His contribution, therefore, is that government is trust for the benefit of men. The awkward question what was to happen if the ruler committed a breach of trust is skated over rather lightly.

Natural Rights

Even today, many theories of natural law have a religious base, but in the eighteenth century we notice an increasing secularization of the approach to legal and political questions. This ultimately makes more difficult the solution of the question whence comes the binding force of natural law, for the easy solution that it is based on the will of God does not prove acceptable to all men. In it was found what the Middle ages had found in religious faith, and what the nineteenth century was to find in science—a key to unlock all doors, a panacea for all the ills of the world.[18]

In the eighteenth century the theory of natural rights become the spearhead of revolutionary activity. There had long been a tendency to set up natural law as body of principles superior to positive law, and, if pursued too far, such a tendency may easily lead to anarchy. The doctrine arose there were certain innate rights, arising from the very nature of the man, which were beyond the assaults of positive law—in the famous words of the Virginian Declaration of Rights, 'all men are by nature equally free and independent and have certain inherent natural rights of which when they enter a society, they cannot by any compact deprive or divest their posterity.'[19] On the whole, theories of natural rights tended to be individualistic, to consider man as a unit rather than as a member of society. The liberty that was protected was that of the middle classes to run their businesses as they willed, that of the peasants to till their land free of the burdensome exactions of privilege.

There had been a theory that natural law was immutable, and even today most theories of natural rights retain a trace of individualism. But times have changed, and hence the same gospel which was once the cry of the revolutionary is now the cliché of the conservative who wishes to check attempts on the parts of governments to remedy inequalities. The middle classes, having won freedom, did not desire that freedom to be hampered by restraints imposed in the interests of the labouring classes. Thus the doctrine of natural rights has had great influence in America. The early American judges had a strong regard for the liberty of the individual.

The Fourteenth Amendment,[20] whatever may have been its object,[21] has been interpreted to give the courts power to safeguard natural rights and to declare unconstitutional any statute that unreasonably interferes with life, liberty, or property. Grant submits that the modern definition of due process is merely the natural law of story and field under a new name, that of reasonableness. Too often the courts tended to adopt fixed views of natural rights based on the doctrine of laissez-faire and boldly wrote these doctrines into the Constitution itself.[22] Holmes J. has pointed out the dangers of this policy:

'A Constitution is not intended to embody a particular economic theory, whether of paternalism ... or of laissez-faire. It is made for people of fundamentally differing views and the accident of our finding certain opinions natural and familiar, or novel and even shocking, ought not to conclude our judgement upon the question whether statutes embodying them conflict with the Constitution.'

Thus under the guise of the supremacy of law, America has achieved the supremacy of the judges,[23] and some of the political conflicts over Roosevelt's New Deal were transferred to the courts. It is true that the courts did not directly rely on a doctrine of natural right, but the interpretation of what was an unreasonable interference with liberty or property was sometimes affected by the older doctrine that certain rights were fundamental or innate.[24]

Modern Theories

To place the basis of law in an instinctive sense of rights seems but to outline, instead of solving, the fundamental problem of the relationship of justice of law.

Hence to deal with the question of the rational and moral basis of law, new theories of *ius naturale* have arisen; but, thanks to the historical school, they are free from the worst vices of their predecessors. Instead of searching for immutable rules, the thinker attempts to find ideal standards or principles, which will give direction to law, but also be capable of adaptation to different circumstances—hence the phrase, 'natural law with a variable content.' The same principle of justice may require one rule for London, another for Colombo. Although many theories of natural law were static, there is no inherent necessity why this should be so. Reason does not assume that the world remains the same, and a theory based on reason can easily be made progressive. The opposition between natural law and positive law is frequently solved by regarding the former as the ideal by which law should be tested, the latter as the actual law in force. Kant is the bridge between the earlier theories and those of days.

But there are still many different approaches, and it is perhaps unfortunate that the old terminology of natural law is used. But, whatever the terminology we use, the same problem must be faced. For all Bentham's scorn of natural law, his standard of *utility* is typical of mush natural law writing and the actual term utilitas was used in Middle Ages.[25] For those who which to go beyond formal theories basing the validity of law on the will of sovereign, or on an examination of the nature of legal system investigated objectively whether as system of rules or as system of more complex nature, there may be only three solutions—force, the will of the majority, or the needs of community life.[26] Thus, Goodhart defines law as 'those rule of conduct on which the existence of the society is based and violation of which, in consequence, tends to invalidate the existence of the society.'[27] This (in clearer language) is a solution similar to those of many natural law theorists, for the close relationship between law and the essential foundation of the community life is stressed. Le Fur describes natural law as law discovered by reason working by the light of ethics on the data provided by social facts.[28]

In the twentieth century we see the beginning of a functional and relativist approach. Theories of law become secularized: pragmatism emerges as a legal philosophy and the advance of science turns the minds of men into materialistic channels. New economic conditions and social philosophies made it impossible to apply literally the older doctrines, and until they could be restated in modern terms there was a tendency to reject them *in toto*. Moreover, Freud and the psychoanalysts introduced new theories of human mind—the doctrine that we 'rationalize' our actions introduced cynicism towards absolute ideals. The first result of the widespread adoption of the functional approach was destructive—many lost their faith in reason and religion as the basis of natural law, but there was nothing constructive to put in its place.

Natural law is rejected, for very different reasons, both by Kelsen and Kohler. Kelsen realizes that the fundamental thesis of natural law is that the validity of law is sought elsewhere than in a formal postulate (e.g. the will of the sovereign). The jurist cannot accept two standards of validity, for in case of conflict his pure science would contradict itself. To Kelsen, justice is an irrational ideal, as it cannot be proved by rational cognition. If we are content with the formal approach, such a theory is unanswerable, but, since we can understand the development of law and its relationship to society only by digging deeper into the mind of man, we find the results of Kelsen's theory rather scanty. And when Kelsen treats the problem of international law there seems to have crept in the 'ghost of natural law', for the primacy of international law is based on the needs of man rather than on any logical theory.[29]

Kohler[30] builds on the work of the historical school and adapts the premises of Hegel, but his modifications are so extensive that cynics say that there is little Hegelianism and less philosophy. Law is essentially a social fact and jurisprudence is a branch of that philosophy which deals with man and his culture—which term he defines as the greatest possible development both of human knowledge and of human control over nature. But culture is relative to time and place, and, as it varies, so must law. Evolution is thus the keynote of his work. 'There is no eternal law. The law that is suitable for one period is not so for another: we can only strive to provide every culture with its corresponding system of law. What is good for one would mean ruin to another?' But Kohler does not regard law as being automatically created. Jurisprudence must be a creative science—the legal order must be perpetually creating new values which are in accord with the advancement of culture, and those who are far-sighted should struggle with the masses whose views are more mundane. He is therefore opposed to the juristic pessimism of the historical school.[32] Kohler seems to make two points: firstly, reason (or the idea of culture) lies at the basis of law; secondly, the actual rules must be adapted to the state of development of any particular society. Stripped of its

Hegelian trappings, this is only to say that law is based on the needs of community life, on the reasonable demands of man as a civilized being. Thus, although Kohler expresses hostility to the doctrine of natural law, his basic ideas are somewhat akin to some modern forms of that theory: the jurist must draw from the civilization of his time those 'jural postulates' or necessary laws which are essential to achieve the purpose desired.[33]

The neo-Kantain approach is illustrated by Stammler, who seeks for the a priori form of law and of justice.[34] Stammler considers that the purpose of law is not to protect the will of one but to unify the purpose of all, to create a society in which each member will share adequate means of self-expression. But if this is the purpose of law is not also the purpose of just law, which attempts to effect a reasonable reconciliation of men's purpose? Hence a just law is that which agrees with the purpose of law as such. In seeking to elaborate the form of just law, Stammler has no difficulty in showing the confusion and ambiguity of previous theories of natural law. But in order to secure certainty he takes the heroic step of rejecting the view that a basis for law can be discovered by analyzing the nature of man—it can be found only by analyzing the nature of law. There is no law of nature in the old sense of the word, but there may be formal principle implied in the notion of law, which are universally true. Hence the cliché, 'nature of law with a variable content', explains Stammler's view so long as we remember that natural law is a mere logical form. Is the necessary mark of law—this is much the view of Salmond,[35] although the latter does not cumber his writing with the neo-Kantain technique. Indeed Stammler's method proves nothing concerning the nature of justice, and the only conclusion that we can draw is that even a philosophical technique does not make the writer immune from being influenced by his own prejudices.[36]

Geny seeks the foundation of natural law in the truths of religion.[37] He wishes to discover directive principles, which will act as a guide to the judge where there is no authority in point. Can the disturbing element of justice, ethics, social interest (call it what you will) be so reduced to order that it will prevent arbitrary caprice? As a philosophic basis Geny chooses so many elements from different streams of thought that it is difficult to weld his heterogeneous material into a consistent whole. He denies that reason alone can solve the problems of the universe. Hence a modern doctrine of natural law can supply merely directive principles, which must be applied by the constructive work of the jurist, who must never forget that legal technique is not an end in itself but only a means of putting into effect the fundamental truths on which human life is based.

The clearest modern Catholic exposition is that of Heinrich Romen.[38] Law is not mere will—it is based on reason. But he rejects the excesses of the rationalists. The fundamental principles he finds to be 'What is just is to be done' and 'Give to everyone his due'. These directive principles he fills out with Christian teaching and a consideration of the rational and social nature of man. But he agrees with Geny that the further we descend from these first principles to particular rules, the more difficult becomes the decision and the greater the controversy. He regards the legal institution of private property and inheritance as part of the natural law, but decisions as to the exact forms of property and of inheritance are subject to economic conditions. Thus severe restrictions on private property may be necessary in certain conditions—property must be made to fulfill its real function to serving the individual. His doctrine does emphasize the moral supremacy of the natural law: but rejects the anarchical individualism of some earlier theories. Man exists only in society and he owes a duty not to disrupt the social structure. If a law is only unjust, it is the citizen's moral (as well as legal) duty to obey. Only those laws are devoid of obligation, which are immoral.

Moreover, Romen claims that there is no essential divergence between the historical and the natural law schools, if both are properly understood. All law must take account of the peculiarity of individual people and their legal genius, the course of historical development and economic evolution. Only the fundamental ends of society can be claimed as universal. On the other hand, politics cannot be divorced from the moral universe—natural law remains the criterion by which the just of law is to be determined. 'Just as the real and the true are one, so too the true and the just are ultimately one. *Veritas facit legem*...True freedom consists in being bound by justice.'

The modern deification of the State leads naturally to a denial of the existence of natural law, since the State is placed above moral rules, which bind the individual alone. Such an approach is not confined to modern Fascist theories, for its roots lie in the Hegelian conception of the State as an end in itself. Modern doctrines have carried to its logical end this older philosophy, and both Fascism and Communism condemned as outmoded and bourgeois any doctrine that natural law should bind or guide the lawmaker.

All action must be guided by the needs of the community as a whole. Whether we can prove the validity or not of ideals based on the unique value of human personality, it is unlikely that democracy will succeed unless they are respected. All attempts to establish absolute values on any other than a religious base have failed—but religion is essentially a matter of faith rather than intellectual proof. The nature of human communities seems to be such, however, that each to survive must recognize some fundamental values and must devise means to protect those values and, in the long run, not only to protect them but to permit them to grow and change.

The Common Law Approach

Finally, let us consider the attitude of the common law towards this question of value. We cannot adopt the easy solution of saying that the actual law in force lays down all the standards that are to be applied and hence that such problem need not trouble us. For, while of necessity there are many detailed rules, which adopt certain ideals, there are two means by which modern views may influence the law laid down by the past: firstly, where there is no authority, the court's view of what is socially expedient will influence the law; and, secondly, many accepted rules lay down broad standards which are mere moulds that can be filled with changing contents. Thus public policy is 'a principle of judicial legislation or interpretation founded on the current needs of the community'.[39] The standard of reasonableness is elastic enough to be adapted to present views. Yet in applying these principles and standards, the English doctrine is that the judge should not apply his own view, nor even that of philosophy, but the opinion of the average right-thinking member of the community. If the House of Lords interpreted public policy by Marxian standards, there would not only be surprise but a feeling that the proper bounds of the court had been exceeded.[40]

Hence while there has been some repetition of natural law learning in the English Books, the English judge prefers to use more humble tests. Bracton, Coke, and Blackstone use the doctrine of natural law as the rhetorical figment, but do not incorporate it into their theories of law. Nevertheless, English law was open to the same ethical influence as were those system that relied on natural law; but, where the continental lawyer would flourish a philosophy, the English jurist pins his faith to common sense, natural justice, reason, convenience, practical considerations, public policy, or humanity. As Scrutton L.J. pithily observed: I am sure it is justice. It is probably the law for that reason.[41]

The whole conception of equity is, of course, akin to natural law, but Chancellor postulated, not a philosophy, but rather an Englishman with a conscience slightly more sensitive than the average. Bentham's hedonistic calculus fits in well with the practical approach of the common lawyer. He is not interested in ultimate metaphysics but in framing a utilitarian test which could be used to encourage law reform.

The continental equivalent of public policy is the conception of *ordre publique*, but it is interesting to contrast the English doctrine of public policy with the theory of natural law, for that throws light on the true nature of each. Compared with continental doctrines, the rule of public policy is practical and conservative, related to concrete cases rather than to abstract theory. The doctrine of public policy cannot be set in opposition to law (as was *ius naturale*), for it is part and parcel of the common law itself-it is respectable and respected. Nor could it be regarded as a universal or immutable body of rules, for the diversity of the heads of public policy is equaled only by the development of the rules under each head as circumstances changed. Once cornering the market was regarded as 'a most heinous offence'[42]—now (if the operation be successful) it leads to universal admiration.

The common law determination of the ends that the courts should follow has thus been a work of practical adaptation to what is conceived to be the community rather than a philosophic study. It is akin to the spirit of Pound's analogy of social engineering—that the law should satisfy as many wants as possible with the least sacrifice.[43] But there can never be an exact correlation between the rules of law and the views of the average man. There are no precise methods of discovering what the community really thinks,[44] So we must trust the judge to be a typical representative of his day and generation.[45] Concerning many legal problems, we can hardly regard the average man as having any view at all. And occasionally the law has not hesitated to set a standard far higher than that actually observes. While jurisprudence is dispensed by many as some jargon of the continent, an appropriate dose of legal philosophy would stimulate the development of the subject. Even if we admit that philosophy has not yet evolved an acceptable scale of values, that its answer to the fundamental problems of jurisprudence are still confused, yet at least a study of philosophy shows us the facility of a dogmatic, unconscious assumption of a view that has already been shown to be false. Duguit is not the only writer who was most metaphysical when he attempted to divorce his writing from philosophy and ethics. Ignorance of the contribution of the philosopher causes us to stumble when we might walk with reflected light—even if the rays are not very powerful, they are preferable to the darkness which otherwise would be our lot.

Whatever be the problems of philosophy, the law must actually translate a set of values into working rules of law. Pound points out, in reply to those who argue that a measure of values cannot be achieved, that the law has been forced to evolve a working test of values without waiting for all theoretical difficulties to be solved.[46] In this evolution the law cannot but be influenced greatly by the philosophy of life which a community holds.

It is how clear that directly or indirectly the purpose of law was justice. Generally, today also the purpose of law is justice. It is also definite that purpose of law in future shall also remain the adherence of principles of faster in any form what so ever, as I had described.

Subject to certain exception about the real purpose of law, Justice Krishna Iyer described that the integral yoga of law and religion is the genius of Indian culture, which blends in dharma the finer components of legality and spiritual values. The Hindu sages, the Buddhist and Jain Seers as well as the Sikh Saints and other socio-religious reformers regarded law and religion not as divorced from each other but as mutually inter-acting and cross-fertilizing. For that matter, the teaching of Jesus Christ and the Quranic texts emanation from Prophet Mohammed, divinised the rules of conduct so much so the legal and religious have validity rooted in higher values beyond the materialist norms and secular guidelines. The lofty perspective lends a profound meaning to the humanism, which binds law and religion. To an Indian mind the study of the two departments of knowledge relating to the regulation of worldly affairs and the pursuit of matters of the spirit has a common foundation and the goodness of life, and any understanding of Law and Religion must therefore be informed by this seminal principle. Indeed, there is an Indian identity, a Bharatiya flavour for every religion extant in our land and every personal law, which has its fountain force in the respective faith. A creative mutuality and fertile fellowship have moulded family laws and godly faiths, which have flourished in our country over the centuries. Akbar even attempted a synthesis between the two.

The brooding omnipresence of vedic wisdom and an eclectic readiness to be hospitable to all cultures are obvious to the discerning scholar who studies insightfully how, beneath the bleeding communalism and aggressive godism, a lovely cultural tapestry of secular-sacred community of laws and religions lends depth and beauty to the basic humanism underlying the diversity of teachings.

True, the raw realities of conflicts, fear, hatred and feuding episodes mar the sublime unity in diversity, which is the fundamental feature of India's age-old spirit. Even so, my thesis, which enlivens my consciousness about the future of Law and Religion in India, is that the continuing process secularly expressed in law and ecclesiastically manifested in religion, has a higher personality. That is the discovery of cultural India which should not be confused between the living being with a survival value of values and the cadaver, which is, but anatomy without the vital breathe.

The story of civilization has two dynamic components, among many, namely Law and Religion. From ancient times, Law and Religion have interacted, jointly operated and, at times, mutually fought to overpower each other. In many vintage cultures and bygone societies, the two have been a blended brew and, even to this day, in many communities and countries, religion actively or passively affects law or is a component thereof; but while law holds religion in leash, generally speaking, in no country has law succeeded in extinguishing religion. Khomeni's Iran is an instance of religion dominating but not defeating law, although a sizeable number of secular Iranians demand revolutionary deliverance from Islamic rule. A case in contrast in the Soviet Union where the October Revolution put religion on the retreat, but

65 years after, there are working churches, constitutional freedom to practice one's faith and even conferences of religious leaders. Some states, with secular veneer, have state religions and, on the contrary, several states, where religious communities flourish, are secular in character. Another point to be noticed in this jurisdiction is that profession and practice often vary. The fact, however, is that even in loudly secular societies and states, religion survives after death, as it were, though as an apparition, even in theocratic states many departments of social and economic relations are free from ecclesiastical or allied stranglehold or control. Broadly stated, religion, vis-à-vis law, is fighting a losing battle but it is still die-hard. From the perspective of the secular-sacredotal symbiosis, India, a land of ubiquitous 'holies,' fighting faiths and rationalist rebels, occupies a middle-position. It may be an interesting study to examine the Religion-Law equation in a country notorious for multiple religious and proliferous pantheons projecting into politics, state and the Law, and yet, constitutionally harmonized in 'Law India.' The picture in real life is somewhat unlovely and the rhythm of secularism is a wee-bit wobbly even as law bends before God's lobby. Yet, a historical, jurisprudential, political and pragmatic examination of Law and Religion in India may be instructive, even illuminating, revealing the pathology of secular distortions when pressurized by religious and the technology of management of hostile religions and denominations in the context of a crowd of communities, castes and minorities drawing dividends from religion-related backward status. The Indian experiment in constitutional secularism and conflict resolution, a study in the social dynamics of Justice, in the perspectives of frictional religious relationships and fundamentalist rigidities in family laws, bring into play a viable blend of sacred secular values and a jurisprudence of peaceful religious pluralism.

Law and religion the world over have quarelled and combined in varying degrees. A glance back in time lights the issue clearly.

There are many instances where the function of priests, lawgivers, and judges have overlapped. Law springs from custom, and many of the customs regulate relations depending on religion. Promises, contracts, and treaties are frequently made invoking religion. When legal rules take the form of written records embodying what is believed to have been delivered to a people directly by the deity, or through sages inspired by a divine power, the sanctity of law attains its maximum and it is virtually a part of religion, and those who knew it have both a legal and a religious function. The Roman pontifices early had legal powers. Offences against the community may be deemed offences against the deity, and punishment takes the form of devoting the culprit to the wrath of the powers of the underworld. Trial by ordeal, the appeal to the judgment of God, has been in various forms a widespread institution in underdeveloped communities. In some cases religious revelations and sacred writings have included rules for secular conduct.

Mosaic law is an amalgam of religious and secular rules: To the Mohammedan, the Quran provides both a body of beliefs and ritual and a comprehensive code of behaviour. It prescribes both religious and legal observances. The Quran is the primary expression of Islamic Law, though not a code of law, as well as the basic formulation of religious ethics. Jewish law comprises rules of worship and ritual, private and social behaviour and, as the personal law of Jewish citizens in question of status, is part of the law of modern Israel.

In Christian Western Europe in the Middle Ages the power claimed for the spiritual and lay authorities came into sharp conflict on many occasions, notably in the investiture contest. . . . The long conflict between Church and State is essentially a conflict between the authorities in the religious and legal spheres of national life.

There have also been instances where the state has been theocratic and religious; persons, beliefs, attitudes and rule have been the major controlling force in the community, acting through state law; example have been Calvin's Geneva and, a times, Puritan England and Presbyterian Scotland.

The reformation in England produced profound changes in the law, not least in that supreme exercise of parliamentary power, which overthrew the papal supremacy and made Henry VIII supreme head under God of the Church in England. As a result of these changes English ecclesiastical law, even in purely spiritual matters is part of the law of the State, and it is only in the twentieth century, by delegation by Parliament to the Church Assembly, and later to the General Synod, that the Church of England has had practical legislative independence. In America separation of church and state did not come about till after the Declaration of Independence.

Even in the modern world, many secular processes are tinged with religious rituals. For example, taking the oath of office or oath to deliver the truth still has a religious flavour, although an atheist may make solemn affirmation instead. On the whole, religion still has a hold on the life of the law in most countries of the world.

A global view, a wide spectrum of secularism of varied hues, so much so, each is peculiar in its own way. Despite this profusion and confusion of colours, some conceptual fundamentals of practical significance are available across the board which make of generalizations and help us hold whether a State is secular or not. In a discussion where secularism and religion are involved, the distinction between State and Society must be kept in view. The State may keep its processes secular, while the people may practice one or more religions and may even face the problem of the cold war and hot war among gods and their human battalions. It is surprising but true that in several instances while the Law of Constitution declares temporal affairs as out of bounds for religions and forbids the State from taking steps with or slant towards religion or against religion, yet a given society may be a jungle of religions, castes, sects, cults engaged in rivalry and operating through crypto-political procedures and pressures to use State power to their own advantages. The Indian religious syndrome and constitutional control may offer lessons for others too in the role of law vis-à-vis religion.

When freedom from the British came to the Indian sub-continent, Hindu-Muslim massacres maddeningly mounted. Pakistan went Islamic but India stubbornly remained secular and refused to be stampeded into Hindu Raj. With a proportion of population, 85% of Hindus, 10% of Muslims plus other tiny minorities, India's inviolable secularism is a great tribute to the leaders of struggle for freedom, like Gandhi, Nehru, Ambedkar and Azad. But when millions are seized by communal convulsions and countless lives are lost in religious carnage the law can't wish away macabre bitterness. Secular Law had to face this sensitive challenge of degenerate religion.

The role of Law in disciplining religions into peaceful co-existence is under strain because of the provocative anti-Hindu policy of Pakistan and Bangladesh and the militant communal politics inside India. Even so, Indian Law has a better record of keeping peace than in other countries with feuding religious pluralism.

Any objective will agree that Indian Law, procedural and substantive, are secular, that the judiciary is substantially free from religious bias, that the legislative and administrative processes are, by and large, functionally uninfluenced by caste and creed. A government of laws may be secular in soul but when its operators are infected, the processes get polluted.

Mohammad Ghouse[7a] has criticized the dubious politics of communal secularism:

Though our Constitution seeks to establish a new policy founded on secularism—communalism and violence pervade our society. Our major religions seek to regulate all human activities, disregarding the difference between the secular and the sacred. The caste and religion-oriented behaviour of the people, the existence and emergence of communal organizations have slowed down the process of de-communalization of the process engineered by the substitution of joint for separate electorates.

The tragic portents for Law to keep secular sanity and sanitation are obvious and ominous. Why? Dr. Ghouse[8] is right:

Some of the political parties have vested interest in communalism and communal violence to gain power, others tolerate it to retain power. Some ride on the crest of communalism; others fear to swim against it. The electorate, stamped in tradition, is responsive to appeals based on caste, religion and languages. It has not realized the value of the vote.

While communalism and fascism are tightening their hold on the life of the nation, no organized, dedicated and determined effort is being made to loosen that hold and to nourish and strengthen secularism. There are Hindus who identify secularism with Muslim appeasement, and Muslims who dismiss secularism as un-Islamic.

National integration, which in the Indian setting, means dissolving communal-religious divisiveness and defusing blow-ups, is an ineffectual process because the law is left without social invigoration and political will.

It is a creed of the Constitution to promote a scientific temper and cultivate a humanist spirit (Vide Art. 51-A).

Future Shock or Human Tomorrow is the black and white alternatives for Law and Religion in India. They have a future if they are constitutionally functional in a fresh secular spiritual embrace. The dynamics of survival and the tryst with destiny compel the nation into a cultural strategy of jettisoning confrontations among Gods and, instead, cross-fertilizing Law with the values of divinity implicit in the worth of the human person. The highest function of Law and Religion is to offer creative opportunity to everyone to unfold his full potential. The Indian Constitution is a signpost in that noble direction.

Vistarmic visions of Law and Religion under the Indian sun yield deeper perceptions than have been articulated in the past. Indeed, Indian brotherhood in a stable society can never be an enduring value unless we are able to arrive at a grand synthesis of the essentials of the plurality of religions and laws (revolving round religion). This is the new discovery of India, which Indians have yet to make. Indeed, such an adventure in humanist synthesis and secular cross-fertilization may well be described as the spiritual dimension of Indian unity and patriotism. If we fail here or drift aimlessly, stark disaster stares us in the face as a nation, what with blood-thirsty gods vampirism sects and begotten cults over-powering fraternal secularism and scientific spiritualism, compelling the people of India to divide themselves into warring camps. It is a pity that by a perversion of history, fanned by colonial and feudal forces, gods have become barbarous and men inhumanly religious. If an honest man is the noblest work of God, and honest God is the noblest work of man. India awaits an universal wave of humanism where all religions and faith live in harmony and atheism, skeptical rationalism and god-fearing religion of man have a place in the pantheon of civilization.

Reality is order and harmony in nature and society. Entropy is disorder, which upsets the balance and beauty of inner and outer nature. Thus Law and Religion, though operating in dual dimensions, have an inner nexus, which, once grasped, will stabilize the truth about the complimentary character of the science of Society and the Spirit of Man.

Salmond has concluded that, law is an instrument of society, and no discussion would be complete without some inquiry as to its object. What then has, or should, law achieve?

One answer is justice. Aquinas and Salmond have claimed justice as the goal of law: indeed for them it is a logical part of the very notion of the law. Secondly Aquinas[47] following Augustine, an unjust law is no law, while to Salmond[48] law is those principles applied by the state in the administration of justice. Others, such as the positivists, who would deny any essential or logical connection between the two concepts, would nevertheless regard justice as highly relevant to a critical evaluation of law.[49] It is therefore, a concept which legal theory must investigate.

Justice can be used in a wider or a more restricted sense.[50] In the wide sense, such as is used by Aquinas in his contention that an unjust law is no law, justice appears to be roughly synonymous with morality. In the narrower sense, as in the expressions "court of justice", "natural justice" and "denial of justice", the term refers to but one area of morality.

That "justice" has this narrower sense can be seen by examining the converse concept, that of injustice. An unjust man, act or law is automatically immoral, but the converse is not true. Wickedness can take other forms than injustice. Rape is an abhorrent act, but the last description to be applied to it is that of being unjust. Injustice is rather the charge leveled against men, acts or laws that treat one or more persons more harshly or more favourably than others in the same situation. A father who picks on one child and makes a favourite of another is an unjust parent. For justice consists precisely in not singling persons out for special treatment in the absence of significant differences, but in treating cases alike and meting out fair and equal treatment to all.

Now justice operates at two different levels.[51] As "distributive justice," it works to ensure a fair division of social benefits and burdens among the members of a community. One of the most important of democratic rights is the right to vote of an adult. Distribute justice then serves to secure a balance or equilibrium among the members of society.

This balance, however, can be upset. Suppose one citizen, X, is prevented by another, Y, from exercising his right to vote. Now the balance is upset because Y has deprived X of a right that should be equally enjoyed by all. At this point "corrective justice" will move in to correct the disequilibrium by forcing Y to make X some compensation. Then, in its distributive aspect serves to secure, and in its corrective aspect to redress, the balance of benefits and burdens in a society.

Hence, the function of the courts is chiefly that of applying justice in its corrective sense. In a just system of law, then, we shall expect to find, on the one hand rules aiming to procure equality of distribution, and on the other specific rules relating to the application of corrective justice by the courts. Consequently, in a fair legal system we should look for procedural or other rules to afford each party an equal opportunity of presenting his case and calling evidence and to prevent judicial prejudice in favour of either.

But fair and equal dispensation of justice demands more than equality between the parties to individual lawsuits; it requires that all be equal before the law. What this means is not that all should enjoy equality of legal rights, for the distribution of these has little or nothing to do with judicial function. It means rather that the legal rights, which each person has, should be given equal protection by the courts. This entails then, not just that in each case both plaintiff and defendant get an equal "crack of the whip," but that today's plaintiff and tomorrow's receive the same sort of hearing; in other words, that the judges should mete out justice without distinction between high and low, rich and poor, and so forth.

But this in turn entails that like cases are treated alike not only as regards the bearing but also in respect of the finding. Major discrepancies in sentencing mean in fact inequality before the law. This requirement, then, that like cases be treated alike in this sense, points away from a system of "palm tree" justice, whereby each case is decided on its merits according to what the judge thinks fit, to a system of general rules prescribing what is to be decided in whole classes of similar cases; and these rules we shall expect to find in the substantive provisions of the law.

Now once we have a legal system operating via such general rules, we can see that there is yet another sort of balance to be achieved by distributive justice. Once general rules of substantive law appear on the scene, however, whether they result from legislation or from judicial creation, a balance is beginning to be struck, not between persons, but between interests. It is no longer concerned with whether this plaintiff's right to his good name should prevail over this defendant's right to speak his mind, but with the balancing and reconciling in general of the right to reputation and the right of freedom of speech. Similarly in property law, in those cases where an innocent victim's goods are dishonestly acquired and sold to an innocent purchaser, the law is compelled to adjudicate not just between the two interested parties but also between the conflicting social interests of security of property and ready marketability of goods.

This has led jurists such as the American writer Roscoe Pound[52] to regard law as the species of social engineering, whose function it is to maximize the fulfillment of the interests of the community and its members and to promote the smooth running of the machinery of society.

But the basic notion of like treatment of alike cases is but the formal aspect of justice. The material aspect concerns the determination of what makes like cases alike. Those who described, not justify their practice on the basis that such factors are so important so as to render unequal, those who differ with regard to them; while those who condemn such discrimination do so on the grounds that such factors are irrelevant to the measurement of human equality. Which factors are, and which are not relevant is in the ultimate a question not of fact but of outlook and attitude; and in so far as the law must answer such question, it must do so by accepting and enshrining value judgement rather than by applying simple rules of law.

Justice, however, is not the only possible or desirable goal of law. Indeed the notion of law represents a basic conflict between two different needs, the need for uniformity and the need for flexibility. Uniformity is needed partly to provide certainty and predictability. Where rules of law are fixed and generalized, the citizen can plan his activities with a measure of certainty and predict the legal consequences of his behaviour.

On the other hand there is a need for flexibility. The existing rules may not provide for the exceptional case, and as legal realism has shown, no rule can provide for every possible case. Some measure of discretion, therefore, is valuable where circumstances alter cases. Furthermore, flexibility is necessary to enable the law to adapt itself to social change.[53] As a society alters, so do its needs, and a serviceable legal system must be able in its development to take account of new social, political and economic requirements. Givén an unalterable system of law, the necessary changes can only be brought about by violence and upheaval; law that is capable of adaptation, whether by legislation or judicial development, allows for peaceful change. This reconciliation of stability with flexibility is a permanent problem for any legal system.

Law And Fact

It is commonly said that all question which arise for consideration and determination in a court of justice are of two kinds, being either question of law or question of fact. In a sense this proposition is true, but it is one, which requires careful examination.

The term question of law is used in three distinct though related senses. It means, in the first place, a question, which the court is bound to answer in accordance with the rule of law—a question which the law itself has authoritatively answered, to the exclusion of the right of the court to answer the question as it thinks fit in accordance with what is considered to be the truth and justice of the matter. All other questions are questions of fact—using the term fact in its widest possible sense to include everything that is not law. In this sense, every question which has not been predetermined and authoritatively answered by the law is a question of fact—whether it is, or is not, one of fact in any narrower sense, which may be possessed by that term.

In a second and different signification, a question of law is a question as to what the law is. Thus, an appeal on the question of law means an appeal in which the question for argument and determination is what the true rule of law is on a certain matter. Question of law in this sense arise, not out of the existence of law, but out of its uncertainty. If the whole law could be definitely ascertained[54], there would be no question of law in this sense; but all questions to be answered in accordance with that law would still be question of law in the former sense. When a question first arises in a court of justice as to the meaning of an ambiguous statutory provision, the question one of law in this second sense; it is a question as to what the law is. But it is not the question of law in the first sense, but a question of fact. The judicial interpretation of a statute, therefore, represents a progressive transformation of the various questions of fact as to the meaning of that statute into question of law (in the first sense) to be answered in conformity with the body of interpretative case law so developed.

There is still another and third sense in which the expression question of law is used. This arises from the composite character of the typical English tribunal, at any rate until recent years, and the resulting division of judicial functions between a judge and a jury. The general rule is that questions of law (in both of the foregoing senses) are for the judge, but those questions of fact (that is to say, all other questions) are for the jury. This rule, however, is subject to numerous and important exceptions.

Though there are no cases in which the law is left to jury, there are many questions of fact that are withdrawn from the cognizance of a jury and answered by the judge. The interpretation of a document, for example, may be, and very often is, a pure question of fact, and nevertheless falls within the province of a judge. So the question of reasonable and probable cause for a prosecution—which arise in actions for malicious prosecution—is one of fact and yet one for the judge himself. So it is the duty of the judge to decide whether there is any sufficient evidence to justify a verdict for the plaintiff; and if he decides that there is not, the case is withdrawn from the jury altogether; yet this is a mere matter of fact, undetermined by any authoritative rule of law.

We proceed now to consider more particularly the nature of questions of fact. The term question of fact has more than one meaning. In its most general sense it includes all questions, which are not question of law. Everything is matter of fact, which is not matter of law. And, as the expression question of law has three distinct applications, it follows that a corresponding diversity exists in the application of the contrasted term. A question of fact, therefore, as opposed to a question of law, means either (1) any question, which is not predetermined by a rule of law; or (2) any question except a question as to what the law is; or (3) any question that is to be answered by the jury instead of by the judge.

There is, however, a narrower and more specific sense, in which the expression question of fact does not include all question that are not questions of law, but only some of them. In this sense a question of fact is opposed to a question of judicial discretion. The sphere of judicial discretion includes all questions as to what is right, just, equitable, or reasonable, so far as not predetermined by authoritative rules of law but committed to the *liberum arbitrium* of the courts. A question judicial discretion pertains to the sphere of right, as opposed to that of fact in its stricter sense. It is a question as to what ought to be, as opposed to a question of what is. Matters of fact are capable of proof, and are the subject of evidence adduced for that purpose. Matters of right and judicial discretion are not the subject of evidence and demonstration, but of argument, and are submitted to the reason and conscience of the court. In determining questions of fact the court is seeking to ascertain the truth of the matter, in determining questions of judicial discretion it seeks to discover to the right or justice of the matter. Whether the accused has committed the criminal act with which he is charged, is a question of fact; but whether, if guilty, he should be punished by way of imprisonment or only by way of fine, is a question of judicial discretion or of right.

There is yet a third meaning of the expression "question or matter of fact" in which it is contrasted with a question or matter of opinion. Alternatively, the answer to a question of opinion may be matter of assessment or evaluation, which can neither be proved by evidence nor determined by law, since the law may not provide criteria for assessment.

A distinction is also drawn between primary and secondary facts. Primary facts are proved by oral, documentary and other evidence; secondary facts can be inferred from primary facts.

Matters and question, which come before a court of justice, therefore, are of three classes:

(a) Matters and question of law - that is to say, all that are determined by authoritative legal principles;

(b) Matters and question of judicial discretion- that is to say, all matters and questions as to what is right, just, equitable, or reasonable, except so far as determined by law;

(c) Matters and questions of facts - that is to say, all other matters and questions whatever.

In matter of the first kind, the duty of the court is to ascertain the rule of law and to decide in accordance with it. In matters of the second kind, its duty is to exercise its moral judgement, in order to ascertain the right and justice of the case. In matters of the third kind, its duty is to exercise its intellectual judgement on the evidence submitted to it in order to ascertain the truth.

The existence and development of a legal system represents the transformation, to a greater or less extent, of questions of fact and of judicial discretion into question of law, by the establishment of authoritative and predetermined answers to these questions. This process of transformation proceeds chiefly within the sphere of judicial discretion, and only to a smaller extent within the sphere of pure fact. In respect of question as to what is just, right, and reasonable, the purpose and effect of a system of law is to exclude and supersede to a very large extent the individual moral judgement of the courts, and to compel them to determine these questions in accordance with fixed and authoritative principles which express the established and permanent moral judgement of the community at large. Natural or moral justice is to a very large extent transmuted into legal justice; *is natural* becomes *us positivum.* The justice which courts of justice are appointed to administer becomes for the most part such justice as is recognized and approved by the law, and not such justice as commends itself to the courts themselves. The sphere of judicial discretion is merely such portion of the sphere of right as has not been thus encroached upon by the sphere of law.

Questions of opinion too are transformed into questions of law. This is largely the result of replacing trial by jury in civil actions by trail by judge alone. Future progress in the common law may well lie in the re-transformation of questions of law into question of opinion and discretion. In many areas judicial discretion has been freed from fetters of law. The occupiers; Liability Act 1957, replaced a mass of particular rules by a few broad, simple principles. Such developments, providing the courts with fixed decisions on the merit, allow rules of law to function as "guide-posts rather than hitch posts".

To a lesser extent, even questions of pure fact are similarly transformed into questions of law. Even to such questions the law will, on occasion, supply predetermined and authoritative fact must be deemed to be such and such, whether it be so in truth or not. The law is the theory of things, as received and acted upon within courts of justice, and this theory may or may not conform to the reality of things outside. The eye of the law does not infallibly see things as they are. Partly by deliberate design and partly by the errors and accidents of historical development, law and fact, legal theory and the truth of things, may fail in complete coincidence. We have ever to distinguish that which exists in deed and in truth from that fraud in fact, and vice versa. That is to say, when the law shall be deemed fraud and what shall not, this principle may or may not be true, and so far as it is untrue the truth of things is excluded by the legal theory of things.

This discordance between law and fact may come about in more ways than once. Its most frequent cause is the establishment of legal presumptions, whereby one fact is recognized by law as sufficient proof of another fact, whether it is in truth sufficient for this purpose or not. Such legal presumptions-*presumptiones juris*-are of two kinds, being either conclusive or rebut table. A presumption of the first kind, sometimes infer the existence of one fact from the existence of another, even though this inference could be proved to be false. A presumption of the second kind requires the courts to draw such an inference even though there is no sufficient evidence to support it, provided only that there is no sufficient evidence to establish the contrary inference. Thus a negotiable instrument is presumed to be given for value, a person not heard of for seven years is sometimes presumed to be dead, and an accused person is presumed to be innocent. A fact which by virtue of a legal presumption is deemed by law to exist, whether it exists or not, is said in the technical language of the law to exist constructively notice, for example, means fraud or notice which is deemed to exist by virtue of an authoritative rule of law, whether it exits in truth or not.

Another method by which law on occasion deliberately departs from the truth of things for sufficient or insufficient reasons, is the use of the device known as a *legal fiction-fictio juris.* This was a device familiar to primitive legal system, though mostly fallen out of use in modern law.[55]

An important legal fiction recognized by modern system is that of the adoption of children - a fiction which played a great part in the law of primitive communities. An adoptive child is a child who is not in fact the child of its adopting parent, but is deemed to be such be a legal fiction, with much the same results in law as if this fictitious parentage was real.

The same question may be partly one of law and partly one of fact or judicial discretion. This is so in two senses. In the first place, the question may be in reality composite, consisting of two or more questions combined, and the several components may be of different natures in this respect. The question, for example, whether a partnership exists between A and B is partly one of fact (viz., what agreement has been made between them) and partly one of law (viz., whether such an agreement is sufficient to constitute the legal relation of partnership). Similar composite questions are innumerable. In the second phase, there are many cases in which the freedom of judicial discretion on any point is not wholly taken away by a fixed rule of law, but is merely restrained and limited by such a rule, and is left to operate within the restricted sphere so allowed to it. In such a case the question to be determined by the court is one of law so far as the law goes, and one of fact or judicial discretion as to the rest. The proper penalty for a offence is usually a question of this nature. The law imposes a fixed maximum, but leaves the discretion of the court to operate within the limits so appointed. So, in many cases, judicial discretion, instead of being, is merely limited and controlled by rules of law which determined the general considerations which are to be taken into account as relevant and material in the exercise of this discretion. The discretion of the court has not been taken away, but it must be exercised within limits, in the manner, and upon the considerations thus authoritatively indicated by law.

The Territorial Nature of Law

The answer to this question is somewhat surprisingly complex, and we must begin by distinguishing between the territorial enforcement of law and the territoriality of law itself.

The enforcement of law is undoubtedly territorial in the same way as a state in territorial; that is to say, the state power is in time of peace exercised only within the territories of the state and on its public ships and aircraft and on vessels and aircraft registered under its law.

The territoriality of law in this meaning flows from the political division of the world. No state allows other states, as a general rule, to exercise powers of government within it.

The enforcement of law is therefore confined to the territorial boundaries of the state enforcing it. A person who commits a crime or a tort in state A, and who then removes himself and his property to state B, cannot, so long as he is in state B, be reached by the authorities of state A. He has certainly violated the law of state A, by an act committed within its territory, but the enforcement of that law, while he and his belongings are outside the territory, is impossible.

In the case of crimes this situation is largely remedied by the practice of extradition. States conclude treaties with each other, by which each agrees to surrender to the other persons found in its territory who are wanted for crimes committed in the territory of the other parties to the treaty, extradition is not practice in civil cases, but as general rule every state gives a remedy in its own courts for civil wrongs wherever they may be committed.

In other words, to say that a legal system belongs to defined territory means partly that its rules do not purport to apply extra-territorially, partly that those who apply and enforce them do not regard them as applying extra-territorially and partly that other state do not so regard them.

The proposition that a system of law applies only to person, things, acts and events within a defined territory is not a self-evident truth; it is a very rough and imperfect generalization. To take English criminal law, there are several offences with which English courts will deal and to which they will apply, English law, though committed elsewhere than in England: for example, piracy, and treason, murder or bigamy committed by British subjects in any part of the world. Some states, such as Turkey, go much beyond this, and apply their criminal law even to foreigners in respect of crimes committed abroad if the victims are their subjects and the foreigner concerned ventures within their territory.[55] Next, the rule that title to land is governed by the *lez situs* is not invariable. An English court of equity will apply certain equitable rules even to land situated abroad. Italian law rejects the *lex situs* in favour of the law of the owner's nationality, in case of succession on death.[56] Turning to pure personality, this is governed in several respects, in Anglo-American jurisdictions, by the law of the owner's domicile. According to this rule English law may be applied by English courts to chattels that are not in England and that belong to a person who is not at the time in England, if the owner is regarded as having his permanent home in England. This is a slight move away from the strict territorial principle.

The English law of torts knows comparatively little of any territorial limitation. If an action for damages, for negligence or other wrongful injury committed abroad is brought in an English court, it will in general be determined in accordance with English law and not otherwise. Then again, the law of procedure is hardly in any respect territorial. The English law of procedure is the law of English courts rather than the law of England. It is the same for all litigants who come before those courts, whatever may be the territorial connections of the litigants or of their case of action. Finally, a great qualification upon the territoriality of law is the existence in every legal system of a department known as the conflict of laws. The avowed object of the various system of conflict of laws is to help to regulate situations that have a foreign element.

If a contract is made in France between German and American, and is meant to be performed in Italy, the English courts, if they have to consider a system of law applies to it. The answer is supplied by the department of English law known as the conflict of laws. Suppose that the English system of conflict of laws indicate that French law is to be applied, the English courts will then apply to the contract not the English law of contract, what may be called the domestic law, but the French law of contract. Yet the French law is applied only in virtue of a rule of the English system of conflict of laws. Thus although the English courts do not apply domestic English law to the contract, they do apply the English system of conflict of laws.

It seems, therefore, that the territoriality of law, if considered as something distinct from the territorial enforcement of law, is an idea that fits the facts only in a very imperfect way. It does not follow from the notion of law, but is simply a rule that may or may not be adopted as convenience or policy dictates.

We must also observe that the territoriality of a particular system of law may be regarded very differently in the courts of the state whose law is in questioning the courts of another state, and in international tribunals applying public international law. In the territoriality of law is a matter of self-limitation by the state in question, and varies from state to state. In it is a matter for each state to decide, in framing its rules for the conflicts of the laws, how far it will recognize the legal rule of other states; here again the solution varies from state to states. In there ought in theory to be uniform solution for all states, though the rules of international law cannot be regarded as settled.

The dependence of the "law of the land" upon the court in which the case is heard has also been strikingly illustrated in the United State of America. In the United States each component state possesses its own system of law and federal system of courts. Before 1938 it was possible for the federal court to take a different view of the law of (say) Kentucky from the courts of Kentucky themselves.[57] What such circumstance was "the law of Kentucky?" The answer could only be that "the law of Kentucky" depended upon the court before which the action is brought.

Since territoriality is not a logically necessary part of the idea of law, a system of law is readily conceivable, the application of which is limited and determined not by reference to territorial considerations, but by reference to the personal qualifications of the individuals over whom jurisdiction in exercised: qualifications such as nationality, or religion. The history of early law shows us system of personal law existing to a higher degree. The early law administrated by the courts of Rome was, in the main, not the territorial law of Rome, but the personal law of the Romans. Foreigners had no part in it. It was the *ius civile,* the law of the civvies. It was only by a process of historical development that the *ius gentium* was superadded to the *ius civile* as applicable to civvies and peregrini equally.[58] In Europe, after the dissolution of the Western Roman Empire, the laws were to a large extent conceived as personal rather than territorial, the members of each race or nationality living by their own national laws.[59] A similar process of thought and practice was observable until recently in the ex-territorial administration of the national laws of European states in the consular court abroad was to be regarded rather as the personal law of English men, than as being in any proper or intelligible sense the territorial law of England.

It may be added that in India personal systems of law survive even at the present day, though they are gradually being superseded by legislation which either unifies the law of two or more races (particularly, of course, Hindus and Muslims or applies to the country on a territorial basis. Conflicts to personal law still cause difficulties, for which there are no satisfactory rules.[60]

Constitutional Law

Constitutional law is, as its name implies, the body of those legal rules, which determine the Constitution of the state. It is not possible to draw any hard and fast line between the Constitution and the remaining portions of the state's organization; neither, therefore, is it possible to draw any such line between constitutional law and other branches of the legal system. The distinction is one of degree, rather than one of kind, and is drawn for purpose for practical convenience, rather than in obedience to any logical requirement. The more important, fundamental, and far-reaching principle or practice is, the more likely it is to be classed as constitutional. Conversely, the more special, detailed, and limited in its application, the less likely it is to find a place in any exposition of the law and practice of the

Constitution. The structure of the supreme legislature and the methods of its action pertain to constitutional law; the structure and operations of subordinate legislatures as those possessed by the colonies, are justly entitled to the same position; but those of such subordinate legislature as a borough council would by general consent be treated as not sufficiently important and fundamental to be deemed part of the Constitution. So the organization and powers of the supreme courts of judicator, treated in outline and not in detail, pertain to constitutional law; while it is otherwise with courts of inferior jurisdiction, and with the detailed structure and practice of the Supreme Court itself.

In some states, may be in England, the distinction between constitutional law and the remaining portion of the legal system is accentuated and made definite by the embodiment of the former in a special and distinct enactment, the terms of which cannot be altered by the ordinary forms of legislation. Such constitutions are said to be rigid, as opposed to those, which are flexible, that of the United States of America. The provisions of this document cannot be altered without the consent of three-fourths of the legislature of the different states. The English Constitution on the other hand is flexible; it is defined and set apart in no distinct document, and is not distinguishable from the residue of the law in respect of the methods of its alteration.

We have defined constitutional law as the body of those legal principles which determine the Constitution of a state—which determine, that is to say, the essential and fundamental portions of the state's organization. We have here to face an apparent difficulty and a possible objection. How, it may be asked, can the Constitution of the state be determined by law at all? For constitutional law includes amongst other things the basic rules of recognition of a state's legal system. Does this mean that the State and its Constitution are necessarily prior to the law, and that what passes as constitutional law is in reality not law but a matter of fact and practice?

Admittedly, in certain cases a Constitution may be determined by pre-existing law. On the grant of independence to a colony, the mother country may in accordance with its own legal system enact a Constitution for the new state. Again, the existing Constitution in a state may allow for its replacement by a new Constitution. But apart such cases, every Constitution has an extra-legal origin and the resulting constitutional law depends on the pre-establishment de facto of actual usages and operation.

As an illustration of the proposition that every Constitution has an extra-legal origin, we may take the United State of America. The original constituent states achieved their independence by way of rebellion against the lawful authority of English Crown. Each of these communities thereupon established a Constitution for itself, by way of popular consent expressed directly or through representatives. By virtue of what legal power or authority was this done? Before these constitutions were actually established, there was no law in these colonies save that of England, and it was not by the authority of this law, but in open and forcible defiance of it, that these colonial communities set up new states and new constitutions. Their origin was not merely extra-legal, it was illegal. Yet, so soon as these constitutions succeeded in obtaining de facto establishment in the rebellious colonies, they received recognition as legally valid from the courts of those colonies. Constitutional law followed hard upon the heels of constitutional fact. Courts, legislatures, and law had alike their origin in the Constitution; therefore the Constitution could not derive its origin from them. So, also, with every Constitution that is altered by way of illegal revolution. By what legal title did William III assume the Crown? Yet the Bill of Rights is now good law, and the successors of King William have held the crown by valid titles. *Quod fieri non debet, factum valet.*

But the fact that Constitution of extra-legal origin are not determined by pre-existing law does not prevent the fundamental rules of such constitutions from qualifying as legal rules. From ordinary legal rules, however they differ in one important respect: their authority cannot logically be derived from some more basic legal rule, because they are themselves the basic rules of the legal system. For suppose the constitutional provisions regarding the authority of the legislature were to be enacted by legislation. What would this add? If the legislature has no legal authority, the enactment is void. If it has legal authority, then the enactment is valid but it owes its authority, not to itself, but to the already existing rule conferring authority on the legislature.

The basic rules of a Constitution, then, and of a legal system must ultimately be of customary nature. Even in the case of written Constitution this is so; for here the Constitution in the document owes its validity to the fact that there is in the state in question either a simple customary rule to the effect that this written Constitution has authority, or else a pre-existing customary rules that the method in which the Constitution was made was valid. But any such basic customary rules differ from ordinary customary rules of law in that strictly they are not amenable to alteration be legislation or judicial decision. Ordinary customary rules can be amended or abrogated by such methods. The basic rules of the system too can in fact be altered, but the new rules arising from such alteration owe their validity to the former basic rules, which remain like axiom, from which the whole legal system is derived. On the other hand these fundamental rules are not in the same category as rules of morality. First, as we have seen, there may be no moral justification for having one particular rule of recognition rather than any other; morality may dictate the acceptance of some system of law, but does not tell us which. Secondly, our basic rules share with other legal rules the characteristic of being capable of detailed formalization. The customary rules relating to legislation for example, may descend into a mass of precision and detail. Morality, as we saw, is not susceptible to this kind of development.

Nowhere is this discordance between the constitutions in fact and in law more serious and obvious than in England. A statement of the strict legal theory of the British Constitution would differ curiously from a statement of the actual facts. Similar discrepancies exist, however, in most other states. A complete account of a Constitution, therefore, involves a statement of constitutional custom as well as of constitutional law. It involves as account of the organized state as it exists in practice and in fact, as well as of the reflected image of this organization as it appears in legal theory.

Although the Constitution *de jure* and the Constitution *de facto* are not necessarily the same, they nevertheless tend towards coincidence. Constitutional law and practice react upon each other, each striving to assimilate the other to itself. The objective facts of state organization tend to mould legal theory into conformity with themselves. They seek expression and recognition through legislation, or through the law-creating functions of the courts. Conversely, the accepted legal theory endeavors to realize itself in the facts. The law, although it necessarily involves a pre-existing Constitution, may nevertheless react upon and influence the Constitution from which it springs. It cannot create a *Constitution ex nihilo,* but it may modify to any extent one which already exists. Constitutional practice may alter, while constitutional law remains the same, and vice versa, but the most familiar and effective way of altering the practice is to alter the law. The will of the body politic, as expressed through the legislature and the courts, will commonly realize itself in constitutional and the courts, with constitutional theory by the analysis of opinion of Salmond, as a whole. Now it is clear once again that real purpose of law is justice subject to certain exception as described above. It may be condemned that primary base of law is justice and it takes to maintain balance and stability in society just to keep pace with time for regular changes using to time.

Hibbert defines[61] Constitutional Law as "the body of rules governing the relation between the sovereign and his subjects and the different parts of the sovereign body."

According to Dicey[62]: "Constitutional law includes all rules which directly or indirectly effect the distribution or exercise of the sovereign power of the State. Hence it includes (among other things) all rules which define the members to each other or which determine the mode in which the sovereign power or the members thereof exercise their authority."

Wade and Phillips[63] write: "There is no hard and fast definition of constitutional law. In the generally accepted use of term, it means the rule of law, including binding convention, which regulate the structure of the principle organ of government and their inter-relations and the position of the members of the community in relation to those organs and functions of the State."

The conclusion of Austin is that constitutional law is not positive law or law in the strict sense but is merely positive morality. Constitutional law derives its force only from public opinion regarding its expediency and morality. It belongs only to the class of moral rules and cannot be regarded as a part of positive law.

Salmond writes that the organization of a modern State is of extraordinary complexity. It is usually divided into two distinct parts. The first part consists of the details of State structure and State action. The first part is known as the Constitution of the State.

In some States, though not in England, the distinction between constitutional law and the remaining portions of the legal system is made definite by the embodiment of the former in a special and distinct enactment, the terms which cannot be altered by the ordinary forms of legislation. Such constitutions are said to be rigid, as opposed to those, which are flexible. The Constitution of the United State is set forth in a document agreed upon by the founders of the Commonwealth as containing all those principle of State structure and action sufficiently important to be deemed fundamental and therefore constitutional. The provisions of this fundamental document cannot be altered without the consent of three-fourths of the legislatures of the different

States. The English Constitution is flexible and is not to be found in a document. The method of its amendment is easy.

Salmond points out, if constitutional law is the body of those legal principles, which determine the Constitution of a State, the problem is how the Constitution of a State can be determined by law at all. There can be no law unless there is already a State and there can be no State without a Constitution. If the State and the Constitution are prior to the law, law cannot determine the Constitution. Therefore it can be said that constitutional law is not law in reality. The Constitution is both a matter of fact and law. It consists not only of legal rules but also of constitutional practices. Constitutional principles are logically prior to constitutional law. There may be a State and a Constitution without any law, but there can be no law without a State and a Constitution. No Constitution can have its source and basis in the law. It has an extra-legal origin.

The basic rules of a Constitution and of a legal system must ultimately be of customary nature. This is so even in a written Constitution. Basic customary rules differ form ordinary customary rules of law in that strictly they are not amenable to alteration by legislation or judicial decision. Ordinary customary rules can be amended or abrogated by such methods. Fundamental rules are not in the same category as the rules of morality.

A complete account of a Constitution involves a statement of constitutional custom as well as of constitutional law. It involves an account of the organized State, as it exists in practice and in fact, as well as of the reflected image of that organization as it appears in legal history.

The *Constitution de jure* and the *Constitution de facto* are not necessarily the same but they tend towards coincidence. Constitutional law and practice react upon each other, each striving to assimilate the other to itself. Constitutional practice may alter while constitutional law remains the same and vice-versa. The most familiar and effective way of altering the practice is to alter the law. The will of the body politic, as expressed through the legislature and the courts, will commonly realize itself in constitutional fact no less than in constitutional theory.

Administrative Law

According to Prof. Wade: "Administrative law is primarily concerned not with judicial control nor even legislation by delegation but with administration." According to Dr. Jennings: "Administrative law is the law relating to the administration. It determines the organization, powers and duties of administrative authorities."

The view of Austin is that administrative law determines "the ends and modes to end in which the sovereign powers shall be exercised directly by the monarch or sovereign member or shall be exercised directly by the subordinate political superiors to whom portions of those powers are dedicated or committed in trust."

Prof. Holland divides public law into six divisions and puts administrative law in the second category. According to him, constitutional law is concerned with structure and administrative law is concerned with functions.

According to Prof. Robson, the term administrative law implies the jurisdiction of a judicial nature exercised by administrative agencies over the rights and properties of citizens and corporate bodies.

In France, the term *Droit Administratif* is used in place of administrative law. According to Barthelemy, it "consists of all the legal rules governing the relations of public administrative bodies to one another and to individuals". Prof. Rene David defines *Droit Administratif* as "the body of rules which determine the organization and the duties of public administration and which regulate the relations of the administrative authorities towards the citizens of the State".

A distinction is made between administrative law and constitutional law. According to Holland, constitutional law deals with various organs of sovereign power as at rest and administrative law deals with those organs as in motion. The first deals with the structure and the second with the functions of the State. The distinction between the two is one of degree and convenience and not of principles relating to organization and power of organs of the State and their relations inter se and towards the citizens, administrative law is that aspect of constitutional law which deals in detail with the powers and functions of administrative authorities.

Kinds Of Law

Sir John Salmond had classified law into eight groups. These eight groups are as follows:

1. Imperative Law

According to Salmond: "Imperative law means a rule which prescribes a general course of action imposed by some authority which enforces it by superior power either by physical force or any other form of compulsion." The chief advocate of imperative law is Austin who defines law as a command which obliges a person or persons to a course of conduct.

It is in the very nature of the law to be imperative, otherwise it is not law but a rule, which may or may not be obeyed. Imperative law has been classified with reference to the authority from which they proceed. They are either divine or human. Divine law consists of the commands imposed by God upon men and they are enforced by threats of punishment in this world or in the next world. Human law consists of imperative rule imposed upon men. Those are of three kinds: civil law, law of positive morality and law of nations or international law. Civil law consists of commands issued by the state to its subjects and enforced by its physical power. The law of positive morality consists of rules imposed by society upon its members and enforced by public censure or disapprobation. International law consists of rules imposed upon states by the society of states and enforced partly by international opinion and partly by the threat of war.

2. Physical or Scientific Laws

According to Salmond: "Physical law or laws of science are an expression of the uniformities of nature-general principles expressing the regularity and harmony observable in the activated and operations of the universe". Physical laws are so called natural laws or laws of nature. There is uniformity and regularity in those laws. They are not the creation of men and cannot be changed by them. Human laws change from time to time and country-to-country but physical laws are invariable and immutable forever.

3. Natural Law or Moral Law

According to Salmond: "By natural law or moral law is meant the principles of natural right and wrong-the principles of natural justice if we use the term justice in its widest sense to include all forms of rightful action". Natural law has been called Divine law, the law of reason, the universal or common law and eternal law. It is called the command of God imposed upon men. It is established by that reason by which the world is governed. It is unwritten law and is not written on brazen tablets or pillars of stone but by the finger of nature in the hearts of men. It is universally obeyed in all places and by all people. It has existed from the beginning of the world and hence is called eternal. Divine law is also called natural law as its principles are supposed to have been laid down by God for the guidance of mankind. It is called rational law as it is supposed to be based on reason. It is called unwritten law as it is not to be found in the form of a code. All these are not considered to be satisfactory but they point out the various characteristics of natural law. Natural law appeals to the reason of man. It is addressed to intelligent human beings. It does not posess physical compulsion. It embodies the principles of morality. Its principles are common to all the states. Natural law exists only in an ideal State and differs from positive law of a state.

The law of nature puts forward an ideal to be followed. This was actually done by writers like Hegel, Kant, Paine, Aristotie, Locke, and Hume etc. During the Middle Ages, the law of nature was considered to be a higher law, which was imposed on the people by the command of God. The law of nature sets up an ideal, which the legal systems of the countries try to achieve.

The view of Dias and Hughes is that some of the contributions of the philosophy of natural law to human progress are epoch-making.

(a) The various doctrines have always served the social need of the age. They have helped to maintain stability against changes as in the time of the Greeks and the medieval church. They have inspired change against stability, notably after the Reformation and the Renaissance.

(b) The philosophy of natural law has inspired legislation and the use of reason in formulating systems of law.

(c) The period from the Renaissance down to the 18th century witnessed a lasting distinction drawn between positive law and morality.

(d) The same period also brought about the emancipation of the individual.

(e) A strong connection was established between positive law and freedom of the individual.

(f) The natural rights of the individual acquired great significance.

In the United States, they are enshrined in the Constitution. It is not always possible to justify arguments that have been founded on the doctrine of natural rights. Thus, slavery was justified on the ground that the right of property was a natural right. As slaves were property, slavery was a natural right and unalterable. Liberty in the Fourteenth Amendment of the American Constitution has been held to include unlimited freedom of contract and "person" has come to cover corporations. The result is that big corporations have been able to protect themselves behind the cover of the natural rights of an individual.

The influence of natural law ideas on English lawyers was also great. One of the effects was the doctrine of the supremacy of law. Natural law theories are reflected in the writings of certain legal authors such as Fortesque, Blackstone and St. Jerman. The modern law of quasi-contract was erected from avowed principles of natural justice. The conflict of laws was originally founded on natural justice. The judicial control of administrative and quasi-judicial functions is based on the principle that those who administer them must abide by the principles of natural justice.

There is widespread revival of the concept of natural law in the world and there are many reasons for it. There is a general desire to restore closer relations between law and morality. People are not satisfied with the Austinian view of law which ignores morality altogether. It is also felt that there is a necessity for a juristic basis for a progressive interpretation of positive law. The development of sociological theories demand that the theory of law should allow a judicial interpretation of positive law in accordance with changing ideas and circumstances. The development of idea of relativity in modern law has removed the chief difficulty in the way of the old idea of natural law. Laws can be universal and still vary in their contents. No law is eternal and every law must change according to circumstances. There is evolution everywhere. According to Kohler, law is based on reason and the actual law at any time in an country depends upon the stage of the development of the people concerned.

4. Conventional Law

According to Salmond, conventional law means "any rule or system of rules agreed upon by persons for the regulation of their conduct towards each other". It is a form of special law. It is law for the parties who subscribe to it. Examples of conventional law are the laws of cricket or any other game, rules and regulations of a club or any other voluntary society. Conventional law in same cases is enforced by the state. When it is enforced by the state, it becomes a part of the civil law. The view of some writers is that international law or the law of nations is also a kind of conventional law on the ground that its principles are expressly or impliedly agreed upon by the States concerned.

5. Customary Law

According to Salmond, customary law means "any rule of action which is actually observed by men—any rule which is the expression of some voluntary action." A custom may be voluntary and still it is law. When a custom is firmly established, it is enforced by the authority of the state. Customary law is an important source of law. This is particularly so among the conservative people who want to keep as much of the past as possible.

Before codification, almost the whole of Hindu law was based on custom. Then came the Hindu Marriage Act in 1955. More Acts were passed on Hindu law in the succeeding years. The result is that the Hindu law regarding marriage, succession, minority and guardianship, adoption and maintenance is codified and governed by appropriate statutes. Custom can never override statute law. The custom of sati cannot be pleaded to a charge of murder or its abetment.

6. Practical or Technical Law

Practical or technical law consists of rules for the attainment of certain ends e.g., the laws of health, the laws of architecture etc. These rules guide us as to what we ought to do in order to attain a certain end. Within this category come the laws of music, laws of architecture, laws of style, etc.

7. International Law

According to Lord Birkenhead, international law consists of rules acknowledged by the general body of civilized independent States to be binding upon them in their mutual relations. It consists of those rules which govern sovereign States in their relations and conduct towards each other.

According to Starke, international may be defined, for its great part, of the principles and rules of conduct which States feel themselves bound to observe and therefore do commonly observe in their relations with each other and which includes also (a) the rules of law relating to functioning of international institutions and organizations, their relations with each other and their relations with states and individuals and (b) certain rules of law relating to individuals so far as the rights and duties of such individuals are the concern of the international community.

Dias and Hughes write: "International law is the body of principles and rules, which civilized States, consider as binding upon them in their mutual relations. It rests upon the consent of Sovereign States".

Hall observes: "International law consists in certain rules of conduct which modern civilized States regard as binding on them in their relation with one another with a force comparable in nature and degree to that binding the conscientious persons to obey the laws of the country and which they also regard as enforceable by appropriate means in case of infringement".

According to Lord Russel of Killowen, international is "the aggregate of the rules to which the nations have agreed to confirm in their conduct towards one another".

Oppenheim writes: "International law is the name for the body of customary and conventional rules which are considered legally binding (as distinguished from usage, morality and rules of so-called international comity) by civilized States in their intercourse with each other."

According to Salmond, international law is essentially a species of conventional law and has its source in international agreement. It consists of those rules which the sovereign States have agreed to observe in their dealings with one another.

Nature of International Law

There is considerable divergence of opinion regarding the true nature of international law. John Austin, Willoughby and Holland regard international law as positive morality or the moral code of nations and do not concede that it is law properly so-called. If we accept Austin's definition of law as a command addressed to political inferiors by a political sovereign superior and followed by a sanction in the event of disobedience, international law cannot be called law.

According to Holland, international law is the vanishing point of jurisprudence as it lacks any arbiter of disputed question save public opinion, beyond and above the disputant parties themselves. Such rules are voluntary and though habitually observed by every State in its dealings with the rest, can be called law only by courtesy.

According to Lord Salisbury, international law "can be enforced by no tribunal and therefore to apply to it the phrase law is to some extent misleading".

Dias and Huge writes that it is an undoubted fact that the respect which States pay to international law is less than that which individuals pay to municipal law. There has always been a need to enhance the prestige of international law by calling in aid the magic of the word "Law," especially in creating a sense of obligations. This is one reason why international lawyers are sensitive about Austin's exclusion of international law from the scope of law and want to prove that international law is really law.

The view of Professor Hart is that there are sufficient analogies of content, as opposed to form, none bring the rules of international law nearer to municipal law. There are rules prescribing how States ought to behave, which are accepted as guiding standards just as in municipal law. Appeals are made to precedent, writings and treatises as in municipal law and not to rightness or morality. Rules of international law, like those municipal laws, can be morally neutral. Like rules of municipal law, they can be changed by conscious act, e.g., by treaty.

Professor Dias points out that in spite of these resemblances between international law and municipal law, there are two important differences between them, which cannot be overlooked. One difference is that the subjects of international law are primarily States and the disparity in strength between them far exceeds that between individuals in society. Individuals as such are increasingly becoming subjects of international law, which enhance the disparity between the various subjects. The other difference is that whereas the courts of a municipal order appeal to the same criterion or criteria by which to identify "Laws," there is no coordination in the ways in which rules of international law are identified. There is no single criterion of identification because there are unrelated sets of tribunals, each of which identifies international law differently.

The basis of the binding force of international law is commonly ascribed to consent, but this is not a satisfactory explanation. A basic consent presupposes some rule which makes consent obligatory. The basis of that rule requires elucidation. If consent is the basis, it follows that once consent is withdrawn, the obligation to obey ceases. In municipal law, consent is unrealistic. Individuals are never asked if they consent to be found by municipal laws, which are treated as binding regardless of consent. Even if some dissident declares that he no longer accepts a law, his withdrawal does not affect the coercive power of the State, which comes into play irrespective of what the individual thinks. The so-called "binding force" rests in the psychological reactions including people to obey, among which fear of organized force in one factor. In the international sphere there is no effective machinery for applying overwhelming organized force. The great shortcoming of international law is the absence of effective machinery to carry out sanctions. In any case, such action is more likely to influence weak rather than strong States. Whether or not a given State at any time abides by a give rule of international law depends upon various considerations such as a desire to secure fair treatment for its own nationals at the hands of other States, nationalism, tradition, morality, diplomacy, economic interests and possibly fear. This shows that the working of international law is different from that of municipal law. International law continues mainly because States find in it a useful instrument of policy.

According to Oppenheim, international law is law in the true sense of the term. For hundreds of years, more and more rules have grown up for the conduct of the States with one another. These rules are to a great extent customary rules but along with them are daily created more and more written rules by international agreements. Oppenheim admits that there is at present no Central Government above the government of the rules of international law. For this reason, compared with municipal laws and the means available for its enforcement the law of nations is certainly weaker of the two. A law is the stronger, if more guarantees are given that it can and will be enforced. Starke writes: "International law is a weak law. It is mainly customary. Existing international legislative machinery is not comparable in efficiency to State legislative machinery. In spite of the achievements of the United Nations in re-establishing a world court under the name of the International Court of Justice, there still is no universal compulsory jurisdiction for settling legal disputes between States. Finally, many of the rules of international law can only be formulated with difficulty and, to say the least, are quite uncertain. It was on this account that the attempt of the International Conference of 1930 at Hague to codify certain branches of international law suffered a relative break down".

International law is regarded as a part of American Law and is ascertained and administered by the court justice of appropriate jurisdiction. Likewise, the law the Prize Courts administer in England is not municipal law but international law.

8. Civil Law

According to Salmond, civil law is "the law of the State or of the land, the law of lawyers and the law courts." Civil law is the positive law of the land or the law as it exists. Like any other law, it is uniform and that uniformity is established by judicial precedents. It is noted for its constancy because without that, it would be nothing but the law of the jungle. It is enjoyed by the people who inhabit a particular State, which commands obedience through the judicial processes. It is backed by the force and might of the State for purpose of enforcement. Civil law has an imperative character and has legal sanction behind it. It is essentially of territorial nature. It applies within the territory of the State concerned. It is not universal but general. It creates legal rights. Whether fundamental or primary. It also creates secondary rights. Any infringement of law is always attendant with attachments, fine or imprisonment, or some other form of punishment, which the society inflicts on the wrongdoer in order to show its displeasure against the person who violates the law.

The term civil law is derived from *jus civile* or civil law of the Romans. It is not so popular today as it used to be. The term positive law has become more popular than civil law. Sometimes, the term municipal law is used in place of civil law.

Holland prefers to use the term positive law and writes thus: "A law in the sense in which that term is employed in jurisprudence, is enforced by a sovereign political authority. It is thus distinguished not only from other rule which, like the principles of morality and the so-called laws of honour and of fashion are enforced by an indeterminate authority which is either, on the one hand, superhuman or on the other hand, politically subordinate. In order to emphasize the fact that laws, in the strict sense of the term, are thus authoritatively imposed, they are described as positive laws".

However Salmond prefers to use the term civil law instead of positive law and observes: "The term civil law, as indicating the law of the land, has been partially superseded in recent times by the improper substitute, positive law. *Jus positivum* was a title invented by medieval jurists to denote law made or established by human authority as opposed to the *jus naturale,* which was uncreated and immutable. It is from this contrast that the term positive derives all its point and significance. It is not permissible, therefore, to confine positive law to the law of the land. All law is positive that is not natural. International law, for example, is a kind of *jus positivum,* no less than the civil law itself."

Common Law

According to Salmond: "The common law is the entire body of English law, the total *corpus juris angliae* with three exceptions, namely (1)statute law, (2) equity and (3) special law in its various forms.'' The expression common law was adopted by English lawyers from the canonists who used it to denote the general law of the church as opposed to those divergent usages which prevailed in different local jurisdiction and superseded or modified within their territorial limits the common law of Christendom. The development of common law is closely associated with the growth of King's justice in England after the Norman Conquest.

By the beginning of the 14th century, the Court of Chancery arose and began to administer justice by the side of common law courts. Equity was finally absorbed into the general law when the Judicature Act of 1873 united the common law and equity jurisdictions. Though equity and common law have become co-ordinate parts of a single system of general law, the original jurisdiction between them still persists and the term Common Law is even now used in contrast with equity.

Up to 1873, there were two distinct systems of law in England administered by the ordinary courts of justice viz., the King's Bench, the Court of Common Pleas and the Court of Exchequer. In the Court of Chancery, the Chancellor decided cases not according to the common law but according to the principles of equity. The Judicature Act 1873 provided for a High Court of Justice with a Court of Appeal over it. The High Court of Justice was divided into five divisions: the Chancery, the Queen's Bench, Common Pleas, exchequer and the Probate and the Divorce and Admiralty.

Equity

It was found during the 13th century in England that common law had become very rigid and that rigidity should be lessened by supplementing it by rules governed by the conscience of the judge. There were certain rules of natural justice prevalent at that time and those were used to supplement the principles of common law. The result was that a party who could not get any relief in the ordinary course, applied to the King who was the fountain of justice. The king referred those petitions to the Lord Chancellor, considered those applications and gave relief in fit cases, particularly in those of frauds, errors and unjust judgements.

In course of time, the Lord Chancellor advised the judges of the Court of Chancery to supplement the law by principles of equity justice and good conscience. This resulted in a variety of decisions of a conflicting nature. It was found necessary to have uniformity in those judgements. That led to the formation of a body of equitable rules, which were supplementary to the rules of common law. During the reign of Henry VI, the Lord Chancellor developed the remedy of injunction, which emanated from Chancery Courts. By this remedy, the Chancellor prohibited the execution of decrees past by the common law courts. It was in the matter of injunctions that there was a conflict between Lord Chancellor Ellesmere and Chief Justice Coke of the Common Law. Lord Chancellor issued an injunction prohibiting the holder of a decree obtained by fraud from executing it and that decree had been passed by Chief Justice Coke. This dispute was referred to Lord Bacon who was the Attorney-General of England and he decided in favor of the Lord Chancellor. The result was that equitable principles came to be recognized as principles superior to the rules of common law. During the Chancellor ship of Lord Eldon, equity became a body of principles decided on the basis of precedents laid down by the judges in the Equity Courts. Today equity has been merged into law. "The two streams flow side by side but their waters do not mingle". Equitable principles are as effective as the principles of common law.

Equity becomes a source of law. The principle emanating from the conscience of the judge were made uniform and they were made into a body of rules called the rules of equity or equitable law. Out of the equitable principles have emerged laws such as Law of Trusts, the Law of Mortgages, the Law of Quasi-Contracts, the Doctrine in the partnership Act and the companies Act. Several principle of equity is embodied in the Specific Relief Act.

General Law and Special Law

According to Salmond, the whole body of law can be divided into two parts: general law and special law. General law consists of the general or the ordinary law of the land. Special law consists of certain other bodies of legal rules which are so special and exceptional in their nature, sources or application that it is inconvenient to treat them as standing outside the general and ordinary law. General law consists of those legal rules, which are taken judicial notice of by the courts whenever there is any occasion for their application. Special law consists of the legal rules which courts will not recognize and apply them as a matter of course but which must be specially proved and brought to the notice of the courts by the parties interested in their recognition. According to Salmond, the best of distinction is judicial notice. By judicial notice is meant the knowledge which any court, ex officio, possesses and acts upon as contrasted with the knowledge, which a court is bound to acquire on the strength of evidence, produced for the purpose.

The matter can be illustrated by taking an example of one type of special law or custom. The court may not and ordinarily it does not, know what a particular custom is. The parties have to prove such a custom if they rely upon it.

Ordinarily, special laws are the very opposite of statue laws which courts are bound to know. Ignorance of law is no excuse. If a person does not take a license for his dog due to negligence, he cannot take up the plea of his ignorance.

The fact that the sun rises in the east and sets in the west need not be proved by evidence. The court is presumed and bound to know them suo moto. Likewise, the court is bound to take judicial notice of all the statue laws.

Kinds of Special Law

Salmond refers to six kinds of special laws and those are Local Law, Foreign Law, Conventional Law, Autonomic Law, Martial Law and International Law as administered in Prize Courts.

(1) Local Law: Local law is the law of a particular law locality and not the general law of the whole country. There may be customs, which have obtained the force of law in certain localities and within those localities, that customary law superseded the general law. An easement right to privacy does not exist under the general law, but can be claimed by custom in Uttar Pradesh and Gujarat. A right of pre-emption in respect of immovable property cannot be claimed under the general law but such a right is recognized by custom in Bihar, Haryana and Delhi.

In addition to local customary law, there may be local enacted law, which consists of enactments emanating from subordinate local legislative authority. They are recognized as having full force in the locality for which they have been formulated.

(2) Foreign Law: It is essential in many cases to take account of a system of foreign law and to determine the rights and liabilities of the parties on that basis. Ignorance of law is no excuse and everyone is supposed to know the law of the law of the land. However, ignorance of foreign law, of a fact and can be excused.

In some cases, foreign law has to be taken into consideration to do justice between the parties. In the case of a contract entered into in a foreign country, justice cannot be done fully unless the case is decided according to the law of the place where the contract was entered into. Every State has evolved a set of rules, which prescribe the conditions, and circumstances in which foreign law is enforced by its courts. This is done for the sake of international community. There is a sort of reciprocity in this matter and if one State accepts, it can expect the same from other States. The rules, which regulate the application of foreign law, are known as the Conflict of Laws or Private International Law. The rules of Private International Law may vary from state to state. The French have different rules from those of England. The same is true of the United States. While public international law is concerned with States, private international law is concerned with individuals and never with States.

(3) Conventional Law: Conventional law has its source in the agreement of those who are subject to it. Agreement is law for those who make it. Examples of conventional law are the rules of a club or a co-operative society. Some other examples of conventional law are the articles of association of a company, articles of partnership etc.

(4) Autonomic Law: By autonomic law is meant that species of law, which has its source in various forms of subordinate legislative authority, possessed by private persons and bodies of persons. A railway company may make byelaws for regulating its traffic. Likewise, a university may make statutes for the government of its members. An incorporated company can alter its articles and impose new rules and regulations upon the shareholders.

(5) Martial Law: Martial law is the law administered in the courts maintained by military authorities. Martial law is of there kinds:

i. It is the law for the discipline and control of the army itself and is commonly known as the military law. It affects the army alone and never the civil population.

ii. The second kind of martial law is that by which in times of war, the army governs any foreign land in its military occupation. The country is governed by the military commander through the prerogative of the sovereign. The law in this case depends upon the pleasure of the military commanders.

iii. The third kind of martial law is the law by which in times of war, the army governs the realm itself in derogation of the civil law so far as the same is required for public safety or military necessity. The temporary establishment of military justice can be justified on the ground of necessity. The establishment of a military government and military Justice is known as the proclamation of martial law. Courts cannot question the validity of the actions of a military commander if he had acted honestly.

Martial law is not to be confused with military law. The two are different concepts. While military law is a State law, martial law is based on common law. Military law is applicable to soldiers alone and is embodied in the Army Act. Offences under this Act are triable by the court- martial. As an ordinary citizen, a soldier is governed by the ordinary law of the land. While military law is applicable to soldiers alone, martial law is applicable to soldiers as well as civilians in times of war or tumult. Even when there is no war or rebellion, soldiers are governed by military law. Martial law is temporary while military law is permanent law.

(6) International Law as administered in Prize Courts (Prize Law): International law is kind of conventional law. As a special law, it refers to that portion of the law of the nations, which is administered by the Prize Courts of the State in times of war. Prize law is that part of law which regulate the practice of the capture of ships and cargoes at sea in times of war. International law requires that all Sates desiring to exercise the right of capture must establish and maintain within their territories what are known as Prize Courts. It is the duty of those courts to investigate the legality of all the captures of ships and cargoes. If the seizure is lawful, the property is adjudged as a lawful prize of war. If the same is found unlawful, orders are passed for the return of that property. Prize Courts are established by and belong exclusively to the individual State by which the ships and cargoes are captured. In spite of that, the law administered by the Prize Court is not the law of the country but international law. Lord Parker writes: "The law which the Prize Court is to administer is not national law or as it is sometimes called, the municipal law, but the law of nations—in other words, international law. Of course, the Prize Court is a municipal court and its decrees and orders owe their validity to municipal law. The law it enforces may therefore in one sense be considered a branch of municipal law".

Prize courts were set up to decide the fate of the ships and cargoes captured during the war between India and Pakistan in 1971.

Now in conclusion, classification of laws is not only desirable but also necessary.

Classification of laws has been made from time to time. The Romans jurists attempted a classification of laws. The Hindu law-givers gave 18 titles of heads of vyavahara or civil law. They made a distinction between civil and also classified criminal law under various heads.

While classifying laws, we must not forget that no classification of laws is going to be permanent. Every classification is based on the law as it was when the classification was made.

Law may be broadly divided into two classes: international law and national or state law.

International law is divided into two classes: public international law and private international law. Public international law is that body of rules which governs the conduct and relations of the States with each other. By private international law we mean those rules and principles according to which cases having foreign element are decided. Private international law applies to individuals and not to States. Moreover, the rules and principles of private international law vary from State to State and there is no uniformity. Private international law is enforced by municipal courts, which apply municipal law and not international law. In order to avoid controversy, it is suggested that private international law be called Conflict of Laws and should be treated as a branch of municipal private law.

National Law or State Law

It is the law applied within the State. It can be divided into two classes: public law and private law. Private law determines and regulates the organization and functioning of the State and determines the relation of the state with its subjects.

Private law is divided into three classes: constitutional law, administrative law and criminal law. Constitutional law determines the nature of the State and structure of the government. It is superior to the ordinary law of the land.

Constitutional law is written in India and the United States but it is unwritten in England. The modern tendency is to have written constitutions.

Administrative law deals with the structure, powers and function of the organization of administration, the limits of their powers, the methods and procedures followed by them and the methods by which their powers are controlled including the legal remedies available to persons whose rights have been infringed.

Criminal law defines offences and prescribes punishments for them. It not only prevents crimes but also punishes the offenders. Criminal law is necessary for the maintenance of law and order and peace within the State.

Private law regulates and governs the relations of citizens with one another. The parties are private individuals and the State decides the dispute among the people. There is great difficulty in classifying private law. A general classification of general law is the law of persons, the law of property, the law of obligations, the conflict of laws, contracts, quasi-contracts and tort.

The following is general classification of law:-

Some New Kinds of Law: an act which is in contravention to the known electronically developed system of law such as cyber law can be known by vision, nods or electronics devices even sitting at a long distance. Internet, Email or Cyber laws are taken examples of it. These laws can be said to be technical laws because the violation of systematic rule of manufacture or processing of electronic devices by a person for his own benefit or for benefit of others by vision, audio-video visual or by other electronics devices are chief example.

There may be other forms of laws also, which are not apparent today but may be very important for tomorrow in future. Present law may be obsolete tomorrow, even today several laws framed before independence of India are still obsolete and useless. Hence the kinds and classification of laws can not be static, it is dynamic. It is progressive not rigid. It is not permanent or universal; it has to keep peace with society, noting down and taking in view the need of time & society.

Classification of law by Holland as follows:-

From one point of view: -

1. Private Law
2. Public Law
3. International Law

Another point of views: -

Law of persons, Law of things from another points of view:-

1. Substantive & Adjective Law
2. Private, public, international law
3. Normal and abnormal law
4. Law of rights in rem and rights in pesonam
5. The laws of rights Antecedent and of rights remedial

Classification of law by Austin is as follows:-

1. Divine Law
2. Human Law
3. Positive morality (improperly called law)
4. Laws metaphorically or figuratively so called:-

   i. **Divine Law**

      a) Revealed

      b) Unrevealed

   ii. **Human Law**

      a) Positive Law

      b) Positive Moral Law

(Rules set by a non-political superior e.g. international law)

   iii. Not Classified

      a) Law of Art

      b) Self prescribed rules of conduct

      c) Laws of Nature

Purposes Of Law

According to Pound, sociologists there are 4 purposes-

1) Purpose of Law is to maintain law & order situation.
2) To maintain the status in society, to keep standard of living every person well firm without fear.
3) Purpose of law is to enable individual to have the maximum freedom to assert themselves, to have the people natural liberty.
4) Maximum satisfaction of needs of people.

Purpose of Law by Gilbert is as follows-

"Law is the embodiment of everything that is excellent."

Stamonler-"The object of law is to give every person adequate means of self expressions."

Purpose of Law by Justice Holme is as follows-

"The object of law is not the punishment of sins but to prevent some external results".

One school only regards purpose of law for the purpose of maintaining law and order situation. Hindu Law regards welfare of people as purpose of law. While Muslim law regards purpose of law as discipline of soul, the improvement of moral & preservation of life, property and reputation.

Law & Morality

The ultimate purpose and object of the law is to maintain the morality in society. Law and morality have had a long marriage with occasional desertion and judicial separation but all together never a divorce. Pound has discovered four stages in the development of Law with respect to morality. The first stages of undifferentiated ethical a custom, customs of popular actions, religion and law. Then law was not different from morality but the analytical jurist says that it was pre-legal stage. Second stage is modified or crystallized which in time out striped by morality and has not sufficient power of growth to keep abreast. Third stage is reshaping of law by intrusion of morality into law. In that stage both the ideas of equity and natural law are effective agencies of growth. The fourth stage is of conscious, constructive law making the maturity of law in which it is said that the morals and morality are for the lawmakers and that law alone is for the judge.

It is definite that the religion and religious customs have formed definite sources of law and justice. From this point of view jurisprudence is closely allied with religious morality.

Lord Denning discusses the influence of Christianity. In the laws of England first search from the truth is the basis of justice-secondly he indicates good faith and reasonableness in law as mark of religious Christian influence on English law, thirdly he sees the reflection of the biblical injunction "Love thy neighbor" in justice & civil wrong by pointing out that primary ends of social organization is justice and love is both the basic and frame the reference of civil wrong, fourthly the principle of Christianity of sanctity to human life and individual responsibility and sees its influence in new trends of criminal jurisprudence. Fifthly the principle of unselfishness in the modern laws and jurisprudence trying to restrain narrow individualism. Sixthly marriage as an institution under Christian Church and principle of family life has found their recognition in laws.

Lord Denning also indicated that Lord Atkin and Justice Coke spent one fourth of each day in prayers and also pointed out about the contribution of these jurists of religion in law. He also pointed out that the whole truth and no half-truth's principle in law is illustration of Christian influence in English law as case law it was same held by House of Lord King v/s Kylsant.

Recently professor Hart has examined this question in recent book by analogizing the significant aspect of problem of moral & laws. Here he discusses the use of criminal law so before morality in particular reference with the offences of rape (sexual offences) and he examine the observation of John Stuart Mill "the only purpose for which power can be exercised rightfully over any member of the civilized community is to prevent holism to others," this has been in the last 100 years a subject of sharp challenge from Sir J.M.

Stephen. The conclusion of Pro. Hart is that they failed to recognize the distinction of vital importance for legal and political theory and their views of the functions of legal punishment are not shared by many. There is no doubt that development of the law has been influenced by the morals and this is acknowledged by Prof. Hart. He, however, raises the question whether development of morality has been influenced by law.

Justice Mukharjee says that law has not only developed moralities by reforming and clarifying old moralities. But also creating new moralities or widening the old moralities. Many new moralities has been created in the sphere industrial, social and administrative sphere and in other ways of jurisprudence.

Prof. Hart acknowledges that moralities often into adequate definition of law and legal system. But poses the question where it is a contingent fact, law & morality often overlaps as far instances in their common prescription of certain forms of violent and honestly and because of the fact that they share vocabulary of right obligation and duty. And lastly, Prof. Hart opens a very fundamental problem "is law open to moral criticism. "But the whole problem as discussed by Hart is the problem of legal enforcement of morality. In other words he raises the question "in the fact that certain conduct is by common standard immoral sufficient to justify making that conduct punishable by law." Is it inertly permissible to enforce morality as such. Ought immorality to as such be a crime. The question of professor Hart was the suicide act 1961- he described this act as a landmark in English legal history because it is first act of parliament for at least it embodies to remove all together the penalties of criminal law from a practice both morality condemn by conventional moral Christianity and punishable by law. He expressed the hope that suicide act might be followed by further measures to reform to the extent that certain forms of homosexual behavior and abortion between consorting advents in private life will cease to be crime offenses. But this may create hue and cry as it has created in India by legalizing the abortions up to 3 months pregnancy. If law is good part of sociology and social control then such sociology is not an unequivocal support of such new morality.

Law has to be an anchor somewhere and is not merely a servant of the passion of the day but is also the censor of certain standard and also an ideal conduct.

About the purposes of law, socialistic, communistic and soviet views are different. A.Denisov (64) says that- Law expresses the state will of the economically and politically dominant class determined in the final count by the dominant mode of production. The class with character of law consisting in it, not only reflecting the given economic basis, but also actively promoting the protection, strengthening and development of a given social relations in the interests of the prominent class.

Because law is a system of universally mandatory norms and rules of behaviour, established or recognized (sanctioned) by the state, protected from in fragment with the help of the state apparatus of coercion.

Irrespective of the forms in which they are manifested, rules of law are general and abstract in character. They constitute general rules for typical situations, and are applicable to all members of the society or to specific categories of people.

Law differs from the other social norms of a class society(those of morality, customs, traditions, non-government organizations, and so on) in its inseparable link with the state: it expresses the state will of the dominant class. With the help of the state, the dominant class makes its will the law that is mandatory and independent of the arbitrary powers of the individuals. Observance of rules of law is ensured by a special apparatus of coercion – the state supervises and controls the observance of rules of law, punishes those who violate legal prohibitions, restoring, if possible, the infringed rights and settles legal disputes by force.

Law regulates not all social relations and people's actions, but merely those that, first, seem particularly important to the dominant class from the point of view of its own interests, determined by the material conditions of its life; second, the relations that can be protected by an apparatus of state coercion, and permit supervision and control by state bodies over the actions of the participants in these relations. Legal regulation cannot embrace absolutely all social relations and people's actions, since any attempt to implement such regulation would make law virtually boundless, and the state machinery impossibly expensive and unwieldy.

Law is not the only regulator of social relations in a class society. These relations and people's behavior are also regulated by the norms of morals, customs, traditions, religious and other norms. When raising its will to the status of law, the dominant class takes account of the prospects for the interaction between law and other social norms and the ideology of the class society, exerting an influence on people's behavior with the help not only of law, but also other norms expressing the will of the same class.

Historically, the first class society was the slave-owning one, which openly expressed the class division of society by viewing slaves as belonging completely to their masters. The basic provision of law in slave-owing society was "slaves are things," which secured the full might of the exploiters and their economic, political and personal power over enormous numbers of slaves. The essence of slave-owing law was also expressed in the establishment of legal inequality among the freemen, the granting of a number of special rights and privileges to the upper echelons of slave-owing society (the nobility, rich people, priests, and so on). Thus, according to the laws of Manu in Ancient India, there existed four varnas Brahmans (priests), Kshatriyas (military men), Vaishyas (merchants, artisans and peasants) and shudra; the first three varnas enjoyed different rights and privileges, while the shudra had only duties to perform.

The essence of feudal law is will of the feudal lords, raised to the status of law, geared to protecting, maintaining and developing feudal ownership of the land and the non-economic coercion of the peasant class. The content of this will is determined by the specifics of the feudal mode of production, under which agriculture is the basis of the national economy and, correspondingly, the main means of production is the land; the economic domination of the feudal lords is conditioned by their ownership of the land and ability to force the main mass of the peasantry to perform a number of service duties.

Bourgeois law recognizes all members of society as being legally equal and free. Under capitalist production, however, legal equality and freedom are merely a form for fixing the actual economic inequality between capitalist and proletarians. The rights and freedoms proclaimed by bourgeois law are not provided with material guarantees, the result being that in practice they can be exercised primarily by representatives of the propertied classes. By securing the relations of capitalist property and exploitation, bourgeois law is essentially the legalized will of the dominant bourgeoisie. It is designed to protect and strengthen the capitalist mode of production, based on exploitation of the working people, who are forced to sell their labour power to the owners of the tools and means of production.

Socialist law differs fundamentally from all exploiting legal systems in its essence, purpose and enforcement. It expresses the state will of the working class and toiling masses led by it, that is, during the building of socialism -the will of the vast majority of society, while in developed socialist,- the will of the whole people.

In socialist society (the first phase of communism), law is necessary "in the capacity of regulator (determining factor) in the distribution of products and allotment of labour among the members of society". Under socialism, law serves the implementation of the principle of "from each according to his abilities, to each according to his work". The productive forces have not yet attained the level of development necessary for distribution according to needs, and labour has not yet become a primary vital requirement of all members of society. For this reason, under socialism it is necessary to stimulate labour, control the measure of labour and the measure of consumption, distribute the output produced by society in accordance with the quantity and quality of the workers' labour. This underlies the use of law that is essentially different, since it is based on social ownership of the means of production, which excludes the possibility of exploiting people.

Socialist law secures a broad range of socio-economic, political and personal rights and freedom of citizens. Moreover, these rights and freedoms can be really exercised since they are provided with a system of material and other guarantees. The socialist improvement of the living conditions of citizens as the programs for socio-economic and cultural development is fulfilled.

In socialist society, where there are no antagonistic classes and the process of legislation is organized in such a way that the will and interests of the working masses are revealed and taken into account to the maximum, the chief methods of law enforcement are persuasion, control, preventive measures and social influence. Socialist law, like any other law, is protective against infringements by means of special apparatus of coercion. It is specific, however, in that, in socialist society, coercion is applied not to some given class, but to the minority who are offenders and do not make up a particular social group.

The types of law in social formations based on exploitation and oppression have four inherent common features; they express the state will of the dominant minority of society; they secure private and exploitation of man by man; they are designed to oppress the popular masses, and legally or in practice deny the rights and freedoms of the working people; they are backed up by the threat of punishment, systematic coercion and oppression of the majority of society. The differences between these types of law are seen in the way the slave-owing and feudal types of law have a class character and openly secure the domination of class of slave-owners or feudal lords, exploitation and oppression of the working masses, while bourgeois law is officially equally applicable to all. Deprived of material guarantee for the majority, however, it legally secures economic inequality and exploitation of the proletariat by the bourgeosie.

The socialist type of law has the following inherent specifics: it expresses the state will of the majority of society (the working class and toiling masses led by it) during the building of socialism, and the state will of all the people in developed socialist society; it secures social property, precludes exploitation of man by man; it serves to strengthen and develop democracy and the full power of the people; it grants the working people, a broad range of rights and freedoms, guaranteed materially; it is to back up the working people's belief in the justice and expedience of the rules of the law; it is protected from infringements by measures of state coercion, relying on the support of the broad population.

A special place in the classification of law belongs to the legal systems in force in societies that are transitional from one socio-economic formation to another, historically hire one. At present, these include the legal systems of countries that have chosen a non-capitalist path of development.

The purpose of law is expressed in its function. There is several classifications of these.

The most specific classification of law's functions is according to their social orientation. It expresses the social purpose of the legal system of various socio-economic formations and is, in content, similar to classification of function according to type of state. Thus, one of the chief function of slave-owing law is the legal formulation of the slave-owners, ownership of the instruments and means of production and the full power of the slave-owners over the slaves, expressed as the dominant class's ownership of the working people-the slaves. Inherent in feudal law is the function of securing ownership of the land and the non-economic coercion of the peasants to work for the feudal laws. The chief function of bourgeois law includes the protection and strengthening of the relation of capitalist ownership and commodity production within the framework of which the bourgeosie exploit the proletariat and makes capitalist profit.

One of the chief functions of socialist law is the regulation (determination) of the measure of the labour and the measure of consumption for the purpose of development of socialist production, the all-out stimulation of socialist useful labour, and the creation of the necessary conditioned for cultivation-a universal requirement for labour.

The function of law in countries that are following a non-capitalist path of development include the implementation of radical agrarian transformation in the interest of peasantry, the forcible suppression of the agents of imperialism and reactionaries who resist the national-democratic revolution, and others. According to the role of law in the development and change of social relation, the following functions are distinguished: the static function (securing of relations favorable and profitable for the dominant class, including, above all, those conditioning its domination); the dynamic function (Creating a development of social relation corresponding to the state will of the dominant class), the suppressive, negative functions (elimination of relation contradictory to this will).

According to the means of legal impact and social relation and people's behaviour, the following functions are distinguished: the regulated function (regulation of a number of the social relations inherent in the given mode of production by allocating certain rights and duties to their participants), the protected functions (Legal prohibition on actions contradictory to the will of dominant class, applying legal sanction-measures of state coercion-to people who have committed such actions) and the stimulating function

(Encouragement of actions corresponding to the will and interest of the dominant class, the granting of privileges and advantages to people who behave in this way).

Connected with classification of law's functions are such concepts as legal impact and legal regulation.

Legal impact means all forms of influence exercised by law on people's behaviour, not necessarily connected with the use of specifically legal means and categories.

Law exercises a motivational impact on people's behaviour as system of information on the juridical (and thus social, too) outcome of given actions, events, situations and consequences, against which the members of society measure their behaviour. In class antagonistic societies, the informational aspect of law is geared primarily to preventing and curbing actions, which are illegal from the point of view of the dominant class. Acts, law's and other sources of law of an exploitative type contain a multitude of prohibitions on various actions (infringement of the law), as well as punishment applied for such infringements. This aspect of exploitative law is addressed to the consciousness of the oppressed masses.

In socialist society, it is the creative aspect of legal impact that comes to the fore-maintenance of socially useful behaviour, stimulation, encouragement, information about real opportunity for citizens to apply their creative abilities and talents, about materially guaranteed possibilities, defined by law, for the all round development of the individual.

The functioning of law is closely linked with the ideology of society. The forms of social consciousness (especially political consciousness, morals and, in number of societies, religion) affect law, its content and forms of realization. In term law is a mighty ideological and organizing force. The reflection of exiting law in social consciousness, as well as assessment in legal concepts and categories (subjective law, duty, prohibition, a legally important fact) of existing social relations (conception concerning desirable law) from legal consciousness, which has a class character.

Further law may be classified as follows: -

Laws properly called and laws improperly so-called.

Strictly speaking all improper laws are analogous law, proper and the term law as applied to any of them is a metaphorical or figurative expression. What the meaning of metaphorical (we usually mean our in which analogy is faint the alliance between the primitive and the derivative significant remote)

The situation of laws proper with such in proper laws. All as are closely analogous to the proper under three capital classes: -

1. Law properly so called which are set by God.
2. Law properly so called which are set by new as political superior or by men as private person in pursuance of legal rights.
3. It is of two kinds: -
   - a) Law which are set by men to men but not as political superior or inferior nor in pursuance of legal rights.
   - b) The laws, which are closely analogous to laws proper but are merely opinion or sentiments held or felt by men in regard to human conduct.

So there is clear cut distinction between positive law or positive morality (which are set by political superior are positive law rest by positive morality)- those laws which are set by private person in pursuance of legal right are also positive law.

Science of jurisprudence is concerned with positive law or with laws strictly so called with out regard to their goodness & badness.

Science of positive morality as considered with out regard to it goodness & badness might be the subject of science closely and analogous to jurisprudence, the name moral or science of morals would denote it ambiguously. These names are commonly joined to the department of ethics or deontology.

Meaning of good or bad as applied to human laws. Meaning of good or bad as applied to laws of God.

By the theory of utility every law is good which is useful and every law is bad which is pernicious.

To an atheist a human law is good if it is generally useful if pernicious then bad. Then in conclusion the theory of utility is good enough.

The three essentials (command, sanction, duties) of law properly so-called together with certain following consequences: -

1. Law of law or positive law is laws properly so-called.
2. The gneissic character of positive moral rules. (No law belonging to this class is a direct or circuitous command of a monarch or sovereign number in the character of political superior.)
3. The positive moral rules, some are laws proper (they are set by men to men-they are set by private person in pursuance of legal right). But others are laws in proper. The positive moral rules which are laws properly so called are commands.

The positive moral rules, which are laws improperly so-called (are laws set or imposed by general opinion) rule of honour, fashion, international law.

- A law set by general opinion merely the opinion of an indeterminate body of person in regard to a kind of conduct.
- A determinate body that opines or feels by very opinion or sentiment. To command that conduct of the kind shall be punished but the command expressed by that determinate partly is not. Law or rule by general opinion but it is law properly so-called set by determinate author.

So law set by general opinion is not law - and there is a brief semblance and analogy between a law proper and law set by general opinion. (So the entire question rounds whether body is determinate or indeterminate group of persons).

Distinction between determinate and indeterminate. Determinate bodies are of two types: -

a) A body is composed of persons determined specifically or individually

b) It is composed of all the persons who belong to given class or who belong respectively to two or more such classes.

But indeterminate body is not determinable and assignable to partnership firms, Parliament is a determinate body.

For example by indeterminate body it will save the nature of a law set by general opinion.

An indeterminate body is incapable of corporate conduct because it's persons could not be identified.

So in brief, law is of three kind—law of lord—positive law—positive morality (it is of two type which are law in proper sense—and improper sense).

The corresponding sanction-duties and rights of all the three above mentioned law-religious, public point, governable, legal, moral etc.

Sometimes these body of laws coincide, sometimes they do not and sometimes conflict.

Mostly law of God and positive morality conflict and law of God and positive law conflict for example customary laws.

Is the tendency to confound positive law with the science of legislation and positive morality with deontology?

As Blackstone says laws of God are superior to all in obligation, that the human law should be suffered to contradict it. If these are contradictory they are of no value.

Writers on international law like Grotins, Puffenaorff, Hausaid jut as above. Blackstone has given instances of it.

Secondly, tendency to confound positive law with positive morality and both with legislation and deontology.

Mansfield has given several examples of it.

Judicial legislation-(possible by Brown, and Mansfield) but Bentham, who refuted the theory of judge made law is shut down by Brown and Mansfield.

The foregoing division of law is allies in the main theme with the division of professor. Locke divides in three parts

1) Divine law (law set by god to the acting of new whether formulated by the light of nature or the voice of revolution) and is the sanctioned for sin or duty).
2) Civil Law-Positive law as discussed sanction of positive law will by grotto and reward (criminal or innocent).
3) Law of opinion or reputation-sanction is virtue or vice.

Locke "which good or evil, pleasure or pain attending our observance or branch of law by nuderes of lawmaker is that we call reward or punishment i.e. sanction (this theory of sanction for reward is not accepted by Brown)."

The analogy borne to a law proper by a law which opinion imposes lies mainly in the following point of resemblance – in the base of law set by opinion as well as in the case of law properly so called the rational being are or subject to contingent evil. In the event of their not complying wish known are presumes desire of another being or being of a like nature. So analogy between a law in the proper acceptations (law metaphorical or figurative so-called) and law improperly so-called which opinion sets or imposes is therefore strong. The defect which excludes the latter from the laws of law is only the wish or desire of its author has not been duly signified

(Examples–law of gravity–uniformity and stability of conduct etc.) the atheist also require uniformity and stability.

Every law properly so-called has two parties by whom it is established-and a party to whom it is set.

Laws metaphorical or figuratively so called are often blended and confounded wish laws imperative and properly so called.

Sanction

Three types

- Laws of God. Religion
- Positive law. Legal
- Positive Morality. Moral

But Brown, Bentham have added one more group of sanction to it that is –physical or natural sanction. Bentham defines it "A physical sanction is an evil brought upon the suffering party by an act or omission of his own. But it is not brought by the sufferer by divine law or positive law or rules of positive morality. For example if a house is burnt by negligence of his own. Such sanctions are related by the following analogy to sanctions properly so-called. When they achieved suffered they are suffered by rational being by act or omission of his own. The party may avert such sanctions from being occurred in other cases by avoiding the litigation or quarrellings.

The three exceptions of positive law recognized by Austin and Brown are (in the sense of Roman lawyers) and ought to be classed respectively with laws metaphorically or figuratively and rules of positive morality because they are closely connected with the positive law. But Brown sets them as improper laws of anomalous sorts and excludes them from the classes of laws so which in strictness they belong.

Notes

1. E. Bodenheimer, Jurisprudence
2. Lon. L. Fuller, The Law in Quest of Itself
3. P. Vinogradoff, Historical Jurisprudence
4. W.D. Ross, Aristotle
5. H. Kelsen, Interpretations of Modern Legal Philosophies
6. Dig.1.1.9; Inst.1.2; Inst.1.3.
7. N.M. Korkunov, General Theory of Law
8. Romans ii.
9. F. Kern, Kingship and law in the Middle Ages
10. M.J. Adler, Essays in Thomis
11. H. Grotius call these methods the more subtle a priori and the more popular a posteriori

12. A convenient summary of T. Hobbes's views is found in Huntington Cairns, Legal Philosophy from Plato to Hegel, ch.vii: M. Oakeshott, Hobbes's Leviathan.

13. Leviathan, ch.xxxii.

14. Op.cit.ch.xiv

15. Hobbes altogether lays down nineteen rules of nature

16. Op.cit.ch.xvii

17. 1632-1704

18. J. Dickinson, Administrative Justice and the Supremacy of Law

19. D.G. Ritchie, Natural Rights, J.W. Jones in Combridge Legal Essays, Declarations of rights are not confined to the eighteenth century-the United Nations has produced a Universal Declaration of Human Rights.

20. Passed in 1868, No State shall 'deprive any person of life, liberty, or property without due process of law, nor deny to any person within its jurisdiction the equal protection of the laws.'

21. 47 Yale L.J. (1938)

22. Thus in Lochner v. New York (1904), 198 U.S. 45, the majority decided that it was unconstitutional for the legislature to limit the hours of work in a bakehouse to ten hours a day

23. J.A.C. Grant, 31 Col. L.R. 56:C.G.Haines, Revival of Natural Law Concepts

24. R.H. Jackson, The Struggle for Judicial Supremacy, points out that only two acts of Congress were held unconstitutional by the court in the first seventy years of its existence. 1890 and 1938 State legislation was set aside under the Fourteenth Amendment 228 times.

25. F. Pollock, Essays in the Law

26. L. Le Fur, in Droit, Morale, Maurs

27. Transactions of the Grotius Society

28. Droit, Morale, Maurs,

29. E.g. J. Charmont, la Renaissance du drit naturel

30. H. Lauterpacht, in Modern Theories of Law

31. Lehrbuch der Rechtsphilosophie, translated by A. Albrecht as Philosophy of Law

32. R. Pound, Interpretations of Legal History, J. Kohler, Philosophy of Law

33. Castillejo y Duarte, Filosofia del Derecho (1910); Appendix to J. Kohler's Philosophy of law
34. Die Lehre von Richtigen Rechte: Theory of Justice (trans.I.Husik): M.Ginsberg in Modern Theories of Law
35. F. Geny, Science et technique; M. Cohen Law and the Social Order
36. H. Goldschmidt, Archives de phil. Du droit
37. Methode Dharamasastra'interpretation et sources en droit prive positif, and Science et technique.
38. The Natural Law, K.N. Llewellyn (in reviewing R. Pound; jurisprudence)
39. P.H. Winfield
40. Stuart v. Bell, [1891] 2 Q.B. 341 at 350; in the Estate of Bohrmann, [1938]
41. Gardiner v. Heading, [1928] 2 K.B. 284
42. R. V. Waddington (1800), 1
43. Interpretatin of Legal History, 152.
44. J. Dickinson, 29 Col. L.R. (1929)
45. Cf. P.H. Winfield, 54 L.Q.R. (1938)
46. Contemporary Juristic Theory
47. Pollock, Jurisprudence and Legal Essays S.K. Allen, Aspects of Justice; Dowrick, Justice according to English Common Lawyers; Hart, The Concept of Law,
48. See Salmond, Jurisprudence (7th ed.), 39: "the law may be defined as the body of principles recognized and applied by the state in the administration of justice. In other words, the law consists of the rules recognized and acted on by courts of justice."
49. Austin, "the science of jurisprudence."
50. Dowrick, op.cit., Discusses seven meanings of the word "justice"
51. This distinction is made by Aristotle, Nichomochean Ethics, 11306-11326
52. Pound, Philosophy of Law,
53. Friedmann, Law and Social Change in Contemporary Britain,
54. Maine, Ancient Law
55. See Berge, "Criminal Jurisdiction and the Territorial Principle." (1932)

56. See Lorenzen, "Public Policy and the conflict of Laws"
57. Swift V. Tyson (1842) 16 Pet. 1; overruled in Erie R.R. V. Tompkins, 58 Sup.ct. 817: 304 U.S. 64 (1938).
58. Buckland and Mcnair, Roman Law and Common Law
59. Story, conflict of laws (8th ed. 1883)
60. A. Gledhill, Whither Indian Law, (School of Oriental and African Studies, Univ. of Landon, 1965).
61. Britian Constitutional Law
62. Law and consitution
63. Constitutional & Administrative Law
64. A Theory of Siats

CHAPTER 5

Administration of Justice and Morals

In the words of Jeremy Taylor: "A herd of wolves is quieter than so many men, unless all have one reason in them or have one power over them." Spioza writes: "Those who persuade themselves that a multitude of men can be induced to live by the rule of reason are dreamers of dreams and of the golden age of poets." Hobbes says that without a common power to keep them all in awe, it is not possible for individuals to live in society. Without it, injustice is unchecked and triumphant and the life of people is solitary, poor, nasty, brutish and short.

Administration of Justice always works on the foundation of Legal system:

Once we abandon the view that the foundations of a legal system consist in a habit of obedience to a legally unlimited sovereign and substitute for this the conception of an ultimate rule of recognition, which provides a system of rules with its criteria of validity, a range of fascinating and important questions confront us. They are relatively new questions; for they were veiled so long as jurisprudence and political theory were committed to the older ways of thought. They are also difficult questions, requiring a full answer, on the one hand a grasp of some fundamental issues of constitutional law and on the other an appreciation of the characteristic manner in which legal forms may silently shift and change. We shall therefore investigate these questions only so far as they bear upon the wisdom or unwisdom of insisting, as we have done, that a central place should be assigned to the union of primary and secondary rules in the elucidation of the concept of law.

The first difficulty is that of classification; for the rule, which, in the last resort, is used to identify the law, escapes the conventional categories used for describing a legal system, though these are often taken to be exhaustive. Thus, English constitutional writers since Dicey have usually repeated the statement that the constitutional arrangements of the United Kingdom consist partly of laws strictly so called statutes, orders in council, and rules embodied in precedents and partly of conventions, which are mere usage, understandings or customs. The latter include important rules such as that the Queen may not refuse her consent to a bill duly passed by peers and commons; there is, however, no legal duty on the Queen to give her consent and such rules are called conventions because the courts do not recognize them as imposing a legal duty. Plainly the rule that what the Queen in Parliament enacts is law does not fall into either of these categories. It is not a convention, since the courts are most intimately concerned with it and they use it in identifying the law; and it is not a rule on the same level as the 'laws strictly so called,' which it is used to identify. Even if it were enacted by statute, this would not reduce it to the level of a statute; for the legal status of such an enactment necessarily would depend on the fact that the rule existed antecedently to and independently of the enactment. Moreover, as we have shown in the last section, its existence, unlike that of a statute, must consist in an actual practice.

This aspect of things extract from some a cry of despair. How can we show that the fundamental provisions of a Constitution, which are surely law, are real laws? Others reply with the insistence that at the base of legal systems there is something, which is 'not law,' which is 'pre-legal','meta-legal', or is just 'political fact.' This uneasiness is a sure sign that the categories used for the description of this most important feature in any system of law are too crude. The case for calling the rule of recognition, 'law' is that the rule providing criteria for the identification of other rules of the system may well be thought a defining feature of a legal system, and so itself worth calling 'law', the case for calling it 'fact' is that to assert that such a rule exists is indeed to make an external statement of an actual fact concerning the manner in which the rules of an 'efficious' system are identified. Both these aspects claim attention but we cannot do justice to both by choosing one of the labels, 'law' or 'fact'. Instead, we need to remember that the ultimate rule of recognition may be regarded from two points of view: one is expressed in the external statement of fact that the rule exists in the actual practice of the system; the other is expressed in the internal statements of validity made by those who use it in identifying the law.

A second set of questions arises out of the hidden complexity and vagueness of the assertion that a legal system exists in a given country or among a given social group. When we make this assertion we in fact refer in compressed, portmanteau form to a number of heterogeneous social facts, usually concomitant. The standard terminology of legal and political thought, developed in the shadow of a misleading theory, is apt to oversimplify and obscure the facts. Yet when we take off the spectacles constituted by this terminology and look at the facts, it becomes apparent that a legal system, like a human being, may at one stage be unborn, at a second not yet wholly independent of its mother, then enjoy a healthy independent existence, later decay and finally die. These halfway stages between birth and normal, independent existence and, again, between that and death, put out of joint our familiar ways of describing legal phenomena. They are worth our study because, baffling as they are, they throw into relief the full complexity of what we take for granted, when in the normal case, we make the confident and true assertion that in a given country a legal system exists.

One way of realizing this complexity is to see just where the simple, Austinian formula of a general habit of obedience to order fails to reproduce or distort the complex facts which constitute the minimum conditions which a society must satisfy if it is to have a legal system. We may allow that this formula does designate one necessary condition: namely, that where the laws impose obligations or duties these should be generally obeyed or at any rate not generally disobeyed. But, though essential, this only caters for what we may term the 'end product' of the legal system, where it makes its impact on the private citizen; whereas its day-to-day existence consists also in the official creation, the identification, and the official use and application of law. The relationship with law involved here can be called 'obedience' only if that word is extended so far beyond its normal use as to cease to characterize informatively these operations. In no ordinary sense of 'obey' are legislators obeying rules when, in enacting laws, they conform to the rules conferring their legislative powers, except of course when the rules conferring such powers are reinforced by rules imposing a duty to follow them. Nor, in failing to conform to these rules do they 'disobey' a law, though they may fail to make one. Nor does the word 'obey' describe well what judges do when they apply the system's rule of recognition and recognize a statute as valid law and use it in the determination of disputes. We can of course, if we wish, preserve the simple terminology of 'obedience' in face of the facts by many devices. One is to express, e.g. the use made by judges of general criteria of validity in recognizing a statute, as a case of obedience to orders given by the 'Founders of the Constitution,' or (where there are no 'Founders') as obedience to a 'depsychologized command' i.e., a command without a commander.

Alternatively we can push out of sight the whole official side to law and for go the description of the use of rules made in legislation and adjudication, and instead, think of the whole official world as one person (the 'sovereign') issuing orders, through various agents or mouthpieces, which are habitually obeyed by the citizen. But this is either no more than convenient shorthand for complex facts which still await description, or a disastrously confusing piece of mythology.

It is natural to react from the failure of attempts to give an account of what it is for a legal system to exist, in the agreeably simple terms of the habitual obedience, which is indeed characteristic of the relationship of the ordinary citizen to law, by making the opposite error. This consists in taking what is characteristic of the official activities, especially the judicial attitude or relationship to law, and treating this as an adequate account of what must exist in a social group, which has a legal system. This amounts to replacing the simple conception that bulk of society habitually obey the law with the conception that they must generally share, accept, or regard as binding the ultimate rule of recognition specifying the criteria in terms of which the validity of laws are ultimately assessed. There the 'Constitution' was so simple that no fiction would be involved in attributing knowledge and acceptance of it to the ordinary citizen as well as to the officials and lawyers. In the simple word of Rex we might well say that there was more than mere habitual obedience by the bulk of the population to his word. There it might well be the case that both he and the officials of the system 'accepted,' in the same explicit, conscious way, a rule of recognition specifying Rex's word as the criterion of valid law for the whole society, though subjects and officials would have different roles to play and different relationships to the rules of law identified by this criterion. To insist that this state of affairs, imaginable in a simple society, always or usually exists in a complex modern state would be to insist on a fiction. Here surely the reality of the situation is that a great proportion of ordinary citizens–perhaps a majority, have no general conception of the legal structure or of its criteria of validity. The law, which he obeys, is something, which he knows of only as 'the law.' He may obey it for a variety of different reasons and among them may often, though not always, be the knowledge that it will be the best for him to do so. He will be aware of the general likely consequences of disobedience: that there are officials who may arrest him and others who will try him and send him to prison for breaking the law. So long as the laws, which are valid by the system's tests of validity, are obeyed by the bulk of the population, this surely is all the evidence we need in order to establish that a given legal system exists.

But just because a legal system is a complex union of primary and secondary rules, this evidence is not all that is needed to describe the relationships to law involved in the existence of a legal system. It must be supplemented by a description of the relevant relationship of the officials of the system to the secondary rules, which concern them as officials. Here what is crucial is that there should be a unified or shared official acceptance of the rule of recognition containing the system's criteria of validity. But it is just here that the simple notion of general obedience, which was adequate to characterize the indispensable minimum in the case of ordinary citizens, is inadequate. The point is not, or not merely, the 'linguistic' one that 'obedience' is not naturally used to refer to the way in which these secondary rules are respected as rules by courts and other officials. We could find, if necessary, some wider expressions like 'follow','comply', or 'conform to' which would characterize both what ordinary citizens do in relation to law when they report for military service and what judges do when they identify a particular statute as law in their courts, on the footing that what the Queen in Parliament enacts is law. But these blanket terms would merely mask vital differences, which must be grasped if the minimum conditions involved in the existence of the complex social phenomenon, which we call a legal system, is to be understood.

What makes 'obedience' misleading as a description of what legislators do in conforming to the rules conferring their powers, and of what courts do in applying an accepted ultimate rule of recognition, is that obeying a rule (or an order) need not involve thought on the part of the person obeying that what he does is the right thing, both for himself and for others to do: he need not have a view of what he does as a fulfillment of a standard of behavior for others of the social group. He need not think of his conforming behavior as 'right',' correct', or 'obligatory.' His attitude, in other words, need not have any of that critical character which is involved whenever social rules are accepted and types of conduct are treated as general standards. He need not, though he may, share the internal point of view accepting the rules as standards for all to whom they apply. Instead, he may think of the rule only as something demanding action from him under threat of penalty; he may obey it out of fear of the consequences, or from inertia, without thinking of himself or others as having an obligation to do so and without being disposed to criticize either himself or others for deviations. But this merely personal concern with the rules, which is all the ordinary citizen may have in obeying them, cannot characterize the attitude of the courts to the rules with which they operate as courts. This is most patently the case with the ultimate rule of recognition in terms of which the validity of other rules is assessed. Thus, if it is to exist at all, must be regarded from the internal point of view as a public, common standard of correct judicial decision, and not as something, which each judge merely obeys for his part only. Individual courts of the system though they may, on occasion, deviate from these rules must, in general, be critically concerned with such deviations as lapes from standards, which are essentially common or public.

This is not merely a matter of the efficiency or health of the legal system, but is logically a necessary condition of our ability to speak of the existence of a single legal system. If only some judges acted 'for their part only' on the footing that what the Queen in Parliament enacts is law, and made no criticisms of those who did not respect this rule of recognition, the characteristic unity and continuity of a legal system would have disappeared. For this depends on the acceptance, at this crucial point, of Dommon standards of legal validity.

In the interval between these vagaries of judicial behaviour and the chaos, which would ultimately ensue when the ordinary man was faced with contrary judicial orders, we would be at loss to describe the situation. We would be in the presence of a **lusus** nature worth thinking about only because it sharpens our awareness of what is often too obvious to be noticed.

There are, therefore, two minimum conditions necessary and sufficient for the existence of a legal system. On the one hand those rules of behavior which are valid according to the system's ultimate criteria of validity must be generally obeyed, and, on the other hand, its rules of recognition specifying the criteria of legal validity and its rules of change and adjudication must be effectively accepted as common public standards of official behaviour by its officials. The first condition is the only one which private citizens need satisfy: they may obey each 'for his part only' and from any motive whatever; though in a healthy society they will in fact often accept these rules as common standards of behaviour and acknowledge an obligation to obey them, or even trace this obligation to a more general obligation to respect the Constitution. The second condition must also be satisfied by the officials of the system. They must regard these as common standards of official behaviour and appraise critically their own and each other's deviations as lapes.

Of course it is also true that besides these there will be many primary rules, which apply to officials in their merely personal capacity, which they need only obey.

The assertion that a legal system exists is therefore a statement looking both towards obedience by ordinary citizens and to the acceptance by officials of secondary rules as critical common standards of official behaviour. We need not be surprised at this duality. It is merely the reflection of the composite of a legal system as compared with a simpler decentralized pre-legal form of social structure, which consists only of primary rules. In the simpler structure since there are no officials, the rules must be widely accepted as setting critical standards for the behaviour of the group. If there, the internal point of view is not widely disseminated there could not logically be any rules. But where there is a union of primary and secondary rules, which is as we have argued, the most fruitful way of regarding a legal system, the acceptance of the rules as common standards for the group may be spit off from the relatively passive matter of the ordinary individual acquiescing in the rules by obeying them for his part alone. In an extreme case the internal point of view with its characteristic normative use of legal language ('This is a valid rule') might be confined to the official word. In this more complex system, only officials might accept and use the system's criteria of legal validity. The society in which this was so, might be deplicably sheep like; the sheep might end in the slaughter-house. But there is little reason for thinking that it could not exist or for denying it the title of legal system.

Evidence for the existence of a legal system must therefore be drawn from two different sectors of social life. The normal, unproblematic case where we can say confidently that a legal system exists, is just one where it is clear that the two sectors are congruent in their respective typical concerns with the law. Crudely put, the facts are that the rules recognized as valid at the official level are generally obeyed. Sometimes, however, the official sector may be detached from the private sector, in the sense that there is no longer general obedience to the rules, which are valid according to the criteria of validity in use in the courts. The variety of ways in which this may happen belongs to the pathology of legal systems; for they represent a breakdown in the complex congruent practice, which is referred to when we make the external statement of fact that, a legal system exists. There is a partial failure of what is presupposed whenever, from within the particular system, we make internal statements of law. Such a breakdown may be the product of different disturbing factors. 'Revolution', where rival claims to govern are made from within the fro up, is only one case, and though this will always involve the breach of some of the laws of the existing system, it may entail only the legally unauthorized substitution of a new set of individuals as officials, and not a new Constitution or legal system.

Enemy occupation, where a rival claim to govern without authority under the existing system comes from without, is another case; and the simple breakdown of ordered legal control in the face of anarchy or banditry without political pretensions to govern is yet another.

In each of these cases there may be halfway stages during which the courts function, either on the territory or in exile, and still use the criteria of legal validity of the old, once firmly established system; but these orders are ineffective in the territory. The stage at which it is right to say in such cases that the legal system has finally ceased to exist is a thing not susceptible of any exact determination. Plainly, if there is some considerable chance of a restoration or if the disturbance of the established system is an incident in general war of which the issue is still uncertain, no unqualified assertion that it has ceased to exist would be warranted. This is so just because the statement that a legal system exists is of a sufficiently broad and general type to allow for interruptions; it is not verified or falsified by what happens in short spaces of time.

Of course, difficult questions that may arise after interruptions have been succeeded by the resumption of normal relations between the court and the population. A government returns from exile on the expulsion of occupying forces or the defeat of a rebel government; then questions arise as to what was or was not 'law' in the territory during the period of interruption. Here what is most important is to understand that this question may not be one of fact. If it were one of fact it would have to be settled by asking whether the interruption was so protracted and complete that the situation must be described as one in which the original system had ceased to exist and a new one was set up, similar to the old, on the return from exile. Instead the question may be raised as one of international law, or it may, somewhat paradoxically, arise as a question of law within the very system of law existing since the restoration. In the latter case it might well be that the restored systems included a retrospective law declaring the system to have been (or, more candidly, to be 'deemed' to have been) continuously the law of the territory. This might be done even if the interruption were so long as to make such a declaration seem quite at variance with the conclusion that might have been reached, had the question been treated as a question of fact. In such a case there is no reason why the declaration should not stand as a rule of the restored system, determining the law, which its courts must apply to incidents and transaction occurring during the period of interruption.

Administration Of Justice

In the words of Prof. Sidgwick: "In determining a nation's rank in political civilization, no test is more decisive than the degree in which justice as defined by the law is actually realized in its judicial administration." Lord Bryce writes: "There is not better test of the excellence of a government than the efficiency of its judicial system." George Washington said: "Administration of justice is the firmest pillar of government. Law exists to bind together the community. It is sovereign and cannot be violated with impunity." Salmond and Roscore Pound have emphasized the importance of justice in their definitions of law. They have defined law in terms of justice. According to Salmond: "Law may be defined as the body of principles recognized and applied by the State in the administration of justice." Roscoe Pound observes: "Law is the body of principles recognized or enforced by public and regular tribunals in the administration of justice." Blackstone wrote: "Justice is not derived from the king as his free gift but he is the steward of the public to dispense it to whom it is due. He is not the spring but the reservoir from whence right and equity are conducted by a thousand channels to every individual."

The most essential functions of a State are primarily two: war and administration of justice. If a State is not capable of performing either or both of these functions, it cannot be called a State. According to Salmond, the administration of justice implies the maintenance of right within a political community by means of the physical force of the State. It is a modern and civilized substitute for the primitive practice of private vengeance and violent self-help. The definition of Salmond has been criticised on the ground that it is not the force of the State alone that secures the obedience of law. There are a number of other factors such as social sanctions, habit and convenience that help in the obedience of law. In civilized societies, obedience to law becomes a matter of habit and in very rare cases the force of the State is used to secure it. The supporters of the definition of Salmond point out that if the force of the State is not used in all cases to secure obedience, it does not mean that the control of the State has disappeared. It merely indicates the final triumph and supremacy of the control of the State.

Salmond points out that men do not have one reason in them and each is moved by his own interests and passions. The only alternative is one's power over men. Man is by nature a fighting animal and force is the ultima-ratio of all mankind. Without a common power to keep them all in awe, it is impossible for men to cohere in any but the most primitive form of society. Without it civilization is unattainable. However orderly a society may be, the element of force is always present and operative. It may become latent but still exists. A society in which the power of the State is never called into actual exercise does not mark the disappearance of the control of the government but its final triumph and supremacy. It is suggested that force, as an instrument for the coercion of mankind is merely a temporary and provisional incident in the development of a perfect civilization. To a large extent already, the element of force has become merely latent and for the most part it is sufficient for the State to declare the rights and duties of its subjects. This is clear from the increasing popularity of the cases for mere declaration, which do not seek any other relief except the declaration of law or the rights of the parties. The force of public opinion is a valuable support and even indispensable for a system of law because without it there can be no stability and permanence. However, public opinion alone is no substitute for legal sanctions. The influence of public censure is a very weak one. The influence of the national conscience, unsupported by the force of the State, can be counteracted by small societies or associations possessing separate interests and separate antagonistic consciences of their own. A man cares more for the opinion of his friends and immediate associates than for the opinion of the rest of world. The censure of ten thousand may be outweighed by the approval of ten. The honour of thieves finds its sanction and support from those belonging to their profession.

Social sanction is an efficient instrument only if it is associated with and supplemented by the concentrated and irresistible force of the community. Force is necessary to coerce the recalcitrant minority and prevent them from gaining an unfair advantage over the law-abiding majority in State. The conclusion is that the administration of justice with the sanction of the physical force of the State is unavoidable and admits to no substitute.

Evolution of Administration of Justice:

The evolution of administration of justice is identical with the origin and growth of man. The social nature of man demands that he must live in society. While living so, man must have experienced a conflict of interests and that created the necessity for providing for the administration of justice.

To begin with, every individual had to help himself to punish the wrongdoer. Personal vengeance was allowed. He avenged himself upon his enemies by his own hand, probably supported by the hands of his friends and kinsmen where necessary. At that stage, every man carried his life in his hands. He was liable to be attacked at any time and he could resist by overpowering his opponent. In those days, every man was a judge in his own cause. There was no guarantee that crime would certainly be punished and that also in proportion to the gravity of the crime. Very often one crime led to another. Not only an individual was involved, even the member of his family and tribe could be the victims of retaliation. There were group conflicts and tribal conflicts. Blood feuds were common. When blood feuds became disastrous, primitive societies provided for the payment of some money or its equivalent as compensation to the victim of the crime or the relatives of the victim. The system of compensation was developed until a regular sliding scale was fixed. In the case of murder, the vengeance of the relatives of the deceased could be bought off by paying blood money according to the importance of the victim.

The second stage in the history of administration of justice started with the rise of political States. However, those States were not strong enough to regulate crime and inflict punishment on the criminals. The law of private vengeance and violent self-help continued to prevail. The State merely regulated private vengeance and violent self-help. The State also prescribed rules for the regulation of private vengeance. The State enforced the concept of "a tooth for a tooth","an eye for eye" and "a life for a life". The State provided that a life would not be taken for a tooth or a life for an eye. Vengeance was not totally abolished in the Anglo-Saxon period of the history of England but was merely restricted and regulated.

With the growth of the power of the State, the State began to act as a judge to assess liability and impose penalty. It was no longer a regulator of private vengeance. It substituted public equity and punishment for private vengeance. The civil law and administration of civil justice helped the wronged and became a substitute for the violent self-help of the primitive days. The modern administration of justice is a natural corollary to the growth in power of political State.

As regards advantages, legal justice ensures uniformity and certainly in the administration of justice. Everybody knows what the law is and there is no scope for arbitrary action. Even the judges have to give decisions according to declared law of the country. As law is certain, citizens can shape their conduct accordingly. Another advantage is that there is impartiality in the administration of justice.

There are certain disadvantages of legal justice. One disadvantage is that it is rigid. Another defect of legal justice is its formalism or technicalities. Judges attach more importance to legal technicalities than they deserve. They give importance to form than to substance. Another defect of legal justice is that it is complex. Sir John Salmond concludes: "The law is without doubt a remedy for greater evils, yet it brings with it evils of its own."

Public Justice:

Public justice is that which is administered by the State through its own tribunals. Private justice is distinguished as being justice between individuals. Public justice is relation between the courts on one hand and individuals on the other.

Civil And Criminal Justice:

Blackstone writes: "Wrongs are divisible into two sorts or species, private wrongs and public wrongs. The former are an infringement or privation of the private or civil rights belonging to individuals, considered as individuals, and are thereupon frequently termed civil injuries; the latter are a breach and violation of public rights and duties which affect the whole community considered as a community and are distinguished by the harsher appellation of crimes and misdemeanours." A crime is an act deemed by law to be harmful to society in general. Murder injures primarily the particular victim but its disregard of human life does not allow the same to be a matter between the murderer and the family of the murdered. Those who commit such acts are proceeded against by the State and they are punished if convicted. Civil wrongs such as a breach of contract or trespass to land are deemed to infringe only the rights of the individual wronged and not the society in general. The law leaves it to the victim to sue for compensation in the courts.

English law has certain features, which prevent us from drawing a clear line between crimes and civil wrongs. There are some wrongs to the State and therefore public wrongs, but still they are regarded as civil wrongs by law. A refusal to pay taxes is an offence against the State and is dealt with in a suit to the State, but it is a civil wrong, in the same way as a refusal to pay money lent by a private person is a civil wrong. The breach of a contract made with the State is not a criminal offence. An action by the State for the recovery of a debt, or for damage, or for the restoration of public property, or for the enforcement of a public trust is a civil wrong although in each case the person injured and suing is the State itself. Some civil wrongs can cause greater general harm than some criminal offences. The negligence of a contractor may cause greater damage and loss than a petty theft. The same act may be civil injury or a crime.

However, Salmond points out that from a practical standpoint, the importance of distinction lies in the difference in the legal consequences of crime and civil wrongs. Civil justice is administered according to one set of forms and criminal justice according to another set of forms. Civil justice is administered in one set of courts and criminal justice is administered in a somewhat different set of courts. The outcome of the proceedings is generally different. If successful, civil proceedings result in a judgement for damages, or in a judgement for the payment of a debt or penalty or in an injection or decree for specific restitution or specific performance, or in an order for the delivery of possession of land, or in a decree of divorce, or in an order of mandamus, prohibition or certiorari, or in a writ of habeas corpus, or in other forms of religion known as civil. If successful, criminal proceedings result in one or a number of punishments, ranging from hanging to fine or in a binding over to keep the peace, release upon probation or similar other results belonging distinctly to criminal law. However, even here the distinction is not clear-cut. Criminal proceedings may result in an order against the accused to make restitution or compensation. Civil proceeding may result in an award of exemplary or punitive damages. However, the basic objective of criminal proceedings is punishment and the usual goal of civil proceedings is not punitive.

One view is that the object of civil proceedings is to enforce rights, while the object of criminal proceedings is to punish wrongs. There is an element of truth in this view. Punishment is more a feature of criminal proceeding than of civil proceedings. However, punishment is not always present in criminal proceedings and not always absent in civil proceedings, a juvenile offender may be just warned and not punished in a criminal proceedings whereas in an action for torts, damages may be awarded by way of punishment. When a man disobeys an injuction of the court, he may even be punished with imprisonment in civil proceedings. Therefore, this distinction does not go to the root of the matter.

Another distinction made by some writers is that crimes are more harmful in their consequences than civil wrongs. While crimes injure the public at large, civil wrongs injure the private individual. However, this distinction cannot always be maintained. Some acts may be considered both as crimes and civil wrongs. This is so in the case of defamation. It is also not always true that crimes are more harmful than civil wrongs. Negligence of a contractor is a civil wrong but it may result in more loss of life and property than a simple assault or petty theft, which are crimes.

According to some writers, the State constitutes itself as a party to the proceedings in a crime, but in civil proceedings private individuals are parties. This distinction is also not true in all cases. There are crimes in which private individuals can be parties. It is sure that no hard & fast distinction can be founded.

The purpose of criminal justice is to punish the wrongdoer. He is punished by the State. The question arises, what is the purpose of punishment or in other words what is the end of criminal justice. From very ancient times, a number of theories may be broadly divided into seven cases which are as follows:-

Theories Of Punishment

There are five theories of punishment: deterrent theory, preventive theory, reformative theory, retributive theory and theory of compensation, theory of social boycott and theory of repentance.

(a) **Deterrent Theory:** Salmond considers the deterrent aspect of punishment to be the most important. To quote him: "Punishment is before all things deterrent and the chief end of the law of crime is to make the evildoer an example and a warning to all that are likeminded with him." A similar view was expressed by Locke when he stated that the commission of every offence should be made "a bad bargain for the offender."

According to the deterrent theory of punishment, the object of punishment is not only to prevent the wrongdoer from doing a wrong a second time but also to make him an example to others who have criminal tendencies. A judge once said: "I don't punish you for stealing the sheep, but so that sheep may not be stolen again." The aim of punishment is not revenge but terror. An exemplary punishment should be given to the criminal so that the others may learn a lesson from him. The view of Manu was that "penalty keeps the people under cantrol, penalty protects them, penalty remains awake when people are asleep, so the wise have regarded punishment (danda) as a source of righteousness." Again, "people are in check by punishment, for it is difficult to find a man who by nature sticks to the path of virtue and this world is unable to afford sources of enjoyment through fear of punishment." Paton writes: "The deterrent theory emphasises the necessity of protecting society, by so treating the prisoners that others will be deterred from breaking the law."

The deterrent theory was the basis of punishment in England in medieval times and continued to be so till the beginning of the 19th century. The result was that severe and inhuman punishments were inflicted even for minor offences in England. In India also, the penalty of death or mutilation of limbs was imposed even for petty offences.

There is a lot of criticism of the deterrent theory of punishment in modern times. It is contended that the deterrent theory has proved ineffective in checking crime. Even when there is a provision for very severe punishments in the penal law of the country, people continue to commit crimes. It is pointed out that with the increase in the severity of punishment, crimes have also increased. Excessive harshness of punishment tends to defeat its own purpose by arousing the sympathy of the public towards those who are given cruel punishments. Deterrent punishment is likely to harden the criminal instead of creating in him the fear of law. Hardened criminals are not afraid of punishment. Punishment loses its horror once the criminal is punished.

Beccaria writes: "The more cruel the punishment becomes; the more human minds hardened, adjusting themselves, like fluids, to the level of objects around them; and the ever living force of the passions bring it about that, after a hundred years of cruel punishments, the wheel frightens men only just as much as at first did the punishment of prison." Hobbes expresses himself in these words: "People are not deterred from murder by the sight of the murderers dangling from a gibbet. On the contrary, what there is in them, of lust for blood is tickled and excited, their sensuality or ferocity is aroused and the counteracting impulses, the aversion to bloodshed, the compunction for suffering are arrested."

(b) Preventive Theory: Another object of punishment is preventive or disabling. The offenders are disabled from repeating the offences by such punishments as imprisonment, death, exile, forfeiture of office etc. By putting the criminal in jail, he is prevented from committing another crime. By dismissing a person from his office, he is deprived of an opportunity to commit a crime again. Paton writes: "The preventive theory concentrates on the prisoner but seeks to prevent him from offending again in the future. Death penalty and exile serve the same purpose of disabling the offender." Justice Holmes writes: "There can be no case in which the law-maker makes certain conduct criminal, without his thereby showing a wish and purpose to prevent that conduct. Prevention would accordingly seem to be the chief and only universal purpose of punishment. The law threatens certain pains if you do certain things, intending thereby to give you a new motive for not doing them. If you persist in doing them, it has to inflict the pains in order that its threats may continue to be believed."

An example of preventive punishments is the cancellation of the driving license of a person. As he has no license, he is prevented from driving.

(c) **Reformative Theory:** According to this theory, the object of punishment should be the reform of the criminal. Even if an offender commits a crime, he does not cease to be a human being. He may have committed a crime under circumstances, which might never occur again. The object of punishment should be to bring about the moral reform of the offender. He must be educated and taught some art or industry during the period of his imprisonment so that he may be able to start his life again after his release from jail. While awarding punishment, the judge should study the character and age of the offender, his early breeding, his education and environment, the circumstances under which he committed the offence, the object with which he committed the offence and other factors. The object of doing so is to acquaint the judge with the exact nature of the circumstances so that he may give punishment, which suits the circumstances.

The advocates of the reformative theory contend that by a sympathetic, tactful and loving treatment of the offenders, a revolutionary change may be brought about in their characters. Even the cruel hardened prisoners can be reformed and converted into helpful friends by good words and mild suggestions. Severe punishment can merely debase them. Man always kicks against pricks. Whipping will make him balk. Threat will result in resistance. Prison-hell may create the spirit of defiance of God and man. Hanging a criminal is merely an admission of the fact that human beings have failed to reform the erring citizen. Corporal punishments like whipping and pollory destroy all the finest sentiments and tenderness in man. Mild imprisonment with probation is the only mode of punishment approved by the advocates of reformative punishment.

The view of Salmond on the reformation theory is that if criminals are to be sent to prison to be transformed into good citizens by physical, intellectual and moral training, prisons must be turned into comfortable dwelling places. There are many incorrigible offenders who are beyond the reach of reformative influences and with whom crime is not a bad habit but an instinct and they must be left to their fate in despair. The theory of reformative punishment alone is not sufficient and there should be a compromise between the deterrent theory and the reformative theory and the deterrent theory must have the last word. The primary and essential end of criminal justice is deterrence and not reformation. In the past, the deterrent theory alone was considered and crime alone was taken into consideration and not other circumstances. In modern times, there is a tendency to ignore or minimize the deterrent aspect of punishment. What is required is that the value of the deterrent element must be given its proper place. In most cases, criminals are sub-normal persons and that is largely due to the fact that the fear of law has its effect on normal minds. Salmond writes: "The deterrent motive should not be abandoned in favour of the reformative altogether since the permanent influence of criminal law in this stern aspect contributes largely to the maintenance of the moral and social habits which shall prevent any but the abnormal from committing crime and also directly deter any but the sub-normal, apart from exceptional circumstances, from committing crimes."

In spite of the view of Salmond, a lot of emphasis is being put on the reformative aspect of punishment in modern times. In progressive States, provision is made for the prevention of habitual offenders. Borstal schools have set up. Provision is made for a system of probation for first offenders.

Reformation theory is being fastly adopted in the case of juvenile offenders. The oldest legislation on the subject in India is the Reformatory Schools Act, 1980 which aimed at preventing the depraved and delinquent children from becoming confirmed criminals in the coming years. It applied to children under the age of 15 years. Section 4 abolished all criminal proceedings for offences other than homicide against children. The entire responsibility of dealing with delinquent children was put on the local authorities. Section 5 authorised the provincial government to establish and maintain reformatory schools. Section 6 provided that the reformatory schools must provide sufficient means of separating the inmates at night, proper sanitary arrangements, water supply, food clothing and bedding for the youthful offenders detained therein, the means of giving industrial training to youthful offenders and proper places for the reception of youthful offenders when sick. Section 8 provided that if a youthful offender was sentenced to transportation or imprisonment, the court may direct that instead of undergoing sentence, he shall be sent to a reformatory school and detained there for a period not less than three years or more than seven years.

The Government of India passed in 1960 the Children Act, which applies, to the Union Territories. This Act was amended in 1978. This amendment broadened the aim of the Children Act, 1960.

The Probation of offenders Act, 1958 had been passed with a similar object in view. About this Act, the Supreme Court observed in Rattan Lal v. State of Punjab that the Act is a milestone in the progress of the modern liberal trend of reform in the field of penology. It is the result of the recognition of the doctrine that the object of criminal law is more to reform the individual offender than to punish him.

The Act distinguishes offenders between 21 years of age and those above that age and offenders who are guilty of having committed an offence punishable with death or imprisonment for life and those who are guilty of a lesser offence. In the case of offenders who are above the age of 21, absolute discretion is given to the courts to release them after admonition or probation of good conduct. In the case of offenders below the age of 21, an injunction is issued to the courts not to sentence them to imprisonment unless they are satisfied that, having regard to the circumstances of the case, including the nature of the offence and the character of these offenders, it is not desirable to release them on probation.

Section 27 of the Criminal Procedure Code, 1973 provides that any offence not punishable with death or imprisonment for life committed by any person who, at the date when he appears or is brought before the court, is under the age of 16 years, may be tried by the court of a Chief Judicial Magistrate or by any court especially empowered under the Children Act, 1960, or any other law for the time being in force providing for the treatment, training and rehabilitation of youthful offenders. The formation of Juvenile Justices act 2000 had given serious concession to youthful offenders – male or female up to age of 18 have been declared to be Juvenile offenders. They cannot be issued by regular courts. They cannot be convicted to regular methods of punishment. They are to be reformed only and made good citizens.

Section 360 of the Code of Criminal Procedure, 1973 empowers the court to order the release on probation of good conduct or after admonition.

The reformative theory wants to punish the criminal as little as possible and improve him as much as possible. Punishments that brutalize the criminals are discarded. It is contended that if we inflict degrading punishment on criminals, there is no scope left for their reformation. The disgrace and loss of self-respect by the criminals are serious obstacles in the way of their reformation.

In the case of habitual criminals, the deterrent theory would like to inflict as severe a punishment as possible on the ground that the previous punishment must have been inadequate and that is why the criminal committed further offences. The reformative theory is going to fail in the case of habitual offenders.

The deterrent theory may impose the punishment of imprisonment, fine or even whipping and death penalty. According to the reformative theory, excepting imprisonment, the other modes of punishment are barbaric. Imprisonment and probation are the only important instruments available for the purpose of a purely reformative system.

The question arises whether a system of penal code is possible which has reformation as the sole standard of punishment. The view of Salmond is that there are in the world men who are incurably bad. With them, crime is not so much of a bad habit and the reformative theory would be helpless in the case of such persons. According to him, the perfect system of criminal justice is based on neither the reformative nor the deterrent principle. What is required is a compromise between the two and in that also the deterrent principle must have the predominant influence. The extreme inclination towards the reformative theory may be as dangerous as the complete acceptance of the deterrent theory. It is true that previously too much attention was paid to the crime and not to the criminal. It is also true that criminals generally are not ordinary beings. They are mentally diseased and abnormal human beings. However, if all the murderers are considered as innocent and given a lenient treatment, even ordinary sane people may be tempted to commit crimes in view of the lenient attitude of law towards crime.

The reformative theory may be effective in the case of very young and completely insane offenders, but the deterrent element in punishment must have the predominant influence.

In his Philosophy of Right, Prof. D. Lioy writes: "Crimes are to be treated as infirmities and the culpable ones. Diseased subjects whose fury might be subdued in solitude, if they had been impelled to the evil deed by the violence of their passion; and it should aim at correcting their vicious habits by the aid of labour, if they had come to them through idleness and to enlighten their minds by means of instruction, if ignorance had led them astray. By this means law from being vindictive had become just and from being just had become charitable and it completed the act of punishing by the art of healing."

(d) Retributive Theory: In the primitive society, punishment was mainly retributive. The person wronged was allowed to have his revenge against the wrongdoer. The principle of "an eye for an eye", "a tooth for a tooth" was recognized and followed. Justice Holmes writes: "It is commonly known that the early forms of legal procedure were grounded in vengeance."

The retributive aspect was recognized in ancient penology. Early criminal law was based on the principle that all evil should be requited. It was believed that the community could be regarded as purged of the evil only in that way. Among the ancient Jews, even animals which killed human beings were regarded as contaminated and were got rid of for the good of the community. Plato was a supporter of the retributive theory. He wrote: "If justice is the good and the health of the soul as injustice is its disease and shame, chastisement is their remedy. If a man is happy when he lives in order, than when he is out of it, it is of importance to him to enter it again and he enters it through chastisement."

Every culpa demands expiation; the culpa is ugly, it is contrary to justice and order; the expiation is beautiful because all that is just is beautiful and to suffer for justice is also beautiful.

Kant, the German philosopher, expressed himself in these words: "Judicial punishment can never serve merely as a means to further another good, whether for the offender himself or for society, but must always be inflicted on him for the sole reason that he has committed a crime. The law of punishment is a categorical imperative." Kant gave the following example: "Even if a community of citizens dissolves with the consent of every member (e.g., the inhabitants of an island decide to separate and spread all over the world), they must first execute the last murderer in the prison so that everyone gets what is his due according to his deeds."

The view of Sir James Stephen is that the purpose of punishment is to gratify the desire for vengeance by making the criminal pay with his body. Punishment gratifies the feeling of pleasure experienced by individuals at the thought that the criminal has been brought to justice. That desire ought to be satisfied by inflicting punishment in order to avoid the danger of private vengeance.

The view of Sir John Salmond is that the retributive purpose of punishment consists in avenging the wrong done by the criminal to society. The retributive purpose of punishment is the elevation of the moral feelings of the community. The emotion of retributive indignation created by injustice is characteristic of all healthy communities. A noble emotion like righteous indignation deserves to be fostered by the state. Through the criminal justice of the state, satisfaction is found for the moral sense of the community. Lilley writes: "the wrong whereby he has transgressed the law of right, has incurred a debt. Justice requires that the debt be paid, that the wrong be expiated. This is first object of punishment – to satisfy the outraged law."

Another view is that retributive punishment is an end in itself. Apart from gain to society and the victim, the criminal should meet his reward in equivalent suffering.

Punishment is a form of expiation. To suffer punishment is to pay a debt due to the law that has been violated. Guilt plus punishment is equal to innocence. The penalty of wrongdoing is a debt, which the offender owes to his victim. When punishment has been endured, the debt is paid and the legal bond forged by crime is dissolved. The object of true punishment must be to substitute justice for injustice. To compel the wrongdoer to restore to the injured person that, which is own by such restoration and repentance, the sprit of vengeance of the victim is to be satisfied.

Critics point out that punishment in itself is not a remedy for the mischief committed by the offender. It merely aggravates the mischief. Punishment in itself is an evil and can be justified only on the ground that it is going to yield better results. Revenge is wild justice. Justice Holmes writes: "this passion of vengeance is not one, which we encourage, either as private individuals or as lawmakers. Moreover, it does not cover the whole ground."

(e) Theory of Compensation: According to this theory, the object of punishment must be not merely to prevent further crimes but also to compensate the victim of crime. The connection is that the mainspring of criminality is greed and if the offender were made to return the ill-gotten benefits of the crime, the spring of criminality would dry up.

The motive of a crime is not always economic. Offences against the State, against justice, against religion, against marriage and even against persons, may not always be actuated by economic motives. There may be other motives involved in the case. In those cases, the theory of compensation may be neither workable nor effective.

If the offender is a rich person the payment of any amount only be no punishment for him.

(f) Theory of Social Boycott: It is one of the oldest theories. As per this theory; the criminals are socially boycotted from society completely or partly. Criminal has to suffer a lot. He cannot talk to anybody, no one can talk to him. All kinds of social relations are prohibited with these criminals. In India even today, in primitive areas, villages, such types of punishments are awarded by the community heads, village heads etc. Even in other countries such a form of punishment has also be seen. Direct results of this kind of punishment are sociological & philosophical but these affect the roots of the criminality & life of the criminal. It does not make any impact upon habitual offenders & Mafias where society cannot implement such kind of punishment.

(g) The theory of repentance: It is completely an ideological theory. The criminal can get rid of his crime upon the simple repentance as to what he has done. The Hindu philosophy doctrine of *Praschayat* is the origin of this theory. As per Hindu philosophy if any person has offered *Praschayat* (Repentance) against the sin committed by him, then he may get rid from that sin; subject to certain conditions. The same doctrine has been applied in original law. If a criminal repents for his misdeeds then he may be forgiven. This theory appears to be more theoretical rather than practical. The practical use of this theory is very limited and little, otherwise there may be chaos in society.

A perfect system of criminal justice cannot be based on any one theory of punishment. Every theory has its own merits and every effort must be made to take the good points of all. The deterrent aspect of punishment must not be ignored. Likewise, the reformative aspect must be given its due place. The personality of the offender is as important as his actions and we must not divorce his action from his personality. The offender is not merely a criminal to be punished. He is also a patient to be treated. Punishment must be in proportion to the gravity of the crime. It must be small for minor crimes and heavy for major crimes. The first offender should be leniently treated. He who behaves better should be given good diet, clothes and leisure and a part of his sentence should also be remitted. The object of this concession is to convince the offender that normal and free life is better than the life in jail. The government should set up mental hospitals and reformatories in place of jails and living conditions in jails should be improved.

Kinds of Punishment:

Let us consider various kinds of punishment. These are as follows: -

(A) Discarded form of punishment: Those forms should be considered discarded form of punishment that are not in use. Flogging or whipping was the corporeal punishment, it was abolished in India by abolition of

Whipping Act 1955. Likewise punishment of pillory and donkey riding was removed on the ground that to a person at present it adds disgrace, which could not be justified except to an insane, or a child who has no sense.

(B) **Concessional Punishment:** Law also distinguishes essential insane, child, youth, deaf, dumb, blind & other severely handicapped criminals on ground for concessional punishment. Section 318 **cr.p.c.** 1973 provides while awarding sentence, the court can take into consideration the mental & physical condition of an offender. Thus the Supreme Court ordered in sakes of a total blind offender (Sohan Singh con **scc** 1907 page 790). Likewise detention in repertories to children, release on probation to offenders U/s 360(3) **cr.p.c**. award of compensation to injured U/s 357 **cr.p.c.** As well as payment of cost to an accused for who censes on other to be arrested by police officer on insufficient grounds are confessional form of punishment applicable now-a-days. This kind of punishment is ordered only on humanitarian grounds in society.

(C) **New Forms of Punishment:** The law commission in India in its 42nd Report suggested introduction of the following new forms of punishment in the **cr.p.c.** (i) Community service (ii) Disqualification from holding office (iii) Order of payment of compensation and lastly public censure, Still today, these kinds of sober punishment have not been included in **cr.p.c.** These are still pending for formation into law.

(D) **Forfeiture of Property:** A forfeiture of property is a penalty by which one looses his right and inheritance in his property. It could be inflicted on person guilty of offences of death penalty but it was abolished in India in 1921. In England and USA it is done away with. Now in India, it has a limited scope of applicability v/s 126, 127, 161 to 169.ipc only namely depredation on the territories of nation v/s 126, 127 recaptunor property in waging war against nation. 161 to 169 ipc and a public servant who improperly purposes property by virtue office, he is legally prohibited from purchasing. Forfeiture of property as a mode of penalty should be distinguished from forfeiture of property as a mode of realization of government money embezzled by the accused. The latter is not meant to punish the person. Its object being the reoccupation of the loss to the government of the money misappropriated or embezzled.

(E) **Capital Punishment:** In the history of punishment, capital punishment has always occupied a very important place. In ancient times and even in the middle ages, sentencing of offenders to death was a very common kind of punishment. Even for what might be consider as minor offences in modern times, death penalty was imposed. In the reign of George III, there were as many as 220 offences. Death penalty was awardable even for offences like shoplifting, cattle stealing and cutting down of trees. When Samuel Romilly brought proposals for abolition of death penalty for such offences, there was a lot of hue and cry from lawyers, judges, parliamentarians and the so-called protectors of social order.

The Lord Chancellor remarked: " So long as human nature remained what it was, the apprehension of death would have the most powerful co-operation in deterring from the commission of crimes; and he thought it unwise to withdraw the salutary influence of that error."

In 1810, a bill was brought forward to abolish death penalty for the offence of stealing in a shop to the value of five shillings. Lord Ellenborough opposed the bill in these words: "Your Lordships will pause before you assent to a measure so pregnant with danger for the security of the property. The learned judges unanimously agree that the expediency of justice and public security required that there should not be a remission of capital punishment in this part of criminal law. My Lords, if we suffer this bill to pass, we shall not know where we stand, we shall not know whether we are on our heads or on our feet." Six times the House of Commons passed the bill and six times the House of Lords rejected the same. The majority on one occasion included all the judicial members, one Archbishop and six Bishops. However, in spite of opposition, the bill was passed and the number of cases in which capital punishment was awarded was reduced year after year and death penalty was reserved for offences like murder and treason.

In his 'Essay on Capital Punishment,' Sir James Fitzjames Stephen, "the draftsman of the Indian Penal Code," maintained that "no other punishment deters man so effectually from committing crime as the punishment of death.... The threat of instant death is the one to which resort has always been made when there was an absolute necessity of producing some results."

Lord Denning stated: "the punishment inflicted for grave crimes should adequately reflect the revulsion felt by the majority of citizens for them. It is a mistake to consider the object of punishment as being deterrent or reformative or preventive and nothing else. The ultimate justification of any punishment is not that it is a deterrent but it is the emphatic denunciation by the community of a crime, and from this point of view there are some murders which in the present state of opinion demand the most emphatic denunciation of all, namely, the death penalty. The truth is that some crimes are so outrageous that it (death penalty) is imposed irrespective of whether it is deterrent or not."

In spite of these views, death penalty was abolished in the United Kingdom in 1965 except for offences of treason and certain forms of piracy and offences committed by members of Armed Forces during wartime. An attempt was made in the United Kingdom in December 1975 to reintroduce death penalty for terrorist offences involving murder but it was defeated in the House of Lords. A similar motion was rejected by the House of Commons on 19 July 1979.

In India, Indian Penal Code provided for capital punishment but the same was to be resorted to sparingly. The position of capital punishment did not change for more than 100 years but the trend in the direction of the abolition of capital punishment in many countries affected legislative as well as judicial thinking of India. The legislative thinking is reflected in some subtle changes in the Code of Criminal Procedure during the last two decades or so. Before the amendment of the Code of Criminal Procedure in 1955, it was obligatory for a court to give reasons for not awarding death sentence in the case of murder. The amendment in 1955 did away with the requirement of assigning reasons for not giving death sentence in an appropriate case. Under the new Code of Criminal Procedure, 1973, the court has to record reasons for awarding death sentence. It is clear that the provisions regarding death sentence have gradually been liberalized in favour of guilty person, even Supreme Court.

India is clearly towards the abolition of death sentence. In Ediga Anamma v. State of Andhra Pradesh, the Superme Court of India observed: "While murder in its aggravated form in the extenuating factors connected with crime, criminal or legal process, still is condignly visited with death penalty, a compassionate alternative of life imprisonment in all other circumstances is gaining judicial ground." [(1974) 4 SCC 443].

In Raghubir Singh v. State of Haryana, although the Supreme Court accepted the contention that the murder was treacherous, death sentence was reduced to life imprisonment. [(1975) 3 SCC37].

In Rajendra Prasad v. State of Uttar Pradesh, the appellant was sentenced to life imprisonment in a previous case but released on Gandhi Jayanti day. He again committed murder and was sentenced to death by the Sessions Judge and his death sentence was confirmed by the High Court. However, the same was also converted into life imprisonment by the Supreme Court. [(1979) 3 SCC 646].

In Bachan Singh v. State of Punjab, the Supreme Court held by a majority of four to one that the provision of death sentence as an alternative punishment for murder in Section 302 of the Indian Penal Code is not unreasonable and is in the public interest. Section 302 violates neither the letter nor the ethos of Article 19 of the Constitution. The provision of death sentence as an alternative punishment for murder does not violate Article 21 of the Constitution. It was argued that death penalty constitutes an unreasonable, cruel or unusual punishment. The court rejected the plea and held that the framers of the Constitution did not consider death sentence for murder as a degrading punishment, which would defile "the dignity of the individual." Death sentence for the offence of murder also does not violate the basic structure of the Constitution. To commit a crime is not an activity guaranteed by Article 19(1) of the Constitution. A very large segment of people the world over, including sociologists, legislators, jurists, judges and administrators still fairly believe in the necessity of capital punishment for protection of society. The penalty has still a recognized legal sanction in most of the civilized countries in the world and the framers of the Indian Constitution were fully aware of the existence of death penalty as punishment of murder under section 302 of the Indian Penal Code. It is not possible to hold that the provision of death penalty as an alternative punishment for murder is not in the public interest. [(1980) 2 SCC 634].

The dissenting view of Justice Bhagwati was that instead of death sentence, the sentence of life imprisonment should be imposed. He pointed out that the international trend was towards the abolition of death penalty and a large numbers of countries have abolished death penalty *de jure* or *de facto*. As on 30th May, 1979, the following countries had abolished death penalty for all offences: Australia, Brazil, Columbia, Denmark, Federal Republic of Germany, Finland, Norway, Sweden, Portugal etc. Canada, Italy, Spain, Switzerland, the Netherlands, Peru and Malta had abolished death penalty in time of peace but retained it for specific offences committed in time of war. Many other States had retained death penalty on their statute books but they did not conduct any execution for many years. Many states in the United State of America had abolished death penalty. The United Kingdom abolished death penalty in 1965. The United Nations had gradually shifted from the position of neutral observer concerned about, but not committed on the question of death penalty to a position favouring the eventual abolition of death penalty. The objective of the United Nations is that capital punishment should ultimately be abolished in all countries.

Justice Bhagwati also referred to the views of Tolstoy, Jayprakash Narayan, Andrei Sakharov, Victor Hugo and Mahatma Gandhi in support of his contention.

Justice Bhagwati has put emphasis on barbarity and cruelty involved in death sentence. Death penalty is irrevocable. It cannot be recalled. It extinguishes the flame of life forever. It is destructive of the right to live, which is the most precious right of all, a right without which enjoyment of no other right is possible. It silences forever a living being and dispatches him to a country from which there is no return. By reason of its cold and cruel finality, death penalty is qualitatively different from all other forms of punishment. If a person is sentenced to imprisonment, even if it is for life, and subsequently it is found that he was innocent and was wrongly convicted, he can be set free. However, that is not possible where a person has been wrongly convicted and sentenced to death and put out of existence in pursuance of the sentence of death. It is impossible to eliminate the chance of judicial error. No possible judicial safeguard can prevent the conviction of the innocent.

I can very safely say that death penalty cannot be said to be appropriate to the offence merely because it may be or is believed to be an effective deterrent against the commission of the offence. Death penalty cannot be regarded as appropriate to the offence of murder merely because the murder is brutal, heinous or shocking. The nature and magnitude of the offence or the motive and purposes underlying it or the manner and extent of its commission cannot have any relevance to the proportionality of death penalty to the offence.

Justice Bhagwati does not accept the argument advanced in support of death penalty that every punishment is to some extent intended to express the revulsion felt by the society against the wrongdoer and therefore punishment must be commensurate with the crime and as murder is one of the gravest crimes against society, death penalty is the only punishment which fits such crimes and hence it must be held to be reasonable. According to Justice Bhagwati, the denunciatory theory is a remnant of a primitive society, which had no respect for the dignity of man and worth of the human person and seeks to assuage its injured conscience by taking revenge on the wrongdoer. Revenge is an elementary passion of a brute and betrays lack of culture and refinement. A society, which is truly cultured, can never harbour a feeling of revenge against a wrongdoer. The wrongdoer is as much a part of the society as anyone else, and by exterminating him the society is injuring itself.

Retaliation can have no place in a civilized society and particularly in the land of Buddha and Gandhi.

Justice Bhagwati rejects the view that death penalty acts as a deterrent against potential murderers. According to him, this view is a myth, which has been carefully nurtured by a society, which is, actuated not so much by logic or reason as by a sense of retribution. Justice Frankfurter of the Supreme Court of the United States expressed the same view in the course of his examination before the Royal Commission on Capital Punishment: "I think scientifically the claim of deterrence is not worth much." A similar view was expressed by the Royal Commission on Capital Punishment: "Whether the death penalty is used or not and whether executions are frequent or not, both death penalty States and abolition States have rates which suggest that these rates are conditioned by other factors than the death penalty." Again, "the general conclusion which we have reached is that there is no clear evidence in any of the figures we have examined that the abolition of capital punishment has led to an increasing homicide rate or that its reintroduction has led to a fall."

The view of Prof. Sellin is that "there is no evidence that the abolition of capital punishment generally causes an increase in criminal homicides, or that its reintroduction is followed by a decline. The explanation of changes in homicide rates must be sought elsewhere."

In Rajendra Singh's case, Justice Bhagwati recommends that there should be an automatic review of the death sentence by the Supreme Court sitting as a whole and death sentence shall not be affirmed or imposed only if the Supreme Court comes to the conclusion that the offender is a serious menace to society and it is in the interests of society that he should be eliminated. [(1982) 3SCC 24].

The views of Justice V.R. Krishna Iyer are like Justice Bhagwati. His lordship described death penalty as "crime upon criminals" He also said that death penalty is nothing but a legal tyranny of the state. His lordship further stated that death penalty can propose no useful purpose in your way. No crime can be checked or controlled by the fear of death penalty.

Justice R.N. Mishra, Venkatchelaya, Ahmedi & A.S. Anand all chief justice of India have shared the common view that except in rare cases, seriously effecting & adversely to the society. There is no need of death penalty of all. Only in offences where society is highly & seriously and adversely affected, death sentence should be awarded to check infiltration of the lawbreaker and to maintain the balance in society.

There is an ongoing debate between those who stand for the abolition of capital punishment and those who want to retain it. Those who stand for its abolition maintain that capital punishment has not served its deterrent object at all.

It is also contended that crimes are committed very often not by normal human beings under normal circumstances. It is not even certain that a murderer would repeat murder again.

Those who want to retain the sentence of capital punishment argue that there are some offenders who are not only incorrigible but also immensely dangerous to society. There is no reason why society should be burdened with maintaining such people. If an offender cannot be cured and the incorrigible element is harmful to human society, the best thing is to carry out the death sentence.

Another argument in favour of capital punishment is that punishment by the state is substitute for private revenge. If a murderer is not punished with death, it is quite possible that other relative of the victim might murder the murderer and thus a chain of murders may start. So long as human emotion is powerful and the powers of vengeance prevail, capital punishment is a necessary kind of punishment.

The view of Lord Denning is that Capital Punishment is the way in which society expresses its denunciation of the wrongdoer. It is necessary to maintain respect for law. Some crimes are so outrageous that society insists on adequate punishment for the wrongdoer.

Justice Stewart observes; "I can't agree that retribution is a constitutionally impermissible ingredients in the imposition of punishment. The instinct for retribution is part of the nature of man, and channeling that instinct in the administration of criminal justice serves an important purpose in promoting the stability of a society governed by law. When people began to believe that the organized society is unwilling or unable to impose upon criminal offenders the punishment they deserve, then there are sown seeds of anarchy–of self help, vigilance, justice, and lynch law."

J.J Maclen of Canada defends the right of the state to award capital punishment for murder. According to him, if the state has the right & duty to defend the community against outside aggression such as in time of war & and within the country for instance, in case of treason etc. & that to the extent of taking the life of the aggressors and guilty parties, if the citizen want to protect his own life by killing whoever attacks without any reason, the state can do the same when a criminal attacks and endangers the life of the community by deciding to eliminate similarly another human being. Capital punishment must be retained to prove the sanctity of that most precious thing, the gift of life. It embodies the revulsion and horror that we feel for the greatest of crimes. As a deterrent, death penalty is playing its part for which there is no substitute.

Even in England, death penalty has been retained for high treason. In the aftermath of assassination of Prime Minister Bandaranaike in 1959, Ceylon reintroduced capital punishment for murder. Likewise, Israel sanctioned that penalty for crimes committed against the Jewish people and executed Eichmann in 1962 on the ground that he was responsible for the death of many Jews. In 1979, Israel sanctioned the use of death penalty for acts of inhuman cruelty."

The Law Commission of India in its 35th Report has given reasons for the view that Capital punishment has deterrent effect. Basically, every human being dreads death. Death, as a penalty, stands on a totally different level from imprisonment for life or other punishment. The difference is one of quality and not merely of degree.

(F) **Deportation:** Another way of punishment is the deportation of incorrigible or dangerous offenders. This method used to recalled transportation in India. However, this is not a solution to the problem. If a person is dangerous in one society and if he is let loose in another society, he is likely to be equally dangerous there also. Punishment in the form of deportation was abolished long ago in Britain and it has now been abolished in India also.

(G) **Corporal Punishments:** Another form of punishment is corporal punishment. This punishment included modulation, throwing hot elements upon criminal or criminal is thrown in hot elements and other major or minor kind of torture. Previously, this was a very common form of punishment. Right up to the middle ages, whipping was one of the commonest forms of punishment. It was also a very severe form of punishment. Many died as a result of the wounds received by them on account of flogging or whipping. Whipping in public used to be common during the ancient and medieval times in India.

The main object of this kind of punishment is deterrence. However, critics point out that this kind of punishment is not only inhuman but also ineffective. Pakistan has recently introduced flogging as a form of punishment.

A few criminologists have suggested that whipping should be reintroduced in India as a kind of punishment. Their contention is that simple thing, as imprisonment itself does not have the deterrence effect as whipping. This is particularly so in the case of rich offenders. There is opposition to the suggestion on the ground that whipping is a barbaric form of punishment and it should not be introduced in the civilized society of today. Whipping produces only the rougher kind of criminal.

(H) Imprisonment: Another form of punishment is Imprisonment. If properly administered, imprisonment can serve all the 3 objects of punishment. It may be deterrence, it makes an example of the offenders to others. It may be preventive because it disables the offender, at least for some time, from repeating the offence. If properly used, it might give an opportunity to the problem of fixing the period of imprisonment. Both short term and long term imprisonment have their inherent disadvantages. Short-term imprisonments are regarded not only useless but also dangerous. They are useless because no institutional training or treatment is possible in short terms like one-month or six months. They are dangerous because jails provide ideal surroundings to the novices and the minor offenders for further training in a criminal career.

Some kind of accused are sentenced to both imprisonment and fine and some times fine only. The view of Lord Gaddard is that fine should not be used to give an opportunity to persons of means to avoid the punishment of heading.

In judging the adequacy of sentence, the nature of the offence, circumstances of its commission, the age and character of the offender, injury to individuals or to society, effect of punishment on the offender, eye to correction and reformation of the offender, are some amongst many other factors which should ordinarily be taken into consideration by the court.

(I) Solitary confinement: Another kind of punishment is solitary confinement, which is an aggravated kind of punishment. Solitary confinement exploits fully the sociable nature of man. By denying him the society of his fellow beings, it seeks to inflict pain on him.

Critics point out that this kind of punishment is inhuman and perverse. There is every possibility of a man of sound mental health being turned into a lunatic. If used in excess, it may inflict permanent harm on the offender. However, if used in proportion, this kind of punishment may be useful. If those limits are surpassed, it becomes cruel.

Sections 73 & 74 of the Indian Penal Code lay down the limits beyond, which solitary confinement cannot be imposed in India. The total period of solitary confinement cannot exceed three months in any case. It cannot exceed 14 days at a time with intervals of 14 days in between or 7 days at a time with 7 days interval in between.

(J) Indeterminate Sentence: Another kind of imprisonment is indeterminate sentence. In this case, the accused is not sentenced to imprisonment for any fixed period. The period is left indeterminate at that time. When the accused shows improvement, the sentence may be terminated.

(K) Payment of Fine: Punishment of fine, in addition to serving its deterrent object, also serves three more purposes. It may help to support the dependents of the prisoner. It might provide expenses for the prosecution of the prisoner. It may be used for compensating the aggrieved party. This kind of punishment may be very useful if the criminals are not hardened. Care must be taken that heavy and excessive fines, which result in the forfeiture of the property of the offender, should not be inflicted. Facilities for collecting fines must be created in such a way that levying of the fine does not inevitably drive the offender to the prison on account of his inability to pay the fine.

Civil Justice

Primary and Sanctioning Rights

The rights enforced by civil proceedings are of two kinds viz. primary rights and sanctioning rights. Primary rights are those rights, which exists as such. They do not have their source in some wrong. Sanctioning or remedial rights are those rights, which come into being after the violation of a primary right. A primary right is a right arising out of conduct or as a *jus in rem.* A sanctioning right is one, which arises out of the violation of another right. **If A enters into a valid contract performed is a primary right.** If the contract is broken, his right to damages for the loss caused to him for the breach of contract is sanctioning right. A primary right may be enforced by specific enforcement. Specific restitution (restoring a person to his status quo). Where primary rights can be enforced, there is no question of any sanctioning right for that purpose. The cases of the enforcement of a primary right are where a defendant is compelled to perform a contract or to pay a debt. The enforcement of the primary right is called specific enforcement.

Sanctioning rights are (i) the right to be compensated by damages by the wrongdoer, or (ii) the right to exact the imposition of pecuniary penalty on the wrongdoer by penal action. The first is divided into two types: restitution and penal redress. Restitution lies in restoring the plaintiff to his original position. Penal redress involves restitution of all benefits the offenders derives from his wrongful act, plus a full redress for the plaintiff's loss.

Penal and Remedial Proceedings

All legal proceedings can be divided into five categories viz, action for specific enforcement, action for restitution, action for penal redress, penal action and criminal prosecution. Actions for penal redress, penal action and criminal prosecution are called penal proceedings because their ultimate purpose is punishment. Actions for specific enforcement and restitution are called remedial proceeding, as their object is to remedy a wrong. In the case of penal proceedings, the ultimate purpose of the defendant. **Matter missing.** That is so where a person is imprisoned or held liable in damages to the person injured by him. In the case of remedial proceeding, the idea of punishment is entirely absent.

Secondary Functions of Courts of Law:

As we have seen that the primary function of a court of law is the administration of justice. It has to enforce rights and punish wrongs. In every case, there are two parties, viz., the plaintiff and the defendant or the prosecutor and the accused. However, in addition to this order functions are also performed by courts of law.

(1) Courts adjudicate on the claims of citizens against the state. It seems logically impossible to conceive of the forces of the state being used against itself. However, the laws of all modern state provide remedies for individual citizens against the state to be pursued in its own courts. In the case of India, a suit can be brought against the Union of India and of the Government of a State. In England, no action could be brought against the Crown up to the passing of the Crown Proceedings Act, 1947. However, even then, in the case of contractual liabilities, a British subject could put in a petition of Rights Act, 1980. The Crown Proceedings Act, 1947 provides that where a person has a claim against the Crown, that claim can be enforced.

(2) Another function of the courts is the declaration of the rights of individuals. This is done where the rights of the parties are uncertain. What a court does is that it gives an authoritative declaration of the rights of the person concerned. Examples of declaratory proceedings are the declaration of legitimacy, declaration of nullity of marriage, advice to trustees or executors regarding their legal powers and duties, authoritative interpretation of wills etc.

(3) In certain cases courts of justice undertake the management and distribution of the property of a deceased person and also of minors whose property is put under the court of Wards. Other examples of administrative functions are the administration of the trust, the realization and distribution of an insolvent estate, liquidation of a company by the court etc.

(4) In certain cases, judicial decrees are employed as the means of creating, extinguishing and transferring rights. Examples of such function are a decree of divorce or judicial separation, adjudication of bankruptcy, a decree of foreclosure against a mortgager, appointment or removal of trustees, grant of letter of administration etc. In such cases, the judgment of the courts operates not as the remedy of a wrong, but as a title of right.

(5) Superior courts are often armed with the power of supervising the courts below them. Article 227 of the Constitution of India gives such a power to the High Courts in India.

CHAPTER 6

Law and Justice (Dharma and Nyaya)

The concept of 'dharma' was all pervading and brought in its fold not only the duty to be performed by every individual comprising the social groups in those times but was also the ideal of those who were charged with the function of administering justice to the disputing parties. It was, therefore, said that to do justice, in truth as well as in deed was the 'dharma' of the King. If he failed to perform this duty, it was even permitted by the shastras to ask such a king to step down from the throne or if he was unwilling to do, he could be dethroned by force. It was thus understood that 'dharma' is law, 'dharma' is truth, 'dharma' is justice, it is virtue as opposed to vice; it is rightful conduct as against a wrongful one and a moral act in contradiction to an immoral or amoral one.

It would, thus be clear that the ancients had no need to propound any theory or concept of justice, as the Westerners have done for the simple reason that 'dharma' itself was a repository of justice par excellence.

The Nyaya and Vaisisika philosophy, that developed the science of logic and reasoning, that the concept of 'Nyaya' found a place in treatises. 'Nyaya' meant a reasoned conclusion, a proved conclusion. Nyaya, literally a judgment, became then, a method of deciding learned disquisitions paying full regard to systematic methods of proof. By analogical extension this method was found fruitful for deciding disputes in courts, where a proof was necessary. Thus 'Nyaya', which originally was a logical method of deciding a controversy (theory of knowledge), became by extension an application, a method of deciding disputes (theory of justice). Basically 'Nyaya', or the so-called justice, is neither the root nor the fruit of Indian thought and culture but an enquiry about truth or knowledge. Unlike Rit, Dharma, Vrata, Danda, Yajna, Karma, the word Nyaya has no theological and metaphysical basis in Vedic literature. Yama, who is the God of justice, is called 'Dharmaraj' not 'Nayayaraj.' The equation of Nayaya with Dharma is only due to the usage of language.

The formulation of the doctrine of justice, and subsuming the total philosophy of life and ideals of socio-political existence under 'justice', is a peculiar characteristic of western thinking? The debate about 'what is justice?' started in Greek thought, is still going on in the west, but without any conclusion. The fact is that the concept of justice is constituted of diverse elements, like ethical, social, political, logical, psychological, and consequently any method or theory which emphasizes one or some of them by ignoring other or others is bound to be insufficient or incomplete. It seems that by discussing justice writers tend to agree or disagree. This disagreement is the direct result of the attitude of distrust or anxiety developed in the west about the government, State and law. Now it is difficult for the doctrine of justice to reconcile or balance the interests of a socio-political society wherein individuals and social groups are constantly engaged in scuffles for power, position and privilege. All sections claim different kinds of protections against each other at the threshold of 'justice.' Social justice is sought after for the protection of social harm, political justice is seen to protect political harm and the legal one protects against the legal harm.

The western thought justice couldn't keep in tact its frontiers. It was bound to be encroached upon and broken into by incursions, and instrusions of the general current of ideas. Justice must then comprehend the whole theory of social and political existence. If it does so it then approximates Dharma, which is a synthesis of various diverse elements of thinking. It is in the habit of seeing justice particularized, i.e., as a justification of some political or social or economic or moral or some other theory. The western thinkers have failed to measure the breadth of justice. Even in Greek theory when discussion starts with the perfunctory and general view of justice it is immediately directed to its particularities. Unlike the westerner, the Indian mind has the capacity to comprehend the whole wherein it can see the form, content and spirit. Devoid of this view western notion of justice is only a partial fulfillment of Dharma.

Justice is thus, in its original notion, the quality or aptitude of joining; it ties together whatever it touches. Primarily, it ties men together, by common bond of right and fitting order of relations, under which each has his position in the order and receives his due place; each has his rights as his share of the general right pervading and constituting the order; and each owns jura as the exemplification and concrete expression in his own case of the general jus.[1] It is just like 'Dharma' which has its root meaning in 'holding together' and Rit which has its root in 'binding'. From this idea of apportionment of just or rights starts a 'subjective feeling and consequent desire for a fitting order' and Justinian defines it accordingly. His institutes emphasize three aspects of justice:(1) jus as an objective expression of right which is recognized and enforced by rules, (2) living up to one's position, (3) actually and positively respecting another's position and rights.

Purohit [2] describes that justice, then performs the function of 'joining' and fitting together. But there is also a further extension. Justice is joining or fitting together, not only of persons but also of principles. It joins and knits together, and claims of the principles of liberty with those of the principles of equality, and both with those of the principle of fraternity or co-operation; it adjusts them to one another in a right order of their relations.[3] Again it reconciles conflicts and joins together not only different principles but also conflicts within the area of a single principle itself. Justice has been called a term of synthesis. "It is the final principle which controls the general distribution of rights and various principles of their distribution." The theory, as a balancing of interests in all its purity; devoid of standard or measurement is presented by Roscoe Pound who calls it functional justice and emphasizes impartiality minus ideology.

In this ethical meaning justice is considered not in its narrow meaning of "legal justice' but as something, which is good in itself. It is then identified with the ideal of human good. It is seen as an instrument of good life. Legal activities can be evaluated by the standard of good life. Law then becomes a means of procuring good life. In this sense justice is just like Dharma. Though there can be some difficulty in determination of the nature of the good life and right method to ensure it, yet there is no difficulty in realizing that justice is the realization of good through law and the ideal is accepted on all hands.

But when justice is expressed in terms of any other ancillary ideal, it becomes only a partial fulfillment of life and controversy starts. Then it ceases to be a 'total good' and 'ought of life.'

What is Justice-by western thinkers? The idea of justice in the Holy Christian scriptures is a transcendental one. Justice is not known through reason. It is one of the mysteries of faith. There are two elements of justice, which are found in scriptures and are in opposition to one another. One is the doctrine of love, which is the avowed doctrine of the love, which is the avowed doctrine of the law testament and was propagated by Jesus Christ.

In the philosophy of Plato[3] the doctrine of justice holds a very important place. Plato identifies justice with retribution, as retribution is instrumental for attainment of 'good'. The idea of justice derives its total value from the idea of good. But when it is to be determined what is good, the dialogues of Plato are of no help. In one word it is a divine mystery. For practical purposes Plato considers justice as the proper performance of one's functions. It is an expression of harmony. Aristotle takes happiness as the starting point of his ethics. To him happiness is the supreme good. Justice is the consequence or reward for virtue but is not identical with it. At first, he rejects virtue as the end of life. But yet according to him, transformation of happiness into virtue can take place by the reason of right performance of activity and one's own function. Then good is happiness and happiness becomes virtue later, in evolution of his doctrine. He gives the doctrine a golden mean. Accordingly, justice is also the observation of the means. "Aristotle distinguishes, at first, between[4] two kinds of justice, one is general justice and other is particular justice." According to him, there are two concepts of justice–lawfulness and equality. The term 'unjust' held to apply both to man who breaks the law and the man who takes more than his due. Hence, it is clear that both the law-abiding and the fair-minded will be just. 'The just', therefore, means that which is lawful and that which is equal or fair, and the 'unjust' means that which is illegal and that which is unequal or unfair. According to Aristotle, law fulfillness is a broader concept, whereas equality is a narrow one. Every unlawful act is not an unequal act but everything, which is unfair, is unlawful. As a result of this, justice includes whole of lawfulness. It is also total virtue, i.e., perfect virtue. By lawfulness Aristotle means conformity to positive law. To him the law-breaker is unjust while the law-abiding is just. Particular justice is divided by him as, distributed and corrective. He introduces here the principle of proportional equality. While distributing things like honours, offices, etc., the State was to look to the difference in individuals, as it could not be just to treat unequal as equals. In his book 'Nichomachean Ethics,' the standard he sets for distributive justice is merit. In democracy, he says, all freemen are considered equal, in an oligarchy, the consideration is made on 'the basis of wealth and nobility of birth,' and aristocracy, virtue is taken as measurement of distribution.

Corrective justice is concerned with restoration of equality, which has arisen due to violation of law. It has application to transaction, like that of selling, lending, etc., which are called voluntary, and cases of fraud and theft which are involuntary transactions, these may also be the cases of criminal wrongs but Aristotle treats them as civil wrongs. In these cases the aim of the judge, according to Aristotle, is not to punish but to give redress. In cases of offences against state (and not against individuals), Aristotle calls for the application of the principle of general justice. Here the principle is that of arithmetical proportion. It makes no difference whether a good man defrauds a bad man or a bad man a good one. The law looks only to the difference created by the injury; the parties themselves being treated equally.

Aristotle points out a third kind of justice, which he calls 'commutative' justice. This kind governs the exchange of commodities and takes into consideration as its measure the skill of the parties and corresponding value of their products.

Justice is identified in his 'Politics' as the function of the State. For the law is the order of the political community; where the law determines what is just. It comes to this that justice is lawfulness, and if justice is the function of equality, then justice is only equality before law. It seems that justice cannot be defined by rationalistic or moral philosophy. Augustine puts an end to the rational argument when he considers that justice is Christianity and injustice is paganism.

Natural Law Theory of Justice

Natural law theory is also a theory of justice because it considers what is right and wrong in relations between men, in society. According to this view all the natural processes are directed towards some end and they are determined by final causes. Nature is seen pervaded with will and intelligence. If the natural law doctrine is consistent, it must assume a religious character. It can deduce from nature 'just' rules of behaviour only because so far nature is conceived of as a revelation of God's will. As a matter of fact, there is no natural law doctrine of any importance, which has not a more or less religious character. Natural law theory considers that value is imminent in reality and that value is absolute in character. On this presupposition the doctrine of natural law is absolute justice. It identifies laws of nature with rules of law in human society. Nature is considered here as a just social order. If positive law is considered unjust, natural law entitles the individual to offer resistance and violate that unjust law. This is another way in which natural law asserts a theory of justice. On the issue, whether private property is just or not, all natural law theories, from Grotius to Kant, support the right of private property. This view seems somewhat surprising when we see that the Holy Scriptures, as interpreted by the Church, enjoin and ordain that God gave all things to men in common. But man through sin and greed brought private property into existence. Accordingly, natural law is considered one of the powerful opponents of communism. Natural Law doctrine is also used to abolish private property, which is adjudged against nature and a source of all ills. Morally, Fourier, etc. consider private property as a monstrous division of products of nature and something against the wise intentions of nature and God.

As a matter of fact natural law satisfies the deeply felt need of human mind–the need for justification. Auguste Comte and Herbert Spencer who are leading Nineteenth Century Sociologists develop their theories on the assumption that, like natural phenomena, social life is determined by causal laws. These writers evince a reformative trend of thought and begin to see a romantic vision of the future where there will be no idea of rights and people will work on the principle of duty, erasing the distinction between private and public functions with complete socialization or nationalization of human life.

Hegel[6] and Marx[7], the outstanding representative philosophers of the last century incorporated the technique of natural law in their theories. The idea of teleological universe govern Hegel's philosophy of history which shows that reason is the spirit of the world, which is gradually enfolding with the march of time. To him, 'reason' includes morality, and the laws, which are expressions of this world spirit as personification of Reason. Real is rational and rational is real. Kelsen says, "The history of the world is not intelligible apart from a Government of the world. Hegel's so-called philosophy is but a theology of history." Marx employs the dialectical method of Hegel's and to him also, evolution works by means of contradiction but instead of spiritualism he turns to materialism.

The dynamic theory of natural law represented by John Wild and others is founded on the belief that a universal pattern of action, applicable to men everywhere, requires its completion. This theory claims to be empirical as it derives its principles from observation of experienced facts. The facts are tendencies inherent in reality or existence itself. Finite existence requires completion and has a tendency towards fulfillment. Here, value and existence are merged into one another. The fundamental norm is that human life ought to be lived.

Natural law doctrine, as doctrine of justice, is an expression of law as: 'ought to be' or 'just law' or 'good law.' But it puts forth generally only a formal ideal. It cannot convincingly provide any material standards for knowing what is just. Classical Natural Law doctrine introduces two elements of just law. One is that of `value' and the other is that of 'universality.' But these have not proved to be very helpful for the determination of what is just law. Universality, as a theory of valid law is now a lost hope in face of increasing growth of diverse systems of positive law, based upon differences of cultural developments and environmental conditions together with socio-political and economic considerations of its administration and enforcement. Again, the assertions of universal principles, based on reason, are not true guides for consideration of the problems of law.

Natural law, by fusing universality and value has also given birth to the doctrine of natural rights. It gives reason to the owner of 'natural rights' to defend these rights against the interference of law and State. On analysis this theory of 'natural rights' also proves inadequate. Natural law, as the ideal of justice, is only a formal standard and cannot be of any practical use for bringing social justice and social order as it claims, because it does not give answer to what is social justice and how will it be a priori determination of social justice and the ways of its realization. According to Saleilles, answer to all these questions "depend upon certain social facts with which law comes in contact. These facts change, evolve and are transformed. But that depends, in turn, upon conceptions one forms as to justice and order as to authority and liberty, as to right of the community, and the rights of individuals, as to the proportion to be established in the incessant strife between these opposing forces and this proportion varies and alternates."

As a result of the realization of this requirement, Natural Law itself has acquired a name in modern times as "Natural Law with variable content." The concept of natural rights obliterates the distinction between legal rights and moral rights; is and ought; and wish and power; Natural Law represents ideal of justice without awareness of practical needs and possibilities. It fails as a complete theory of justice.

Similarly, liberty as an ideal of justice fails to convince one with all its fervor because of its ambiguity of meaning. In one sense, it professes an unbridled freedom but which is dangerous and foolish; in another sense liberty grants freedom but with restraints, in such measure as may be necessary for happy and peaceful existence. Yet the important problem still remains unsolved. How to determine the quantum of restraints and freedom? It is obvious that for a good life of a citizen there must be a mean between political or legislative despotism and regimented freedom of anarchy. The ambiguity arises from the fact that the ratio between freedom and restraint cannot be determined for all times to come. Freedom by itself is not an adequate ideal unless it is put as freedom to do or enjoy good things. Without this moral element present in it the doctrine of liberty cannot become the doctrine of justice. As moral part cannot be logically derived from liberty, justice cannot be identified with liberty.

There is one more view of justice, which refuses to be assessed by any formula of definition. It is a kind of instinct, which, without appealing to the reasoning of the mind, goes of its own accord straight to the best solution, the one most conformable to the aim of all judicial organization. In fact, we know that there is no such sentiment in human soul. If at all such a sentiment is to be cognized; it is necessarily a mixture of moral doctrine resulting in a moral sentiment. This complex of moral belief is as open to criticism as the belief or doctrines of which it is a composite. To identify such a sentiment with justice is only one's own admission of moral ignorance.

The utilitarian standard of justice is general happiness. The clearest formulations of this view are found in Sedgwick. According to him the main idea of justice is "that society is rightly ordered, and, therefore, just, when its major institutions are arranged so as to achieve the greatest net balance of satisfaction summed over all the individuals belonging to it." Social justice, in this context, is looked upon as a principle of rational prudence applied to an aggregative conception of the welfare of the group. Sir John Rawls says the principle of utility defines 'good' as satisfaction of rational desire and social co-operation is directed to achieve greatest satisfaction of rational desire of individuals. It does not matter directly how one man distributes his satisfaction as long as it gives him maximum fulfillment.

By this reasoning, justice has to protect the elementary good in such a way that it provides the conditions for higher or subtler values. Both Mill and Sedgwick[17] consider that over the above equality and impartiality the nation of 'requital to desert,' i.e., good for good and evil for evil is required, but both are not clear on this point. Later moralists and some of the utilitarian intuitionists, reject the theory that there is duty to reward the virtue and punish the vice. David Ross considers the principle of desert relevant only so far as it is helpful in fulfilling the task of producing as much a combination of moral worth and happiness as we can by its use. Rashdall also prefers a combination of virtue and happiness and not happiness alone as a result of the principle of retribution. It seems that principle of retribution has no great relation to the task of human justice, though some times it may seem that it is necessary for making the offender to realize the degree of moral condemnation that his conduct has evoked and thus to motivate him to amend himself.

There is also another view called pragmatic doctrine of justice, which, instead of the elusive end of happiness, prefers the more concrete one, as satisfaction of as many desires of human beings by balancing their interests without friction and waste or with least friction and waste. The problem of harmonizing the satisfaction of desires and wants is put forth as an urgent need. This is the doctrine of Roscoe Pound who rejects the necessity for any standard or ideology to harmonize the satisfaction of wants and balancing of interests. To E. Barker[8] this "seems to reduce justice to a mere *de facto* balance of different social wants, controlled by no criterion, but attained by the registration of any actual equilibrium which the clash of equally valuable wants has attained for itself at any given time." It would justify a balance in which the wants of one particular type, if it were the most powerful or the most numerous or both had titled the scale. It leaves us accordingly with a pragmatic justice if seen here in its literal meaning of pure balancing adjusting, and ordering. It fails to be conceptualized and understood and seems more of a reaction against different ideologies of justice.

Lundstedt[9] dismisses all that cannot be proved as a fact. All traditional concepts of jurisprudence are to him mere emotive reactions or mirage of language. He rejects completely legal ideologies or the speculation about justice. Hence all those, who look to the material objectives of law and common sense or feelings of justice, to fill in the gaps in a legal system are accused of metaphysical non-sense. Lundstedt holds that any attempt to develop law on the basis of the common sense of justice is to assume that natural justice represents a kind "material law." This he dismisses as non-existent metaphysical construction. To him those who incline towards natural law or justice to gain an objective valuation of law are misled by their subjectivity because all values are subjective to one's own feelings and emotions and as such are incapable of having any scientific objectivity. He considers that even the theory of balancing of interests of the sociological positivists is based upon a faith in natural justice and, therefore, he rejects it as lacking in legal reality. If legal machinery stopped functioning, the feeling of justice would lose all bearing and control and the social structure would be fully disorganized. He is not prepared to accept the oft-applied dictum to go beyond the law or to go contrary to law by means of equity or natural justice as he holds this to be purely imaginative. Thus, in the absence of comprehensive legal theory the concept of justice has reached its vanishing point in the materialistic and positivistic western legal theory, due to Scandinavian realism.

The traditional idea considers and recognize the institutions e.g. monogamy, family, status of parents and children, private property, inheritance, contract, etc. These institutions are taken for granted. As positive law establishes these institutions; the traditional idea is a positivistic one. The positivist accepts such institutions; he uses them for the basis of logical reasoning and draws conclusions, accepts laws, and regulations meant for expediency and certainty; and argues against abuses. When there is a clash between the two principles or two institutions of law and contradictory implications are reached by logic, the traditional sense of justice fails.

Trans-traditional idea of justice detaches one from traditional institutions in different degrees and makes him to criticize these institutions on the basis of the principles of justice taken from outside the legal system. One's personal conviction or creed about what is the most valuable state of affairs or goal or what is the way to realize improved conditions of life. There are various standards, which have been set by different writers, which intermingle and overlap. Arnold Brecht has pointed out important standards as a result of which the jurist appears as a believer of one or more than one of them. The ideal types are – (1) Equalitarian, (2) Libertarian, (3) Revelationist, (4) Conservative or Traditionalist, (5) Authoritarian, believing in leadership principle, (6) Majority Worshipper, (7) Hedonist, (8) Group Worshipper, (9) Harmonizer, (10) Pyramid builder believing in aesthetic values of works of art, (11) Man of duty (12) Peace and order fanatic. Upon these top values the most of the concepts of justice in the 20th century are founded.

If for a moment we look to the Indian juristic scene of today, we witness a strange conglomeration of ideas, which are neither western in the strict sense of the term, nor are they oriental. We are faced with a hybrid culture and consequent hybrid juristic system. Having gone through this hotchpotch of legal philosophy during all these centuries, the Indian mind is still clinging though precariously to metaphysical reality, firstly because it has actually experience; the unity of existence in its spiritual experiences. This has been manifested through the lives of Indian seers and sages who obliterated the distinction between subject and object. Secondly, in India, unlike as in the west metaphysical principles have not been exploited to suit political ideologies of revolution or despotism. Naturally we are not yet scared of these principles. Thirdly, the popularity and progress of science, which has resulted in almost a craze for material advancement in the west, has not been able to solve all the problems of life because of the sole emphasis on exploration of matter. This is an ample and irrefutable testimony of the indispensability and inseparability of spiritual aspect of law from the general theory of law. The truth of the above statement, was completely appreciated and realized by the ancients and the general happiness and peace which reigned in those times is an eloquent testimony of it.

In Judicial Court proceedings the theory of justice, to a great extent, has been a movement of protest against the law's delays, against arbitrary application of law, and against the inequity of the laws themselves.

Justice, as impartiality was recognized in ancient Egypt and in the land of early Hebrews is expressed in the injunctions given to judges to administer the law impartially. Law then begins to be changed to remove arbitrary discrimination like that of race, colour, religion, and sex, as far as possible. Thereafter, the nation of impartiality is extended to wider range of legal relations and rights and duties. In ancient Rome equity is equivalent to equality in Aequitas is Aequilitas together with this is the realization of 'fair exchange' of service as just, on the basis of fairness and social responsibility, for ensuring to the parties at least minimum conditions of physical and mental well being. Thirdly, the notion of justice may be viewed as applicable in relation between states. States are, to put in mildly, expected not to be judges in their own cause, and should not resort to force to settle their grievances. It is also realized that control and distribution of world-resources should be done with justice and the creation of modern economic organization, is a step towards this realization. In all these ways the notion of justice according to law is gradually pervaded by the notion of justice in the law. Once we have recognized exclusion of arbitrary inequalities we see a necessary direction towards justice. We also look to the exclusion of arbitrary power of one man over another. "Justice has, therefore, been mainly concerned with the control of aggression and of domination made possible by natural, inequalities or by inequalities generated by institutions."

The exclusion of arbitrariness grows gradually also in the sphere of criminal law. The historical development in this regard can be traced according to the principle of justice: (1)

At first, early law does not give equal protection. Certain groups, like slaves, and serfs, were not having equal protection of law. The protection which was granted to great nobles and high officials was greater than that extended to the poor masses; (2) Punishments were also unequal and varied according to the gradations in social ranks; (3) In authoritarian states the methods of criminal justice was liable to be arbitrary and oppressive. In modern times the principle of distributive justice of Aristotle has its use for equitable distribution of means of physical and mental well-being in a 'highly differentiated and, large scale society.'

The principle of distributive justice, which has its administration in proportion to merit; to relevant resemblances and differences and what is relevant or not is to depend upon the particular right which is under consideration. "For example, in the case of economic rights, differences in need are relevant, including the conditions necessary for the performances of specific functions and the more general conditions of well-being. In the case of educational rights differences in capacity or interest are relevant; in the case of electoral rights, principle of 'one man, one vote' is adopted in the interest of securing participation by all and in the absence of any agreed method of estimating differences of political capacity. In general, the criteria of relevance adopted by a society varies with the moral outlook prevalent in it and are thus a good index of the level of moral development attained by it."

Isena Justice, as a legal concept, has been found hard to define. It is a composite of concepts, or an ideal proportion of them, which can never be prefixed. More than that, it may be one's own ideological construction, or intellectual preference or critical reflection or emotional reaction. Its appeal to human beings is so great that no legal theory can ignore it without the risk of being incomplete and inadequate. Though justice is not amenable to logical and scientific approach as there is no unanimity about its settled content and meaning, yet it is a sort of demand notice which we direct against our legal systems, social orders, and political institutions and agencies. It is our theory of expectation, the net result of our desires and demands. Justice is also then the theory of the ends or values of law, which are assessed by objective determination in the light of the practical working of law.

The ancient Indian mind tries to solve any particular problem; firstly by comprehending it in the context of the whole reality and then draws conclusions or forms judgement or propounds any theory relating to it. In other words, it sees unity in the whole existence with all its phases. All the important concepts are oriented on this basis. They viewed law in all its diverse aspects. To them law is; positive law as well as ideal law. Law is the nature of this world as well as of man. It is textual prescription as well as *de facto* virtuous conduct and practice. It is administration as well as interpretation. It is an ideal norm (dharma) as well as political expediency (Arth). It is the bond, the duty, or that which holds us together, as well as the character of freedom or Right, or which is determined according to one's own reason and conscience. It is relative as well as absolute. It is an intelligible concrete rule of conduct as well as a mysterious aspect of the whole reality. Our concept of justice is included in our concept of *Dharma* or Law, which covers the whole metaphysics, epistemology, and ethics of law. As the Indian thought, feeling and will are oriented on this view of reality; it is better if we try to understand justice in the light of the total view of reality. Justice, to the ancients was dharma. Now order, harmony, security, punishment and prosperity are important from the point of view of action of justice; and happiness, freedom, and welfare are important from the point of view of ethics.

1. JUSTICE AS KNOWLEDGE (GYAN)

In order to know the ends of law or realize the theory of justice, we will have to deal with law together with social, religious, moral aspects of ancients Indian thought and values which have a complete correspondence with Reality which is in ancient phraseology the 'Sat-Chit-Anand.' Knowledge of justice lies in truth, reason, impartial performance of judicial function, and sense of duty.

(a) Satya (Truth) as a theory of Justice

'Sat' is existence itself, which in itself is a value. When it exists in social, moral, and jural life it exists as (Satya) truth. Ethic legal norm of truth is then, a derivative of metaphysics. 'Satya' or truth has a practical importance in individual social life. "Satya contributes to the welfare and harmony of society, as a whole. It engenders mutual truth and love, and binds the individuals together. The ethics of 'Satya' is also based on the conception of the unity of self as identical with or at least similar to other selves. Satya promotes unity. It is at once ethical and social virtue." Truth is thus the end of law. When truth operates upon the facts and propositions of law it emerges as justice. Thus justice is truth in action.

Truth has in itself all the juridical idealism because it is reflected in all the key concepts of Indian law and they can be interpreted or re-discovered in the theory of truth. Vidyaranya,[10] the great commentator of Rig-Veda considers 'Rita' to be the mental perception and realization of truth. Shankaracharya,[11] commenting upon the text of *Brihadaranyakopanished,* observes "Satya is the speaking of truth while Dharma is the observance of truth in action. The author[6] of *Hindu Ideals* says, "While 'Rita' denotes the mental perception and realization of truth and 'Satya' denotes the exact expressions of words of truth as perceived by the mind, *Dharma* is observance of truth in conduct of life. In fact, *Dharma* is the way of life, which translates into action the truth as perceived by the man of insight and as expressed by him truly. In short, Rit is truth in thought, Satya is truth in words and Dharma is truth in deed. Hence, the *Brihadaranyakopanisad* proclaims that which is *Dharma* is truth. Therefore, according to Indian thinkers *Dharma* and truth are interchangeable expressions and denote the fundamental aspiration of man which is the pursuit of truth in thought, word and deed." This pursuit of truth becomes the primary aim of life as it is bound to contribute to the prosperity and well being of mankind. Mahabharata considers the authority of truth to be even higher than the Vedas. Virtuous conduct of Veda-knowing people and prevailing customs which have become a true part of life have been recognized from time to time as law, to a very great extent. All the concepts of law and its ideals converge on truth. The Rig-Veda says, "By truth is earth upheld."(X.85.1) The supreme Brahman itself is the Right, is the Truth. (Nrisimhottaratapini Upanishad-I. 6).

Truth has great convincing power. It can bring a change of attitude in our view about what is just and what is not just. It is due to this tendency that some of the evils of history have been done away with because on rational enquiry they were found to be false. We, today, are again implementing justice by knowing the truth of social life. Through the agency of law we are abolishing discrimination on the basis of caste, creed and colour. We are trying to raise the status of the untouchables, the backward classes and scheduled tribes by restoring them the true social respect by means of social justice. This is so because we have realized now that their status is not in accord with truth, i.e., it is not worthy of them as human beings, though at one time it may have been considered as just.

We have still to realize the other untruth on unequal distribution of wealth. We have to do away with privileges and disparity of income because both these are unjust. A great change and transformation will take place if we expose the evils of the day and earnestly pray like the Rig Vedic seer: "Lead me from 'asat' (untruth) to 'sat' (truth)." Great Indians, from the past to the present, have tried to follow the path of truth in various fields of life. Mahatma Gandhi even identified God with truth. He forged the doctrine of 'Satyagrah', literally to seize or hold truth, to give passive resistance and non-cooperation. He vindicated truth and justice through it and declared: "if a man will only realize that it is unmanly to obey laws that are unjust, no man's tyranny will enslave him. This is the key to self-rule or home-rule. As long as the superstition that man should obey unjust laws exists, so long will their slavery exist. And a passive resister alone can remove such a superstition."

This theory proves that there is in the minds of human beings, a permanent and universal equation between unjust and untruth. In this lies not only the sanity of our mass-mind but also a warning to administrators, legislators and politicians; not to depart from the basic concept of truth which is just and not to misuse political legislative, and executive power for their personal ends.

(b) Reason

However, we need not be too dogmatic about truth. It needs to be understood in the light of justice. For this, we should travel into the realm of Reason or 'Viveka' which has been expressed by Manu as *'Atmatusti'* (self-satisfaction) and was enumerated as one of the sources of law. We should seek living and dynamic truth and not lifeless and static truth. Political lies may also be told to keep up the morale of the soldiers in war. So, falsehood is justified when it serves some higher values like mercy, respect for grief, the good of public or the nation as a whole. Similarly, for the sake of convenience and utility legal fictions and presumptions, are allowed to prevail in the interest of workability of a legal system. But it is difficult to provide a theory to know how far should these untruths, presumptions and fictions be allowed. It can only be said that they may be allowed to the extent that they serve the ends of justice. In such case they have to be considered as reasonable.

'Viveka', thus moderates the rigor of truth. By virtue of this Vivek, i.e., reason and logic, our *Mimansakas* made workable the legal system that was oriented on the Vedas and the Smiritis. By this method they kept alive the spirit of justice by de-recognizing obsolete customs and concepts and gave admittance to new ones.

Like truth, *Viveka* is also an end of law and is a means of justice. Any theory, which formulates law, has to be refined and purified by reason. To a very great extent, reason has been able to make law a means of justice, because reason is the power of justice. Reason has also its broader conception in which it can serve the cause of justice. In this aspect it embraces the whole field of enquiry and the span of our purposes. It is through this reason that we seek 'convincing grounds,' for our opinions and proofs, of our conclusion. All this is done in the spirit of detachment and impartiality to seek the solution of any legal problem. Reason, thus, becomes a vehicle of Dharma or justice. By this means also, we can discuss and determine the relevance of empirical facts for providing more just solutions.

In Vedic times women had equal rights; *niyoga* was practiced and widow marriages were permitted; and daughter's share in inheritance was recognized. But due to the deterioration of times these rights began to seem unjust and reason was sought to hold it so. It was because of this fact that women began to be looked upon as inferior beings. Now in modern India, recognizing and realizing the worth and dignity of the women, we have given them equal status. This is nothing but the role of reason, which has helped us in implementing justice. In this sense reason has the power to change the social situation with the corresponding ideas of justice.

It would thus seem that the justice or dharma couldn't be explained or determined by reason alone. So Mahabharat a declares that no one can completely know what is *dharma*. To some extent, it may be mentioned that *dharma* is shrouded in mystery. This shows the limitation of reason to explore the nature of *dharma*. Reason was to the Indian mind only a means not an end. There was neither an exclusive rationalistic era in India nor was there the need for its antidote, the irrationalism. When *dharma* is not knowable through other sources; when it is not possible what is justice and what is injustice, the only alternative is to leave it to one's judgment and experience. To this extent, it is submitted; *dharma* or justice is a dynamic concept.

(c) Impartial Performance of Judicial Function (Nyaya or Positive Justice)

Justice in courts is called Nyaya. There it represents the characteristic impartiality and the supremacy of the rule of law, which are both the pillars of justice.

According to Manu (VIII. 3) justice consists of the application of law to the cases arising between the members of a state. Law is known from customs and from smritis e.g. those of Gautama, Yajnavalkya, and others. Justice, as interpreted by Sukra, consists two elements: First, it consists a discrimination of the good from the bad (of course according to the law). Second, it has a utilitarian basis, in as much as it is calculated to minister to the virtues of the rules ad the ruled, and promotes common well. According to Kane[12], the primary duty of the King was to administer justice impartially and to punish the guilty. The king was considered as the fountain of justice. To Manu, protection of subjects was in itself the highest dharma. Yajnavalkya points out that protection consists in punishing internal aggression, in meeting external aggression. Manu personifies that the administration of justice is administered through the dart of *dharma* pieces; *adharma* or falsehood taken out from the body of *dharma*. Yajnavalkya declares that impartial administration of justice yields the same rewards as solemn Vedic sacrifices. (I. 359-360). In this way, administration of justice was held to be a sacred duty. According to Manu, a truthful, thoughtful and a wise king who knows *Dharma, Arth* and *Kama* alone is entitled to use the power of *danda* rightfully. Manu declares that a king who punishes those who do not deserve to be punished incurs great obloquy and goes to hell.

Again, in the Mahabharata (Anusasna 6.38 and Chapter 70) and the Ramayana, it is said that the king who does not show up himself for administering justice and suffer the litigants waiting for him would suffer like king Nrga. The quick and speedy justice was thus the aim, though adjournments were also granted in special and compelling circumstances. It was realized by Sukra and Katyana that delay in deciding cases was as good as denial of justice. The purpose of legal procedure was to ascertain the truth of the matter. Manu states that "the king who decided the causes of people unjustly through greed is soon subjugated by enemies, while the king who is curbing his own temper and desires and impartially decides causes to the dictates of Sastra becomes of one mind with his subjects as rivers merge in the ocean." Brahaspati and Narad lay emphasis on both the secular and spiritual effects of doing justice, saying, "when the king gives decisions according to Shastrà he spreads his fame in this world and secures Heaven." King should not come to hasty judgement. After rejecting the chicanery (Chala), the king should decide according to the real state of facts, for without proper presentation even a well-founded case fails. According to Brihaspati, for justice, reliance should not be placed upon 'Shastras alone without taking into consideration of the circumstances of the case, otherwise it may lead to loss of *dharma* (injustice or sin).' When the king is seated on the seat of justice (dharmasana) let him be devoid of passion, equal towards all, performing the view of *Vivasvat*. Yajnavalkya declares: "the king, freed from anger and greed, should give justice assisted by learned Brahmins in conformity with the (Percepts) treatises of *dharma*. The king has liberty of the State. It is his duty to see that rules of *dharma* are not exploited for the personal ends of litigants and in derogation of the interests of the States.

The above analysis of the concepts of justice leads us to say that justice is an enforcement of law, which is laid down by *dharmashastras* or is directed by it. It is that justice who is administered by the court, and is characterized as impartiality, foresightedness and wisdom. Here the problem of justice is not to know law, but to apply it.

(d) Justice as Performance of One's Own Duties

Dharma (justice) is not merely an attitude of impartiality and detached objectivity with which one must decide cases but it is also duty or obligation. It is *swadharma* or one's own nature, in which lies one's own fulfillment. *Swadharma* is, then, performance of one's own duties according to one's own station in life. Gita says: "Devoted each to his own duty man attains perfection." "Better is one's own imperfect *Dharma*, than the *Dharma* of another well performed." In this sense, *Dharma* or justice is duty in the functional sense according to the *Varna-system*. Thus *Varna*, in ancient times was based on one's own aptitudes, i.e., one's nature. It is only later that *Varnas* degenerated into hereditary classes and undermined the progress of our society. Hence realization of one's own duties and performing them is in itself justice. In this context, Plato was of the view that justice in a State is nothing but a manifestation of the sense of duty of a citizen's public action. It can be here asserted that in this respect Plato's idea of justice in a State comes nearer to approximate the functional notion of *dharma* or justice of the ancients. If this sense develops in our people, there is no need of remedy justice of the other type, i.e., corrective justice of the ancients. If this sense develops in our people, there is no need to repair the loss or harm caused by a failure to perform one's own dharma or duty. Gita heightens this notion of justice by reaching the highest point in morality when it says that duty is the end and it should be performed for its own sake.

II. Justice As Power (Shakti)

In order to realize justice in life it must perform some active role by establishing peace, order and a state of security by protection of life and property. Let us consider theory of *Karma* as natural justice.

(a) Theory of Karma as Natural Justice

The idea of justice is rooted in the law of *Karma*, a variation of *Rit*, and a conception of the whole universe as an ordered whole. The order or law on the physical, social and moral level is *Rit*. In the same way, the order established on the basis of law, called legal system, has also *Rit* as its genesis. As this universe is dynamic, because of its *Swadha* (energy or potency), this order works through causation i.e., in succession of actions and reactions. This aspect of *Rit* is called *Karma*. Justice, consists of re-establishing the order or punishing those who have violated the order by their actions (Karmas), recompensating those who have suffered at the hands of the disturbers of order. Justice thus becomes '*Dandaniti*' (theory of punishment). Without the theory of *Karma* one cannot have logical and theoretical grounds for awarding punishment and so administering legal justice. The logic of *Karma* establishes a link between punishment and the act (wrong) done.

According to the theory of *Karma*, the reality, which is order as well as existence, is self-sufficient on the natural or cosmic plane and has its own potency. As this universe is conscious and is progressively manfolding itself, it determines our individual, social and moral life. In man, with his free will, it allows him to determine his own moral progress or regress. The doctrine of *Karma*, as causation, allows our action to determine our future. It appears as principle of retributive justice which is an extension of the principle of causation in nature and becomes the principle of natural justice. From this emerges a general principle– 'a man reaps what he sows.' This law of *Karma* was conceived as inexorable, that man might not escape it even by early death in life. The doctrine of *Karma* is not fetishistic. Man can undo the bad effect of Karmas by knowledge, right conduct and thus can reverse the course of regression. Law of Karma, then, is also the law of practical reason, which can bring about moral regeneration. The Law of Karma is the universal moral law, which governs the life of the individual and society and becomes the moral book-keeping. It is based on the principle of merit or desert and is the incarnation of eternal justice.

In the Gita, two views of *Karma* are given to us. In a wider sense, *Karma* is conceived, as the creative world is the *Karma* of the Absolute. In the narrow view, *Karma* is actions done by the individual soul on account of *'Prakriti'* and *'Gunas'*. The tendency of all such *Karmas* is to bind a man and he is liable to fall an easy prey to attachment if the *Karma* is 'actuated by desire or self-conceit' or when 'done through delusion without regard to consequences.' If the action is 'done without love or hatred and without any desire of its fruits and free from attachment', it is good *Karma*. As one cannot avoid doing *Karma* for worklessness or non-activity in life is impossible, what is needed is to work 'with a controlled mind and in an unattached manner' (III.7). If we ask what actions are to be performed, Gita says that a man's obligation is to do his duty enjoined upon him by *'dharma'*. He should perform his function well without desire of rewards or fruits. This concept of Justice is the aspect of *Rit* or law, as order which, is again illustrated by doctrine of *Karma* and explained by the propriety of actions on which the order maintains itself. The duty should be done with the sense of sacrifice like *Yajna*, i.e., *'Yajnarthkarma'*, without any desire for reward, because in God's nature there is no causal connection between virtue and happiness. In this sense justice is, that *Karma* or duty which is performed by judges, administers, rulers interpreters, commentators, etc., is the proper and honest performance of their duties, without favour, fear and prejudice and without any desire for reward. This is an impartial adjudication. In this way just order in society is established and maintained. Gita gives expression to the socialistic principle of social and economic justice when it declares that: 'He who enjoys objects given by God without making offerings in return to them is a thief (III-12). The same idea has been expressed in *Ishavasyopanished.'* `There is the dwelling place of God in everything that is moving in this world. Enjoy the world with a sense of selflessness; do not hanker after another man's wealth.' In the language of social ethics, it means that he, who enjoys wealth more than necessary for him, is really stealing it because it also belongs to his fellow beings with whose help he has acquired it and it is, therefore, a trust property with him.

The doctrine of *Karma* is interpreted by Lokmanya Tilak[13] as a principle of collective justice because *Karma* does not merely influence individual but also the society as a whole.

According to him "in as much as every human being is born in some family, some community, or some country, he has to some extent suffer on account of the actions not only of himself but also of the community and society such as the family etc. to which he belongs." The necessary conclusion is then that, because of this idea of collective justice, as applied to nations and countries, the people of nations and countries suffer for the wrong and foolish *Karmas* (actions) of their leaders. This may appear to be an unusual extension of the doctrine of justice but it does look logical.

Again Gita gives us the theory of divine justice. This is implicit in the concept of *'Daiva'* (XIII. 14.). It means that 'over and above all the materials, objects, instruments and means which come into play in the doing of all acts, there is one incalculable element, viz. *Daiva*.' In the view of Dr. Radhakrishnan "*Daiva* or super-personal fate is the general cosmic necessity, the resultant of all that has happened in the past, which rules unnoticed. It works in the individual for its own incalculable purpose." It is not to be interpreted as fatalism. As man has risen from the state of pure animalism, he has the capacity to overcome the limitations or heredity and enviroment by the force of his will.

(b) Justice as Dandniti or Positive Justice

This is a philosophic justification for the infliction of punishment. If an offender does not suffer punishment at the hands of the king, or in this life, he has to suffer the evil effects of his *Karmas* in the next life. It is also stated that if he suffers penance imposed by *Shastras* or learned men he is absolved from his sins. By punishment, a sort of repayment of debt due to *Karmas* is made. This is sanctioned by *dharmasastrakars*. According to the view of *Vashistha* (XIX. 45) which has been re-stated by Manu (VII. 318) and Narad (48), men "who have committed crimes and who have been punished by the king are purified, go to heaven like those who have performed good deeds." The king as this theory shows, seems to possess in addition to the secular power, some religious power. One reason for this is that the king has been created to uphold *dharma*. The other is that punishment is but another name for *dharma* and by punishment the *dharma* is restored. The punishment by the king has the same value as penance has and thus becomes a retributive (expiatory) justice. It is also said that if the king does not punish properly, it is he (king) who incurs sin but the sinner or the wrongdoer is certainly absolved from the wrong. However, this aspect of punishment is the implementation of *dharma* and is different from that which is dealt with by the aim of *Kantak-Sodhana* and is meted out on the basis of *'Arth'*, i.e., the political interests of the State. Theory of *Karma* then provides an explanation to the theory of punishment. But punishment can also be explained on the basis of the characteristic human nature and practical needs of social order.

Rita and Dharma are the expressions of eternal order. On cosmic level, this order maintains itself, but on human level it has to be maintained by the human agency of *danda. Danda* becomes a theory of positive justice. By administering positive justice this order is maintained. The truth is that without justice no order is preserved and without order justice is not possible. Justice and order are complementary to each other. Man, by his very nature, is not always inclined towards the maintenance of order. Our ancient sages were conscious of the evil potentialities of man. They considered coercive force of punishment necessary to maintain order. Order is maintained by protecting the life and property and by securing the performance of duties. When it is maintained through punishment it is called justice, which guarantees protection and security. Kane rightly observes that *Danda* was raised to the position of divinity by Manu, Yajnavalkya and Vyas. *Danda,* it is said, rules over all people, it protects all of them, *danda* is awake even when the guardians of law have gone to sleep; the wise men treat *danda* as *dharma* (Manu VII-18) etc. In *Bhagavatgita* (X-38), Lord Krishna says that He (God) is danda in the hands of those who control others. He is *niti,* i.e., *rajniti* (politics) for the conquerors. King then becomes the protector of the helpless, the home of the homeless, the son of the sonless and the father of the fatherless. Manu (VI-27-28) also says that by the proper application of *Danda* three *purusharthas* of *Dharma, Arth* and *Kama* are advanced. To some, *Danda* has the status of God, but to many it is indispensable for preservation of society.

In this way justice becomes the expression of order, peace and security. It is the business of law to secure safety for its people. According to Hobbes, the safety of the people is the supreme law. Security and justice are mutually related. Law or *Dharma* by its prescriptions, procedures, and institutions preserves and secures the interests of individuals and society. By making available the material requirements the frequent violations of law can, to some extent, be avoided; hence law is maintained by security.

Again, law is not merely an ordering device but also works as means of social security. Social security was the part of *dandniti* in the times of Kautilya. The ancients were not only actuated by a desire to adjust their law to the changing circumstances of the times but were also conscious that stability alone could ensure peace and good government. They were also alive to the fact that both stability and change are necessary for justice. *Danda* performed the one, and interpreted the other.

Justice, in order to be real and true, must provide equal opportunities and conditions of life by removing differences of wealth and living conditions. Ideal equality is not possible. In a different way, the ancient legal theory has been the expression of equality before the law. The law was considered superior to any human authority. At the initial stage the *Varna-system* was based upon equal opportunities, which were provided to persons according to their aptitudes. In the society of early Rig Vedic period women were equal in rank with men; the king governed by the advice of assemblies; republican form of government was also popular; widows were free to remarry; daughters got a share in father's property. There were inter-caste marriages; people were free to preach and adopt any doctrine, religion and could adopt any mode of worship. It is only due to historical reasons and later, social deterioration that unequal conditions of life began to prevail. Present government shows the harm that has been done to us by centuries of political enslavement and social stagnation.

(c) Arth as Justice

Ancient Indian mind was not only concentrated on *dharma* alone but also looked to arth, which was also recognized as one of the important ends of life. There are four ends of life: *Dharma, Arth, Karma, and Moksa*. The ideals of *dharma* and *moksha* work for spiritual benefit and are related to the other world but *Arth* and *karma* are more concerned with *arth* which includes within its range all the economic functions and material conditions and objects of life, e.g., attainment of riches, worldly prosperity, material advantages, wealth and all that which concerns commercial life, business affairs, work, prices, etc. *Arth* in the sphere of law means plaint, action, and petition; in politics it is the interest of the state, i.e., expediency. In life in general it is utility, that is, what is useful. "It means the whole range of tangible objects that can be possessed, enjoyed and lost; work we require in daily life for the upkeep of the household, raising of the family and discharge of religious duties, i.e., for virtuous fulfillment of life's obligations." If *Arth* is considered as an end of the individual life, it certainly has an important bearing on doctrine of justice. The sources of '*Arth*' are economic activity, commerce and agriculture all of them were called '*Vrata*'. This *Vrata* was thought necessary for the state of **matter missing**...... the advancement in the economic sphere. The *Kamandàka, Nitisara* declare, "when *Vrata* is destroyed this world is surely dead though it seems to breathe."

According to Mahabharata, wealth has been given an important place. This is evident from the fact that 'he who robs another of wealth robs him of his *dharma* and poverty befalls one who is sinful because lack of wealth is the root of all-evil.' 'Wealth has its enhancement.' All these views show that in ancient India material aspect of life was not neglected. There was harmony between *Dharma* and *Arth*. It was considered unjust for the individuals to amass wealth without giving a portion of its charity. This dictate of justice was nothing but a boosting of the socialistic principle and we have evidence enough to show that the ancients did not neglect the welfare aspect of justice in their legal theory.

Thus, on the basis of social ethics, Mahatma Gandhi developed economic idea of a just-economic order in society. He has brought about a perfect synthesis of *'Dharma and Arth'* by his concept of trusteeship. "Gandhi ji rejects class war and pleads for class conciliation. He argues in favour of a concept of 'trusteeship' whereby the owners of the means of production would regard themselves more as trustees of their property rather than absolute owners.

III. JUSTICE AS FELICITY (ANAND)

(a) Kama or Bliss

This bliss or happiness has been also understood as comprising grades and degrees, depending upon variations of culture, material advancement, individual or personal aptitudes and values. The philosophic justification for any theory of justice, which takes into account the welfare and happiness of the people, lies in the view that *'kama'* is a part of reality, because from it ensue desires, satisfaction, pleasure, happiness and welfare. These are the very ends of life, the legitimate activity. *'Kama'* is the *'lila'* or *'maya'* or manifestation of reality in its varied forms. It may manifest itself in joy, in the enjoyment of pleasures, and in the satisfaction of one's desires. Thus happiness, the beneficial aspect is revealed in welfare (Loksamgrah or Kalyan). Happiness (Sukha), bliss (Anand) etc. all these are the aspects of the reality which in its pure form expresses the joy of *Kama*. Man, who is the part of this reality and partakes in its process cannot be without happiness or *'Anandam'* or *'Anand'*. *Kama* is then, the content of this world, the aspect of the reality and the recognized and legitimate end of human life.

In spite of the fact that due to the prominence given to spiritual side of life and due to its identification with the coarser pleasures of life, the importance of *Kama* cannot be belittled. At the lowest stage this *Kama* is sensual or animal pleasure, and at the higher state it is aesthetic enjoyment and delight of artistic experience and at the highest, it is bliss, beauty and enlightenment, i.e., of God's realization. *Kama* is said to be one of the 'Vibhutis' of God. It is not inconsistent with *Dharma*. It is grounded in the very nature of man. Manu considers human nature not free from desires. The inclination towards pleasure is recognized, it is the attribute of the self and is sought for its own sake. Mahabharat a also upholds this when it says that all acts have there and, the attainment of happiness (Shantiparva, 190, 6-7, 9). Even *Dharma* can be looked upon as an instrument of securing ultimate happiness. To the ancient Indian thinkers "the world was too real to be ignored persistently. The needs of the body and the mind were too insistent to be completely suppressed and it was recognized that such suppression would finally lead to serious disorders in the patterns of organized social life. The inclusion of *Kama* as an ideal of life was a sign of this recognition." Man has to proceed progressively from the physical, the biological, the mental, intellectual and to the spiritual well-being which is infinite joy and bliss and is called the *'Anand-Maya-Kosh'* of the self (Taittrya-Upanisad III). Again self-love, at the higher stage becomes love of others. All the ideas of welfare and good of others are the refinements of this initial self-love of man. If welfare is the expression of this happiness *(Kama), dharma* itself becomes the aspect of *Kama*, because it is said that one who knows welfare of others knows *dharma*. Thus *'Kama'* in its purest sense was an embodiment of virtuous living but due to historical circumstances it acquired an inferior status.

The Indian concept of *Kama* as happiness is quite different from that of sensual and quantitative happiness of Bentham, which is illusive and is the by-product of the satisfaction of desires. It (happiness) can be justified only as a reaction against natural law and historical theories of law, and served only as theory of law reform in the 19th century England, which has suffered a long period of legislative stagnation. Real happiness is not animal, sensual and momentary pleasure or the finite happiness. It is not the greatest good of the greatest number. That which is infinite, is (the true pleasure) happiness; there is no real happiness in the finite sense. The infinite alone is happiness. "Joy and consciousness, a limitless ocean of joy greater than which there is no happiness–such is *Anand*". This happiness has to be realized at the initial stage by intelligence and rational discrimination. In it lies the knowledge of the one who controlleth all, the inmost self of all beings, who maketh many forms of one form–they who see that one in the self, only to those rulers of intelligence belongth the Eternal Happiness, unto none else."

The knowledge and realization of Reality of happiness is not only the personal, subjective, and limited consciousness; it is not also the individual consciousness unaware of the good of humanity. It is saturated with the sense of service and the will to do good to others. The urge for common human welfare and service is the natural outcome of such realization. This concern for common human welfare ensues from the concept of the brotherhood of man and common parenthood of God.

It thus seen that the ancient Indian Literature is full of the expression of the need of welfare and service. The service and welfare is expressed also by nature. "The trees bear fruits for others, the streams flow for the good of others and so do cows yield milk for others. The human birth is likewise meant for doing well to others." It is our duty to do well for its own sake. "A righteous man is likened to a sandal tree which affords scent even to the axe that cuts it."

This is the cultural foundation from which Indian theory of justice arises, which means that one cannot deny the need of minimum joy or happiness of human existence. This happiness has three sources. At the political level it is the theory of justice. The King, being the fountain of justice, is asked to "bear himself towards his subject as a mother towards the child of her womb–as the mother disregarding those objects that are more cherished by her, seeks the good of her child, even so, without doubt, should kings conducts themselves (Shantiparva LVI).

On the social level, this happiness is the result of the co-operative effort, co-ordinate and goodwill of other members. On individual level, it is the submission of one's own desire gradually by rational discrimination of different kinds of pleasures. The life of individual then becomes "a confluence of two principles that make it a continuum of inner conflicts and man's natural endeavour is to resolve and transcend them. This may be achieved by *Samsiddhi*. The two together contribute to the realization of the individual's freedom. The society, in ancient India, is an organization, which supplies these two needs, i.e., of the spirit and of the body and the State is ordained to satisfy them. The entire literature of the *Dharmashastras* and the *Arthshastra* expresses its primary concern with welfare.

The concept of *Yajna* is oriented on the idea of sacrifice, service and welfare. *Yajna,* for this reason is identified with God, because welfare aspect is the necessary aspect of the supreme. On this basis Vinoba Bhave has started two movements called the *Bhoodan-movement* and *Sampatidan movement* (Ref. Ist Chapter), the aim of which is to do justice to the landless and the poor, by making available to them land and wealth. The concepts of *Rit* and *Dharma,* as we have seen, are also oriented on welfare. The concept of authority-called *Vrata* also has its basis in welfare of the world. Punishment is also wielded for the good of the individual and the society. In this way al the important concepts lead to this one view of welfare.

(b) Freedom

Man is a free-willing agent. He is free to choose the path of good or evil. Under the influence of western culture man exercises this freedom by controlling nature, development of technology, satisfaction of wants, acquisition of property, entering into contractual relations with others, etc. Hence there are pleas for freedom. It was considered by the theory of justice as a natural right. But when it was known that individual freedom is liable to be abused by unscrupulous individuals and groups the theory of justice allowed limitations on it. But synthesis between freedom and responsibility is not yet complete and its proportion is variable according to different men and their ideas. The net result is that, what is available to the western man is limited freedom but not full freedom. There is no denying the truth that the essence of freedom consists in allowing man to develop his personality. But this truth must be rightly realized. The Indian mind seeks freedom by higher spiritual realization and in fact experiences unbounded freedom. The freedom carved by western mind is the evil effect of exaggerated individualism, or a means of exploitation of other individuals and their property. On true analysis, this freedom is the rationale for giving sanctity to property. The Indian concept of freedom is negation of one's own ego. In this sense freedom becomes more real and true.

This freedom is bliss and is more positive in its content and has more intensity in its actual experience. It is of a higher kind and is not tainted with exploitation of others. It provides opportunities for human development to the point of perfection. It is not acquisition but realization. This freedom is not expressed in rights but services; not in accumulation but distribution, not in competition but co-operation, not in agreement but understanding; it is not the civilization of the ways and means of living but the civilization or culture of the ways and means of realization of the very worth, and significance of life and its potency for perfection.

Justice and Justice-According-to-Law

In view of Western thinker or present jurist. Let us consider the difference, if any between both. Justice, in its purely ethical aspect, is justness, a moral quality and good character. But law is not necessarily justness. It has no relationship at all to morality or even to utility. It may be, in the view of the moralist, grossly wrong, and yet be law. In the appiication of law, however, justice is an absolute requirement, whatever the quality of the law may be. When we speak of the 'administration of justice,' we really mean the application of the moral principle of justice to existing laws when rights and duties are disputed by rival claims. Whatever the beauties of the one and the shortcomings of the other, the principle remains steadfast; but in the rules of law creating the situations on which justice has to operate there is no necessary consistency of principle at all.

There is nothing inherently paradoxical in the notion of an unjust law, despite Hobbes's famous dictum to the contrary. An unjust law may be administered justly, and a just law unjustly. All of us in fact criticize as unwise and unjust laws that we nevertheless obey because we believe that it is more righteous to do this than to bring confusion on society by insubordination. Socrates himself bowed to what he considered injustice, and there is reason to think that he might have availed himself of means to escape the penalty–because, having made his protest unavailingly, he considered it the part of virtue to submit to the prevailing opinion of his community. The judges who applied this unjust law acted justly. In the vast mass of modern legislation there are many enactments, which judges consider unjust in principle or harsh in consequences, or perhaps both, but they would fail in their duty if they did not apply them to the best of their understanding.

Every man is entitled to hold his own opinion of justice or injustice, wisdom or foolishness, necessity or futility, of a law, which he is required, at his peril, to obey. Whether he thinks it right to obey it for the general peace of society, or to defy it because it raises a question of principle which admits no compromise, is a matter for his own conscience. He will hesitate before being too dogmatic about the essential rightness or wrongness of any particular legal institution. There is, little consensus of opinion among men on that subject. The question becomes even more difficult in modern conditions, when laws are frequently prompted not by the aim of regulating or adjusting private rights, but by purely utilitarian and especially economic considerations. He would be a bold man who would pronounce dogmatically upon the justice or injustice of all the provisions of modern Finance Acts.

The Technique of Justice-According-To-Law

According to Allen[14]" in the operation of justice-according-to-law, subjective variances also exist, but are better disciplined. It is obvious that some judges have a keener appreciation than others of the true principle of justice to apply to the problem before them. But all of them have a great deal of guidance from the "taught tradition" of the law in which they are bred. The worst judge, with the least innate sense of justice, can nearly always find an example, and often many examples, of how a particular situation has been handled by other judges; and this accumulation of experience is the strongest argument in favour of the English system of precedents. It is true, and it daily becomes more observable, that the examples and analogies placed before the judge are often in conflict, and he has no easy task in choosing between them, but even that very conflict, together with the opposing arguments of counsel also steeped in the "taught tradition," at least acquaints him thoroughly with the relevant considerations on which his decision is to be based; and that is often far from true of individual, unschooled opinions of the justice or injustice of laws. Sometimes, and indeed more often than might be supposed; there is no exact authority to cover the instant case; then, it is often said, the judge must resort to "natural justice," and some codes explicitly enjoin him to do so. But even in these cases the judge seldom relies for illumination solely on an "inner light." In the absence of positive authority, he generally reasons by analogy as nearly as possible to authority, and his decision is not the child of mere inspiration but of a highly trained technique in weighing rival considerations.

Law and Mores

Allen once again describes that Austin has often been criticized because his well-known definition of law as sovereign command included no reference to justice. This seems to me to be beside the mark. Austin was offering a description of law as it is, or as he conceived it to be. The weakness of that description, as has been many times observed, is that it is too limited in its view of the sources from which law may spring and of those from which it derives its obligatory force; but he does not seem to have been wrong in omitting a moral element from his definition. As he has suggested, no ethical character, whether of justice or of any other moral principle, is essential to the nature of law.

Laws are, in general, made for the sake of government, order, security, tranquility, and prosperity. But law need not take account of any beneficial object. A tyrant, no doubt, can legislate solely for his own benefit. He may, by wholly arbitrary and immoral rule, use law simply as a means of plunder and aggrandizement. His dominion may not even pretend to justice in any degree. I doubt whether there have been many tyrants in history who have ever governed in such manner, and I am sure that if they have existed, they have not long survived. However, the thing is conceivable; if the despot possesses irresistible power, and is wholly unscrupulous, people may live under a regime of law, which is uninfluenced by any moral, expedient or even sane principle whatever.

These are extravagant examples, though not so extravagant as we might have thought them a generation ago; but in communities with any pretence to constitutional equilibrium or to government "by consent of the governed," the fate of arbitrary law is even more certain. Law must therefore accord, in the main, with prevailing ideas of justice, morality and expediency, or it will not receive obedience. There is thus, in practice, a constant and a necessary accord between law and those generally prevailing beliefs and sentiments, of any and changing kinds, which we may compendiously call "morality," in the sense of mores rather than of sapientia, for many of these current beliefs are more automatic-by habit, environment and tradition-than reasoned. Without some such general concurrence of law and mores, a community will not posses or retain what Austin called the "habit of obedience" lacking which, sooner or later, law will cease to maintain its binding force.

In most civilized communities, the irresistible power of the State restrains itself by what German jurisprudence call "auto-limitation," growing from that hidden tap-root of the social tree, a root lying deeper than any explicit Constitution–which in Kelsen's system is the Grundnorm. We have very clear examples of it in our own society. The Sovereign possesses prerogative powers, which it is almost inconceivable that she should ever exercise. But everybody knows that it is in fact limited by a multitude of restraints, which lie ultimately in the "consent of the governed." No ruling authority in the civilized world dares to be merely authoritarian.

All this is the well known, not to say elementary, foundation of what we call "law-abidingness," but it does not, affect the general contention that justice is not inherent in the notion of law and that unjust law may still be law, though it has less prospect of survival and enforcement than law which, in its design and effect, has regarded to justice and many other considerations which moderate the naked exercise of power. On the other hand, justice is the immutable dictate in the administration of law, as well as being the standard by which we may form individual estimates of the goodness or badness of laws actually made (de lege lata) or of laws which we believe ought to be made (de lege condenda).

The distinct, and often opposed, elements of justice and justice-according-to-law have played different roles in different legal systems. There is, for example, a marked contrast in this respect between Greek and Roman ideas. Both Plato and Aristotle were far more interested in the theoretical aspects of justice than in the rationale of its practical applications. It is, no doubt, a modern habit of thought, now discredited in some quarters; to conceive the principal branches of government as the legislative, the executive and the judicial–a trichotomy which, after all, corresponds with the process of most planned and fulfilled human action. We can hardly expect Plato to anticipate Montesquieu, but it is a little surprising to find that in the three chief public function of his ideal republic he gives no place to the administration of justice. To him legal decisions are "the shadows and images of justice"–which is, perhaps, no bad description of them; but it must be confessed that when he offers his own ideal code, as he does in the laws, the shadows become very dark and the images very indistinct.

To modern eyes law are a strange medley of innovation and conservatism, of reform and acquiescence, of boldness mingled with mere customary observance and even with superstition. Here Aristotle says "but it is a different matter to say that law itself is the embodiment of justice and virtue," and so he tells us when he predicates that "the law commands us to live according to each virtue and forbids us to live according to each vice." It seems to imply that the whole of virtue may come by mere law-abidingness, and this is inconsistent with what follows; for Aristotle goes on to say that the factors which make for complete virtue lie in those parts of the law which concern "education towards the common good. Righteousness, then, lies ultimately in the trained individual disposition, not in the mere commandments of the law."

It is never possible to analyze exactly the mysterious qualities of national or personal genius, but it seems clear that one of the principal factors in the astonishing development of Roman law was that its jurists and its judges never confused justice with justice-according-to-law.

The Romans, as everybody knows were not pre-eminently a philosophical nation. It is open to doubt whether the great classical jurists had more than a tepid interest in philosophy at all. Much has been written about the influence of Greek on Roman law, but actually it does not seem to have amounted to much more than this, than when the Romans, in the

Mediterranean intercourse which was the essence of the ius gentium, or in their own provinces, found a Greek legal expedient which seemed useful and convenient, they did not hesitate to borrow and adapt it. If they were not otherwise eclectic in their law, and they do not seem to have been so, but, on the contrary, somewhat severely nationalistic–that was because few known legal systems had anything to offer which was superior to what they could devise for themselves. The whole course of Roman jurisprudence was the working out of sensible solutions of practical problems. It was essentially a technique of justice-according-to-law, and it was, on the whole, the most efficient, which the world has seen. Roman law, in short, grew by trial and error, and there was never a better example of Professor Pound's "reason tested by experience and experience developed by reason." It never had, in theory, any doctrine of the binding force of precedents. It is impossible to resist the impression that the rules attributed to the jurists, and stated with clarity and precision, which have been the envy of the world, were based on the day-to-day experience of lawyers who had to find principles of justice-according-to-law to fit the fluctuating circumstances of legal relationships.

Our own law has grown on similar lines, though with nothing like the consistency of the Roman law. England grew from a feudal to a contract State, and from a contract to an industrial State, and the adoption of her law to these changes was a less uniform process. Trial and error has been the method, and error has taken the form of anomalies chiefly due to the caprices of social evolution. But in the main principles of the common law, judges have been jurists, elaborating solutions with the aid of a strong, traditional sense of the requirements of justice-according-to-law, without favour to any and without fear of any. Perhaps if it had, and if most English lawyers had not been so skeptical of it, reform in many branches of our law would not have been so tardy. Certainly it is not to credit that for so many centuries hardly a protesting or reforming voice was raised among our great "institutional" expositors of law, who, though they often paid perfunctory deference to an ideal justice in the shape of law of nature or law of God, for the most part accepted with equanimity many patent discrepancies in our law between the ideal and the real.

While vigorous criticisms of pars of English law, and especially criminal law, had been voiced by others before him, Jeremy Bentham was the first Englishman who undertook a systematic critical examination of English legal institutions in gross and in detail, and his disciple John Austin was the first of his race to attempt a scientific analysis, which was often highly critical, of our law's "leading conceptions." Bentham's contempt of history and of evolutionary processes was his greatest fault and led him to injudicious conclusions; but the very strength of his reaction against the inevitability of "whatever is, is right" inspired a new approach to law for which the time was more than ripe. About English law Allen remarked "Since the day of Bentham and Austin we have never lacked constructive critics of our law, and we do not lack them today; and yet it cannot be said that a philosophic approach to law has gained much ground among us. We are still cautious of rarefied abstraction in legal theory, and, as I have said, we have reduced the notion of natural justice to a minimum. While other countries have abounded in new philosophies of law, no Englishman in his century has founded a new legal 'school of thought,' and we are sometimes accused of inertia, or even sheer myopia, in this infertility. Perhaps we are the poorer for this defect of originality, though we can take a little comfort when we reflect how nebulous some of the more 'advanced' theories seem to be and how the strenuous effort after originality for its own sake leads often to a darkening of counsel. Yet, there is substance in the charge that in the higher criticism of the legal scriptures we show a certain lack of intellectual enterprise. In all our history we have never produced any overtopping legal philosopher of world reputation, for not even Austin could claim that distinction. Further Allen described that the essence of their present law-abidingness is that they are prepared to accept the defects of justice-according-to-law because they believe that on the whole it approximates with a reasonable measure of success to absolute justice, in the same way that they are prepared to accept many restraints on their personal liberty because they believe that by so doing they best secure the common good. Vigilance is always necessary to ensure, that temper of voluntary submission does not degenerate into a mood of supine subjection, but so long as the citizen preserves a due balance of acceptance and independence, he is at least in the way of virtue. Even if, in vision of the sublimer justice, he is still in Plato's cave, he is not losing sight of the glimmer beyond, and groping towards the glimmer is the only human way to reach the plenitude of light."

Justice and Liberty

Except justice itself, no human boon has been more vociferously and continuously demanded, than liberty.

This dominant aspiration towards liberty has been not only the constant theme of the friends of humanity but a favourite instrument of its enemies; for, played upon unscrupulously, it is a fertile source of popular delusion and hysteria.

It has often been observed, for example, by Lord Bryce in his well-known essay on "Obedience"–which the most effective demand for liberty has generally come from minorities. Revolutions against oppression always find their starting-point in the active few, for the many, whatever their sufferings may be, have not the initiative or the intelligence to organize resistance. The Palace, not the market place, is the usual launching-ground of revolt. Even when men like Rousseau or Karl Marx create a tremendous social ferment, it is to the intellectuals that they appeal. The majority of men will dumbly endure a great deal for the sake of a "quiet life." The prospect of convulsion in all the settled ways is more disagreeable to them than their accustomed disabilities: Such, in general, is their first reaction to the hazard of insurrection; but it must be added that, once aroused by the promise of a new and glittering, though undefined, liberty, they will pursue it with a ferocity which seems to stop at nothing.

Is Natural History complete emancipation from all restraints? If so, they chase a phantom, for there is no such thing as absolute liberty on earth. Not only is it unattainable, but it is inconceivable. There has never been in all history a more misunderstood generalization than that "man is born free." Rousseau[15] did not mean, as he has so often been represented as meaning that man is born with some heaven-sent attribute of liberty. In the same chapter, which contains his famous aphorism-perhaps the most quoted in literature–he continues: "the social order is a sacred right, which serves as a basis for all others. But this right does not come by nature; it is founded on conventions, and it is therefore necessary to understand what the conventions are." (He then goes on, by what purports to be historical exposition, but is for the most part pure fancy, to explain how the "conventions" of government have grown from primitive to civilized societies.) Of course man is not "born free!" He is everywhere in chains because, at the very moment of his birth, he is chained by an umbilical cord; and when that is severed, for the rest of his life he is navel-bound to the society into which he is born. He is the product of his heredity and environment, and his destiny is largely governed by his physical endowment and by the genes, which are an ineradicable element of his composition. Man is highly complicated organism who, for the most part, has no control over his own marvellous mechanism. He may do good or ill, if he possesses sufficient capacity of choice, to the processes, which maintain his life, but he cannot alter them by a jot. He can reinforce, or he can impair, the chemistry of his body by wise or unwise behaviour, but he cannot alter the chemistry itself. He cannot, by taking thought, supply himself with a new and better liver or lungs or bowels, often though he may wish that he could. He cannot wholly protect himself against invasion by unseen, deadly enemies, which can work fearful evil upon him in secret-devastation which he may not even suspect and which he can do little to prevent. In this twentieth century he is only beginning, dimly and speculatively, to understand the working of his most potent, indispensable instrument–that miraculous electrical power-station which he calls his brain; and, knowing so little of it, he is still content to think of himself as an imaginary trichotomy of body, mind and soul–distinctions to which he can attach no really intelligible meaning."

He further says, "Even the limited degree of control which he can exercise over his organism is determined by such area of his will as is 'free'." I will not be foolhardy enough to embark upon that endless controversy, which in the view of some philosophers presents no problem at all, except an artificial one of dialectic. I would only say that there seems to me to be great danger in thinking of "free-willing man," as some philosophers tend to do, as a uniform, established (not to say abstract) type. Not even Pan gloss can believe that every man is as much master of his fate as every other man. To take the extreme contrast, nobody would maintain that 'will' is the same for the insane as for the sane; but one need not point only to extremes, for between them lie infinite gradations of "responsibility" which as yet as every judge know, we can assess only in the crudest manner.

What's done we partly may compute, but know not what's resisted, nor, indeed, what real power of resistance the individual possesses. "The fated sky gives us free scope;" but it is the eternal and unresolved problem of existence how free is the scope and how fated is the sky; and it may be that when all the philosophers and theologians and moralists have said their say–if they ever finish saying it–it will be the geneticists and the bio-chemists who will give us some faint inkling of the answer."

Let us now consider Social Liberty. It is not possible to conceive man as socially free, because he cannot exist in isolation. That is surely too manifest to need emphasis in any complex "civilized" society. There have, of course, been many fictional descriptions of men in a state of uninhibited liberty. There is no escape in the world from the world. Some day, perhaps, there will be, for those who yearn for it, escape to other worlds, but it remains to be seen whether the migration will be for well or woe.

Liberty has often been viewed in one or other of these two aspects–as an attribute or aspiration of *man qua man*, or as a quality of status or "human right" of man; and it seems to me that in a great deal of the discussion of freedom these two conceptions of it are frequently intermingled, so that it is difficult to know whether we are being asked to consider freedom as some immanent quality of the human creature, without which he is so much the less human, or as a condition, though certainly a personal condition, existing relatively to social circumstances–in other words, as essentially a political institution or ideal.

At the other extreme from this is the utilitarian jurisprudence, as in Von Ihering and many modern sociological writers, which concentrates on the social ends, purposes and values of legal institutions. Here the danger is that individual liberty, though still regarded as a human good, is swamped or lost to view. All "social values" exist ultimately for the individual, since the State, or Society, is a bloodless entity, incapable of feeling good or ill, joy or sorrow; and the world happens to be populated by creatures. It is they, and they alone, who can suffer good or ill by social regulation, and it is their destiny, not that of principalities and powers, which alone matters under the species of both time and eternity. Assuredly, all utilitarians, from Bentham onwards, have recognized this expressly or implicitly; the greatest happiness of the greatest number obviously reverts to individual experience, for there can be no sensation of pleasure or pain. The paradox is best shown in the case of Jeremy Bentham himself, who, in his solicitude for the well-being of the individual, became in large measure the sponsor of a collectivist etatisme which would probably shock him to the soul if he were alive today.

It is true, that vast numbers of men can accept severe restrictions on their liberty without much protest or resistance.

Repression is less painful to them than the perturbations of radical change. A limited nature may even be happier under circumscription than under freedom, with all its personal problems. The barefoot man–a thing; the shod man–a mortal, not ashamed of his place in the order of creation. Such and doubtless many less unsophisticated were the visions always before the eyes of the American slaves. So, too, it was in the ancient world, where many domestic bondmen enjoyed circumstances and responsibilities of more advantage than hardship; but freedom was always the goal to be attained even at a great price; and it is needless to remark how many freemen of the ancient world, having achieved their ambition, made notable contributions to art, philosophy and public affairs.

Liberty-the Fulcrum of Personality

Liberty is a perennial aspiration of the human being because it is the keystone, the ultimate vindication of his ego, or, as Ihering calls it, "the moral affirmation of the individual." No man who is master of himself, however imperfectly in fact he may exercise that mastery, can be in his own eyes other than a moral eunuch. It is for this reason that in nearly all philosophical discussion freedom becomes part, under different guises, of the kingdom of the will. Liberty does not consist in the mere enjoyment of powers, capacities and opportunities; it is an inner being and becoming, a state of mind produced not so much by actual advantage as by the consciousness of its possession and its possibilities. An absolute potentate may have complete "freedom" to do what he wills; but we have learned in a startling manner, that "the governing passion of tyrants is fear." What shall it profit a man that he gains the whole world and loses his peace of mind? The peasant ploughing his furrow enjoys more true liberty than the despot with unrestrained "freedom" to command men and events.

Liberty, then, is that reinforcement of the ego, which all men crave for, in order to justify their existence in their own eyes. It may take the positive form of an addition to existing powers. But it is plain that either of these two forms really amounts to the same in result, for the negative, which is cancelled increases, the sum of the positive. Usually, the acquisition of liberty consists in the breaking down of barriers. These are many and irksome and, in the order of nature, none can escape them. We are hedged in by so many limitations both of physical existence and of moral obligation that few can resist the mood of rebelling against them, either by weeping or railing at the way of all flesh, or by kicking not only against the pricks but over the traces. Liberty is not a wholly uninhibited state of existence, but the diminution to the utmost practicable minimum of impediments to self-realization.

Allen described, "it is not however, universally accepted that liberty consists essentially in removal of restraint. We must also look, it is sometimes said, at the objective of liberty. Liberty confers or augments power, but it is not the same thing as the power itself, which remains to be exercised at the option of the individual. It may be employed in different ways, or it may not be employed at all. When, therefore, we speak of freedom for, we are in danger of confusing an opportunity–for that is what liberty offers, with the highly variable manner in which the opportunity may or may not be fulfilled. Yet, the power which is thus made available, is still something distinct from the conferment of it, for it is at the will of the beneficiary whether he exercises it or not. Similarly, married women today have rights over their property which they did not enjoy a hundred years ago; but we seem to be moving from one plane of concept to another if we begin to look at this new freedom as existing for the innumerable purposes to which property rights may be put. The essence of that reform was the removal of the unjust and uneconomic dominion, which a husband could exercise over his wife's property; and, with the greatest respect to those who forcibly argue otherwise, I suggest that we shall greatly confuse our conception of liberty if we include in it the variable objectives of enlarged autonomy. The essence lies, as Hobbes observed with his usual pith, in "removal of opposition."

The human beings cannot live without restraints. A man who desires complete "freedom" to indulge his appetite seeks merely to destroy himself. He violates a restraint which is imposed by nature itself so as he himself is concerned, and, since by completely uninhibited self-indulgence he is almost certain to injure others as well, he is also violating a restraint imposed upon him by social co-existence. Liberty has frequently been invoked on the ground, which turns out to be the very contradiction of it. If freedom is conceived as complete unrestraint, then it is misconceived, and is certainly not a human good. It is true that one school of thought has found the idea of political liberty in anarchy; but it has never commanded much following. If, then, liberty is to be regarded as a good, it must consist in the release not merely from restraints, but from harmful restrains, by which I mean restraints, which are either unnecessary impediments to rational action or denial of faculties without which no human being can readily be said to live.

Spiritual Liberty

Allen once again said that the human beings couldn't live without restraints. But is it not possible to discard all material restraints? If, as has been suggested, true liberty resides, or results, in a state of mind, cannot the mind attain complete freedom from all material circumstances? Mystics are reputed to have achieved this feat; it is familiar in much Eastern philosophy; and something not unlike it was the core of the Stoic "equilibrium attained through strife."

It is not to be denied that remarkable enfranchisements of personality may be experienced through the joint influences of contemplation and corporeal discipline; and those who can arrive at this imperturbable inner serenity approach as near to entire human release as can be imagined. There is in history no more poignant reminder of mortality than the cry which physical agony wrung from him on the cross–the cry of doubt, which, if it had been well-founded, would have meant the negation of his whole mission and sacrifice.

Political Liberty

Allen describes that whether or not a state of mind may truly 'stand in freedom loosened from the world,' for most mortals it is powerfully influenced and circumscribed by material circumstances. Hence freedom must be regarded as an attribute of man, the political animal. Liberty, said Lord Acton, is the highest political end, not happiness or efficiency, as the utilitarians have claimed. It is the highest political end for a reason long since given by John Stuart Mill in a famous dictum, which is, indeed, almost a truism–that ultimately the worth of a society depends on the worth of the individuals who compose it. If that be true, then a political order which ensures the maximum of personal liberty strengthens itself through the vitality of its individuals who, as we have seen, can grow to full stature only through the consciousness of free personality. "They make a rout," said Dr. Johnson, "about universal liberty, without considering that all that is to be valued, or indeed can be enjoyed by individuals, is private liberty. Political liberty is good only so far as it produces private liberty."

Variable Spheres of Liberty

Allen again said that private liberty, however, must depend on that degree of it, which a particular social order deems compatible with the sum of liberty. Thus it becomes a distributed good and the allocation varies enormously with time and place. Every society exhibits in its history profound transformations in the permitted spheres of personal liberty–or in what it is now fashionable to call the "norms" of liberty; we are apt to forget how recent are many of our famous British freedoms. To Locke, and to his whole school of thought, the very foundation of society was the security of property. Today, nobody is secure in that respect and indeed in one political doctrine the whole institution of private property is distasteful. Today, it is no longer true to say that the average man is entirely free to sell his services, as he will's. "Freedom of the press" is now one of the most familiar slogans of libertarians. Unhappily, it provides lamentable examples of those abuses of liberty it constantly invokes, with hypocritical fervour, by those who, for no other motive than their own self, employ every means within their power and ingenuity to debauch the public mind. Yet freedom of the press is not doubted today as an essential principle of democracy.

So it has been, again, with "freedom of the person," which today is regarded as so fundamental a liberty that an application "concerning the liberty of the subject" takes precedence over any other business in our courts. The so-called "presumption of innocence," is apt to regard as aboriginal in our society, is really of modern growth. Today, we surround the accused with so many safeguards–at his arrest, his questioning, his examination before magistrates, at the conduct of his trial, in his rights of appeal and in our law of evidence, that doubts have been expressed, even by judges, whether our criminal law does not provide too many opportunities for the guilty to escape conviction. Even if that be true, public opinion undoubtedly prefers it to the risk of the innocent, insufficiently protected, suffering unjustly. Nearly all this is the product of the nineteenth and twentieth centuries.

Many other examples might be given–notably the revolution in the status of women, married and unmarried. Dicey wrote about his law and opinion in England, "When we look at that celebrated treatise, we seem to be living in a social order almost as remote as the Middle Ages; and yet it was first written little more than 100 years ago. Whatever the diagnosis of the causes may be, and whether we believe them to be for good or ill, they have happened, many of them within our own lifetimes. They have consisted not simply in material changes, but in new moods in what may be called the social philosophy of liberty. As population has increased–and this, in my belief, has been the most powerful factor of all, it has been necessary to re-think some of the "self-evident" social axioms. The difference, in essence, was between a determinist and a perfectionist view of the human being; it was at the heart of the Liberal philosophy, and although Socialism took its origin in economic theory, this attitude of mind, which we may call sentimental or humane according to taste, was always a hemisphere in the whole Mercator's projection of Socialism."

There have been equally great fluctuations in those accepted standards, which, though few would maintain that they actually beget, at least greatly influence, what we call "morality." The two chief regulators of liberty for man-in-society, besides legal ordinance, are the individual sense of right and wrong and the opinion of one's fellows about rightness and wrongness; and the two overlap at so many points that it is often difficult to distinguish their reciprocal influences. It is certain that prevalent notions of good conduct, even though quite arbitrary and disputable from the point of view of pure ethics, may be galling fetters on freedom of behaviour, since only exceptional persons can be totally indifferent to their neighbours' opinion; and the penalties for social non-conformity may be even more drastic "sanctions" than the punishments of the law. In this regard too we have seen a marked change, amounting almost to a volte-face, in the provinces of liberty. When Mill wrote his famous essay "On Liberty" in 1859, he, unlike most of the Liberal publicists, was even more concerned with the tyrannies of public opinion than with those of government.

The other approach to the problem of State interference has as its starting-point the belief that liberty is the private possession of each individual and not merely a unit of the public property vested in the State. Authority and the necessity for regulation must be acknowledged by every well-affected citizen, provided, as has been said, that he has some say in the kind of authority to which he is willing to submit. Limitations on his personal freedom of action he must accept, unless he is prepared to be an uncompromising solipsist, which, at least in social and legal relationships, is equivalent to adopting a criminal attitude of mind and conduct; but at least he is entitled to ask that such limitations be justified in his eyes, and, if he considers them excessive or irresponsible, to protest against them, if necessary to the point of trying to change his government. Unless this tendency is kept under constant review and criticism, it can very easily develop into that cult of State infallibility.

Habit of action, temptations of immediate convenience, all the insidious influences of system and precedent, can produce that condition of mind even more easily, and perhaps more ineradicably, than considered conviction. The vigilance which is necessary to counteract these influences is not easy to maintain, for constant questioning of encroachments produces in time a certain fatigue, a certain hopelessness against olds, and no little fear of coming to be regarded as a mere crank or bore. If this mood once becomes settled and general, the pass is sold; for, trite though the observation is, it remains true, on all human experience, that liberty is more easily bartered away by retail than by wholesale.

Liberty, Law and Justice

Allen describes that if social man is to be assessed and guarded on this principle, we must now ask what relationship it bears to law and justice. It is too well known to need elaboration than Kant and his numerous disciples have seen in law, the counterpart in the political sphere of the categorical imperative in the moral sphere. In part of a work, which was written towards the end of his life (in 1947), Kant attempted an examination of the "metaphysic" of law. He approached the question ex-hypothesis as one of Pure Reason, and his tentative formal definition of law was "the idea which proceeds from the conditions under which each man's freedom of action of others, in accordance with a universal law of liberty. This seems to differ from the moral principle of the categorical imperative only in relating itself to the conditions which govern free action; and it is because of the indefinably various conditions of legal systems that this concept has been most heavily attacked."

It was against the "conceptual" approach to law that the whole Historical School of Savigny and his disciples revolted, maintaining that legal systems are not the product of Pure Reason but of evolutionary processes differing with the history and circumstances of each community.

A similar criticism rejects the assumption of a "universal law of freedom" in the legal sphere. Apart from the fact that many perfectly valid laws have been directed against rather than for freedom, it is objected that law cannot be rightly conceived or defined in terms of any general end or aim, because here again there is the utmost variation in its objectives from people to people and from epoch to epoch, and all such fluctuations powerfully influence the spheres of human liberty.

Again modern exponents of "functional" jurisprudence see the focus by concentrating too much attention on the individual and too little on the social value and aims of law. The reaction against any priori approach to law has in some quarters been so vehement that Realists distrust any "principles" at all in the operations of law and prefer to regard them merely as series of facts–as things done rather than as logical processes. This is the reaction, which the law has brought upon itself by a tendency towards too facile and too artificial dogmatism, and though this antithesis can hardly be described as the prevailing fashion, it has considerable vogue among modern jurists who are not content, like previous generations, to accept old "conceptual" orthodoxies without scrutiny.

Thus Sir Paul Vinogradoff[16] observes: "The notion of freedom, however, was not happily selected, since it is obvious that the adjustment effected by law must consist in the curtailment of individual freedom, and freedom, as usually understood, merely opens the way for possible action, but does not indicate the course action should take." But surely the curtailment is as inherent in the Kantian conception as the enfranchisement, since the individual freedom must be consistent with the equal freedom of others.

The Paradox of Law

Let us see what Allen said: this is the perpetual paradox of freedom according to law. It was really at the whole Social Contract theory, which sought to place on an artificial basis of calculated agreement, the perennial barter between individual and general liberty in the whole process of government. "Every law diminishes liberty," said Bentham; but it would be equally true to say that law augment liberty, because what is taken away from one is contributed to the common stock, in which everybody is a sharer. If I am not at liberty to enjoy my property, as I like, it is because my unrestricted use of it may be to the general detriment, and also because part of it is required for public purposes intended for the common advantage of which I, like everybody else, shall have the ultimate benefit. What I lose directly I gain indirectly; and conversely, if I were under no restraint at all, I should lose in the end, because others following my example might behave so selfishly that we should all be equal sufferers. Thus every legal right is simultaneously a gift with one hand and a taking away with another, since the power which it confers on one involves a duty or liability imposed on another, or upon all others, which is a diminution of their freedom; and this is illustrated by the very language of the law, for rights, though they enlarge the opportunities of power, are described in their adverse aspect.

Law, therefore, may be rightly viewed from either of these angles, with the emphasis laid, at choice, on the one or the other, but without mutual exclusion. One judge says: "the function of law is to free and not to fetter liberty, in the true sense of the term. Another says: "the common law, in principle, imposes obligations on the individual for the benefit of the public, and not on the public for the benefit of the individual." A dictum of Coke has become a settled maxim of the law: "the law will sooner suffer a private mischief than a public inconvenience." On Bentham's principle, every law is a "private mischief" in so far as it limits liberty, but it is so only in order to minimize "public inconvenience." All these predications are really asserting the same thing, or, perhaps it would be more accurate to say, are looking at different sides of the same thing; and it is important not to confuse our thought by splitting them into two separate conceptions and establishing a false difference, which may grow into an antinomy, between them.

Thus, every legitimate restraint, imposed by law, on the "free scope" of man-in-society is to be regarded as a contribution to the general sum of distributive liberty, in which everybody, including the person deprived, is the ultimate beneficiary; and perhaps the position has never been more succinctly described than in Cicero's paradox: "we are the slaves of the law in order that we may be free." It is no new or startling conception that freedom may be found in service or even in sacrifice; the idea is dominant in a great deal of religious thought. In all this, however, I necessarily assume that we are considering a rational, developed and civilized system of law. It is, of course, possible for a potentate to make laws, which are related to no private or public advantage except his own.

Liberty and Justice

Allen again told that what is justice? Is the idea of freedom inherent in the idea of justice? The function of justice as the harmonizing or equalizing influence in human relations. Without that tempering influence, it is obvious that the boundaries of individual freedom becomes obliterated, so that the notion of freedom itself ceases to have any meaning for anybody; for, as we have seen, there is on earth no freedom without bounds, save perhaps in the inner spirit of some exceptional men. The balance which justice strives to maintain between the competing claims of men upon "the good life" is a delimitation of their spheres of power and opportunity, and therein lies their liberty. As for justice-according-to-law, if it be true, as I have contended, that law is ever seeking to regulate the dispersion of liberties, reconciling the freedom of the one of that of the many, to the ultimate advantage of each sharer in the common stock, then it is again manifest that the judge in his office, by impartial administration of the law which he serves, is daily assigning the relative freedoms of those between whose claims he is called upon to decide.

Freedom and English Law and Justice

Allen lastly described that the English judge is especially conscious of this aspect of his function when the issue before him touches upon what may be called the more elementary freedoms. Montesquieu said that it was in the idea of political liberty that the English nation had expressed its genius. "I do not know whether Englishmen are in fact free or not, but with such a Constitution they ought to be free." Englishmen certainly did not enjoy the same measure of personal liberty as they do today; and it is questionable whether the English people, throughout the greater span of its history, has evinced a special genius for personal liberty as the goal of existence. It is difficult to find much "free scope" under a feudal system, and we should not like today to live under a Tudor regime. And yet it was in that age that Shakespeare was able to put into the mouth of John of Gaunt a Declaration of Independence, which was still valid when in 1940 we were threatened with helot age. There were many personal restrictions which today we should vehemently repudiate; but to an observer like Montesquieu, who had seen and experienced the absolutism of Louis XIV, what counted most, was our long and unremitting struggle to establish a form of polity which gave the individual at least an appreciable measure of self-government. Therein, at the cost of much strife and pain, we had justified the foreigner's appraisal of our aspiration. The example was more contagious than he or we had calculated; for it was in the same spirit that our hardy emigrant to the New World established their nationhood and their "self-evident" rights.

I have referred to the development in modern times of our sensitiveness about those elementary personal freedoms, which in some countries are buttressed by "constitutional guarantees," but which our nation has been content to build up through the common law. On the whole, it may be said that in England the scales come down in favour of individual right; in the United States, on the other hand, where the press enjoys a latitude of comment (especially in causes sub judice) which would be impossible in our society, the scale seem to tip the other way. Yet, liberty has always been the watchword of the American nation, and she is the patron saint whose gigantic effigy is the first sight to greet the eyes of the foreigner as he enters the Hudson River. Each country, believing equally in an ordered society and in personal freedom, must find its own poise between the two.

In his famous essay on "Freedom in Antiquity" Lord Acton discussed the numerous experiments in "mixed" and "balanced" constitutions, and observed, "there is no example of such a balanced Constitution having lasted a century. If it has succeeded anywhere it has been in our favoured country and in our time; and we know not yet how long the wisdom of the nation will preserve the equipoise." The weights and measures have changed, but equilibrium can still be preserved with different units of gravity; he further observed:

"Liberty and good government do not exclude each other; and there are excellent reasons why they should go together. Liberty is not a means to a higher political end. It is in itself the highest political end. It is not for the sake of a good public administration that it is required, but for security in the pursuit of the highest objects of political society, and of private life. Increase of freedom in the State may sometimes promote mediocrity, and give vitality to prejudice; it may even retard useful legislation, diminish the capacity for war, and restrict the boundaries of Empire.... A generous spirit prefers that his country should be poor, and weak, and of no account, but free, rather than powerful, prosperous and enslaved. It is better to be a citizen of a humble commonwealth in the Alps, without a prospect of influence beyond the narrow frontier, than a subject of the superb autocracy that overshadows half of Asia and of Europe."

Notes

1. Radha Krishnan-Indian Philiosophy.
2. Indian Philosophy.
3. Plato in Republic
4. Politics
5. Hegel's Philosophy.
6. Das Capital
7. On Liberty
8. LAW
9. Principles of Law
10. Rig-veda-in English
11. Shankaracharya or Aryanya Kopanishad Ancient Indian Scriptures
12. P.V. Kane-Ancient Indian scriptures
13. Gita Rahasya
14. Aspects of Justice
15. Social Contract
16. Principles of Jurisprudences

CHAPTER 7 Conclusion and Epilogue

The ancient Indian legal philosophy has revealed to us its metaphysical base and spiritual character, from which ensue the concepts and theories which make it an integrated whole and a great synthesis of law, life and experience. From its metaphysical base ensues the theory of reality as Existence pervaded by consciousness, which the Upanishads proclaim as *'Atman'* or *'Brahman'*. This Reality is eminent. Behind all the names and forms, facts and experiences, theories and ideas, there is one which is the substratum of all and that alone lends unity inspite of diversity. The reality is not the material essence but with its spirituality, consciousness, and purposiveness, allows man who is endowed with rational will and capacity for highest knowledge, to participate in the conscious purposes of this universe. He can identify himself with the reality itself, merge in it, and thereby can attain oneness and unity in the realm of actual experience which is called spiritual experience. In such experience lies man's highest realization.

But in order that a greater part of mankind can attain such a state of spiritual realization, all our institutions, organizations, ideas, and human relations have to be oriented in such a manner as would make this realization possible. Law is an instrument of social control and organization and means of human welfare and happiness. But at the same time, it is a virtual part of the reality itself. The ancients were therefore, able to formulate a legal theory that served the highest purposes of life. In the present age, this aspect of law has been totally ignored.

The consequences of this lapse are disastrous for the whole human race, despite all advancement, which is claimed for it. It is, therefore, necessary that law must be so understood, interpreted and constructed as to perform the therapeutic function of saving us from the baneful influence of this materialistic civilization, which has already dehumanised us. Law can perform this function only if the legal theory itself is to be rescued from the octopus of western influence and spiritualised in the light of ancient legal philosophy and concepts.

The necessary consequence of a spiritual view is that all divisions, departmentalism, watertight compartments and reactionary views become unnecessary and our limited views are changed into a total perspective, which brings interaction, harmonisation and synthesis. Spiritual jurisprudence in India does not give a distorted and broken view but a higher perspective, synthetically understandable, and an integrated study.

Law, in order to be law, must exist as a reality, which manifolds itself in different forms, which manifests and grow's endlessly to realise the higher purposes of life. It is not merely precept or formulation but is a living law, a working principle and an enlightened guidance that is conducive to happiness and welfare. Law partakes the Reality; nay it is the Reality itself. In the Vedas, law is expressed as Eternal law or Order (Rit), and is identified with Reality or God. The vision of law is not a revelation of a limited particularised truth. Jurisprudence is not a run-away attempt in solitude or seclusion. Even the analysis of concepts has to serve as the method of understanding of the whole. When we consider law in this prospective, it appears fruitless to quarrel about theories and schools, as it would then be tantamount to a negation of jurisprudence and its integrative potentiality.

To our ancients, true knowledge of science of law does not arise mere from its precept, authority, organization, administration, and enforcement etc., but from a total concern with life and its problems. It is knowledge, practice and welfare activity. The way of study of law lies through logic, history, and ethics but does not end with them. All the particularistic manifestations cannot reveal the inexhaustible "Beyond" and the implicit "Within" or "Behind". Reason, faith, practice, experience, value, expediency, utility are means for its study and understanding and realization without any exclusiveness, or sovereignty of any one of them. It is a healthy union of form and matter, theory and technique, interpretation and adjudication, manifest and mysterious, stability and change.

Modern antagonisms of schools and theories are nothing but the projections of our individual and social imbalances and complexes. We need an interpretative science of jurisprudence that resolves all problems, removes all confusion, reconciles all conflicts and re-channels our energies to the task of legal development and law-reform. That is how jurisprudence can become meaningful to us. It becomes the yoga of law, life and experience; hence a theory of individual and social existence and an expression of progress and a project of welfare and happiness. The jurist; as logician, historian, moralist, utilitarian, pragmatist, liberalist, pacifist, engineer, solidarism, Libralism, practitioner etc. is partner and a participant with others in the great 'Yajna' of law. Spiritual jurisprudence of ancient India looks to law as the multi-dimensional reality with all its forms, functions and meanings. Law is the manifestation of one that is the Truth, the Good and the Beautiful; which is *sat* (Existence), *chit* (Consciousness) and *anand* (Bliss). Its knowledge lies in its realization alone. In this knowledge lies man's real happiness. Law as part and parcel of reality has to be known from within as well as from without. The truths of Indian legal philosophy are grounded in the theory of existence and are realized through spiritual experience of our sages, seers and legal philosophers who actually said, and felt in their moments of spiritual experience the throbs of the great 'Existence,' as an irrefutable fact.

The authenticity and verifiability of this experience was so greatly valuable that all their conception of law, prescriptions and regulations about behaviour theories of man and society are founded on this truth of spiritual experience. It is due to this that it enables knowledge, refines sentiment, sublimates passions and inculcates the sense of service and sacrifice and thus transforms our social and political existence. By evolution of a method called 'Yoga' they have opened the doors of spiritual realization to all those who have spiritual thirst. It is under the impact of this spiritual thirst and spiritual culture that Indian mind merges and obliterates differences and integrates all in one and seeks in them great unity in all its diversity. This is reflected in all the facts of Indian culture and law.

Today, if we want that we should live in this world in peace and harmony, with mutual concern and mutual respect; that goods of existence are apportioned and shared by all in the interest of all; that people should participate in plans, and projects of government; that the worth and significance of human life be recognized and valued; that governments be run in the interests of its people; that classes and individuals cease to exploit each other; that citizens think in terms of their duty and become responsible; that there be no distrust between the individual and the State; all resources of matter and energy and human organization be pooled for the great benefit of the whole–if we aspire for all these, we should spiritualise all our jural, social, political and economic existence in all its theory and practice.

In pursuit of science the prevalent trend of the western culture is more towards the exploration of matter and phenomena. The dominant characteristic of materialism is that it considers atomistic plurality as final and ultimate, which is disconcerting to unity and integration. As a result of this, in life, a particularistic and separatist viewpoint is asserted. In the field of law arises one-sided theories; self-interest is boosted; schism and departmentalism is justified; conflicting interests become the permanent subjects of jurisprudence, which cannot be reconciled, and no workable theory is put forth. 'Duty' is viewed as bondage or slavery and 'Right' is pluralized into rights to be appropriated by individuals to forge the weapon in the war against state and other individuals. Law is viewed, either as an aspect of government and the enforcement of its policies or is viewed as a mere ritual devoid of all reality and sanctity. In the absence of the master-concept the contract, property, procedure and rule of law are heightened to such an extent with their 'smuggled ideological' content that the integrated or synthetic view of law becomes impossible.

The irony and tragedy of this materialistic civilization is that inspite of the progress of science and accrual of the greatest amount of material comforts, it lurks with disquiet, dissatisfaction, frustration and weariness amidst all the so-called prosperity and affluence. There is reaction against this overpowering influence of materialism. To make this thralldom more graceful and honorable, the ideas of self-preservation, co-existence, interdependence, social solidarity balancing of interests, the greatest good of the greatest number, perforce are propagated and adopted, and a somewhat different and wider perspective of law is taken and its canvas is made large and a certain mystique is employed in disguise and is expressed in guarded language to bring about harmony, integration and cohesion. The natural law doctrine thrives upon this felt-insufficiency of materialistic jurisprudence. But all these devices by which unity is sought, fail in a large measure, because they are incomplete and imperfect. If there is no conviction and faith in the spiritual reality of law or if there is no conception of law as a total human concern, all these broad and liberal approaches are liable to be in vain and are bound to be exploited by the state, society, individual or class.

However, being conscious of its weakness 'Scientism' and 'Positivism' have been modified to a very large extent in such a way that ethical or other value-considerations have been introduced in one form or the other. The legal theory is taking dangerous turns. Historicism, putting more credence on instinct and feeling, has faith in collective consciousness, general will and spirit of the people, etc., as a result of which irrationalism has begun to undermine the systematic study of law. American realism, as judicial empiricism, puts the whole theory of law in a melting pot. All these abnormal developments and juristic hostilities are due to the extraordinary course, which has been taken by conflict-ridden civilization of the west. All the conflicts, between State, individual, society and church inter se, have been reflected in juristic, political and social theories. This is the reason why there is separation between law, morality, religion, and metaphysics. All the distractions, in the theory of law, are the progeny of materialistic approach to life, which has reached its saturation point.

It seems that a counter-reaction, against mechanical uniformity and commercialization of human relationships and erosion of human values has also started. In the field of law, jurists have begun to realize the need for a wholesome view of law. Efforts are being made for a constructive juridique, which can take integrating and synthetic view of jurisprudence. But the jurists have not yet left the materialistic pretensions and are still haunted by positivistic viewpoints. Herbert Spencer realized that unification of knowledge should be the mission of philosophy. Jerome Hall pleaded for an integrative jurisprudence and has castigated the particularistic tendency in jurisprudence. "What is needed today, in the opinion of Hall, is an integrated analytical jurisprudence, realistic interpretations of social and culture facts, and the valuable ingredients of natural law doctrine. All these divisions of jurisprudence are intimately related to, and dependent on, one another." He sees integration of fact and thought in man who is 'simultaneously rational–valuing, physical' animal. In the human mind there is unification of 'otherwise disparate processes.' Wrich Fechner finds in law a mixture of idealistic and realistic elements. He has tried to demonstrate the inter-relations and connection between these elements in a legal order. Timesheff has shown 'in law there is ethic-imperative co-ordination.' Law presents a combination of organized power and group conviction. The power mechanism is not more important than ethical and social considerations of law. In fact, it seems that people are dismayed by the 'single track and one-dimensional theories about law.'

Professor Dennis Lloyd has also realized the need of a synthetic approach to the study of jurisprudence. In our own country, as early as 1955, Dr. Sethna has laid the foundation of the Indian School of Synthetic Jurisprudence. Sethna wants to synthesize and harmonise conflicting ideas by merely taking a mid-way view by avoiding extremes and affecting compromises. He is in search of connecting links and wants to steer only a middle course. His endeavour is to bring compromises amidst rival extremes. All that he wants is to see all jurisprudence aspects at one time or at one place. In view of Boscoe Pound; Sethna wants to bring all the approaches to a common focus. Jurisprudence is viewed as the harp that "produces the melody of law, and the legislation, judges and lawyers are musicians who play (and sing) on the strings (the fundamental principles) of this harp." To him, the end of law is the greatest good for the largest number of society. The greatest value of law is love. "Love is truth, love is beauty; love is sublime." Again he wants law to represent "the general will of people, and that judges would respect reasonable traditions, customs, and usages of long standing."

All these approaches to juristic schools, theories, attitudes and method, without having a theory of unity of the whole Existence with law, are liable to fail. These efforts are directed; it seems to make a digest to jurisprudence theories, schools and methods that may serve as 'Reader's digest.' This is an admixture of various theories, and with due respect to the learned author, it has to be stated that it is far from being synthetic jurisprudence. All these attempts represent a materialistic reaction against a materialistic jurisprudence. They are inspired by utilitarian motive and do not provide us with any philosophic justification. What is needed is a complete recasting and overhauling of views about jurisprudence and its problems.

Without faith and belief in the unity of the whole existence, which is represented and reflected in law, we cannot provide rational grounds for forging the bonds of social unity through law. In absence of metaphysical and spiritual approach all the approaches to law are half-hearted and inadequate. They are also alien to us because they do not take into consideration our culture, which is predominantly spiritual. As spiritualism has unravelled the mystery of life it will certainly engage in unravelling the mystery of law. Thirst for knowing what is mysterious and unknown is still in us. Law has derived its power and holds in the past from magic, myth, music, ritual and religion and still, in a measure, assisted by them. The Indian juristic mind of the past has also cognized supersensible world and a state of spiritual realization that transforms man's view about man, society and universe. The enlightened sees the whole world as one and the mankind as brotherhood and on this basis devotes his life in service. He has compassion for all. All the property, power, position, and authority, which create legal problems, hard to solve, become irrelevant. All the differences appear unreal and with this they seem to vanish. Man, in such a state, gets the real and unadulterated knowledge. If law has to accomplish the goals set by it for the development, progress and reformation of the individual and society it must develop according to the spiritual vision of one world, one community and one law. Man's life, then, will be full of love, sacrifice and service.

We have to realize that matter divides, disintegrates, isolates and frustrates, while spirit unites and integrates. Spiritual jurisprudence gives such a unity that all the views, doctrines and parts of law are 'one' from the point of view of their nature and many only for the sake of convenience and they never cease to represent the whole. All the distinctions and divisions then become provisional because, in essence, they represent the one. The matter of law is impregnated with spirit or reality or higher purposes of life. What is real is what is good and conducive to welfare. The real is the truth as well as ideal, i.e., value. Existence itself is value; value is inherent in existence.

The spiritual base of the Indian jurisprudence is quite manifest and clear. Law arises, as has been mentioned above, as an expression of this sentient universe, possessing consciousness or *'Karma'*. *Rit* is not only the order but is said to have magical binding force. *Dharma* is also described as the mystic force of this world. Satya or Existence is the existence and Reality itself, which has to be realized by the truth of spiritual experience. *'Danda'* is not only a raw force but is the variant of *Dharma*. *Yajna* is not mere Sacrifice or ritual but a participation in the higher purposes of the spirit; it is as good as Yoga or meagre by means of action. *Karma* is also a causative aspect of the conscious reality, which becomes the principle or moral retribution. The ultimate authority of law lies in the Vedas that are known as the revealed texts and are said to be impersonal. Even *Mimansa* or interpretation, with its faith in *Apurva*, and *Vyavahar* as analogical extension of *Yajna* and *Satya* (inquiry for truth) are indicative of spiritual elements.

Thus, ancient Indian legal philosophy can be seen as the spiritualization of the reality of law which other legal philosophies are seen as temporalization or the maleealization of the reality of Law.

The peculiar characteristic of spiritual jurisprudence in India is that all the important concepts partake of the nature of each other. *Rit* (or Dharma), *Satya* and *Yajna* express order, right, duty and welfare. They can be substituted for one another. They enforce each other. In them, there is interconnection, interpretation and mutual relevance. These are the aspects of the same reality, i.e., law.

If we believe that Indian Culture is predominantly a spiritual culture and the Indian bent of mind is still attuned to the spiritualistic thinking; if we realize that spiritualism unifies and dissolves all differences and merges man's interests into those of the community or society, and encourages co-operation and co-ordination, and resolves conflicts; if its cult does away with all the injuries, harms, malpractices and wrongs of human life; if it provides the outlet for the highest type of pleasure, called bliss; if law can be a doctrine as well as practice, and a way of life and living: then let there be spiritual jurisprudence to fulfill the needs of spiritual culture of India and thereby to rescue it from degeneration and degradation. Let us model our concept of law on the spiritual foundation of our culture. But we should not over look the temporal & matearialistic foundation. It shall be better we model our Concept of Law on the Joint Basic of sipirtual as well as temporal (materialistive) foundations altogether. Leter hope for a good legal system are the way.

Index